GOVERNMENT BEYOND THE CENTRE

SERIES EDITORS: GERRY STOKER AND DAVID WILSON

The world of sub-central governance and administration – including local authorities, quasi-governmental bodies and the agencies of public–private partnerships – has seen massive changes in the United Kingdom and other western democracies. The original aim of the **Government Beyond the Centre** series was to bring the study of this often-neglected world into the mainstream of social science research, applying the spotlight of critical analysis to what had traditionally been the preserve of institutional public administration approaches.

The replacement of traditional models of government by new models of governance has affected central government, too, with the contracting out of many traditional functions, the increasing importance of relationships with devolved and supranational authorities, and the emergence of new holistic models based on partnership and collaboration.

This series focuses on the agenda of change in governance both at sub-central level and in the new patterns of relationships surrounding the core executive. Its objective is to provide up-to-date and informative accounts of the new forms of management and administration and the structures of power and influence that are emerging, and of the economic, political and ideological forces that underline them.

The series will be of interest to students and practitioners in central and local government, public management and social policy, and all those interested in the reshaping of the governmental institutions which have a daily and major impact on our lives.

Government Beyond the Centre
Series Standing Order
ISBN 0–333–71696–5 hardback
ISBN 0–333–69337–X paperback
(*outside North America only*)

You can receive future titles in this series as they are published by placing a standing order. Please contact your bookseller or, in the case of difficulty, write to us at the address below with your name and address, the title of the series and an ISBN quoted above.

Customer Services Department, Macmillan Distribution Ltd
Houndmills, Basingstoke, Hampshire RG21 6XS, England

GOVERNMENT BEYOND THE CENTRE

SERIES EDITORS: GERRY STOKER AND DAVID WILSON

Local Government in the United Kingdom

Fourth Edition

David Wilson
and
Chris Game

First edition 1994
Second edition 1998
Third edition 2002
Fourth edition 2006

Published by
PALGRAVE MACMILLAN
Houndmills, Basingstoke, Hampshire RG21 6XS and
175 Fifth Avenue, New York, N.Y. 10010
Companies and representatives throughout the world

PALGRAVE MACMILLAN is the global academic imprint of the Palgrave Macmillan division of St. Martin's Press, LLC and of Palgrave Macmillan Ltd. Macmillan® is a registered trademark in the United States, United Kingdom and other countries. Palgrave is a registered trademark in the European Union and other countries.

ISBN-13: 978–1–4039–9786–9 hardback
ISBN-10: 1–4039–9786–1   hardback
ISBN-13: 978–1–4039–9787–6 paperback
ISBN-10: 1–4039–9787–X   paperback

This book is printed on paper suitable for recycling and made from fully managed and sustained forest sources.

Catalogue records for this book are available from the British Library and the US Library of Congress.
Library of Congress Catalog Card Number: 2006047488

10   9   8   7   6   5   4   3   2
15 14 13 12 11 10 09 08 07 06

Copy-edited and typeset by Povey–Edmondson
Exeter and Rochdale, England

Printed and bound in Great Britain by CPD (Wales) Ltd, Ebbw Vale

To **Jamie**
whose courage in adversity has
been an inspiration to many

Contents

List of Figures

List of Exhibits

Preface to the Fourth Edition

Readers familiar with previous editions of this book may notice, on reaching Chapter 9, that something is missing. There is no organisation chart of the upper echelons – the minister and senior civil servants – of the government department responsible for national policy on local government in England: at the time of the writing of this preface, the Department for Communities and Local Government (DCLG). The reason has, as it happens, nothing to do with devolution and our trying to avoid appearing excessively Anglocentric. Rather, it is because, until after the whole of the rest of the book had been completed, proofread and was *en route* to the printers, the DCLG had not been invented.

In its place, literally, was its predecessor, the Office of the Deputy Prime Minister (ODPM), referred to frequently throughout the book, as well as in Chapter 9. It had, however, from the start of the 2005 Parliament, been widely assumed to be unlikely that the ODPM would survive, in any relevant form, very long after the anticipated resignation of Tony Blair as Prime Minister. Hence our omission of an organisation chart that would probably become redundant early on in the book's expected life. What no one had foreseen was that Blair, in his most radical ministerial reshuffle – following, as it happened, an exceptionally damaging set of local election results for Labour in May 2006 – would 'disappear' the ODPM, if not the DPM himself, well *before* his departure.

Profound as was our personal irritation at the inconsiderateness of the PM's timing, we recognise that, in the great scheme of things, our inconvenience is comparatively inconsequential set alongside the disruption to other people's lives and careers, and, perhaps, the future of local government reform. Uncomplainingly, therefore, we have revised our text at not so much the eleventh hour as the thirteenth. We have done so, wherever possible, according to two principles: sufficiently to remove what would have been factual inaccuracies, but minimally enough to avoid upsetting what is known in publishers' jargon as the existing 'pagination'.

The episode does, though, have its illustrative value, for it is in its way one of many possible measures of the impermanence and unpredictability of the contemporary world of UK local government. In this fourth edition of our book, the ODPM is the fourth 'local government department' we have described. In the first edition (1994) it was the Department of the Environment (DoE). In the second, completed shortly after New Labour's election in 1997, Transport and the Regions had been added to form the DETR – see the list of abbreviations (p. xx). Following the 2001 Election it was restructured again into the Department for Transport, Local Government and the Regions (DTLR) and featured as such in our third edition. We had not allowed, though, for the misdemeanours of the Secretary of State, Stephen Byers. By May 2002 he had resigned, his department had been reorganised into the ODPM, and our DTLR organisation chart consigned to the same irrelevance that an ODPM chart would have had in this present edition.

In most other western governmental systems, politicians may come and go, as national ministers or local councillors; that, after all, is what elections are about. In our system it can seem as if *institutions* come and go almost as frequently. For, as well as the ODPM/DCLG changes, there is also the possibility in no more than the medium term of a fundamental rearrangement of the whole structure of local government, in quite possibly all four nations of the UK state. This would involve a change in the number of councils, their boundaries, and their responsibilities in the first such reorganisations since ... as long ago as the mid-1990s.

Then there are all the changes in policy and practice – many stemming from local authorities themselves, but all too frequently imposed upon them from above, by central government. An outstanding recent example would be Comprehensive Performance Assessment (CPA), also covered in Chapter 9. Though completely unmentioned in Labour's 2001 election manifesto, CPA came, more than any other single initiative, to dominate the lives of leading local government practitioners in the ensuing four years.

Dealing as it does, therefore, with a local government world in a state of apparently constant flux, this edition, like its predecessors, is exactly what it says on the jacket; comprehensively revised and updated. No chapter has survived intact, and, while the three-part structure has been retained, the content of Part 3 in particular is substantially new, much of the former Chapters 17 and 18 having been incorporated into the main body of the book. Chapter 16 has been retitled, as well as rewritten and refocused, and other chapters with an above-average share of new material include 5, 6 and 8, with their respective coverage of regional governance, the institutions of executive local government, and the Triffid-like growth of local partnerships.

Another innovation is our linked website – **www.palgrave.com/politics/ wilson**. A principal purpose of this site is obviously to enable readers to keep up with the major changes and developments in UK local government without having to wait for the book's next edition. It will contain, therefore, periodic updating briefings – covering, for example, White Papers and other ministerial initiatives, legislation, official and academic publications, local elections, and key changes in postholders. Second, there are guides to further reading; these, too, will be regularly updated. Third, the site contains a few of the exhibits from earlier editions that have been dropped for the present one but which may still be of some intrinsic interest.

Still on the topic of websites, one unchanged feature in this edition is the policy on website references. For reasons previously explained – principally the magnificence of Google, the ultimate public–private partnership (see Chapter 8) – there are no strings of website references to all mentioned institutions, as found in some introductory texts. Almost invariably, these can now be easily Googled and, perhaps with the help of their own 'Search' facilities, beneficially explored by our readers – just as we ourselves have done in producing this book. Generally speaking, we have restricted references to sites that are non-obvious, or where we have drawn material from a specific page.

There are also some more profound things than website referencing policy that, pleasingly, stay constant in this uncertain world – one being the debts of gratitude incurred in producing a volume of this attempted type and range. First come our academic colleagues, headed, as ever, by now Emeritus Professors John Stewart and George Jones. The influence of their published work is witnessed by the justly celebratory volume referred to in the Chapter 3 reading guide on our website. Publication lists and citation indexes, though, however vital to Research Assessment Exercises, are flimsy indicators of the day-to-day stimulus of one's academic associates. They are, of course, far too numerous to name individually, but two who must be mentioned, having worked closely with both authors in their respective institutions, are Professors Gerry Stoker and Steve Leach. Two others who would feature more prominently than they themselves might imagine in an Oscar-style acceptance speech by the second-named author would be Professors Richard Rose and Tony King.

Which brings us to our most heartfelt thanks of all. One of us at least must have done something right, in order to have been blessed with the quality of administrative and secretarial assistance on which we have drawn so heavily in the preparation of previous editions of this book. It is no slight whatever, therefore, on the dedication of her predecessors to thank Margaret Spence for a commitment to and enthusiasm for this project so far beyond any call of duty as to be almost eerie. Quite simply, no expression of our appreciation could be too high.

Our publisher, Steven Kennedy, comes, very nearly, into a similar bracket. That he was the Political Studies Association's first – and to date only – Political Publisher of the Year in 2004 was no surprise whatever to all those of us who have known and have worked with him over the years. Local government is but one of many fields of political science whose debt to him is immense. If there were awards for editorial consultants, we would certainly be delighted to nominate Keith Povey; as it is, we express our overdue public thanks for his tremendous work on this and previous editions.

Lastly, though anything but least, we must express our admiration of and gratitude to our under-rewarded artists and their respective publications for permission to reproduce their cartoons and caricatures: Patrick Blower for Figures 5.1 and 9.3; Malcolm Willett for Figures 9.1 and 17.1; Adrian Teal and CartoonStock for Figure 9.4 – all of which first appeared in the *Local Government Chronicle*; Brick for Figure 10.1, and Harry Venning and *The Guardian* for Figure 13.1.

We trust these and the other illustrations contribute both to the book's merit and our readers' interest. For whatever defects and errors you detect and for the views expressed, we, of course, are responsible.

DAVID WILSON
CHRIS GAME

List of Abbreviations

ACSeS	Association of Council Secretaries and Solicitors
BC	Borough Council
BME	black and minority ethnic
BV	Best Value
BVPI	Best Value Performance Indicator
BVPP	Best Value Performance Plan
CC	County/City Council
CCT	compulsory competitive tendering
CIPFA	Chartered Institute of Public and Finance Accountancy
CIPR	Chartered Institute of Public Relations
CPA	Comprehensive Performance Assessment
DC	District Council
DCLG	Department for Communities and Local Government (2006–)
DEFRA	Department for Environment, Food and Rural Affairs
DETR	Department of the Environment, Transport and the Regions (1997–2001)
DfES	Department for Education and Skills (1997–)
DSO	Direct Service Organisation
DTLR	Department for Transport, Local Government and the Regions (2001–02)
EU	European Union
FTE	full-time equivalent
GDP	gross domestic product
GLA	Greater London Authority (2000–)
GLC	Greater London Council (1963–86)
GO(R)	Government Offices (for the Regions)
IDeA/I&DeA	Improvement and Development Agency
IPPR	Institute for Public Policy Research
LAA	Local Area Agreement
LEA	Local Education Authority
LGA	Local Government Association
LGCE	Local Government Commission for England
LGIU	Local Government Information Unit
LGMA	Labour Government's Modernisation Agenda
LPSA	Local Public Service Agreement
LSC	Learning and Skills Council
LSP	Local Strategic Partnership

LSVT	Large Scale Voluntary Transfer (of housing)
NDC	New Deal for Communities
NLGN	New Local Government Network
NNDR/UBR	National Non-domestic Rate/Uniform Business Rate
NRF	Neighbourhood Renewal Fund
ODPM	Office of the Deputy Prime Minister (2002–06)
OFSTED	Office for Standards in Education
ONS	Office for National Statistics
PFI	Private Finance Initiative
RDA	Regional Development Agency
RSG	Revenue Support Grant
RSL	registered social landlord
SOCPO	Society of Chief Personnel Officers
SOLACE	Society of Local Authority Chief Executives
UA	Unitary Authority
VCS	Voluntary and Community Sector
VFM	value for money

Part 1

Local Government: The Basics

Chapter 1

Introduction: Our Aims and Approach

The licence plate view of local government

For most Americans, British vehicle licence plates tell them all they feel they need to know about British local government:

> [British] licence plates are unimaginative and uninformative. There is no 'Kent: The Garden County' or 'Cumbria: Land o' Lakes'. I wonder what games British children play on long trips. (Seitz, 1998, p. 270)

The author of this observation was Raymond Seitz, one of the outstanding and most Anglophile of recent American ambassadors to Britain. The reference to children's games came from his recollections of being driven across the USA as a young boy and playing an 'I-spy' game of spotting licence plates, each displaying some slogan or nickname related to its state of origin: 'New York: The Empire State', 'Tennessee: The Volunteer State', and, more disconcertingly, 'New Hampshire: Live Free or Die'. The early lesson in government that Seitz learned from this experience was that every state had its own special character and identity. State, and even local, governments had real authority, and their residents had a fierce pride in being different from their neighbours across a shared boundary. American states had their own constitutions and legislatures. They could raise capital and tax their citizens, with taxes that varied from state to state. America was a federal and genuinely pluralist country.

By comparison, Seitz found the United Kingdom to be unitary and uniform. He was both right and wrong – constitutionally right, observationally wrong. The UK is indeed a *unitary state*, governed constitutionally as a single unit, through the national Parliament at Westminster. Parliament is constitutionally sovereign, and any sub-central governments – the Scottish Parliament, the Welsh and Northern Ireland Assemblies, and Britain's several hundred local authorities – are necessarily subordinate. All are literally creatures – or creations – of Parliament. Britain is fundamentally different, therefore, from the USA, Canada, Australia, India, Germany and Switzerland, which are *federal states*: associations of largely self-governing regions united by a central or federal government.

3

Seitz went further, though, and equated Britain's unitary form of government with uniformity – and here, we suggest, he was wrong. He would probably have been mildly surprised to learn that, thanks to Plantlife International, all our counties have their own 'county flowers' – Bedfordshire: the bee orchid; Herefordshire: mistletoe; Rutland: the clustered bellflower and so on – in a kind of pale mimicry of the way that American states have their own trees, birds, mammals, insects, gemstones and even beverages. He would have been entirely unsurprised, though, that our own two local authorities, Leicestershire and Birmingham, have apparently so little sense of individuality that they share the same flower: the foxglove (see www.plantlife.org.uk). It would have confirmed all his suspicions. For UK local government, it seemed to Seitz, was under almost constant reorganisation, with boundaries changing and councils coming and going without anyone apparently caring very much. Services, benefits, taxes and even licence plates are more or less the same everywhere:

> Central government divvies up the public purse and distributes the funds evenly across a homogeneous society. Who gets what is a national responsibility and a national preoccupation. (Seitz, 1998, p. 270)

The egalitarianism may be admirable, but the cost, concludes Seitz, is a 'feebleness' of local government and a 'super-centralism' of policy making in which 'local government is directed from London in a semi-colonial fashion' (p. 274).

Centralism doesn't eliminate local difference

Despite naturally being distressed about our local authorities sharing the same flower, we cannot let Seitz's perceptions of uniformity go unchallenged. Get out of London more, and get real, would have been our respectful advice to the ambassador. Of course, there are not the same extremes of government in the UK as in the USA, nearly 40 times its size, as well as being a federation. He is right too – as we show in Chapter 9 – about councils in this country being subject to much greater central government control and direction than even most of their European counterparts. But look a bit more carefully and you will quickly see forces of diversity as well as forces of uniformity: differing sizes, locations, histories, cultures, economies, social class structures, politics – all of which militate against even neighbouring councils being the undistinguishable 'administrative units' that Seitz thought he saw (1998, p. 271).

Shared foxgloves notwithstanding, Birmingham and Leicestershire and their respective councils do have their own characters and identities, just as do American states. They also 'do' local government in very different and distinctive ways, and always have done. The first message of this book, therefore, is the importance of getting the balance right. Don't understate the real and pervasive centralism that characterises the British system of government, but don't ignore either the equally real differences and local variations that stubbornly remain.

Narrow, dull? You're joking!

There is a modish view, widely found, unfortunately, among political commentators, that local government is boring, and that the world of local government is narrow, uniform and dull. This is another misconception we shall attempt to dispel, as it is, in fact, quite the reverse.

Narrow is something local government has never been. That local authorities 'look after you from the cradle to the grave' – or from sperm to worm – is both a cliché and an outdatedly paternalistic view of councils' wide-ranging responsibilities. But it is also literally true, in that they will register your birth, death and, if necessary, any intervening marriage or civil partnership, and then finally dispose of you, in cemetery or crematorium according to taste. Prince Charles and Camilla, you may recall, forgot this and, having failed to arrange with the council registrar an exclusive wedding licence for St. George's Chapel, Windsor Castle, had to get married with the hoi polloi across the road in the albeit still rather splendid Guildhall. They, though, are the exceptions with their probably rather arm's-length contact with most public services. For the rest of us, our local councils and the services they provide have a far more immediate, continuous and comprehensive impact on all our own lives than many of the so-called 'bigger' issues that make the national political headlines.

Nor have these local councils ever been uniform – except in the sense that the whole land mass of our planet would look uniform if viewed from far enough away. 'Africa', we have had to try to learn, is not an undifferentiated continent of wars, starvation, disease and misery, but rather 54 countries, each with its particular blend of natural resources, terrain, history, economy, form of government, languages, and so on. Similarly, local government in the UK is the government of 468 localities, and an institutionalised recognition of their widely varying characteristics – geographic, demographic, social, economic and, by no means least, political. Throughout this book we shall illustrate, wherever possible, the differences that exist even among councils of the same type and of a similar size, and encourage you to discover for yourselves the uniquenesses of your own councils, or what you might call the microcosmos of local government.

As for being dull, the very suggestion would be likely to raise a pitying, and self-pitying, smile from most of those working in or with local government over the past few years. What area of the private sector, they would ask, has had to come to terms with more change and upheaval on every front: privatisation and the contracting out of services; compulsory competitive tendering (CCT), Best Value, and Comprehensive Performance Assessment (CPA); the introduction and almost instant abandonment of a 'poll tax', followed by a council tax and tax capping; neighbourhood offices, one-stop shops, enabling councils, beacon councils, private finance initiatives, area-based initiatives, strategic partnerships, inspectorates, e-government, performance indicators and league tables ... all against a backdrop of continuous financial constraint and the actual or threatened rearrangement of the country's whole local government structure.

Few of these ideas and developments would or could have found their way into a book on local government published twenty years ago. Their origins are mixed. Some have come from within the world of local government. But many, as Seitz noted, stem from central government and from the unprecedented quantity of legislation directed at local councils in recent years. It has been this interventionist and legislative attention of central government that has, directly and indirectly, raised the profile of local government and made it regular front-page news – whether it be the Mayor of London, Ken Livingstone, spending an alleged £28 per pigeon to keep them away from Trafalgar Square, or protesting pensioners being sent to jail for refusing to pay their council tax.

If, notwithstanding its diversity and inherent importance, local government has in the past conveyed an image more insipid than inspiring, presumably those chiefly to blame must be councils themselves, who have all too often failed to project themselves in such a way as to stimulate the awareness – let alone the interest or political support – of those they supposedly represent and serve. To be fair, this criticism is one that many of them would now acknowledge and claim to be doing their best to rectify – though still not very often to the point of keeping town halls and civic centres open in the evenings and at weekends! We shall be drawing attention to some of the better efforts at user-friendliness throughout this book.

When it comes to the study of local government, authors too have their responsibilities. Part of our job must be to stimulate the interest of *our* public in the activities of local government: to convey, as directly as possible, a sense of its 'feel' and atmosphere. So who are our public?

Facts and 'feel'

We assume that most of our readers will not themselves have worked in local government, or at least not for any great length of time. We assume that, for most readers, your principal experience of local government will have been as customers, consumers, clients and citizens; perhaps also, to add a fifth C, as complainants. You will probably have had various more or less memorable contacts over the years with council officials and employees, and perhaps also with your locally elected councillors. You will certainly be at least one and probably several of the following: council tax payers, education grant recipients, state school or college students, council house tenants, social services clients, library borrowers, sports and leisure centre users, pedestrians, bus travellers, car drivers, taxi riders, planning applicants or protesters, domestic refuse producers, and so on. You will probably be registered local electors, and possibly actual voters. Yet perhaps oddly, given this degree of personal involvement, you are likely to consider yourselves 'outsiders' in relation to the world of local government.

If so, then in this sense we too are outsiders. We are not employed in local government either; but we do work very closely *with* local government. In various ways – through teaching and lecturing, research and consultancy – we are in virtually daily contact with local councils, their members and staff. A key part of our jobs involves trying to link together, or at least narrow the gap between, the 'academic' and 'practitioner' worlds of local government, and that is the task we have set ourselves in this book.

The classic 'problem' of local government in the United Kingdom has been described by Ben Page, from the polling company MORI (Market and Opinion Research International), as people seeing politicians they don't quite trust, doing things they don't quite understand, and getting a direct bill for it. This book addresses Page's problem head-on. It will introduce you to the most important 'things' about Britain's local governments and, we hope, increase your understanding of them. It will, particularly in Chapter 10, decode and set in context the 'bill' that all council tax payers receive each year. And, while we can't guarantee to increase your trust in local politicians, we will provide an insight into the kinds of people they are and some of the not always appreciated difficulties of the job they seek to do.

Returning to the question of balance, our aim is to present a picture of local government comprising and balancing both facts and 'feel'. We are concerned that our readers acquire a factually accurate knowledge of what local government is about and how it works. We are equally concerned, though, that you acquire too something of its 'feel': an appreciation of the interests, viewpoints, motivations, satisfactions and frustrations of those involved, and an awareness of the range, the nature and the complexities of the issues they face. With this latter objective in mind, we now put forward a few suggestions or recommendations.

Welcome to gov.uk

First, make whatever use you can of the fact that you yourselves will, depending on where you live, be residents of at least one local council, and possibly two or three. These councils produce a mass of information in different forms about the services they provide and the activities in which they are involved. They may produce and circulate their own council newspaper, or insert a couple of pages regularly into one of the local papers. They will certainly deliver to you personally a statement of their annual budget to accompany your council tax demand. They will also produce all sorts of other leaflets, brochures, cards and pamphlets about particular services that should be available from your local town or county hall. So go along and scavenge – or, if necessary, ask!

Better still, all principal councils now have their own websites, and there really is no more efficient and enjoyable way of finding out about both your own council and local government in general than by surfing the net and comparing these hugely assorted council sites (see Exhibit 1.1).

University websites – what we might call 'ac.uk' sites, ending as they do in .ac.uk – vary greatly, from those offering little more than long lists of courses and departments to those with virtual tours of campuses, webcams, and much else besides. Council sites – almost all ending in .gov.uk – vary much more and are correspondingly more informative. If your council proves to be one with a website that seems little more than a glorified online brochure-cum-telephone directory, and/or proclaims, directly or indirectly, that it was last updated several months ago, it is in its own way making as eloquent a statement about itself as those councils with much more ambitious and genuinely *transactional* sites. Judge for yourself, by comparing sites, or by testing them using our short list of questions in Exhibit 1.1, how useful, practical and enterprising your council's site is.

An early definition

Just about every council website nowadays should offer an A–Z listing of services, something about the way in which the council organises itself, and a news page of recent initiatives and forthcoming activities. Our guess is that after no more than, say, twenty minutes' surfing and browsing in the way we have suggested, even if you were to have started with no previous knowledge at all about local government, you would be able to piece together a reasonable preliminary impression of the kind of institution a local council is (Exhibit 1.2). It is by no means a fully comprehensive definition of what a council is and how it operates, but it is a useful jumping-off point for the more extended discussion of these matters in Chapter 3.

Exhibit 1.1 Test out your own council's website

Three (of the many) ways of finding your council's site

1. *Most comprehensive*: the Government's official website
   – www.direct.gov.uk
   Find a job, a school, a course, child care, a government department –
   and your own council. A hugely improved site since the previous
   edition of this book; it's bound to come in useful sometime.

2. *More fun*: the Oultwood Local Government Web Index
   – www.oultwood.com
   Commendable little private company, whose local government index
   was pioneering. Sites are retrievable by both maps and initial letter,
   and can be compared with council sites in other countries. Check
   especially its 'good practice' sites, bus traffic signs – 'heavyweight
   sites, with busloads of good content' – webcam and disabled icons, but
   remember too that, as a still quite small company monitoring a now
   large world of very rapid change, it may not be bang up-to-date.

3. *Easiest*: Google or guess it: council name + .gov.uk

A dozen test questions for any council site

1. Would you say the site is essentially *promotional* – an online
   brochure/telephone directory – or genuinely *transactional*, offering a
   significant range of services online?
2. Is there stuff clearly past its sell-by date?
3. Could you find your own councillor(s) using only your address or
   postcode – that is, if you don't happen to know the name of the ward
   you live in?
4. Can you find any account of how your councillors have spent their
   time on different aspects of council work over the past couple of
   months?
5. Is there a clear statement of which political party or parties control the
   council?
6. Does the A–Z of services include those provided by other councils or
   organisations in the area?
7. Is there a listing for 'wheelie bins' or only 'refuse collection' or even
   'wheeled bin'? Could you find out which day your wheelie bin would
   be emptied simply by typing in your street name?
8. What information, if any, is available in languages other than English?
9. Could you download useful maps of the council area?
10. Are committee papers – agendas, reports, minutes – available online?
11. Could you find details of how to complain to, or compliment, the
    council?
12. Could you find out who is the largest employer in the area, and what
    the current unemployment rate is in your own ward?

Exhibit 1.2 Your local council

Your local council is:

- a large, geographically-defined, multi-functional organisation,
- pursuing a variety of social, political and economic objectives,
- either through the direct provision,
- or through the sponsorship, indirect funding, regulation, or monitoring of
- a very extensive range of services to its local community.

Organisation of the book

Which brings us to the way in which this book is organised. It is divided into three parts. Part 1 is concerned with the *basics* of local government. The aim is to provide you with a good foundation knowledge of the purposes and origins of local government, its structures, functions and finances, and the context in which it operates.

Part 2 looks at the *dynamics* that drive the system. What makes local government 'tick'? The focus moves on to the people and institutions that make decisions, provide services and seek to influence the activities of their locality. We become more directly concerned with politics, since our aim is to understand how various local government players perceive their situation and try to realise their objectives.

Part 3 turns to the agenda of *change*: changes that in 2005/06 were already being implemented and, more speculatively, possible changes in the less foreseeable future. The absence from the re-elected Labour Government's first Queen's Speech of anything actually labelled a Local Government Bill fooled no one who has followed the subject in recent years. 'Localism' and 'engaging with people at the neighbourhood level' were prominent, if unclarified, themes of the election campaign, and the likelihood is that by the end of the decade local government will have evolved and changed at least as much as during the 1980s or 1990s. The book concludes, therefore, with some suggestions of 'the shape of things to come'. Remember our own website (www.palgrave.com/politics/wilson). As noted in the Preface, this is where, in this edition, you will find the 'Guides to further reading' for each chapter, also relevant updating information.

Chapter 2

Themes and Issues in Local Government

Introduction – follow those headlines!

This chapter introduces some of the main current themes and issues in UK local government and the key defining characteristics of the local government system. We start by attempting to demonstrate the value of our own advice about the benefits of following local government in the national and local media. If, for example, you had been on media watch during the summer of 2005, the headlines that might have caught your eye would almost certainly have included some of those shown in Exhibit 2.1.

Constant change – with more to come

Our headlines collectively illustrate several of the most prominent themes of contemporary local government in the UK, starting with its state of apparently perpetual motion. In almost every aspect it continued in the early twenty-first century, as during the 1980s and 1990s, to be subject to change, much of it of the most fundamental kind (Items 1, 2 and 7 in Exhibit 2.1). Through much of the 1990s, as we describe in Chapter 5, even the total *number of councils* was changing – or, to be specific, falling – from year to year. The 540 councils in existence when the first edition of this book was published in 1994 – already a very small number by comparative international standards – had by the time of the second edition in 1998 fallen to 468. One in every seven had disappeared, the victims of national governmental reorganisation (Wilson and Game, 1998, p. 14, plus Exhibits on linked website).

In Wales, 45 counties and districts had been cut by more than half, to just 22 'unitary' (single-tier or all-purpose) councils. In Scotland 65 former regions and districts were reduced to 32 unitaries. In England, 46 new unitary councils replaced five counties and 58 districts. Only Northern Ireland's local government structure remained intact, and that now looks likely to change with the anticipated ending of direct rule from London,

---

Exhibit 2.1 Selected news headlines, 2005

1. **CITY REGIONAL GOVERNMENT AFTER NE REFERENDUM REBUFF?**
   Local Government Minister, David Miliband, promises a 'fundamental debate' on devolution to England's core cities, following the November 2004 referendum rejection of the Government's proposed elected North East Regional Assembly.

2. **TORBAY VOTES FOR ELECTED MAYOR**
   Following a successful petition and campaign, referendum voters of Torbay in Devon opt by 18,074 to 14,682 for their council to be led in future by a directly elected mayor – the 13th in England – rather than a party-elected leader as at present.

3. **'TIME, GENTLEMEN, PLEASE', INSISTS MINISTER**
   As councils take over liquor licensing powers from magistrates, thousands of pubs and clubs miss the August application deadline for new licences, but the Minister responsible, James Purnell, refuses councils' pleas to allow them extra time.

4. **NEW YOUTH POWERS FOR COUNCILS**
   A Government Green Paper, *Youth Matters*, proposes that councils take over the youth advice service from Connexions – the government support service for young people – and give out 'opportunity cards' for free leisure activities to well-behaved 13 to 16 year olds.

5. **SMOKING BAN ON THE WAY – IN SCOTLAND**
   Confederation of Scottish Local Authorities (COSLA) confirms that Scottish councils are ready to implement the comprehensive public smoking ban introduced by the Scottish Parliament – while a partial ban in England is still under discussion.

6. **JAMIE OLIVER, YOU'RE LATE!**
   Hull City Council, ever so slightly envious of the publicity gained by 'Jamie's School Dinners' campaign, reminds the nation that nutritionally balanced lunch menus were introduced into all of Hull's primary and secondary schools in February 2004.

---

the restoration of the Northern Ireland Assembly and its Executive Committee of Ministers, and a transfer of more responsibilities to a smaller number of what should be more powerful councils (see Item 7).

If, as a reader, you think all this structural tinkering might make for confusion and uncertainty, just try to imagine yourself as a council worker, not knowing whether your employing authority will still be in existence in a couple of years' time, let alone what powers and service responsibilities it might have (see Items 3, 4 and 11), or how it might be managed and organised (see Item 2).

Structural change did not, of course, stop in 1998. Quite the contrary, in fact, as in 1997 the New Labour Government came into office with the

7. **FEWER AND LARGER, BUT WILL THEY BE STRONGER, ASKS NILGO**
   Northern Ireland Local Government Association (NILGO) accepts the Government's proposed restructuring of the province's local government, cutting councils from 26 to probably seven, but wants these bigger councils to have more service responsibilities.
8. **EUROPE'S TALLEST TOWER BLOCK GETS MINISTERIAL GO-AHEAD**
   Deputy Prime Minister, John Prescott, overrides opposition of the local planning authority, Lambeth London Borough Council and English Heritage and approves a 49-storey block of flats overshadowing Big Ben and the Houses of Parliament.
9. **CORNISH COUNCILS' SUSTAINABLE ENERGY PARTNERSHIP**
   Home Health, one of the programmes run by the Sustainable Energy Partnership of sixty Cornish organisations, including the county and all six district councils, has provided over 3,000 homes with free energy saving measures in the past two years.
10. **CHINESE INTERESTED IN TAMESIDE'S GLASS CRUSHER**
    Tameside MBC's innovative glass-recycling practice – crushing glass into sand-sized granules, which are then used to prevent the council's sports pitches from flooding – has attracted overseas attention, from Malta to China.
11. **'CONCHIE' REGISTRARS MAY BOYCOTT GAY WEDDINGS**
    Some local registrars may become conscientious objectors and opt out of the permissive part of the Civil Partnerships Act 2004, which requires councils to register partnerships giving gay couples various legal rights, and permits them, if they choose, to host 'gay wedding' ceremonies.
12. **HANTS SOCIAL WORKERS' TSUNAMI RELIEF MISSION**
    Six Hampshire County Council social workers return from three weeks in Hambantota, one of the most devastated areas of Sri Lanka, making use of their experience in child protection, family therapy and bereavement, and adult disability.

century's most far-reaching agenda for constitutional reform, including a radical programme of *devolution*. Within two years, the Scots had, for the first time in nearly 300 years, their own legislative Parliament and Executive (the equivalent of the Cabinet), with Ministers very ready to distance themselves from Westminster policy if they considered it to be in Scotland's interests (see Item 5). Wales too had its own Assembly, though without, at present, the powers to vary tax or pass primary legislation. The Assembly has, however, a say in the implementation of domestic legislation, and Welsh councils, both in the ways in which they conduct their business and in the policies they pursue, have become steadily more distinguishable from their English counterparts.

Northern Ireland's new Assembly, its first since Edward Heath's Government assumed direct rule over the province in 1972, had the most stuttering infancy: elected in June 1998, convened and adjourned in July 1999, reconvened in November 1999, suspended and reinstated in 2000, and re-suspended in October 2002. Like the Scottish Parliament, though, it has (when not suspended) legislative powers, including over what most in the province hope may eventually be a transformed and strengthened system of local government.

There has been further structural reform in England too, with almost certainly more to come. London, without a capital-wide elected Authority since the Thatcher Government's abolition of the Greater London Council (GLC) in 1985/86, now has one again – one capable, moreover, of spearheading a winning bid for the 2012 Olympics. In May 2000, Londoners elected both a 25-member Assembly and the country's first directly-elected executive mayor: the same Ken Livingstone who had been the last (Labour) leader of the GLC, but who now stood and won as an Independent.

London is a special case, though whether a special case of local government or of regional government is a moot point. What is not disputable is that the rest of England remains as the hole in Labour's 'devolution settlement' that has brought elected, democratic government to Scotland, Wales, Northern Ireland and London, but not to the English regions. That was not how the Government had intended things to work out. The plan back in 1997 was that initially Regional Development Agencies (RDAs) would be set up – business-led bodies responsible for developing and delivering economic strategies for their respective regions – overseen by 'chambers' or assemblies of councillors, business people, trade unionists and religious leaders. These chambers would be ministerially nominated, rather than directly elected, but could – and, the Government hoped, would – be transformed in due course into elected regional assemblies, if a region's electors demonstrated in a referendum that that is what they wished. If they did wish it, however, there was a condition: that the creation of this new tier of elected government would be accompanied by a simultaneous move towards unitary local government, as already existed in Scotland and Wales: in short, yet more reorganisation and a further reduction in the numbers of councils and councillors.

In the Government's envisaged scenario, this move towards elected regional assemblies would be a progressive one – starting in those regions where there was felt to be the strongest sense of regional identity, then gradually spreading by imitation across most, if not all, of the rest of the country. The flagship region was to be the North East, but when the regional referendum was held there, in November 2004, the people themselves had other ideas. There was a respectable 48 per cent response to the all-postal ballot, but the proposed assembly was rejected by a ratio of nearly four to one. Regional assemblies are, therefore, now definitely off the Government's agenda, but not necessarily very much else. Extended unitary local government is certainly still there – and so are any number of other possible structural reform proposals, from city regions (see Exhibit 2.1, Item 1) to neighbourhood councils. We shall return to some of the more plausible of these notions in Chapter 18.

An additional by-product of the rejection of elected regional assemblies has been the re-emergence of the idea of elected mayors – another Labour reform to have met with a lukewarm reception, but one favoured by the new Minister of Communities and Local Government appointed after the 2005 General Election, David Miliband. Mayors were intended to be a key feature of the radical *internal structural changes* that councils were required to adopt in the opening years of the twenty-first century, which we deal with in more detail in Chapter 6. Through its Local Government Act 2000, the Blair Government was attempting to 'modernise' the whole way in which, throughout their history, councils had organised themselves and conducted their business. Previously, all elected councillors were involved, through their membership of committees, in the policy-making of their councils. In future, the Government wanted policy determination to be the responsibility of either a single directly elected executive mayor – as in the Greater London Authority – or at least of a small cabinet of leading councillors. The remaining non-executive councillors, as well as representing their communities and constituents, would critically examine and scrutinise council policy – more systematically, rigorously and constructively, it was hoped, than had happened under the committee system.

These highly prescriptive proposals were not generally well received in the local government world, and the Government was forced to make certain concessions to meet the demands, particularly, of smaller district councils. *Elected executive mayors* too, though quite appealing to the general public, were, not really surprisingly, seriously unpopular among councillors, who claimed to foresee the democratic dangers of power being so concentrated in the hands of a single individual, with they themselves being marginalised in the policy-making process. Consequently, at the first time of asking, only eleven English councils – less than 3 per cent – followed Greater London's example of being led by a directly elected mayor; the remainder continued the practice of having their leader chosen by party groups of councillors. By 2005, though, it looked as if the anti-mayoral tide might be turning, with the electors of Torbay ensuring that, if there were to be a second generation of elected mayors, possibly resulting from the Godfather-like 'encouragement' of ministers, theirs would be the first (see Exhibit 2.1, Item 2).

In addition to all this actual or potential organisational change, other government legislation in 2005 was, as ever, adding to or subtracting from local authorities' powers and responsibilities. Of the fifty bills mentioned in the post-election Queen's Speech, at least twenty had significant implications for local government, from animal welfare (strengthened licensing and inspection powers), through child care and education (powers to tackle school under-performance), to identity cards, road safety, and violent crime. Most of local government's concerns in recent years have been about its steady loss of power, variously to the private sector or to other public but non-elected bodies. In 2005, though, it seemed that its prospective new powers were raising more questions in the media: whether the Government would allocate sufficient funding for new youth services, how to police a partial smoking ban involving definitions of a 'bar area' and an 'enclosed public space', and the contentious topic of 'gay weddings' (see Exhibit 2.1, Items 4, 5 and 11).

Far bigger issues, however, also loomed. The conclusions of a long-awaited local financial review were imminent, prompting some 'blue skies thinking' – from, among others, some of our own academic colleagues – about whether local government's future might be one in which councils relinquished control completely of many of their traditional services, such as education, social services, housing management, libraries and leisure centres. For a country once used to long-term stability in its governmental institutions, the breadth, speed and scale of all this change – whether actual or merely aired – are at least remarkable and, to many, constitutionally and democratically threatening. Inevitably, it is one of this book's key themes.

Non-elected local government and 'local governance'

There is a trend detectable in much of this recent change to which we have already alluded, particularly in relation to the English regions: the spread of non-elected or indirectly elected local government. It is not in itself a new phenomenon. The original National Health Service (NHS) structure and the newer self-governing primary care, NHS and other trusts have been completely non-elected since 1974; so too were the New Town Development Corporations and the Scottish and Welsh development agencies, on which the English regional development agencies are modelled.

However, the scale of non-elected government increased enormously during the 1980s and 1990s, frequently at the *direct expense* of elected local councils. Under national governments of both major parties, service responsibilities were removed from local authorities and given mainly to single-purpose Government-appointed agencies: Urban Development Corporations (UDCs) for inner city development, Training and Enterprise Councils (TECs) – since transformed into Learning and Skills Councils

(LSCs) – Housing Action Trusts (HATs), and governing bodies of grant-maintained schools and further education colleges, for example. These single- or special-purpose bodies are conventionally known as *local quangos* – quasi-autonomous non-governmental organisations – and it is no exaggeration to talk of there having been a 'quango explosion', involving the creation of at least 5,000 of them and the appointment of a 'quangocracy' of over 70,000 board members – in both cases, several times the numbers of elected councils and councillors. It has amounted, in the judgement of Jones and Stewart (1992, p. 15), to a 'fundamental change' in our system of local government:

> Government is being handed back to the 'new magistracy' from whom it was removed in the counties more than 100 years ago. Elected representatives are being replaced by a burgeoning army of the selected ... the *unknown governors* of our society (our emphasis).

So fundamental have these changes been, and so fragmented has local service provision consequently become, that some political scientists claim that local government has evolved into something termed *local 'governance'*. This concept, it is suggested, describes more effectively the extensive network of public, voluntary and private sector bodies that are nowadays involved in policy-making and service delivery at the sub-central level (see, e.g., Rhodes, 1997; Stoker, 2000, 2004a; Leach and Percy-Smith, 2001; Goss, 2001; John, 2001).

We would not disagree with the analysis, but neither have we been seriously tempted to retitle or fundamentally refocus our book. While giving plenty of attention to relevant non-governmental organisations, this particular book's focus remains *elected local government*, which itself remains, as democratically accountable service provider and major resource holder, at the very heart of any network or process of local governance.

Breaking up and making up: partnership working

Long, long ago, when we were young, there was a tear-jerking Neil Sedaka song, 'Breaking up is hard to do'. It wasn't, of course, and it certainly isn't if you're a national government with a healthy parliamentary majority at your disposal. You can quite easily pass legislation to break up parts of multi-purpose local authorities into semi-independent, single-purpose bodies in the way we have just described. In public management jargon the process is known as 'disaggregation' or the 'hollowing-out' of, in this case, the local state.

Having disaggregated, though, you soon find that there are certain policy problems – neighbourhood regeneration, crime and disorder, child care, local sustainable development – that require the people, skills, knowledge and experience that are no longer to be found largely within the same organisation, but in a whole range of now generally disconnected ones. So they have to be brought together again – in the jargon, 'reconfigured' or 'joined up' – in *partnerships*. Partnership working (see Exhibit 2.1, Item 8; also Chapter 8 below) has become a central feature of today's local government, and councils are quite likely to find themselves working *with* and *through* external organisations that are now delivering the services for which they themselves used to be responsible. When it works well, it's like the Ronettes, the great girl group also from the early 1960s, sang: 'The best part of breaking up is making up', but getting it to work well can be difficult.

Diminished discretion

As some powers have been taken away from local government, those retained have been increasingly constrained – subject to greater national direction and control. Switchback changes in local government finance, particularly during the 1980s and early 1990s, were accompanied by the imposition of steadily tighter conditions – Government ministers and civil servants becoming more directly involved in declaring what *they* calculate each individual local council ought to be spending on different services. The outcome, as suggested in Figure 2.1, has been a perceptible reduction in local discretion, in the ability of local councils either to decide for themselves or to finance effectively services they would wish to provide for their local communities.

We shall encounter later many of the specific entries in Figure 2.1. We shall also note the contrast between this centralising trend in the United Kingdom and the generally decentralising policies that were being pursued by most other European central governments, but which here have been more the exception than the rule. For the present we merely draw attention to the general shape of what we label the 'funnel of local authority discretion'.

Like a funnel, there is a definite tapering from one end to the other, modified in this latest version by our attempt to represent the deliberately dualistic approach of the Blair Administration towards local government: some relaxation of central control and ministerial interference for those local authorities whose performance is judged to have 'earned' it, but remedial treatment of the toughest kind for any 'backsliders'. But there is deliberately no suggestion in the funnel's shape that all local discretion has been eliminated. Councils still have some opportunity, Figure 2.1 implies, to determine their own political priorities and to embark on their own policy initiatives in response to the needs and wishes of the residents in their particular local communities. They may feel increasingly hemmed in by central government dictates and directives, they may protest their unfairness, but they have by no means been robbed of all initiative and individuality.

Diversity and innovation

Proof of that last assertion may be found in just about any selection of news headlines, and ours, in Exhibit 2.1, is no exception. Examples will range from the momentous and contentious to the barely newsworthy. But Hull's school dinners (and similarly its excellent pencils made from recycled plastic cups), Tameside's glass crusher, and even Hampshire's tsunami relief work (Items 6, 10 and 12) all have one thing in common. They are all examples of local councils deciding freely to do something differently from how it was being done before, different from what other councils are doing, and *not* merely in response to some central government demand or requirement.

Contracting, competing, commissioning

The picture of contemporary local government that is emerging is one of inevitable subordination to central government, but hardly craven subservience: councils with perhaps less freedom of action than previously, but far from emasculated.

As for the future, the goal that the Conservative Governments of the 1980s sometimes appeared to have in mind was expressible as a pun. The combination of the Government's removal of some functions from the control of local authorities and its encouragement of the contracting out of others to the private sector led to the coining of the term: the *Contracting Authority*. Both in size and in the nature of its work, the local authority of the future, it was suggested, would be a contracting one!

If you wanted an illustration of the poet and dramatist T. S. Eliot's assertion that 'humour is a way of saying something serious', you need look no further. The terminology has changed – 'contracting out' having largely been displaced by the equally clumsy 'outsourcing' – but the credo of competition ushered in by the Thatcher Government's Compulsory Competitive Tendering (CCT) has long since become part of the day-to-day life of local government.

Both Cs were defining features of CCT, which required councils to put out for tender, or competitive bidding, increasing numbers of the services that most of them had previously provided themselves, using their own employees, equipment and facilities. The compulsion, therefore, was to

Figure 2.1   *The funnel of local authority discretion*

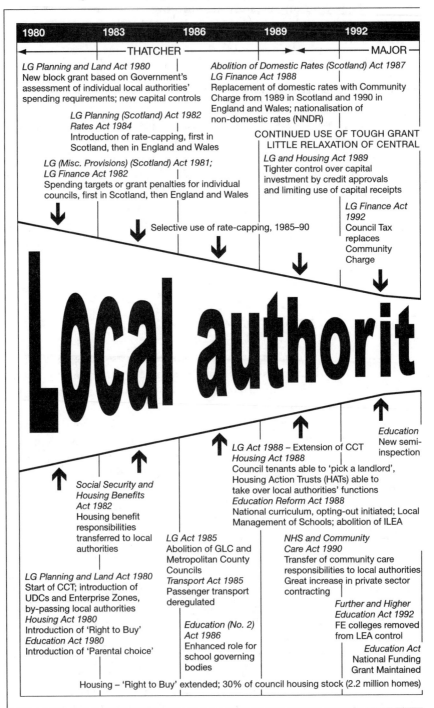

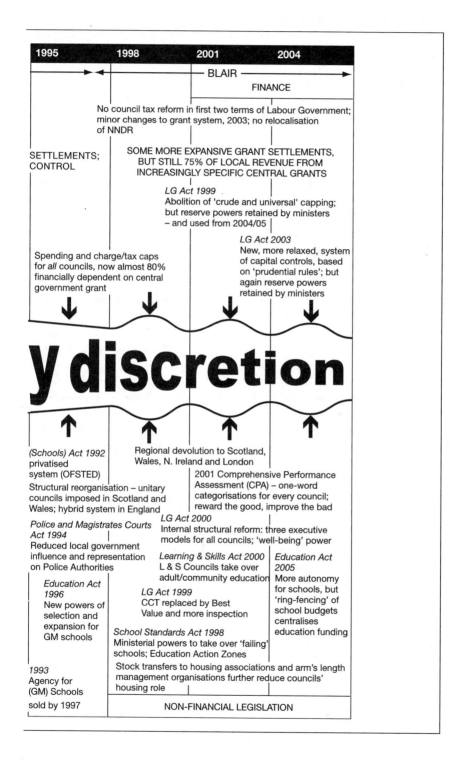

1995	1998	2001	2004

◄──►◄───────────── BLAIR ──────────────────►

FINANCE

No council tax reform in first two terms of Labour Government; minor changes to grant system, 2003; no relocalisation of NNDR

SETTLEMENTS; CONTROL

SOME MORE EXPANSIVE GRANT SETTLEMENTS, BUT STILL 75% OF LOCAL REVENUE FROM INCREASINGLY SPECIFIC CENTRAL GRANTS

LG Act 1999
Abolition of 'crude and universal' capping; but reserve powers retained by ministers – and used from 2004/05

LG Act 2003
New, more relaxed, system of capital controls, based on 'prudential rules'; but again reserve powers retained by ministers

Spending and charge/tax caps for *all* councils, now almost 80% financially dependent on central government grant

y discretion

(Schools) Act 1992 privatised system (OFSTED)

Regional devolution to Scotland, Wales, N. Ireland and London

2001 Comprehensive Performance Assessment (CPA) – one-word categorisations for every council; reward the good, improve the bad

Structural reorganisation – unitary councils imposed in Scotland and Wales; hybrid system in England

LG Act 2000
Internal structural reform: three executive models for all councils; 'well-being' power

Police and Magistrates Courts Act 1994
Reduced local government influence and representation on Police Authorities

Learning & Skills Act 2000
L & S Councils take over adult/community education

Education Act 2005
More autonomy for schools, but 'ring-fencing' of school budgets centralises education funding

Education Act 1996
New powers of selection and expansion for GM schools

LG Act 1999
CCT replaced by Best Value and more inspection

School Standards Act 1998
Ministerial powers to take over 'failing' schools; Education Action Zones

1993 Agency for (GM) Schools sold by 1997

Stock transfers to housing associations and arm's length management organisations further reduce councils' housing role

NON-FINANCIAL LEGISLATION

compete – not necessarily to contract out, which would only happen if the most competitive bid (defined quite simply as the lowest) came from some outside company or organisation, rather than from the council's own workforce.

Other services and functions too were exposed to the bracing breezes of competition. Council tenants were able to choose their own landlords and vote themselves out of local authority control. Similarly, the parents of children in state schools could vote to 'opt-out' of their Local Education Authority and become 'grant-maintained' directly by the then Department for Education. In the case of 1990s' urban regeneration initiatives like City Pride and City Challenge, councils were required to compete against each other for the limited funds that ministers were prepared to make available.

Most of these Conservative Government measures were opposed at the time by Labour, both in Parliament and in local government, where, by the 1990s, it was by far the strongest party political force. When a New Labour Government was elected in 1997, therefore, there had to be changes – but of policy, rather more than of philosophy. CCT went, but in its place came Best Value service provision – the legal requirement placed on councils to deliver a continuous improvement in the standard and efficiency of their services, bringing in outside contractors as appropriate. The process was driven by the four Cs, with councils expected to: *Challenge* the way in which their services were currently being provided; *Compare* their performance with that of others; *Consult* extensively on a plan to deliver continuous service improvements; and *Compete*, wherever practicable, with other potential service providers in implementing that plan. With only a slight adjustment of political emphasis, the Contracting Authority had become the *Competitive Authority* – or, to express what was happening in another way, the *Enabling Authority*.

Traditionally, UK local authorities, in addition to being the elected and representative governments of their localities, were – and were seen as being – large-scale service providers. Throughout the late nineteenth century and most of the twentieth, national governments passed legislation requiring or permitting the provision of all kinds of public services, mainly through the auspices of *other* bodies – and most significant by far of these other bodies were local authorities. Now, however, with some of those services already lost to the private sector or different kinds of single-purpose institutions, and most of the remainder exposed to the force of competition, local authorities' future role, it was argued, would be less as service *providers* and much more as service *enablers*. They might in many instances retain the ultimate responsibility for service provision. But, rather than do everything themselves, with their own directly employed workforces, they would stimulate, facilitate, support, regulate, influence and thereby *enable* other agencies and organisations to act on their behalf (see, e.g., Leach *et al.*, 1996).

As will already have become apparent, the language of local government changes at least as fast as the phenomena it describes, and the Government has decided that it prefers the term *commissioning* over enabling – presumably in a costless attempt to persuade local authorities that they have a more proactive role in overseeing the provision of services for which they themselves were once directly responsible. Confirmation of the arrival of the *Commissioning Authority* and partnership working, and an insight into the Government's thinking about the whole central–local government relationship, were provided by the then Education Secretary, Charles Clarke, in an important speech to the 2004 LGA Education and Social Services Conference:

> Let me say to you directly that your role will not for the most part be concerned with directly providing services. It will be increasingly about commissioning, and working with and through others – through the voluntary community organisations, private companies, co-operatives – whatever it may happen to be.
>
> You face huge and critical leadership challenges: vision and strategy, supporting and training others, joining up services and maximising linkages, increasing choice for users of services, getting people to work in partnership, spotting weaknesses and filling gaps. A role that plays to your historic strengths, to your role as community leaders.
>
> But leaving operational freedom to others, to head teachers, to the managers of children's centres. Using a variety of partners in the public, private and voluntary sectors to deliver day to day services and so offer local people choice and quality. (http://society.guardian.co.uk/conferences/story/0,9744,1331648,00.html)

Choice and quality – 'Customer First'

By no means all recent change in local government has been externally prompted. Increasingly since the 1980s local councils have examined their performance record more self-critically, looking for ways of improving it and thereby enhancing their public image. They have sought to develop – to quote two now rather dated 'buzz' phrases – a public service orientation or customer service culture.

Too often in the past, councils will now concede, they were inclined to act as what in many ways they were: unchallenged monopolistic service providers *to* – rather than *for* or *with* – a largely captive public. The last distinction is a crucial one. Rarely, until fairly recently, were service recipients in fact asked about the type, quantity or quality of service they required, or were prepared, through their own local taxes, to finance. Rarely, in short, were they treated as customers: people able to make choices, with the right to the information on which to base those choices, the right of redress if dissatisfied with the service received, and the right to go to other providers.

Local council services were, for the most part, professionally managed, competently delivered, and tolerably efficient. But the emphasis tended to be on quantity rather than quality, with relatively little consideration being paid to issues of flexibility, variety and consumer choice. In recent years, the pendulum has swung significantly – sometimes, it can seem, to the other extreme, with anybody using any kind of council service being referred to as a 'customer', as if they were making the choice to purchase it at an economic price from *their* local authority shop, rather than any of the others to which they might have taken their custom. It may, we hope, lead to better practice, but it risks blurring the many very different relationships that most people have with the range of local services they use – some of which are 'universal' (street cleaning, refuse collection), some demand-led (information, advice), some defined by eligibility or assessed need (council housing, day nursery places, most social services), and some imposed through legislation (education, trading standards, mental health services). In relatively few cases are they in fact 'customers' in the commonly understood sense of the word.

Notwithstanding the linguistic imprecision, most councils will now have a wide range of 'Customer First' initiatives to improve the quality of their services: neighbourhood offices, 'one-stop shops', call centres (sometimes 24-hour), interactive websites, public internet kiosks, complaints hotlines, council newspapers, community meetings, public attitude surveys, 'focus group' discussions on specific issues with selected groups of residents, public question times at council meetings. As we suggested in Chapter 1 in relation to council websites, it's worth looking out for what your own councils are doing – and perhaps asking yourself whether, in putting the 'Customer First', they might not, at least subconsciously, be putting the 'Citizen Second': overlooking the fact their residents are also members of a local political community, with rights and duties relating to political participation and choice as well to service consumption. It is a rhetorical question to which we shall return.

The present system – defining characteristics

Having identified some of the principal themes and concerns of modern-day local government, we now pause for some stocktaking. If the world of local government is changing as fundamentally as we suggest, what is it changing *from*? What, in broad introductory terms, does the present system look like? What are its main features and its overall rationale? In the remainder of this chapter we introduce some of the key defining characteristics of the UK's local government system.

Local government, not local administration

We should start with a vital distinction, and explain why we have so far been using, unquestioningly, the term 'local government', rather than 'local administration'. It will serve too as a further introduction: to why the university department for which one of us works is called the Institute of Local *Government* Studies (INLOGOV), and not Local *Administrative* Studies.

All countries of any significant size find it necessary to decentralise or disperse some of the basic tasks of governance. Some do so much more extensively and more enthusiastically than others. Switzerland, for example – albeit a somewhat exceptional one – has never had a national Ministry of Education or a Ministry of Health (Allen, 1990, p. 1). The Swiss decentralise these services entirely to the control of local authorities, and mostly very much smaller authorities than those in Britain.

When central governments decentralise, they may choose to do so in different ways and to different degrees:

- *Administrative decentralisation, or delegation*
  They may delegate purely administrative decision-making to dependent field offices of a central ministry. All major policy decisions will continue to be made centrally, but the service will be delivered and routine administrative decisions made by locally based but centrally employed civil servants. The most obvious example in Britain is the Department for Work and Pensions' Jobcentre Plus, whose *cash payments* to the sick, disabled and unemployed are made from local offices of the DWP, or in Northern Ireland the Social Security Agency. They are thus largely separated – unlike the practice in many countries – from the local authority social *services* provided to many of the same people.
- *Functional decentralisation*
  Second, central government can create semi-independent agencies to run specific services. Here, the most obvious example is the NHS, with its structure of strategic health authorities and trusts, overseen by boards of appointed and nominated members. It may look a little like the structure of local councils, and in many countries the health service is a fully integrated part of the local government system. But, though they work closely with and are scrutinised by local authorities, Britain's health authorities and trusts are quite separate: funded by and ultimately accountable to central government, and thus part of the growing 'quangocracy' referred to earlier.
- *Political decentralisation, or devolution*
  Third, central government can devolve policy-making responsibilities in a wide range of service areas to relatively autonomous and directly

elected regional, provincial or local governments. This political decentralisation – the process that produced the Scottish Parliament, the Welsh and Northern Ireland Assemblies, and the Greater London Authority – in which a constitutionally superior body chooses to hand over certain powers to constitutionally dependent ones, is clearly distinguishable from *federalism,* in which *both* the national (or federal) and the local bodies are assigned their powers equally and separately by the constitution. But it is just as clearly distinguishable from local administration.

Local authorities are far more than simply outposts or agents of central government, delivering services in ways and to standards laid down in detail at national ministerial level. Their role, as representative bodies elected by their fellow citizens, is to take such decisions themselves, in accordance with their own policy priorities: to govern their locality. If this were not so, there would not be the often dramatic variations in service costs and performance measures revealed in the increasingly popular league tables of local council statistics. Nor would we have seen in several of our Items in Exhibit 2.1 examples of ways in which councils can, to a certain extent at least, determine and pursue their own initiatives.

Local self-government?

So, does the system of local government – councils of elected politicians making policy decisions on behalf of their local communities – amount to local *self-government*? Do localities and communities have the rights and resources genuinely to manage their own public affairs in what they see as their own best interests? Some writers appear to think so, and use the terms 'local government' and 'local self-government' almost interchangeably.

Others are more hesitant. Local government *ought* to mean local or community self-government, they seem to suggest; it ought to be about democratically elected representatives collectively deciding how best to respond to all the differing needs and wishes of the residents of their area. In practice, though, that is not how it has worked in the United Kingdom.

Many countries do have something legitimately describable as local self-government, especially those formed historically by the coming together of several small communities, for mutual help and support – for example, Switzerland, the Netherlands, Italy, the Scandinavian countries. Local councils or municipalities in such countries have, on average, much smaller populations than do UK local authorities. Yet they have something that British councils historically have not had: a *power of general competence* – a general right to undertake any activities that they feel to be in the interests of their citizens, unless such activities are expressly forbidden or assigned to other bodies. Like private citizens, they can do anything they are not precisely forbidden from doing. In these countries, as Allen puts it (1990, p. 23):

> Local government is not looked upon as just a mechanism. Rather, it is seen as the organic self-expression of the people themselves, whose powers are not yielded to the centre, but retained by the citizens of each community in the country to provide necessary local services for themselves.

In the United Kingdom, with its long monarchical history, the formal constitutional position is almost precisely the reverse: local councils have been able to do *only* what they are statutorily permitted to do. Their rights and competencies are not general, but specific. To quote Allen again (1990, p. 22), almost echoing Ambassador Seitz from our opening paragraphs, or indeed Charles Clarke:

> Local government is looked upon essentially as a subordinate mechanism created by the state for its own convenience. It is no more than one of several alternative agencies through which the paternalist central government can arrange the provision of services for the state's citizen-subjects.

Underlining their subordinate status, the common law doctrine under which councils operate is known as *ultra vires,* a Latin term which translates as 'beyond the powers'. If a local council does something or spends money it is not statutorily authorised to, it will be deemed to have acted *ultra vires*: beyond its powers, and therefore illegally. Moreover, until the practice was finally abolished in the Local Government Act 2000, the elected councillors who collectively agreed to the action became individually punishable and personally liable to refund any money spent illegally.

Another, potentially even more important, measure was introduced in the same 2000 Act – the so-called *power of well-being*. Local authorities were given a new discretionary power, enabling them 'to promote the economic, social and environmental well-being of their areas'. It is not, *per se*, a power of general competence, and does not at a stroke make councils truly self-governing entities, as there are important qualifications concerning the power's use. It cannot be used, for example, to raise money, and it must be exercised with regard to any guidance issued by the Government. But, for enterprising local authorities, it genuinely loosens one of the legal constraints under which they have operated historically – enabling them to think more of the policy outcomes they wish to achieve and the innovations they might make, rather than focusing exclusively on the delivery of existing services (see Chapter 9).

Creatures of statute

Like all local councils' more specific powers and competencies, though, this well-being power is derived from legislation, and in this sense it reinforces, rather than undermines, local government's necessarily subordinate position in Britain's constitution. The doctrine of parliamentary supremacy derives from the fact that the United Kingdom, like more than 80 per cent of the world's nations, is a *unitary* state, not a federal one – as noted in Chapter 1. There is a single source of constitutional power and authority: the Westminster Parliament, in which usually nowadays one party has an overall majority of members and thus forms the Government of the day. Parliament, processing legislation introduced by the Government, can make or unmake law on any subject whatever – including local government.

In federal systems, constitutional power is divided between the federal government at the centre and the governments of decentralised states or regions. No such division exists in Britain. Constitutionally, local authorities are in the same subordinate position as are the Scottish Parliament and the Welsh and Northern Ireland Assemblies. They are literally the creatures, the creations, of parliamentary statute. Their boundaries, duties, powers, memberships and modes of operation are laid down by Acts of Parliament. Naturally, therefore, they can be abolished by Parliament and, as we have seen, restructured and reincarnated at Parliament's will.

Partial autonomy

To summarise: the United Kingdom has a constitutionally subordinate system of local government, without, historically, the wide-ranging competence of many European continental systems, yet which is far more than a network of field agencies of central government. It could be described as semi-autonomous.

There are semantic purists who will insist that a body can no more be partially autonomous than partially pregnant. We find it useful, however, to be able to describe one governmental institution as having relatively less autonomy than another, or less than it possessed at some time in the past. Indeed, such imprecise terminology fits appropriately our uncodified and convention-based constitution. Most European countries have formal, written constitutions, which usually include some provision for, and protection of, the principle of local self-government. In the United Kingdom, with no comparable single constitutional document, there is in theory no limit to the sovereignty of Parliament. There is correspondingly no constitutional protection for local government: neither for the rights of individual councils nor for the system as a whole.

In practice, however, as we shall see in Chapter 4, much of the history of UK local government, particularly during the early decades of the twentieth century, has been about governments determining and Parliaments legislating to devolve powers and responsibilities to local authorities. Local councils have been seen, in Allen's (1990) phrase, as a usefully democratic and effective 'subordinate mechanism' for the delivery of all kinds of services that central government has decided should be provided publicly.

Statutory powers can assume various forms. At one extreme they may be *detailed* and *compulsory,* requiring local councils to undertake certain activities to tightly defined and rigorously enforced standards. Alternatively, they may be *permissive* or *discretionary,* leaving councils to decide for themselves whether or not to provide a particular service, and to what standard. Very frequently they are mixed, as by chance are the three main examples in our news headlines in Exhibit 2.1 (Items 3, 4 and 11). In fact, the chance was less than it might seem, for much of the legislation affecting local government has traditionally had what might be termed a high 'discretion factor'. Local councils have had a considerable say in how they deliver their services and, sometimes, whether or not they do so. But discretion has no guarantee. It can be curtailed and ultimately withdrawn: hence the aptness of the label 'partial autonomy'.

Directly elected

The characteristic responsible above all others for whatever degree of autonomy local authorities do possess is that of their direct election. They are not composed of locally based civil servants or central government appointees. They consist of local people, chosen at regular and regulated elections to represent the interests and inhabitants of the communities in which they themselves also live and work.

These representatives – known as *councillors* or *elected members*, and sometimes just *members* for short – constitute collectively the local council and are the embodiment of its legal authority. On the basis of that authority, they recruit and employ a wide range of staff – professionally qualified 'officers', other administrative, technical and clerical 'white-collar' staff, and various categories of manual or 'blue-collar' workers – to carry out the policies and deliver the services that they, as democratically elected representatives, determine.

Direct election does not, in the UK's unitary system of government, make councillors the constitutional equals or rivals of Members of Parliament. Councillors may have to face their electorates more frequently than do MPs, and there are far more of them: nearly 35 times as many, but elections can always be suspended, just as councils can be abolished, at any time that the Government, through Parliament, decrees. Until that happens, though, councillors' elected status accords them a legitimacy quite different from that of, say, the appointed members of health authorities or any other local quango.

Councillors have had to present themselves and their policy proposals for consideration and approval by the electorate. That local democratic approval represents a uniquely potent bargaining counter in any subsequent negotiations, whether with ministers, Whitehall civil servants or their own local officers. Their critics may, perhaps with some cause, question voters' genuine understanding of the complex issues involved and their relatively low turnout rates in local elections. But the very fact of electoral backing in any even aspiring democratic society has a force of its own.

Multi-service organisations

If electoral accountability is the primary distinguishing feature of local authorities, the second is their range of responsibilities. They are involved in some way or other, it can sometimes seem, with an almost infinite variety of different services.

We referred earlier to councils looking after people from womb to tomb. Another way of illustrating the same point is through the A–Z service directories accessible nowadays on most councils' websites. The directories are designed for the councils' own sometimes understandably confused residents: to publicise the services that may be available to them and, even more importantly, where to go to access them, and who to contact. It has been estimated that a typical unitary authority has at least 700 'lines of business', which is far more than most multinational companies, and, it could be argued, make it correspondingly far more demanding to manage. If you doubt this, take a look at Exhibit 2.2, which lists a selection of just the A-initialled services that such a council might in some way be involved with – all we had room for.

Multi-functional organisations

All the services listed in Exhibit 2.2 have some degree of council involvement. But by no means are they all provided directly by the council itself. Historically, as noted above, it is true that councils' principal function has been that of *direct service provider*. They purchased the land, provided the buildings and equipment, and employed all the staff necessary to deliver their services.

Councils have always, though, had other functions and roles as well, and it is these roles that are becoming relatively more important nowadays. In many cases, the local authority is the *regulator* or *monitor* of the activities of other agencies and organisations. The new liquor

Exhibit 2.2 An A–A of council services

Service	Possible contact department/office
Abandoned vehicles, removal of	Environmental & Consumer Services
Abnormal loads	Highways
Abuse of children	Social Services
Access, for disabled	Planning & Architecture
Accessible transport	Travel Information Centre
Accident prevention	Environmental & Consumer Services
Accidents, road clearance	Highways
Accommodation, hotels and guesthouses	Tourism
Accommodation, for homeless	Housing
Accounts, of the Council	Finance/Treasurer's
Acupuncture, registration of	Environmental & Consumer Services
Admissions and transfers to schools	Education
Adoption, of children	Social Services
Adoption, of roads	Highways
Adult education	Education/Leisure & Culture
Adult protection (vulnerable older people)	Social Services
Adventure playgrounds	Leisure & Community Services
Advertisements and signs, control of	Planning/Development Control
Advice, neighbourhood offices	Neighbourhood Advice & Benefits
Advice bureaux (of ward councillors)	Members' Services
After-school activities	Leisure & Community Services
AIDS/HIV, advice on	Social Services
Air quality, measurement of	Environmental & Consumer Services
Alcohol abuse, advice on	Social Services
Allotments, hire of	Leisure & Community Services
Alteration of buildings	Planning/Development Control
Aluminium recycling	Environmental & Consumer Services
Amusement machines, licensing of	Environmental & Consumer Services
Animal welfare, enforcement of regulations	Environmental & Consumer Services
Antique markets, information on	Environmental & Consumer Services
Ants, control of	Environmental & Consumer Services
Approved lists, of contractors and service suppliers	Finance/Treasurer's
Architecture, listed buildings	Planning
Arts and entertainment, information on	Leisure Services
Asbestos, removal of	Environmental & Consumer Services
Assistance to industry	Economic Development
Awards, student	Education

licensing powers in respect of pubs, clubs, restaurants, takeaways and the like that were causing consternation in 2005 were additional to existing licensing responsibilities for public entertainments, theatres, cinemas, sex establishments, street trading, taxi drivers, animal boarding establishments, hairdressers, late night cafés, performing animals, pet shops, caravan sites and acupuncturists. Similar responsibilities include the *registration* of private residential homes, and the *certification* of sports ground safety, as the public became acutely aware following the Bradford and Hillsborough football disasters.

A further role is as *facilitator,* providing advice, assistance and possibly finance to individuals or organisations undertaking activities consistent with the policy of the council. Thus a Local Action Team of council officers will provide help in setting up credit unions as part of the council's work in alleviating poverty and debt. Start-up grants and loans are available for the establishment of new businesses and workers' co-operatives, and grants are given also to an extensive range of arts, recreation, social and community groups. Finally, moving a further step away from direct service provision, there is that most rapidly developing of council roles to which we have already alluded: that of *service contractor.*

Power of taxation

Vital as we argued that it is, electoral authority is essentially a moral force. To be effective, it needs something more tangible: the right to tax. A further crucial characteristic of local authorities – one that stems directly from the fact that, as multi-purpose organisations, they have choices and priorities to determine, with financial implications – is therefore that they have the power to tax local residents. Other local agencies are funded by government grants and from their own trading income. Local authorities also receive much – too much, we shall suggest in Chapter 10 – of their income from these sources, but for almost 400 years they were also able set the levels of, as well as to collect, their own taxes.

Since 1980, however, the local tax system has undergone an unprecedented series of reforms. Part of the outcome has been that local authorities' taxation power is no longer, as lawyers might say, an unfettered one. As recorded on our funnel of local authority discretion (see Figure 2.1), Conservative ministers in the 1980s used statutory powers to cap or limit councils' levels of spending and their right to tax their own residents, thereby effectively controlling their budgets. The 1997 Labour Government abolished what it called the 'crude and universal capping' system it inherited, but ministers retained and in 2004 resurrected the use of a seemingly arbitrary reserve power to intervene and cap selectively the budget and council tax levels of any council proposing to spend in a way that they decide is 'excessive'. So, while the power to tax still distinguishes local councils from other agencies of public administration, it is a power exercised nowadays with central government constantly looking over its shoulder.

Conclusion

We have identified in this chapter a set of characteristics that, individually and collectively, serve as a definition of UK local government (see Exhibit 2.3). This is a slightly more elaborate definition than the one we arrived at in Chapter 1, and it will serve as a reference point for several of the remaining chapters in Part 1 of the book.

Exhibit 2.3 UK local government defined

Local government is:

- a form of geographical and political decentralisation,
- in which directly elected councils,
- created by and subordinate to Parliament,
- have partial autonomy
- to provide a wide variety of services
- through various direct and indirect means,
- funded in part by local taxation.

Chapter 3

Why Elected Local Government?

Introduction

With the development of that branch of linguistics known as discourse analysis, it can sometimes seem that there is more interest in how politicians deliver their speeches – the phrases and figures of speech they use, their mannerisms and gestures – than in what they actually say. Sometimes this may be justified, but there are plenty of exceptions. One we have already encountered in Chapter 2 – Charles Clarke's message to local authorities that their days as direct education service-providers were over. It may have been unpalatable, but its importance was undeniable.

A few months earlier, in March 2004, Nick Raynsford, the minister then responsible for local government, had delivered an equally important speech. But, fittingly for one more concerned to court his audience and gain their co-operation, his tone was more positive and reasonable than confrontational. He identified four challenges for local government, but he matched these with four challenges for central government, and prefaced both with an identification of 'three unique characteristics of local government which we should value highly'.

Since he used the term 'local government' roughly forty times and 'local governance' not once, it seems safe to assume that his principal focus, like that of this book and particularly this chapter, was on *elected local government*. Indeed, he confirms this by making his first 'unique characteristic':

> local government's democratic accountability to local people. Local government is the only body accountable to the whole community. No other body is answerable to all local people for the decisions it takes. (http://www.publictechnology.net/print.php?sid = 761)

Raynsford's other two nominated characteristics were local government's ability to capture the importance of locality and place, and its capacity for 'joined-up' policy-making. Taken together, as he notes, 'these unique characteristics provide a powerful argument for the value of local government'. They also provide an unmistakably different view of local government from that portrayed by Charles Clarke – a point perhaps acknowledged indirectly by Raynsford (2004, p. 3) in the first of his four challenges for central government, which, he proposes:

> must be better at joining up and presenting a more coherent and consistent approach to local government. [E]ach department should behave towards local government in a way which supports a commonly agreed set of principles. This is not always the case at present.

We shall return to this important point, quite regularly, in later chapters. In this chapter we pick up and expand upon Raynsford's 'unique characteristics' in discussing the rationale and *raison d'être* of elected local government, its value and values.

The problems of local government – some inherent costs and consequences

To central government, it often seems, the commonest 'problem' of local government is when it refuses to do what central government wishes: when local councils pursue demonstrably different goals from those of the party in power nationally. An alternative interpretation of such a battle of wills is that it demonstrates the health and robustness of a governmental system. Far from constituting a problem, it ought to be seen as an affirmation of precisely what local government should be about: locally elected and accountable representatives developing policies embodying *their* judgement of the best interests of *their* local community, not the judgement of the centre. As Nick Raynsford put it in the second of his challenges for central government:

> Local government is not defined as a delivery agent for central government. It is another democratically elected tier of government, with the strengths and responsibilities that come with a democratic mandate. (2004, p. 3)

The challenge is that by no means all his ministerial, and prime ministerial, colleagues would, in practice, endorse this view. Our own reference to 'the problems of local government' is intended to suggest something rather more subtle and complex. We mean the potential costs and considerations involved in any decision to devolve administrative responsibility, let alone political power. In several cases, these potential costs are merely the obverse of possible benefits. But it is still useful to enumerate some of what Allen (1990, ch. 1) terms the 'disadvantages of decentralisation'.

The first argument deployed against decentralisation is that of *financial cost*. It was the principal argument of the victorious opposition in the referendum campaign for an elected North East regional assembly, and is a central element in the ongoing debate about the merits of all-unitary local government in England. Decentralisation duplicates scarce financial resources and staff. Things could be run more cheaply from the centre, critics suggest, whether the centre in question is London or, when considering the case for area or neighbourhood offices, from a council's own headquarters.

Closely linked to finance is *efficiency*. It might be difficult to attract experienced staff and enterprising management, especially if the decentralised units are relatively small and poorly resourced. The argument loses some of its force, however, if there is a national government responsible (or irresponsible) for, among other managerial embarrassments: the Millennium Dome; a Jubilee Line extension costing nearly twice its promised £2.1 billion; army SA80 rifles (in Kosovo) that jam during rapid firing, and Clansmen radios unable either to transmit or receive messages; a Child Support Agency that writes off 30 per cent of the revenue it should have collected; railway signals positioned so badly that there is a jargonised abbreviation ('spads') for the frequency with which they are passed at danger; and a poll tax. In Britain at least, policy inefficiency is not confined to any single level of government.

A different kind of argument is that of *inequality*. The more genuinely decentralised a service, the greater, inevitably, will be the resulting disparities among geographical areas and social groups. These disparities, whether in health or local government services, are condemned as products of a 'postcode lottery', rather than as the outcomes of decisions made by local representative bodies, often elected, responding to their reading of local needs and priorities. The result is public, media and electoral demand for greater 'fairness' and minimum national standards, followed by central government's intervention with resource distribution formulas bringing greater territorial equity but at the cost of local political and financial discretion. This apparent national intolerance of locally varying service provision is a particularly British phenomenon, and perhaps the biggest dilemma facing genuine local government reformers, as opposed to instinctive centralisers or abolitionists.

Finally, there is the charge of potential *corruption*, levelled probably more frequently at local than at national government, and at least as much in the news today as it was in the 1970s, at the time of the notorious 'Poulson affair'. In 1974, several leading politicians and senior public sector employees were found guilty of having improperly and corruptly secured contracts for the private architect, John Poulson. The case led to the important formulation of a National Code of Conduct for the guidance of both councillors and officers. Perhaps for this reason, it is remembered primarily as a case of *local* government corruption, despite the fact that

'Poulson's cadre' (Doig, 1984, p. 142) embraced a Cabinet minister, MPs of two parties, civil servants, health service and nationalised industry employees, as well as councillors and officers.

An equally high-profile case of the 1980s and 1990s – much more to do with political power than personal financial gain in this case – was the 'homes for votes' affair involving Dame Shirley Porter, then Leader of Westminster City Council. Dame Shirley and five councillor and officer associates were found by a local government district auditor to have operated a housing sales policy specifically for the electoral benefit of the Conservative Party, thereby costing their council many millions of pounds. This verdict was eventually upheld by the Law Lords in 2001, who condemned the behaviour as a 'deliberate, blatant and dishonest use of public power', and required Dame Shirley to pay a £37 million surcharge to the council. By that time, aspects of the case had been considered in 1996/97 by the Government's Committee on Standards in Public Life, chaired by Lord Nolan. But it should also be remembered that this Committee was set up in the first place to investigate allegations of misconduct and 'sleaze' in the *Palace,* not the City, of Westminster, and on the part of MPs and ministers, who significantly had no equivalent of the councillors' Code of Conduct to guide their behaviour.

Our point is not that any set of politicians – local or national, male or female, Party A or Party B – is intrinsically more virtuous or more corruptible than any other. It is merely that we should retain a sense of perspective and keep in mind Allen's warning (1990, p. 12) that, despite all the national and international evidence, that

> central agencies are often at least as incompetent, inefficient or corrupt as local bodies, local authorities are perennially in the news for alleged corruption and graft ... one or two notorious cases can suffice to keep the whole concept of local government in disrepute.

The values of local government

These alleged 'problems' of decentralisation are not to be dismissed lightly. But they can be more than balanced by its positive features or, as various authors have phrased it, the justifications of local government (Smith, 1985, ch. 2; Young, 1986b; Clarke and Stewart, 1991, ch. 3). In the remainder of this chapter we group our justifications under the seven headings itemised in Exhibit 3.1. It is a grouping derived from an important and enduring literature – dating back at least 150 years to the still relevant writings of Joshua Toulmin Smith and John Stuart Mill.

Exhibit 3.1 The values or justifications of elected local government

Elected local government is likely to be better than a combination of central government and local administration at:

1. Building and articulating community identity;
2. Emphasising diversity;
3. Fostering innovation and learning;
4. Responding swiftly, appropriately, corporately;
5. Promoting citizenship and participation;
6. Providing political education and training; and
7. Dispersing power.

Building and articulating community identity

In Chapter 2 we concentrated particularly on local *government* and its contrast with local administration. We now focus on *local* government: the government of a particular geographical area and, if the relevant boundaries have been drawn appropriately, the government of a community. The institutions of local government ought both to 'capture the importance of locality and place', as Raynsford put it, and to reflect and reinforce people's sense of community:

> A local authority has the capacity to shape an area, to preserve it, to develop it, to change it, and in doing so to give it a new identity. (Clarke and Stewart, 1991, p. 29)

But of necessity these things take time and need encouragement, both of which have been at a premium in recent years. We contrasted in Chapter 2 the kind of 'bottom-up' local self-government found in some European countries, which grew out of local communities coming together for mutual help and support, and the United Kingdom's more 'top-down' version, deriving from parliamentary statute and the drawing of boundary lines on maps. The inevitable danger of over-frequent 'top-down' restructuring is the severing of any link between a local authority and community identity, the most visible sign of which must be the imposition of alien council names that at best bewilder and at worst infuriate.

The reorganisation of the early 1970s produced countless examples of these 'artificial' names, initially as unfamiliar to their own residents as they still are to many outsiders. Some disappeared, generally unlamented, in reorganisation during the 1990s: the non-metropolitan counties of Avon, Cleveland and Humberside, together with the equally short-lived and much-mispronounced Welsh counties of Clwyd and Dyfed. But countless others remain: the metropolitan districts of Calderdale and Kirklees (respectively the areas around Halifax and Huddersfield), Knowsley (east of Liverpool) and Sandwell (West Midlands); and, among the many non-metropolitan district candidates, Adur, West Sussex (the name of a river – who lives in a river?); Bassetlaw, Notts (an Anglo-Saxon name for an area around Worksop, today not even a village); Gravesham, Kent (another harmless but meaningless Anglo-Saxon name to emphasise that it isn't the real town of Gravesend), Three Rivers, Herts (see Adur); and the doubly confusing Wyre, Lancashire (yet another river) and Wyre Forest (Worcestershire).

Then you can add to all these non-names at least 45 'compass point councils' – where real towns and neighbourhoods considered too small to govern themselves have been lumped together and anonymised by boundary commission bureaucrats into meaningless geographical mongrels – North Hertfordshire, South Somerset, East Northamptonshire, West Lancashire, and so on. As it happens, each of these four contains a town of at least 30,000 population – respectively, Letchworth, Yeovil, Rushden, and Skelmersdale – that would qualify for self-governing status in almost any other country in Western Europe. In Britain, however, they and their like can be seen as testaments to a national political culture that is inclined to build and restructure its local government system 'more on bureaucratic and professional principles than upon local needs and community identities' (Lowndes, 1996, p. 71).

Emphasising diversity – or multiversity

A sense of place and past implies *distinctiveness*: of an area's distinctive geography, history, economy, social and political culture, and of its consequently distinctive preferences and priorities. It is the recognition that even local authorities of the same type, with the same statutory powers and responsibilities, can be utterly different from each other and have completely different governmental needs.

In a federal system like that in the United States, where the states can pass as well as promote their own legislation, the diversity of local demands and circumstances can appear extreme and even bizarre. In Indiana, it is illegal to ride on a bus within four hours of eating garlic; in Kentucky, to carry an ice cream cone in one's pocket; and in Mississippi, to drive with no shoes on. But UK local authorities can also differ so greatly in character that it is possible to imagine their enacting almost equally singular legislation, given the chance.

Basildon, Berwick-upon-Tweed and Bolsover are all English non-metropolitan districts. Yet, apart from their initial letters, they have little in common. Basildon, heartland of 'Essex girl' jokes, was the first of the country's postwar New Towns. After some fifty years, it has grown to include a population of well over 100,000, yet has to share its district council with the two inevitably overshadowed townships of Billericay and Wickford, the total 166,000 population making it the third largest of England's 238 non-metropolitan districts. It is London commuter territory, but the local economy is also thriving – no longer driven by the large Ford car plant, but identified by the government as a key part of the Thames Gateway and an area of potential industrial and residential development. Hence the large-scale investment in a regional shopping centre, Festival Leisure Park, and – not to be overlooked – the National Motorboat Museum. Though there are pockets of deprivation amid the growing prosperity, the Conservatives in 2002 took control of the traditionally Labour-dominated 42-member council and in subsequent elections increased their overall majority.

Berwick-upon-Tweed Borough Council covers nearly nine times the area of Basildon – 370 square miles – but has about one-sixth of its population. By this latter criterion it is almost the smallest council in England. It employs only about 170 staff and has a budget of under £20 million. Notwithstanding its team's membership of the Scottish Football League, the medieval walled town itself lies two miles south of the Scottish border. But most of the borough is deeply rural, its economy based on agriculture, fishing and light industry, plus summer tourism attracted by its picturesque coastline and the Northumberland National Park. The politics of the 29-member council were traditionally Independent and more recently Liberal Democrat, but here too the Conservatives have made advances, and in the 2003 elections emerged as comfortably the largest party, just one seat short of majority control.

Bolsover's voters in North-East Derbyshire, by contrast, haven't elected a single Conservative to their 37-member council in nearly twenty years and never a Liberal Democrat. It is not so much a Labour stronghold as a monopoly. Better known in recent years for its MP – the 'Beast of Bolsover', Dennis Skinner – than for its council, the area was for more than a hundred years a centre of the country's mining industry, although its castle and market charter date back to the thirteenth century. Today there are no mines, nor railways. An enterprise park has replaced the colliery, small businesses are being developed, mining landscapes reclaimed, and heritage sites restored. The council itself, its nearly 600 staff making it by far the town's largest employer, leads the search for a new identity in a coal-less age.

Any other random selection of B-initialled districts would produce just as great a diversity. Yet central government's instinct tends to be to focus on the relatively few similarities of such authorities and to play down their obvious contrasts. Ministers and civil servants struggle to devise formulas that will enable all such councils to be dealt with as a single group. A thriving local government does the reverse. It emphasises and gives voice and expression to the distinctiveness of local communities. It is the *government of difference* or of diversity – or, more accurately still, of *multiversity*.

Fostering innovation and learning

By responding to diverse local circumstances and acting as the government of difference, local authorities are almost bound to enhance the learning capacity of government. They will develop their own solutions and initiatives, some of which may prove unsuccessful or applicable only to their specific locality, but some of which may be adaptable – either by other local authorities or even by central government.

Local authorities are constantly learning from each other – through official bodies like the Audit Commission and the Improvement and Development Agency (IDeA), publicising examples of 'best practice'; through the dozens of local government professional magazines and journals, conferences and seminars; and by simple word of mouth. Refer back to our own selection of news items in Exhibit 2.1. You can be sure that, with or without ministerial encouragement, other councils will have investigated Hull's nutritionally balanced school meals, and have joined the Chinese in exploring the adaptability of Tameside's recycling by glass crusher.

Almost every local authority in the country has developed or piloted some new service that has subsequently been adopted or adapted for use elsewhere. Croydon fits its wheelie bins with microchips, to reveal how much residents are recycling. Barnsley has extended its compulsory retirement age, allowing employees to work until the age of 70. Newport, Gwent was (we think) the first council to introduce streetlights with solar panels. Calderdale hands out on-the-spot fines to anyone throwing cigarette ends on the ground. York has a satellite system capable of signalling to traffic lights as a bus is approaching. The Isle of Wight embarrasses disruptive pupils by driving them to school in 'The Pink Peril', an unheated pink bus. And, possibly despairing of central government's inaction, Southampton and Woking Councils are tackling climate change and cutting carbon emissions by, respectively, harnessing a geo-thermal well to produce electricity and hot water for local businesses, and using micro-generation methods of solar panels, small wind turbines and a static fuel cell (MacGregor, 2006). The list is literally endless, and we defy you to find a council that *cannot* produce some service innovation to boast or bore about.

Responding swiftly, appropriately, corporately

Distance delays. It can also distort perception. Being the multi-service multi-functional organisations that they are, local councils on the spot ought to be able to identify better and faster than can central government the most appropriate response to any local situation. They should also be able to organise that response themselves, quickly, in a co-ordinated fashion, and, possibly, more economically. Sharpe (1970, pp. 155, 165) terms this ability the 'knowledge value' of local government:

> central government is not equipped to grasp the inimitable conditions of each locality. Local government is preferable precisely because locally elected institutions employing their own specialist staff are better placed to understand and interpret both the conditions and the needs of local communities ... out-stationed field agencies could not ... co-ordinate their activities with each other.

An exceptional but vital example of such co-ordination was provided by Kent County Council's emergency support operation following the bomb explosion at the Royal Marines' barracks at Deal in September 1989 which killed eleven bandsmen. The operation involved almost the whole range of council departments:

- the Fire Service
- the Police, who initially notified ...
- the Emergency Planning Unit, who co-ordinated the ensuing support work, calling in, where necessary, organisations such as the British Red Cross, the ambulance service, and Dover District Council
- Social Services, providing temporary shelter for those evacuated from their homes, meals-on-wheels, care and counselling support
- Education, as schools were requisitioned as rest centres
- the School Meals Service, providing food and hot drinks for both the rescued and rescuers
- Building Design and Highways, whose structural engineers were needed to advise on partially collapsed buildings
- Supplies, called upon to provide waterproofs and other protective equipment.

The response to the London bombing incidents in July 2005 differed in certain respects, having been previously rehearsed, and with principal service responsibilities being divided between the Greater London Authority and the relevant London boroughs. But the principle – the benefit to be derived from what is known in management jargon as 'horizontal integration' – is just as applicable as when it was expounded in the Widdicombe Committee Report:

Local authorities can respond corporately to multi-dimensional local issues, such as inner city problems, in a way which national services are less able to do. This is an advantage of multi-purpose units of government which is not easily replicated in a system of local administration. Thus, while the health service might maximise efficiency in its vertical integration of a single service between district health authority and Whitehall, local government will tend to have the advantage in horizontal integration of a range of services at local level. (Widdicombe, 1986a, p. 52)

'Holistic' or 'joined-up' government (see Perri 6 *et al.*, 2002) are the more contemporary terms for the same phenomenon, the contrast being the 'silo' organisation: long, vertical towers making policy pronouncements and attempting to deliver services independently of one another. Those in multi-functional local authorities can find it disconcerting to be lectured about the virtues of joined-up government by ministers in their apparently less effectively integrated Whitehall departmental silos. Many of our most intractable policy problems – crime, community safety, social exclusion, job creation, drugs (see Exhibit 3.2) – require the kind of cross-cutting, multi-service intervention that local authorities, with their wide range of duties, powers and services, are ideally placed to both provide and co-ordinate.

Promoting citizenship and participation

Local *administration* is about acceptance: local officials' acceptance of nationally determined policy, and service recipients' acceptance of those officials' implementation of that policy. Local *government* is about choice and challenge. It actively encourages, particularly nowadays, citizen involvement and participation. It has what Sharpe (1970, p. 160) calls 'democratic primacy' over central government, 'because it does enable more people to participate in their own government'.

Most obviously, elected local government involves citizens as voters and elected representatives. The regularity of local elections means that we have the chance to vote for our councillors far more frequently than for our MPs, even if only a minority of us actually do so. It is interesting, bearing in mind recent low local election turnouts, that, compared to many countries, the United Kingdom has an exceptionally small number of councils and councillors – who are therefore unknown personally to most electors – and an exceptionally large number of MPs. Even so, for every MP or parliamentary candidate, there are roughly forty councillors or candidates in our so-called 'principal' councils – that is, counties, districts, boroughs and unitaries.

Exhibit 3.2 Local government's contribution to a joined-up drugs policy

Social Services departments – plan and provide for social care needs of problem drug users.

Housing departments – provide housing for recovering drug users; manage and control drug use in areas of social housing.

Education and Youth Services – provide drug awareness education, in and outside school; can develop a community drug prevention strategy, using youth and outreach workers and community development officers.

Environmental Services – are responsible for the collection and safe disposal of used syringes; license premises for public entertainment, register door supervisors, etc.

Leisure and Recreation – can provide young people with appropriate and accessible leisure facilities.

Training and Personnel – can contribute to drug prevention strategies; provide help for employees who themselves have drug problems.

Economic Development – provide employment opportunities to deter drug dealing and usage.

Youth Offending Teams – direct young drug-using offenders towards drug treatment.

PLUS, CORPORATELY, local authorities are almost certainly the best-equipped organisations to liaise with representatives from the police, customs and excise, the probation and prison services, health authorities, and the voluntary sector.

These figures, moreover, completely exclude the 90,000 or so elected members of the country's 'local' – that is, parish, town and community – councils. There are about 8,700 parish and town councils in England, and some 2,000 community councils in Wales and Scotland, with an average of nine elected members each, albeit some of them doubling as councillors on principal authorities as well. Some of these councils are larger than our smaller district councils, representing communities of over 30,000 people, and in many countries they would be powerful and important institutions. In the UK, by contrast, as we shall see in Chapter 5, their powers are limited mainly to the discretionary provision of relatively minor and very localised services, and to representing the views of their residents to principal councils and other agencies. Not surprisingly in the circumstances, many elections go uncontested, but these councils remain democratically constituted and accountable bodies, and offer to a great many citizens the means of participating directly in the government of their communities.

There is, in any case, immensely more to participation in local government than standing and voting in local elections. Elections are only the tip of the participation iceberg, as has been shown emphatically by researchers at De Montfort University, who have recorded and categorised the many and varied methods that modern councils use to try to get the populace involved in their decision-making (Lowndes *et al.*, 2001). The data in Exhibit 3.3 come from a follow-up survey based on their work, and, if extrapolated to all English local authorities, show that 'local government as a whole engaged approximately 14 million people via participation and consultation initiatives during 2001' (ODPM, 2002, p. 23).

Such data need, of course, to be interpreted with caution. The fact that, for example, roughly a million people were invited to participate in local referendums during 2001, or that 2.5 million received consultation documents from their councils, does not mean that they all suddenly became excitedly involved model citizens. Even when presented with such initiatives, many, even most, people may decide that they do not wish to take part: that their interests are already adequately represented, and they have better things to do with their lives. If, on the other hand, their interest or curiosity is stirred, there is no shortage of available opportunities – and councils can understandably become irritated at being constantly 'challenged' by ministers such as Nick Raynsford to 'find new ways to engage individuals and local communities' and get 'people to participate more in what the council does' (Raynsford, 2005). You cannot, in a democracy, force people to engage.

Providing political education and training

Participation is itself a form of political education. In the United Kingdom, political education has traditionally been a largely neglected field of study in our schools and colleges. Not before time, this situation is being remedied, with Citizenship Education becoming a compulsory subject on the secondary school curriculum and part of the Personal, Social and Health Education and Citizenship framework in primary schools. In time, these developments will, it is hoped, raise levels of political literacy and community involvement. Even then, though, governmental institutions themselves – particularly at the local level – will continue to have a vital role to play as stimuli of political learning.

Local elections are especially important. Even non-voters are likely to have their political awareness and governmental knowledge increased through the heightened media attention given to local issues and candidates during the campaign period. All UK local elections take place in April or May, shortly after councils have set their budgets for the new financial year and sent out their local tax demands. Councillors and

Exhibit 3.3 How local authorities try to get us to participate

	Approx. percentage of councils saying method used in 2001–02	Increasing (+) or decreasing (–) usage
1. TRADITIONAL METHODS		
• Public meetings/consultation documents	80	–
• Co-option to council committees	50	–
• Public question and answer sessions at council or committee meetings	50	+
2. CONSUMERIST METHODS – concerned mainly with aspects of service delivery		
• Complaints/suggestion schemes	90	=
• Service satisfaction surveys, service-specific or authority-wide	90	+
3. CONSULTATIVE METHODS		
• Interactive websites	65	++
• Citizens' panels – statistically representative samples of 1000+ residents	70	++
• Local referendums	8	+
4. FORUMS – gatherings of residents with a shared background or experience		
• Service user forums	70	+
• Area or neighbourhood forums	65	+
• Issue forums	45	+
• Shared interest forums	35	+
5. DELIBERATIVE METHODS – to encourage the in-depth consideration of issues		
• Focus groups – small discussion groups of 10–12 selected residents	50	+
• Community plans/needs analysis – setting priorities for local service provision	65	+
• Visioning exercises – getting participants to 'vision' some aspect of the future	40	+
• Citizens' juries – extended and evidence-based consideration of a policy area	5	=
6. USER MANAGEMENT – direct citizen control over local services		
• For example, tenant management co-operatives, community-run nurseries and youth clubs	20	=

Source: Data from ODPM (2002), table 2 and charts 1 and 2, pp. 12–13.

candidates, through their election addresses and manifestos, have to defend their actions or propose alternative policies. Statistics are produced, challenged and debated. Surveys may show that many people still remain unaware of who their councillors are and what their councils do, but without elections that ignorance would be almost total.

For its most active and involved participants, local government provides not just education, but also a training and apprenticeship for a professional political career. In recent general elections there has been no single more important recruiting ground than local government – for all political parties. In the 2001 and 2005 Parliaments, over half of all MPs had previously served as local councillors – comprising some two-thirds of Labour MPs, around 60 per cent of Liberal Democrats, and over 30 per cent of Conservatives.

Striking though these figures are, the key term in that last sentence is 'had previously served', for, having become MPs, almost all of them will have resigned from their councils at the earliest political opportunity, even if their parliamentary seats happen to be within their council area. In this respect there is generally in Britain much less career overlap between national and local politics – and local government has a correspondingly less powerful voice nationally – than in many countries.

Dispersing power

Last, though anything but least, we come to arguably the most fundamental value or justification of local government: that of pluralism. To quote the Widdicombe Report on the Conduct of Local Authority Business:

> the case for pluralism is that power should not be concentrated in one organisation of state, but should be dispersed, thereby providing political checks and balances, and a restraint on arbitrary government and absolutism. (Widdicombe, 1986a, p. 48)

Ten years earlier, another Government report, this time by the Layfield Committee of Inquiry into Local Government Finance, had seen local government's role in almost identical terms:

> By providing a large number of points where decisions are taken by people of different political persuasion ... it acts as a counterweight to the uniformity inherent in government decisions. It spreads political power. (Layfield, 1976, p. 53)

It is the same idea that is to be found on the opening page of any dictionary of quotations: Lord Acton's famous aphorism that 'power tends to corrupt, and absolute power corrupts absolutely'. Like many supposedly well-known sayings, it is frequently misquoted, but for our purposes the placement of the emphasis is insightful. The dispersal of power *may* lead to corruption, but Acton's certainty is reserved for its concentration.

Conclusion

Let us be clear. We are not putting forward in this chapter an idealised and uncritical case for decentralised government, certainly not as it currently exists in the United Kingdom. Our local authorities can easily be shown to exhibit the various disadvantages of decentralisation that we enumerated, as well as finding it difficult to live up to its claimed values. As instruments of pluralism, platforms for increased participation, champions of their communities, their deficiencies are manifest and have been argued and documented in the literature (for example, King and Stoker, 1996). They can be bumblingly inefficient, teeth-grindingly bureaucratic, and, on occasion, just plain daft. For example, Camden Council, to protect a fine piece of public sculpture near Hampstead Theatre, encased it behind glass – including the Braille inscription designed specially for the information of blind and partially sighted people. Again, Hampshire County Council's website, urging people to turn out to vote, used a picture of a ballot paper marked with a large black tick – which technically would lead to the vote being counted as spoiled. Such idiocies are part of the inherent price of a decentralised democracy.

Nor are we challenging the ideas we dealt with in Chapter 2 about a unitary state, parliamentary sovereignty and the constitutional subordination of local government in such a state. We are, however, suggesting that a significant dispersal of power away from the centre, by extending choice, encouraging initiative and innovation, and enhancing active participation, is likely to do more for the quality of government and the health of democracy than will its centralisation and concentration. The problems associated with democratic decentralisation are relatively minor compared with those associated with the excessive centralisation of power.

Chapter 4

The Way It Was

Modern institutions, ancient origins

Why have we included an essentially historical chapter in a book on contemporary local government? Why not just concentrate on the present system and structure, as we do in Chapter 5? The answer is disarmingly simple. As John Stewart (2000, p. 15) has observed, 'The nature of local government has been shaped by its history. Shared understandings that have developed over time have become part of the assumptive world of local government.' It is not possible properly to understand the present without at least some appreciation of how that present came about, of how it developed out of and differs from the past. That much would be true for any country. But it is especially true in Britain, where local government, like most other institutions, has evolved gradually and piecemeal over the centuries, uninterrupted by an invasion or violent revolution that might have prompted a formal constitutional settlement.

In Britain there is no codified constitutional document setting out the rights and responsibilities of local authorities and their relationship with national government. Instead, there is a set of institutions and practices, some centuries old, that were created and have been adapted in response to changing circumstances. Thus there are shires, and some shire county boundaries, dating back to Anglo-Saxon or Celtic times – which, in recent debates on reorganisation, many people made clear they did *not* want abolished and replaced by new unitary councils. There are historic cities – such as Bristol, Oxford, Newcastle, Norwich, Aberdeen and Dundee – that were granted Royal Charters during the twelfth century and were centres of genuine municipal self-government until they were forcefully incorporated into their respective counties and regions in the local government reorganisation of the early 1970s.

There are magistrates or Justices of the Peace (JPs), first appointed as local agents of the Crown in the fourteenth century, some 500 years before the emergence of political parties. It is understandable that they cling fiercely to their independent representation on modern-day police authorities – but also that the 'new magistracy' was the phrase chosen by Jones and Stewart to describe the recent spread of non-elected local government agencies (see p. 17 above). There used to be a local property tax – 'the rates' – that originated with the Elizabethan Poor Law of 1601.

Predictably enough, having been abolished by the Conservative Government in 1988, it was recognised as having had significant merits lacking in the new community charge and, when the latter was almost instantly abandoned, was substantially reincarnated in the form of the council tax.

Some sense of history and of historical continuity, therefore, is important. But this is primarily a contemporary account of local government and so we confine ourselves, and you, to a fairly breathless review of indisputably major trends and developments.

French system, British tangle

It is an irony in the history of British local government that the term 'local government' itself was coined only in the nineteenth century – at the very time when it was becoming larger and *less* local than ever before. None the less, the early nineteenth century is our most appropriate starting point. Just across the English Channel, following its 1789 Revolution, France already had not only a clearly defined *system* of local government, but one that in its essentials still exists today:

- A municipality or *commune* in each town, borough, parish or rural community, and all 36,000 and more *communes,* from the smallest hamlet to Paris itself, with the same constitutional status; and
- Each *commune* with its own assembly, elected by universal suffrage, and a mayor responsible to central government as well as to the *commune.*

In Britain, by contrast, there was no such 'system'; nor would there be for most of the nineteenth century. Rather, there was what Patricia Hollis has graphically labelled 'a tangle' (Hollis, 1987, pp. 2–3), comprising principally the three traditional units of British local government: the parish, the county and the borough.

Parishes, of which there were over 15,000 by the 1830s, appointed various unpaid officers – constables, highway surveyors, overseers of the poor, as well as churchwardens – to take responsibility respectively for law and order, road maintenance, and the provision of either work or financial relief for the poor. *Counties,* into which most of the country had been divided in the Middle Ages, were administered by Justices of the Peace (JPs). These Crown-appointed officials had both a judicial role, exercised through the county quarter sessions, and increasing administrative responsibilities, for highways and bridges, weights and measures, and general oversight of the parishes. The 200 or so *boroughs,* or corporate towns, were exempt from this jurisdiction of JPs and effectively governed themselves through Corporations established by Royal Charter. They had the right to determine their own systems of government – sometimes elected, sometimes self-appointed – to decide how to raise the money due to the king, and to run their own courts. This same principle of local self-rule was being developed and extended in Scotland through a considerably larger number of *burghs,* with their councils of burgesses.

There were in addition all kinds of *ad hoc authorities,* established by local Acts of Parliament, each providing a specific service within a particular area whose boundaries might not coincide with those of any other authorities. Thus there were Turnpike Trustees, who could levy tolls on road users to maintain and provide new roads; and Improvement Commissioners, who provided rate-funded services such as paving, lighting, street cleansing, and later fire engines and gas and water supplies.

It was the pressures brought about by the Industrial Revolution – urban poverty and unemployment, overcrowding and poor sanitation, disease and crime – that showed up this 'tangle' for what it was and demonstrated the urgent necessity of reform. The existing patchwork of institutions simply could not cope with the demands of a developing industrial society.

The response of government took two contrasting forms, each reflected in the two major reform acts of the 1830s. On the one hand, the *Poor Law Amendment Act 1834* heralded the creation of *more single-purpose ad hoc authorities*. The Act replaced the parishes for the administration of poor relief, with some 700 unions, or groupings of parishes, under *elected* Boards of Guardians. These Boards were subject to strong central direction from the national Poor Law Commissioners, but the very fact of their election and resulting electoral accountability distinguishes them from most of the single-purpose authorities created more recently. Plenty of other *ad hoc* bodies followed – local health boards, highways boards, elementary school boards, sanitary districts – products in part of the delay in any more comprehensive reform of sub-national government.

The nearest the early nineteenth century came to such a reform was the second of the two 1830s statutes: the *Municipal Corporations Act 1835*. By creating some 78 multi-purpose elected local authorities which were not concerned with the administration of justice, this Act can be seen as the foundation of our present-day local government and thus constitutes the first entry in our summary of structural legislation in Exhibit 4.1. The powers of these new councils were limited and their franchise even more so – restricted to male ratepayers of over three years' residence – but the principle of elected local self-government had been established.

A dual urban–rural system emerges

Despite the reforms of the 1830s, there was nothing until almost the end of the nineteenth century that could even vaguely be called a *system* of local government. There still remained the 'tangle' of literally thousands of

Exhibit 4.1 The evolution of modern local government: keynote legislation

1835   **Municipal Corporations Act** – birth of directly elected corporate boroughs in England and Wales to replace self-electing and frequently corrupt medieval corporations.

1888   **Local Government Act** – established 62 elected county councils and 61 all-purpose county borough councils in England and Wales. Paralleled by Local Government (Scotland) Act 1889.

1894   **Local Government Act** – established within county council areas a network of 535 urban district councils (UDCs), 472 rural district councils (RDCs) and 270 non-county borough councils. Equivalent Scottish structure established by Town Councils (Scotland) Act 1900.

1899   **London Government Act** – completion of the 'modern' structure of local government. Established in London County Council (LCC) area a network of 28 metropolitan borough councils (plus the City of London Corporation) to replace the 38 vestries and district boards.

1929   **Local Government Act** – abolished Boards of Poor Law Guardians and transferred their responsibilities to local authorities. More extensive restructuring and transfer of powers in Scotland under Local Government (Scotland) Act 1929.

1963   **London Government Act** – established, from 1965, the Greater London Council (GLC), 32 London Boroughs, and in the former LCC area the Inner London Education Authority (ILEA). City of London Corporation (33rd borough) survived unchanged.

1972   **Local Government Act** – abolished, from 1974, county boroughs and reduced counties in England and Wales to 47, incorporating 333 non-metropolitan district councils. In urban England, established 6 metropolitan counties and 36 metropolitan districts.

1972   **Local Government (Northern Ireland) Act** – replaced 73 local authorities with 26 single-tier district councils in Northern Ireland elected by proportional representation.

1973   **Local Government (Scotland) Act** – reformed Scottish local government by establishing, from May 1975, 9 regional councils, 53 district councils and 3 island councils to replace over 400 authorities that had existed since 1929.

1985   **Local Government Act** – abolished the GLC and the 6 metropolitan county councils with effect from April 1986. Inner London Education Authority abolished April 1990.

1994   **Local Government (Scotland) and (Wales) Acts** – replaced, from 1996, the two-tier systems in Scotland and Wales with, respectively, 32 and 22 unitary councils. In parallel, 46 new English unitary councils were created by Parliamentary/Statutory Orders, extending the English 'hybrid' system.

1999   **Greater London Authority Act** – created the UK's first directly elected executive mayor and a 25-member Assembly, both elected in May 2000.

appointed and elected bodies, of both single- and multi-purpose authorities.

Rationalisation was clearly overdue, and it came in the form of a group of Acts passed in the last dozen years of the nineteenth century. The *Local Government Act 1888* created 62 county councils, including one for London (the LCC), and 61 county boroughs, all directly elected. *County councils* varied enormously in size, from nearly 3.5 million in Lancashire to 20,000 in Rutland. Initially, they had only a limited range of powers – responsibility for highways and bridges, asylums, weights and measures, and partial control of the police – but these would grow steadily as the twentieth century progressed.

County borough councils were all-purpose authorities, independent of the counties. The county borough status was originally intended only for large towns with populations of over 150,000. During the passage of the legislation, however, the figure was reduced to just 50,000, to the considerable resentment of the counties, whose financial viability could be seriously threatened by the loss of even a single county borough. Parallel legislation in Scotland established 33 elected county councils, with the four largest burghs – Glasgow, Edinburgh, Dundee and Aberdeen – becoming all-purpose *counties of cities*: in effect 'independent islands' like the English county boroughs.

The *Local Government Act 1894* completed the reform of English and Welsh local government outside London by creating elected *urban district councils* (UDCs) and *rural district councils* (RDCs) based on the former sanitary districts. In Scotland, equivalent legislation extended the elective principle to parish and town/burgh councils in 1894 and 1900, respectively, though for a time, as in England and Wales, there continued in existence a complex network of *ad hoc* bodies: school boards, police commissions, county road boards, district and joint standing committees.

The *London Government Act 1899* established 28 *metropolitan borough councils* to provide the capital with a second tier of local government under the LCC. The unique City of London Corporation, with its then 700 years of history, its Lord Mayor, Court of Aldermen and Common Council – a legislative assembly in its own right – remained untouched, as was the case in all subsequent London government reforms.

Between them, these Acts towards the close of the nineteenth century had brought about a small constitutional revolution. There was now a *dual system* of elected local government throughout the country: all-purpose county boroughs/burghs in the largest towns (outside London), and a two- or three-tier system elsewhere, with powers shared between the county, district/burgh and parish councils. With each level or tier of the council protective of its own responsibilities and self-sufficiency, it was not necessarily the most harmonious of systems, but in its essentials it was to last for three-quarters of a century.

Structural tinkering, functional growth

The population of England and Wales was growing by an average of over 1 per cent per annum through the early years of the twentieth century. More significantly, this growth was distinctly uneven: it was concentrated in the towns, which consequently spread or sprawled over the surrounding countryside. Nineteenth-century boundaries began to look outdated and there was an inevitable conflict of interest between urban and rural authorities, as more and more towns qualified for and sought county borough status. To the counties' relief, the minimum qualifying population for county borough status was raised in 1926 to 75,000, the procedure made considerably more difficult, and no new county boroughs were established between 1927 and 1964.

Other structural changes were ushered in by two pieces of legislation in 1929. The *Local Government (Scotland) Act* completed the process of reform and rationalisation described above. The bewildering variety of burghs was reduced to two types – 21 *large burghs*, responsible for most services apart from education, which by now was county-based, and 176 *small burghs*, responsible for housing, public health and amenities – the dividing line being a population of 20,000. Parishes, district and standing joint committees were all abolished and replaced in rural areas by nearly 200 *district councils*, thus completing the creation of a two-tier system across the whole of Scotland outside its four big cities.

In England and Wales, the *Local Government Act 1929* began to tackle the problem of the balance of urban and rural authorities, and particularly the number of very small urban and rural district councils, over 300 of which disappeared following boundary reviews during the ensuing ten years. Nevertheless, many small authorities still survived. Structural reform across all authorities needed tackling in a much more concerted manner, but this did not happen until the postwar years.

A second major consequence of the Local Government Act 1929 was the abolition of what was by then the only remaining *ad hoc* authority, the Guardians of the Poor, whose functions – poor law, civil registration, and the hospital service – were transferred to the county and county borough councils. In a similar measure, responding to the growing number of motor vehicles on frequently inadequate roads, the highways powers of rural districts were also taken over by the county councils.

These kinds of functional change, and the steady acquisition of additional service responsibilities by the county and county borough councils, were what characterised the history of local government in the first half of the twentieth century far more than the comparatively minor structural reforms. The process can be visualised as the rising section of a symmetrical arch (Game, 1991). If the whole arch represents a legislative and functional history of the first hundred years of 'modern' local government, its keystone or pinnacle would come in about the early 1930s, termed by some commentators its 'golden age' (e.g., Byrne, 2000, p. 21).

Almost immediately following their establishment in 1889, the new elected county councils had begun to add to their initially modest portfolios of responsibilities, and the process continued until at least the 1930s: further and technical education, road maintenance, elementary education, vehicle and driver registration, school meals, maternity and child welfare, careers advice, mental health services, secondary education, 'home help' schemes, libraries, unemployment relief, planning and development control, civil defence. At the same time, the county boroughs were spearheading the 1920s' council housing drive and acquiring control of the public utilities – water, gas, electricity and public transport – as well as, in some cases, docks, airports, telephone systems, theatres, crematoria and slaughterhouses.

The turning point, and the start of the falling section of the arch, was signalled by the responsibility for the payment of unemployment relief or the 'dole': it was assumed fleetingly in 1931 and lost three years later to central government in the guise of the Unemployment Assistance Board. But the real downturn came after the Second World War, with the Labour Government's massive programme of health, welfare and nationalisation legislation, all of which took services away from local councils.

Serious structural reform at last

In the postwar years, the structural problems already evident in the 1920s and 1930s were becoming ever more acute. Structures were becoming increasingly irrational as the residential pattern of communities changed, and there were major disparities of size between local authorities of the same type – in particular, many authorities were proving too small, on their own, to provide efficient services. The sheer number of authorities caused public confusion, as did the fragmentation of responsibility for service provision and the need for cumbersome co-ordinating machinery. Reform was invariably opposed by vested interests: the political parties, concerned about electoral consequences, and, of course, local councillors, in favour of the merging of urban and rural councils just as long as it didn't entail the abolition of theirs. Nevertheless, pressure for change was mounting, and it came first in London.

London

Following a three-year review by a Royal Commission, the *London Government Act 1963* created a new two-tier structure: a substantially larger *Greater London Council* (GLC) to replace the old LCC, pushing out into the Home Counties, and 32 *London boroughs* (see Figure 4.1). As in the 1890s, the City of London Corporation survived the reform process unscathed and became effectively the 33rd borough. The boroughs – 12 (or 13) in Inner London to replace the metropolitan boroughs, and 20 in Outer London – were allocated the bulk of services: housing, social services, non-metropolitan roads, and libraries, leaving the GLC with the more 'strategic' functions of fire, ambulances, main roads and refuse disposal. The maverick was education, there being a widespread wish to retain intact the high-reputation service built up by the LCC. So, while the outer boroughs took responsibility also for education, inner London would have its separate service administered by a special committee of the GLC, known as the Inner London Education Authority (ILEA), consisting of elected councillors from the 12 boroughs.

Inevitably, reaction to the 1963 Act was mixed. Some argued that no reform was necessary; others maintained that it did not go far enough, that the GLC boundaries had been too tightly drawn, and that it did nothing to alleviate the problems caused by the division of services between two separate tiers of the council. But, whatever its merits or defects, the reform of London government had at least demonstrated that wholesale change was possible without services being totally dislocated. It also established 'the principle that an entire conurbation, in this case with a population of eight million, should be governed as a single unit' (Elcock, 1991, p. 28). Reform of the rest of the system would surely follow – eventually.

England and Wales

In 1966, separate reforming Royal Commissions were established, one for England (led by Lord Redcliffe-Maud) and one for Scotland (chaired by Lord Wheatley). Both reported in 1969. Wales, as in the later 1990s reorganisation, was treated differently from England. A Commission was not deemed necessary; a White Paper from the Secretary of State for Wales would suffice.

The Redcliffe-Maud Commission produced two reports. The majority of the Commissioners favoured a structure based predominantly on all-purpose unitary authorities embracing both town and country. But a powerful Memorandum of Dissent by Derek Senior, planning journalist and gardening editor of the *Guardian*, advocated a multi-tier system of provincial councils, city regions, district and local councils. At the time, both reports were kicked into the proverbial long grass. Unitary authorities fell along with the Labour Government in its June 1970 election defeat – only to be rediscovered by John Major's Conservative Government in the 1990s. And, with the 2004 referendum rejection of elected English regional assemblies, the same may well happen to Derek Senior's city regions. Sadly, though, the man himself won't be here to see it.

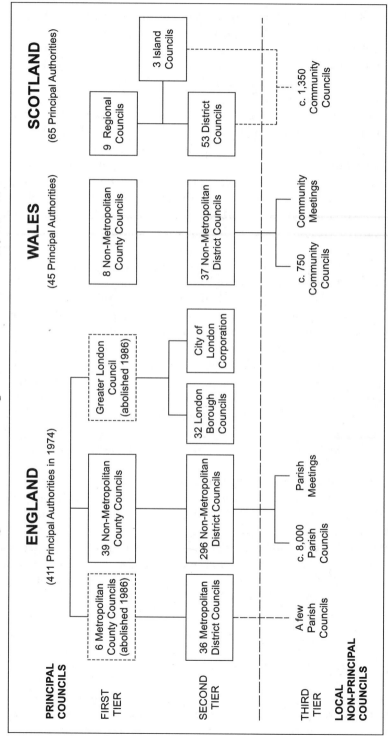

Figure 4.1   *Elected local government in Great Britain, 1974–95*

Rejecting the Redcliffe-Maud Commission's unitary authorities, the Heath Conservative Government opted to retain for the whole of England and Wales a two-tier system based mainly on existing counties – partly on philosophical grounds, but partly too for the obvious reason that the bulk of county councils were dominated by the Government's own party members, supporters and sympathisers.

The *Local Government Act 1972* abolished, from 1974, all county boroughs and reduced the 58 *county councils* in England and Wales to 47, with populations ranging at that time from 100,000 (Powys) to 1.5 million (Hampshire). Within these counties, 1,250 municipal boroughs, urban and rural districts were merged into 333 *district councils* also with hugely varying populations: from 18,760 (Radnor) to 422,000 (Bristol). In the major conurbations, six *metropolitan county councils* were established – Greater Manchester, Merseyside, West Midlands, Tyne and Wear, South Yorkshire and West Yorkshire – and thirty-six *metropolitan districts/ boroughs* with populations ranging from 172,000 (South Tyneside) to almost 1.1 million (Birmingham).

Outside these six metropolitan areas, the former county boroughs, mostly Labour strongholds, were absorbed as district councils into the new counties. These old 'independent islands', often with several centuries of self-governing existence and a fierce civic pride, lost their positions of strength based on large-scale service provision. The loss of education and social services functions to the generally more Conservative counties was an especially bitter blow. Indeed, the maintenance of two principal tiers continued to make co-ordination of policy and administration difficult, and in those services where counties and districts had concurrent powers (e.g., planning, leisure services) the problems in some areas proved to be particularly acute.

At the third, or sub-principal, tier in England outside the major cities the parish was retained, covering areas smaller than districts. Of the more than 10,000 parishes, about 8,700 have elected councils, the more urban of which are known as town councils. Small parishes, with fewer than 200 electors, can instead hold parish meetings which all local electors can attend. In Wales, parishes were replaced in 1974 by *communities,* which have either elected councils or community meetings on a similar basis to English parishes. Additionally, in some urban areas neighbourhood councils have been formed which can provide a sounding board for local opinion.

Scotland

In contrast to its English counterpart, the Wheatley Commission in Scotland proposed a two-tier system, and, not surprisingly, its proposals were largely adopted by the Conservative Government in the *Local*

Government (Scotland) Act 1973 and implemented in May 1975. As in England, the large numbers of small authorities were seen as constituting the fundamental weakness of the existing system, and in the final legislation their numbers were reduced proportionately by even more than in England and Wales. 431 county, city, burgh and district councils were amalgamated into nine *regions*, ranging from 100,000 (Borders) to almost 2.5 million population (Strathclyde); 53 *districts*, from 9,000 population (Badenoch and Strathspey) to 850,000 (Glasgow); and three *'most purpose' island authorities* for Orkney, Shetland and the Western Isles (see Figure 4.1). Additionally, some 1,350 communities set up their own optional *community councils* as a kind of third tier, though these have no statutory powers and a lower status than even parish councils.

The network of regional and district councils Wheatley had proposed fitted with the Conservative Government's preference for two-tier local government. Inevitably, the size and remoteness of the regional tiers were heavily criticised; as in England, shared responsibilities between districts and regions for certain services would also pose difficulties. However, apart from some minor structural revisions, the post-1975 system remained essentially intact until April 1996, with the huge Strathclyde Region comprising almost half of Scotland's total population.

Northern Ireland

It will be noted from Exhibit 4.1 that Northern Ireland's local government was reformed at the same time as that in the rest of the United Kingdom. That reform, though, and the significantly different structures it produced, need to be understood in the context of the political conflicts between the province's Unionist and Catholic communities, which had intensified during the 1960s.

Since the Local Government (Ireland) Act 1898, Northern Ireland had had a structure of local government very similar to that on the mainland. There were two all-purpose county boroughs – Belfast and Londonderry – and a two-tier system of six counties (*not* the nine counties of the historic Ulster province) and 55 urban and rural district councils. The majority Unionist population had ensured that boundaries were drawn in such a way as to give them control of most councils and exclude the Catholic parties from any significant influence.

The resulting inequalities of service provision and particularly discriminatory housing allocations were among the principal grievances of civil rights protesters, and eventually in 1969 a Review Body was set up, chaired by Patrick Macrory. Influenced by the Wheatley Commission, the Macrory Report proposed a reformed two-tier model of elected local government. Most services – education and libraries, planning, roads, water and sewerage, fire, health and social services – would be provided by elected regional bodies, and there would be a greatly reduced number of district councils.

The *Local Government (Northern Ireland) Act 1972* implemented some of these recommendations, but, with the suspension of the Stormont government in the same year and the introduction of direct rule from Westminster, the proposed elected regional tier never materialised. In an attempt to remove sectarian bias at local level, most local authority powers in housing, personal social services, health, education and planning were placed in the hands of various non-elected boards, agencies and departments of the Northern Ireland Office.

Local democracy in Northern Ireland was therefore limited to 26 *district councils*. These are elected, by the Single Transferable Vote (STV) system of proportional representation, but, compared with their mainland counterparts, their responsibilities are very restricted – if not quite to the bins, bogs and burials that is sometimes suggested. In addition to the refuse collection and disposal, public conveniences, cemeteries and crematoria, there are leisure, recreational and cultural facilities, consumer protection, environmental health and safety, and, increasingly, tourism. But, added together, the twenty-six districts' annual spending – around £350 million – amounts to less than 4 per cent of Northern Ireland's total public expenditure. Filling the democratic deficit, or the 'Macrory gap', are the area boards and other quangos providing all other services: 116 bodies in all, 'appointed by a Minister from a government which does not have a single MP anywhere in the six counties' (Vize, 1994, p. 16). District councils nominate up to 40 per cent of the members of some of these boards, but 'policy power remains with Westminster and its Stormont Castle outpost' (Vize, 1994, p. 17).

The Conservative years – politics turns to spite?

By the mid-1970s, then, the dual town/country structure of local government, set up at the end of the nineteenth century and fundamentally unchanged throughout most of the twentieth, had been comprehensively reformed. A two-tier system was in place across almost the whole country. It had its inevitable tensions – competing mandates, resource jealousies, the blurring of lines of responsibility and accountability for service provision – but it would, surely, see us through to the next millennium? Hardly, as you will already have gathered from Exhibit 4.1 and Figure 4.1. Parts of this new structure were to be dismantled almost before they had had a chance to establish themselves.

Despite having at the time far more councillors and controlling far more councils than any other party, the Conservative Government that took office in 1979 was not well-disposed towards local government. Ministers saw it as 'wasteful, profligate, irresponsible, unaccountable, luxurious and out of control' (Newton and Karran, 1985, p. 116). The result was a barrage of legislation aimed at remodelling the finances of local authorities, but not initially their actual structure.

Then in May 1983 the Conservative Party introduced into its General Election manifesto a pledge to abolish the six English metropolitan county councils and the GLC. As Elcock notes (1991, p. 39), the

> official reason given for this hasty proposal was that these authorities had few functions and were therefore redundant: but in 1981 all seven had fallen under Labour control and the GLC Leader, Ken Livingstone, had emerged as a colourful and effective antagonist with his head-quarters just across the Thames from Mrs Thatcher's.

There was, in other words, a party political dimension to this structural reform, just as there had been to the reforms of the 1970s, and as there is bound to be in any reorganisation of sub-central government in a unitary state. We should not be too surprised when politicians behave politically, and certainly this abolition of a tier of elected local government, 'very much a personal decision of Mrs. Thatcher, [was] widely regarded as an act of political spite ... right off the normal political agenda and in almost any other European country ... unconstitutional' (Hebbert, 1998, quoted in Travers, 2004, p. 30).

The Government's arguments and the amplification of its manifesto proposals were set out in a post-election White Paper, *Streamlining the Cities* (DoE, 1983). The title was significant, emphasising the Government's concern to reduce bureaucracy, duplication and waste and generally to 'roll back the frontiers of the state'. By abolishing the top-tier authorities in the metropolitan areas and transferring the bulk of their already limited range of functions to the borough and district councils, it would be bringing government closer to the people, making it more comprehensible and accessible, and thereby enhancing local democracy. In doing so, of course, it would also be removing the irritation of the attendant policy conflicts between the top-tier metropolitan authorities and central government whenever the two were controlled by different political parties.

Despite opposition in both the Commons and the Lords, the *Local Government Act 1985* was eventually passed, and from 31 March 1986 the GLC and the six metropolitan county councils ceased to exist, London having no city-wide government for the first time since 1855. Many of the abolished councils' responsibilities were taken over by the London boroughs and metropolitan district/borough councils, but some continued to be run on the same metropolis-wide scale, by a range of joint boards, joint committees, *ad hoc* agencies and central government departments. The result was a degree of complexity and fragmentation that could seem not so much a 'streamlining' of our cities as a return to the administrative 'tangle' of the nineteenth century.

In the metropolitan areas the picture was a little less perplexing than in London: fewer functions were taken over by quasi-government agencies, but those that were so transferred were among the biggest-spending and highest-profile services. So in each of the six metropolitan areas there were, and still are, three *joint boards* for passenger transport, police, fire and civil defence. In both Greater Manchester and Merseyside there are joint boards responsible for waste disposal. In addition, *joint committees* were established dealing with matters such as recreation, arts and economic development. None of these joint boards is *directly elected*. Most are controlled by councillors *nominated* from the constituent metropolitan districts. Directly elected local government is now weaker and more fragmented than before 1986; indirectly elected and appointed bodies have become increasingly numerous and important.

Part of the 1986 reforms, however, did not even make it through to the 1992 election. The *Inner London Education Authority* had been a sub-committee of the GLC, covering the former London County Council area. So, when it was the GLC's turn to be abolished, a new arrangement was needed. What was created, very unusually for this country in the twentieth century, was a *directly elected unifunctional* council, somewhat similar to the elected school boards in particularly the West and Midwestern USA. It could have provided an interesting study of an alternative form of local democracy. In, the event, though, its almost inevitable Labour domination, allied to its high expenditure levels and perceived enthusiasm for 'progressive' education, led to its early abolition in the *Education Reform Act 1988*. Responsibility for education services passed to the individual Inner London boroughs with effect from 1 April 1990.

Summary – into the 1990s

Later that year, in November 1990, Mrs Thatcher was replaced as Conservative Party Leader and Prime Minister by John Major. Mr Major's biggest inherited local government headache by far was the hugely unpopular poll tax, or community charge, and how to get rid of it. By comparison, the structure of the system might have seemed reasonably straightforward and unproblematic.

A similar structure of elected local government existed throughout the *non-metropolitan areas* of England and the whole of Wales and mainland Scotland (see Figure 4.1). Throughout these areas there were two principal tiers of local authorities, with each tier providing a range of services that were judged to be appropriate to its scale. In England and Wales, the upper-tier authorities were known as *counties*; in Scotland they were designated *regions.* The lower-tier authorities were known as *districts,* some of which were entitled, for historic reasons, to call themselves *cities* or *boroughs.* In much of non-metropolitan Britain there were also third-tier, or 'sub-principal', authorities known as parish councils in England and community councils in both Wales and Scotland.

In *metropolitan* England and London there was only one elected tier of local government – *metropolitan districts* and *London boroughs* – describable, though not actually known, as *unitary* or *most-purpose* local authorities. Instead of sharing responsibility for service provision with other elected authorities, they now operated alongside other indirectly elected or nominated bodies. In practice, single-tier local government, accompanied as it is by a mosaic of joint authorities and boards responsible for major services such as fire and civil defence and passenger transport, is nothing like as simple as it sounds: hence our preference for the term 'most-purpose', rather than 'all-purpose'.

In Northern Ireland there was – and still is – a single-tier structure of 26 district councils with a very much more limited range of service responsibilities than even their non-metropolitan district counterparts on the mainland. The major functions of health and social services, education and libraries are organised through *area boards* made up of approximately one-third district councillors and two-thirds ministerial appointees. Responsibility for public-sector housing is with an appointed Northern Ireland Housing Executive, administered through six regions.

None of these UK local authorities had been in existence for more than 25 years, most for barely 15. The system had been fundamentally restructured in the 1960s and 1970s and substantially tinkered with in the 1980s. Time, you might have thought, for a period of stability, in which they could settle down and establish a presence and identity in their communities, while people could become familiar with who their local governors were, and what they did. If so, you could hardly have been more wrong.

Chapter 5

The Way It Is – External Structures

Mapping change and changing maps

This chapter and the next outline the present-day structure and organisation of UK local government. Chapter 6 deals with what we term *internal* structures: the differing ways in which councils manage themselves and conduct their day-to-day business. First, though, we look at *external* structures, and start by bringing up to date the historical evolution of our local government system that we left hanging at the end of Chapter 4.

We present a map, or maps, of British sub-central – that is, both local and regional – government at the time of writing (2005/06). The account is necessarily interwoven with the progression of the Labour Government's extensive programme of constitutional reform – its devolution of powers variously to the Scottish Parliament, and the Welsh and Northern Ireland Assemblies; its restoration, in a unique form, of an elected city-wide authority for Greater London, and its thwarted attempt to introduce somewhat similar directly elected assemblies to the English regions. Major constitutional change, at least in Britain, is not supposed to, and usually doesn't, happen that fast: in this instance it did, and it makes a remarkable story.

England – hybridity, or a dog's breakfast?

We suggested in Chapter 4 that structural reform, once it becomes part of the agenda of national political debate, can acquire a momentum of its own. That is perhaps as good an explanation as any of why, following the reorganisations of local government in London in the 1960s, in the rest of the country in the 1970s, and in metropolitan England in the 1980s, we saw a further GB-wide structural reform during the 1990s. Unlike thirty years previously, there were no longer large numbers of small authorities struggling to cope with the problems of urban and suburban growth and geographical mobility, and few serious observers in or of local government were enthused by the idea of uprooting a structure that had been in place for less than a generation.

The impetus to reform came predominantly from a single individual, Michael Heseltine, a Conservative leadership contender following Margaret Thatcher's resignation in 1990, who became instead, and for the second time in his career, Secretary of State for the Environment. Determined to make a late-career impact as well as to deflect electoral attention away from the embarrassment of the poll tax, it was he who ensured that local government reorganisation would feature as a prominent commitment in the 1992 Conservative manifesto. 'We will set up a commission to examine, area by area, the appropriate local government arrangements in England', the manifesto proclaimed, the main objective being to decide 'whether in any area a *single tier* of local government could provide better accountability and greater efficiency' (emphasis ours).

That phrasing was revealing. For it seemed to suggest a *structure-led* or *cartographic* approach to any weaknesses or deficiencies of local government: a keenness to draw revised boundary lines on maps, increasing the scale and reducing the 'localness' of local councils, before deciding on their future role or purpose. Mr Heseltine's commission – or, in the case of Scotland and Wales, government ministers – would determine not what local government would do in the future, or how, but the size of the areas within which it would do it. But once set in motion, even though Michael Heseltine's successors as Environment Secretary, Michael Howard and John Gummer, seemed not to share his reformist enthusiasm, the restructuring process lurched on, though with less far-reaching impact than had initially been envisaged.

The Government had wanted the county-by-county structural reviews by its Local Government Commission to produce unitary local government across most of non-metropolitan England, bringing it into line with the all-unitary systems that, through ministerial diktat, were being imposed on Scotland and Wales. At one time, following the Commission's draft recommendations, that looked a likely outcome. The Commission was then required, however, to consult the public – who were unconvinced. Though many of them liked the *idea* of unitary local government, far more, when asked, were opposed to the Commission's detailed plans for their own counties and to their likely upheaval and cost. In most counties the weight of opinion favoured the status quo.

The almost inevitable outcome – against a background of the Major Government's national unpopularity and its minimal parliamentary majority – was a policy retreat. Instead of unitary local government becoming the norm in England, there emerged 'hybridity', to use the technical expression for a mix of single- and two-tier local authorities, or a dog's breakfast – the latter obviously being the view presented in Figure 5.1, showing Sir John Banham, the Commission's first chairman, hammering a final piece of the reorganisation puzzle into place.

Figure 5.1   *Cartoon – a confusing solution*

Source: Local Government Chronicle, 16 September 1994.

To be fair, the true picture, presented in Figure 5.2 and Exhibit 5.1, is not as chaotic as the cartoon suggests. Between 1995 and 1998, 46 new unitary authorities came into existence covering just over a quarter of the population of non-metropolitan England. Only four of the 39 former county councils disappeared entirely: the three 'newcomers', created only in the previous reorganisation in the early 1970s – Avon, Cleveland and Humberside – plus Berkshire. Hereford and Worcester, joined in 1974, was re-divided, and the Isle of Wight became a unitary county in its own right. Fourteen counties remained unchanged, and the remaining 19 assumed hybrid structures: one or two mainly large town unitary authorities in otherwise unchanged two-tier counties (see Exhibits on linked website).

There was thus a second generation of largely urban unitaries to add to the 36 metropolitan districts and 32 London boroughs that became unitary in 1986, following the abolition of the GLC and the six metropolitan county councils. And if that arrangement sounds a little familiar, it is: an at least partial return to the pre-1974 structure described in Chapter 4, when county boroughs were the 'independent islands' within two-tier counties. The biggest difference, and the confirmation of the ultimate lack of any coherent rationale underpinning this latest restructuring, can be seen in the final two columns of Exhibit 5.1. While most of the new unitaries were indeed urban centres and half of them former county boroughs, a few are right up the other end of DEFRA's settlement spectrum: predominantly

Figure 5.2   *The local authority map of England, from 1998*

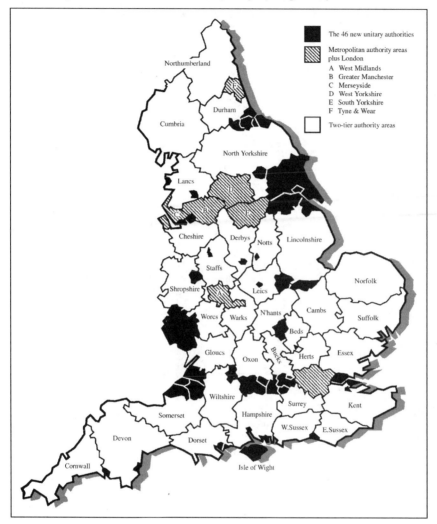

rural and with a unitary status owing rather more to political machination than to any administrative logic.

As for the Local Government Commission, its review functions and associated responsibilities – examining the total number of councillors, the number in each electoral division or ward, the ward boundaries, their names, and the timing of elections – have been absorbed into the Electoral Commission – an independent body, established in 2000, with a remit to keep under review all UK electoral law and practice.

Exhibit 5.1 The second generation of 46 English unitaries

Year created	Former county	'New' unitary	Population (000s)	Urban % of population	DEFRA settlement type
1995	Isle of Wight	Isle of Wight	133	15	5
1996	Avon	Bristol City	381	100	2
		S. Gloucestershire	246	81	2
		North Somerset	188	45	5
		Bath & NE Somerset	169	54	4
	Cleveland	Hartlepool	89	97	3
		Middlesbrough	135	100	2
		Redcar & Cleveland	139	56	2
		Stockton-on-Tees	179	85	2
	Humberside	Kingston upon Hull	244	100	2
		E. Riding of Yorks.	314	29	5
		N. Lincolnshire	153	48	5
		NE Lincolnshire	158	88	3
	North Yorkshire	York	181	83	3
1997	Bedfordshire	Luton	184	100	3
	Buckinghamshire	Milton Keynes	207	89	3
	Derbyshire	Derby City	222	100	3
	Dorset	Bournemouth	163	100	2
		Poole	138	96	2
	Durham	Darlington	98	88	3
	East Sussex	Brighton and Hove	248	99	2
	Hampshire	Portsmouth City	187	100	2
		Southampton	218	100	2
	Leicestershire	Leicester City	280	100	2
		Rutland	34	0	6
	Staffordshire	Stoke-on-Trent City	241	100	2
	Wiltshire	Swindon	180	86	3
1998	Berkshire	Bracknell Forest	110	94	2
		West Berkshire	145	57	5
		Reading	143	100	2
		Slough	119	100	3
		Windsor & Maidenhead	134	81	3
		Wokingham	150	83	2
	Cambridgeshire	Peterborough City	156	87	3
	Cheshire	Halton	118	97	3
		Warrington	191	83	3
	Devon	Plymouth City	240	100	3
		Torbay	130	85	3

Exhibit 5.1 continued

Year created	Former county	'New' unitary	Population (000s)	Urban % of population	DEFRA settlement type
1998	Essex	Southend-on-Sea	161	100	2
		Thurrock	143	86	3
	Hereford & Worcester	Herefordshire	175	34	5
	Kent	Medway	250	90	3
	Lancashire	Blackburn with Darwen	137	95	3
		Blackpool	142	100	2
	Nottinghamshire	Nottingham City	267	100	2
	Shropshire	Telford & Wrekin	158	84	3

Source: Data from DEFRA (2005) and linked LA Classification Dataset.

Notes: DEFRA classification of local authority settlement types (DEFRA, 2005):

1. Major urban: 100,000 or 50 per cent in an urban area with population of 750,000+.
2. Large urban: 50,000 or 50 per cent in any urban area with population of 250,000–750,000.
3. Other urban: Less than 37,000 or 26 per cent in rural settlements and larger market towns.
4. Significantly rural: more than 37,000 or 26 per cent in rural settlements and larger market towns.
5. Rural-50: between 50 per cent and 80 per cent in rural settlements and larger market towns.
6. Rural-80: at least 80 per cent in rural settlements and larger market towns.

Scotland and Wales – fewer councils increase democratic deficit

In Scotland and Wales there were no 'rolling commissions' to examine options and make recommendations area by area. Instead, the respective Secretaries of State were given the task of proposing single-tier structures of authorities which, it was claimed, would have greater local identity, would be more efficient and more accountable. Certain amendments were made following negotiations with local authority associations and during the parliamentary passage of the two bills. But what resulted – thanks, significantly, to the votes of overwhelmingly English Conservative MPs – were the nationwide unitary systems that the Government sought: 32 'all-purpose' authorities in Scotland and 22 in Wales. Following elections in 1995, these councils came into operation in April 1996 – see Figures 5.3 and 5.4.

Figure 5.3 *Scotland's 32 unitary authorities, operational from April 1996*

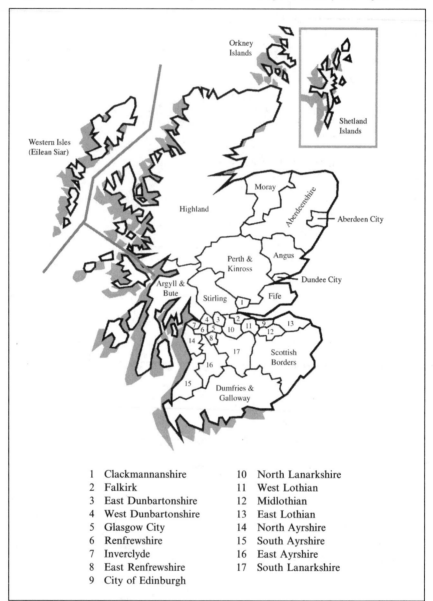

1	Clackmannanshire	10	North Lanarkshire
2	Falkirk	11	West Lothian
3	East Dunbartonshire	12	Midlothian
4	West Dunbartonshire	13	East Lothian
5	Glasgow City	14	North Ayrshire
6	Renfrewshire	15	South Ayrshire
7	Inverclyde	16	East Ayrshire
8	East Renfrewshire	17	South Lanarkshire
9	City of Edinburgh		

Figure 5.4   *The 22 unitary authorities in Wales, operational from April 1996*

1   Swansea
2   Neath Port Talbot
3   Bridgend
4   Rhondda Cynon Taf
5   Merthyr Tydfil
6   Caerphilly
7   Blaenau Gwent
8   Torfaen
9   Newport
10   Cardiff
11   Vale of Glamorgan

In both Scotland and Wales, these ministerially driven reorganisations halved the numbers of councils, which inevitably cover larger areas than the former districts and, though this was not inevitable, have far fewer councillors. England's reorganisation produced the same effect, though on a lesser scale: a reduction of less than 6 per cent in the number of elected councils, though one of more than a quarter in the number of councillors (see Exhibits 5.2 and 5.3). The outcome of the two bouts of reorganisation

Exhibit 5.2 The growing scale of British local government

	Before 1974/75	1974/75– 1996/98	New structure	Increase in scale since 1974/75
England				
No. of councils	1,246	c. 410	388	
Av. population per council	37,000	113,000	121,000	3.3×
Scotland				
No. of councils	430	65	32	
Av. population per council	12,000	78,000	153,000	12.8×
Wales				
No. of councils	181	45	22	
Av. population per council	15,000	62,000	128,000	8.5×
Great Britain				
No. of councils	1,857	520	442	
Av. population per council	29,000	106,000	128,000	4.4×

Exhibit 5.3 Unitary councillors – the missing third

	Number of councillors		The democratic deficit	
	New unitary authorities	In previous two-tier system	No.	%
Non-metropolitan England	2,391	3,476	1,085	31
Scotland	1,245	1,695	450	27
Wales	1,273	1,977	704	36
Total	4,909	7,148	2,239	31

Source for Exhibits 5.2 and 5.3: original tables, calculated by authors.

– in the 1970s and the 1990s – is that Great Britain has, on average, the largest local authorities and the highest ratios of citizens to elected councillors of any country in Western Europe (see Exhibit 12.3). The term 'democratic deficit', often applied to the alleged deficiencies of the European Union, seems more than justified here – and will, if anything, be more justified still in the future. For, while in England ministers hang on to the model of all-unitary local government that would have accompanied elected regional assemblies (see p. 91), in Scotland the search is on for new models of local governance, the most radical form of which would be 'super-councils' unifying all public services under one elected body.

The Greater London Authority – strategic local government

The creation during the 1990s of the second generation of English unitary authorities did not quite complete the sequence of local government restructurings during the last decades of the twentieth century. There was still London – the only major Western capital at the end of the twentieth century without a democratic voice of its own. The Labour Party, in control of the GLC at the time of its abolition, had pledged consistently to restore some form of directly elected government to Greater London, and in 1997 its chance arrived. The party's manifesto promised (p. 34) that:

> following a referendum to confirm popular demand, there will be a new deal for London, with a strategic authority and a mayor, each directly elected. Both will speak up for the needs of the city and plan its future. They will not duplicate the work of the boroughs, but take responsibility for London-wide issues – economic regeneration, planning, policing, transport and environmental protection.

The intention was to produce a novel and unique set of institutions, best seen as a particular form of hybridity – strategic local government, or a mixture of local government reform and embryonic regional government. The Greater London Authority (GLA) would be quite different from the 'modernised' mayoral town and city councils that the Government was planning for the rest of England. But neither would it be permitted the self-governing powers of the devolved administrations emerging in Scotland, Wales and Northern Ireland.

Every local government structural reform, as we emphasised in Chapter 4, has its party political dimension. The GLC had been abolished because of the Thatcher Government's detestation of the way it was being run by 'Red Ken' Livingstone's 'municipal socialist' administration. The creation of the new GLA, and particularly the form it took, owed just as much to party and personality politics – only this time it was the *internal* politics of the New Labour Party and, extraordinarily, the personality of the same man, Ken Livingstone. Following the disappearance of the GLC, Livingstone had become a broadly left-wing, iconoclastic Labour MP, ever ready to snipe at the direction in which his party was being led and at those doing the leading. They in turn still held him, his GLC, and other like-minded Labour councils prominent in the 1980s, heavily responsible for the party's unpopularity and its series of general election defeats.

Justified or not, Tony Blair and his ministers were determined that, under no circumstances, would they permit the creation of a GLC Mark II – a democratically legitimate body with the power and tax base to enable it to challenge seriously the policies of their own national government. Mayors in other cities and towns would be taking over existing, often unitary, councils with wide-ranging services and correspondingly large budgets. In London, most of these services – education, social services, housing, environmental health and consumer protection, leisure, recreation and the arts – would continue to be provided by the 32 London boroughs, several in future probably with mayors of their own. The Greater London mayor would be a significant figurehead and spokesperson for the nation's capital, and would have considerable powers of patronage and influence in making appointments to the new executive agencies through which the Authority would exercise its responsibilities. But the mayor's direct powers and tax-raising opportunities would be modest. Besides which – continued this prime ministerial line of reasoning – the party leadership's control of its own party machine, especially when in government, would prevent the reviled Livingstone from even winning the Labour candidacy for mayor, let alone getting elected.

As obviously ought to happen for a first-term government with a massive parliamentary majority, things went according to plan – up to a point. Ministers produced a White Paper – *A Mayor and Assembly for London* – and a London-wide referendum was held in May 1998, in which 72 per cent – albeit on a turnout of only 34 per cent – approved the Government's proposals. Legislation followed – in fact, the longest piece of legislation in postwar parliamentary history – and eventually, after numerous Opposition attempts to block it, the Government's Commons majority ensured that the Greater London Authority Act was passed.

With nearly 50 per cent of Londoners' general election votes, and 57 out of 74 MPs, Labour was confident of winning the mayoralty, whether against the Conservatives' initial candidate, the soon-to-be-disgraced Lord (Jeffrey) Archer, or his successor, Steven Norris. The next task for ministers, therefore, was to secure the selection of a 'politically acceptable' party candidate. A bitter and cynically manipulated selection process ensued, the sole and unconcealed objective of the prime minister and his colleagues being to 'Stop Livingstone' at all costs. He was stopped, being very narrowly defeated for Labour's candidacy by former Cabinet minister, Frank Dobson, but at the cost of the party's integrity and the scapegoat Dobson's own electability.

Opinion polls suggested that the ministerially victimised Livingstone would be almost unbeatable, prompting him to reverse previous pledges not to run against his own party's candidate and proceed to do precisely that, as an Independent. The opinion polls proved right. In a two-stage (Supplementary Vote) election, Dobson was eliminated in third place after the first stage, and, after the counting of second preferences, Livingstone was elected as Greater London's first mayor, with more than 776,000 votes as against Norris's 564,000. Ken was back, in the remarkable position of being able to say: 'Before I was so rudely interrupted 14 years ago ...'. The turnout, notwithstanding the exceptional media attention, was fractionally lower even than in the referendum; Livingstone's vote, however, was still the highest total ever won by a British politician – a significant mandate for an office with deliberately limited direct powers (D'Arcy and MacLean, 2000; Travers, 2004, ch. 3).

Those limited powers – outlined in Exhibit 5.4 – are, however, a real, if utterly predictable, problem. Even in relation to the 'functional bodies' through which most of the GLA's work is done, the mayor's authority is shared with or constrained by central government departments. As Travers (2004) notes (p. 184):

Any mayor would be rendered largely powerless by the arrangements put in place by the Greater London Authority Act ... Expenditure in London on the National Health Service, higher education, further education, training, the arts, housing and social security are all determined by central government. On the other hand, schools, social care, local transport, environmental services and some social housing are responsibilities of the boroughs. The mayor is squeezed between these two blocs of established financial and political power.

The argument is valid, though 'largely powerless' is perhaps a little exaggerated. Even in his first three years of office, Livingstone had some significant policy achievements: bus usage increased to the highest total in forty years, there were cuts in fares, the Docklands Light Railway extension, the redevelopment and opening-up of Trafalgar Square, and recruitment of additional police officers. And, above all, road user or congestion charging – on this scale, a completely untested approach to traffic management – was introduced successfully in 2003 in the face of massive user and media opposition and the expectation (if not the hope) on the part of ministers that it would fail spectacularly (Glaister, 2005, p. 226). Its success, not to mention the international interest it has created, meant that the time had arrived for an embarrassed prime ministerial

Exhibit 5.4 The Greater London Authority (GLA)

What is it?

A unique form of strategic city-wide government for London. It comprises:

- A directly elected executive mayor – the first in the UK. The first mayor, elected in May 2000 and re-elected in 2004, is Ken Livingstone, now Labour.
- A separately elected 25-member Assembly. Membership following 2004 elections was: 9 Conservatives, 7 Labour, 5 Liberal Democrats, 2 Green Party, 2 UK Independence Party.

The mayor and Assembly are advised and assisted by a permanent staff of about 650, headed by the slightly confusingly named chief executive, Anthony Mayer.

What does it do and how?

Its main responsibilities are *strategic* – principally transport, policing, fire and emergency planning, economic development, planning; secondarily culture, the environment, health. The London boroughs retain responsibility for education, housing, social services, local roads, libraries and museums, refuse collection, environmental health, etc.

The GLA's main responsibilities are exercised through 4 *functional bodies*, members of which are mainly appointed by and accountable to the mayor:

- Transport for London (TfL) – responsible for most public transport in London, including fare structures and future investment.
- Metropolitan Police Authority (MPA) – previously accountable to the Home Secretary.
- London Fire and Emergency Planning Authority (LFEPA).
- London Development Agency – a new body to promote employment, investment, economic development and regeneration in London. Similar to the other 8 English Regional Development Agencies.

Who's in charge – the mayor or the Assembly?

The mayor decides policy – prepares plans on transport, land use, the environment, culture, etc., appoints and sets the budgets for the functional bodies.

The Assembly scrutinises and questions the mayor's activities, and the budget, which it can overturn with a two-thirds majority – significant now that Labour's representation is down from 9 members to 7. It also investigates other issues of relevance to Londoners, and makes policy recommendations to the mayor.

How much does it spend?

The GLA's total (gross) budget in 2005–06 amounted to roughly £9 billion: TfL – £5 bn; MPA – £3 bn; LFEPA – £0.5 bn. Cost of the GLA itself was about £61 million. Net budget requirement (less grants + other income) = £3 billion, most of which comes from central government grants. London taxpayers contributed about £250 on a Band D council tax bill.

Where is it?

'City Hall' occupies one of London's most spectacular new buildings: Lord Foster's award-winning, glass foglamp-resembling construction alongside Tower Bridge – universally known as the mayor's 'glass testicle'. It featured, along with the original 'wobbly' Millennium Bridge, in the Bill Nighy film, *Love Actually*.

climb-down, and, in time for the 2004 mayoral election, Livingstone was readmitted to the Labour Party and adopted as the party's candidate. Whereupon, campaigning largely under his previously Independent colour of mauve, rather than Labour red, he was comfortable re-elected until 2008 with 828,380 votes (55.4 per cent) against 667,178 (44.6 per cent) for the Conservatives' Steven Norris.

Now an asset to the Government, Livingstone began pushing hard for increased powers: the right to propose alternative sub-regional boundaries in London, more planning powers, powers to check on the performance of the boroughs, a single city-wide waste management authority, and, perhaps most significantly, scrapping the Assembly and replacing it with a borough leaders' committee. Given his key role in the successful Olympic bid and its implementation, he made a strong case.

The arrival of the GLA completed – at least for the time being – the structural reorganisation of local government in Great Britain. The 521 principal councils created in the 1970s (see Figure 4.1) had been reduced by nearly a sixth, to 442 (see Figure 5.5), and their average population increased to nearly 130,000 – roughly ten times the average figure for Western European countries.

Joint arrangements

One obvious difference between the reorganisation of London government and most of the other recent restructurings is, of course, that in London an additional, and supposedly co-ordinating, body was being created, whereas the other cases were about merging existing authorities into smaller numbers of unitaries. In London, therefore, one might expect there to have been an institutional streamlining and sharpening of account-ability. But, with borough functions remaining largely untouched, and the GLA's powers being so constrained, the extent to which this has occurred is distinctly limited. Travers (2004, pp. 185–7) maps what he calls 'a rococo layering of government departments, regional offices, appointed boards ... joint committees' in addition to, and often competing with, the institutions of elected government.

If this is the picture in London, it is hardly surprising to find something similar in areas of England where in the 1980s and 1990s the metropolitan and 'newcomer' county councils were broken up and in Scotland and Wales where districts were merged into new unitaries. As we noted in Chapter 4, 'single tier' does not necessarily mean a simplification. Not all of the services and responsibilities of abolished local authorities can be divided up easily or combined and handed over to new or different elected councils. Across much of the UK nowadays, therefore, alongside the

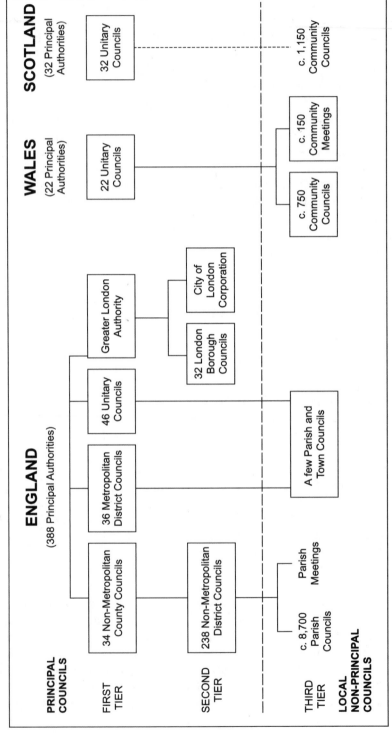

Figure 5.5   Elected local government in Great Britain, 2006

directly elected structures, there are frequently networks of *nominated or indirectly elected joint bodies* and other joint arrangements between councils.

There are three main forms of joint arrangements through which councils work together to provide services:

- *Joint boards.* These are legally required bodies set up by two or more councils to provide statutorily required services. They are created by ministers, and their membership and management are subject to ministerial approval. They do, however, have independent financial powers, including the power to raise money by 'precept' from their constituent authorities. In the English metropolitan areas and in Scotland there are joint boards for police, fire, public transport and waste disposal. There are already some joint police boards in areas where counties are judged too small to justify their own force – for example, West Mercia Constabulary, covering Shropshire, Telford and Wrekin, Herefordshire and Worcestershire – and further amalgamations are high on the Government's reform agenda.

- *Joint committees.* In many ways similar to joint boards, these are *voluntarily* created bodies, where two or more smaller authorities establish joint committees of councillors to carry out specific council functions, such as the provision of specialist schools or residential homes, more effectively than they could on their own.

- *Contracting or agency arrangements.* Local authorities can make contracts with each other for the provision of services. There have long been highways agency arrangements between county councils – the highways authorities – and their district, town and parish councils, whereby the latter carry out minor functions such as grass cutting and vegetation clearance, but they are likely to increase as more councils develop the possibilities of their role as 'enablers'.

As noted at the end of Chapter 4, it is the proliferation of these different kinds of joint arrangements that leads critics to question the labelling of this country's unitary councils as 'all-purpose' authorities. They may constitute the only *directly* elected local authorities in their area, but they are more accurately designated as 'most-purpose' councils. Joint boards and joint committees may often offer efficient and effective services, and some manage to involve their constituent authorities in their decision-making. But they do inevitably add to the *fragmentation* of local government, to the potential confusion and uncertainty of the public, and to the dilution of electoral accountability. Those concerned about such developments are quick to point out that in this, as in many other respects, Britain is unusual: Luxembourg and Finland are the only other Western European countries to have unitary local government systems!

Sub-principal authorities

While this book focuses chiefly on the activities of the 'principal' local authorities in the United Kingdom, there is in non-metropolitan Britain a multitude of 'sub-principal' authorities: parish councils in England, and community councils in Scotland and Wales. Often ancient in origin, they are by no means anachronistic. They have survived the traumas of recent structural reorganisations and, indeed, have seen their roles and powers enhanced. Sometimes referred to as the 'third tier' of our local government, they must not be overlooked.

In England, there are approximately 10,200 parishes, of which some 8,700 – predominantly in more rural areas – have parish or town councils, on which serve some 75,000 elected councillors. These 'civil' parishes – to distinguish them from the entirely separate Anglican parochial church councils of 'ecclesiastical' parishes – are, for about a third of the population, a vital part (frequently in both senses of the adjective) of the British system of local government: independent democratic bodies elected by and accountable to their villages, smaller towns and suburbs. 'Town council', incidentally and confusingly, is synonymous with 'parish council', and any parish council is able to style itself a town council, often entirely appropriately, as some of these parishes are larger than some smaller district councils, with the largest – Weston-super-Mare Town Council – serving a population of over 70,000. Most, however, are much more localised, nearly two-thirds comprising populations of under 1,000, and 40 per cent under 500 (Ellwood *et al.*, 1992). In Wales, there are some 900 'communities', about 750 of which have established community councils, comparable to English parishes. Scotland is also divided into some 1,150 communities, but Scottish community councils are not local authorities in the same sense, as they have no statutory basis, and neither the power to tax nor any access as of right to public funds.

The principal functions of Scottish community councils, therefore, are not in the provision of services, but rather in consultation and representation: ascertaining and articulating the views of their local residents. These roles are obviously just as important for any parish, town or Welsh community council. These latter councils, however, have certain rights – to be consulted, for example, by their district and county councils about local planning applications and footpath surveys. They also have potentially wide service-providing powers, acting either on their own initiative or as agents of their county and district councils. The services that tend to be listed most frequently are the provision and maintenance of village halls and community centres, allotments, playing fields, gymnasiums and public baths, footpaths, parks and open spaces, shelters and war memorials, street lighting, car parks, churchyards and burial grounds.

This permitted list was extended in the final days of the Major Conservative Government to include a range of transport and crime prevention powers. Nowadays, therefore, parishes are as likely to be involved in helping with the provision of meals on wheels, providing recycling facilities, organising community buses, setting up car-sharing schemes, installing CCTV cameras to prevent crime, enabling local post offices and stores to remain open, or arranging local GP clinics. A parish council may in addition spend money on any purpose it considers to be of direct benefit to its area or its inhabitants – up to £5 per local elector.

All these powers, however, are *discretionary*: there is no requirement that the services be provided. Where they *are* provided, they are financed partly by fees and charges and partly through a 'precept' added to the council tax collected by their district council from the area's taxpayers. These precepts vary greatly across the country, from under £10 in some places to £100 per council tax Band D property in others, reflecting the equally great variation in the councils' activities. It is this wholly discretionary nature of parish and town councils' work, and not primarily their size, that accounts for the limited attention they receive in this book. They are *not universal* – encompassing less than a third of the population of England and Wales – and they have *no specific duties* to provide services or facilities. These councils, though, are about far more than delivering services:

> they are about a form of democracy close to the people. They derive their legitimacy from elections, and their power comes through reflecting, mobilising and using public opinion as well as from what they can deliver directly, either on their own or in partnership with larger local authorities. (Coulson, 1998, p. 248)

As Stewart (2000, p. 266) has noted, both counties and districts have developed their relationships with parish councils: 'Partly because of reorganisation, but also because of growing concern to get closer to local communities, there is a new interest in parish and town councils as the elected representatives of the community.' One obvious measure of this interest is the establishment of parish and town councils in urban areas – Leeds, Bradford, Stockport, York, Hartlepool, Newcastle – and the desire of figures such as Ken Livingstone and Sir Robin Wales, Mayor of Newham and Chair of the Association of London Government, to introduce parish councils to the capital. A second measure is the Labour Government's establishment in 2003 of its Quality Parish and Town Council scheme. A Quality Council has to prove itself both able and efficient – through, for example, having contested elections, regular meetings, training programmes for key personnel and effective consultation procedures. Having passed this 'quality test', it can seek, particularly by working in partnership with its principal authorities, community and voluntary organisations, to extend the range of services it provides. By 2006, the number of Quality Status parish and town councils was approaching 300.

All this sounds commendable, but there is a minor source of concern that, at the same time and sometimes being driven by the same ministers, there are several other 'localist' initiatives – area committees, neighbourhood forums, Local Strategic Partnerships, Local Area Agreements – which have the capacity to compete as well as confuse. It is a theme to which we shall return.

Devolution to Scotland and Wales – the road to quasi-federalism

For an administration criticised initially more for its undue caution than for its radicalism, and led by a prime minister with no evident interest in the subject, the 1997 Labour Government's record of constitutional reform was remarkable. Within four years it had reformed the House of Lords, introduced Human Rights and Freedom of Information Acts, codified the financing of political parties and election campaigns, introduced an avalanche of new electoral systems, and, as we have seen, continued the structural reform of local government. Arguably more far-reaching than any of these, however, was its programme of devolution for Scotland, Wales and Northern Ireland, which has changed not just the content of the British constitution but its very nature: Britain is now effectively a quasi-federal state. The Westminster Parliament remains constitutionally supreme, but in practice that supremacy now means different things in the four nations of the United Kingdom. In Scotland, Wales and Northern Ireland – though in differing ways – 'large powers have been removed from the purview of ministers and Members of Parliament' (Bogdanor, 2001, p. 149).

As with the Greater London Authority, the Government's intentions for devolution to Scotland and Wales were outlined in its 1997 manifesto (pp. 33–4):

> As soon as possible after the election, we will enact legislation to allow the people of Scotland and Wales to vote in separate referendums on our proposals, which will be set out in white papers. For Scotland we propose the creation of a parliament with law-making powers, including defined and limited financial powers to vary revenue, and elected by an additional member system. The Scottish parliament will extend democratic control over responsibilities currently exercised administratively by the Scottish Office. The Welsh assembly will provide

democratic control of existing Welsh Office functions. It will have secondary legislative powers, and will be elected by an additional member system. Following majorities in the referendums, we will introduce in the first year of the Parliament legislation on the substantive devolution proposals.

For a party that had been out of power nationally for 18 years, devolution was an unexpected priority. But the manifesto agenda was implemented almost precisely as scheduled. White Papers were published within two months of the Government taking office, and referendums held in September 1997. The Scottish referendum included two questions and, on a 60 per cent turnout, 74 per cent of Scots voted for a Parliament and 64 per cent for one with limited tax-varying powers. The Welsh Assembly, by contrast, was approved by only the narrowest of majorities: just 50.3 per cent on a 50 per cent turnout.

Legislation duly followed, as did the first elections to the new bodies in May 1999. The similarities and differences between the *primary* legislative Scottish Parliament and the *executive* or *secondary* legislative Welsh Assembly can be seen from a comparison of Exhibits 5.5 and 5.6. Both institutions have received at least as much criticism as praise, which was probably to be expected. Nationalists and radical devolutionists are almost bound to be dissatisfied, while unionists see even comparatively modest devolution as an inevitable first step towards an eventual break-up of the United Kingdom. What cannot be disputed is that they have made their presence felt; they have made a difference.

Inevitably, the Scottish Parliament has had the greater impact – as some readers will need little reminding. One of the earliest acts of the Executive was to abolish 'up-front' tuition fees for Scottish students studying in Scotland in favour of a graduate endowment. This was a direct reversal of the Blair Government's policy, prompting the prime minister's revealing outburst that 'you can't have Scotland doing something different from the rest of Britain ... I am beginning to see the defects in all this devolution stuff' (Ashdown, 2001). It was a prophetic remark, though hardly as intended, because by 2001 it was England that was having to come into line with Scotland. There have, though, been plenty of other policy initiatives leading to divergences between Edinburgh and Westminster, as can be seen in Exhibit 5.7 – the last item on the Scottish list being of particular significance. Having already gone their own way on political management and local finance reform, Scottish councils will from 2007 be elected by the Single Transferable Vote (STV) system of proportional representation, eliminating most, of not all, of the nation's one-in-three 'one-party monopolistic' or 'one-party dominant' councils (see Exhibit 14.1).

Notwithstanding its lack of primary legislative powers and its smaller budget, Wales too has produced its own list of distinctive policies –

Exhibit 5.5 Devolved government in Scotland

What is it? A form of legislative devolution: the UK Parliament's constitutional sovereignty remains unchanged, but it will not, by convention, legislate on devolved matters in Scotland: for example, health, education, local government, economic development, transport, law and home affairs, the environment, agriculture, fisheries and forestry, sports and the arts.

The Scottish Parliament – 129 members (MSPs) elected by Additional Member System form of proportional representation (see pp. 231–3). 73 (56.5 per cent) represent individual constituencies; 56 represent eight electoral regions. The second set of elections in 2003 again returned a 'hung' parliament: 50 Labour (−6), 27 Scottish Nationalists (−8), 18 Conservatives, 17 Liberal Democrats, 7 Scottish Green Party (+6), 6 Scottish Socialist Party (+5), 1 Senior Citizens' Unity Party, and 3 'Others'; 48 MSPs (39.5 per cent) are women (compared to 19.6 per cent of MPs).

The Scottish Executive – the government of Scotland for all devolved matters. It comprises:

- The First Minister – elected by the whole parliament; effectively Scotland's prime minister. Initially Donald Dewar; in 2005, Jack McConnell (Labour).
- A Cabinet of 12 ministers, appointed by the First Minister and approved by Parliament. Since 1999, a Labour–Liberal Democrat coalition – 9 Labour, 3 Lib Dems.
- An advisory civil service, organised into 8 main departments – including Finance and Central Services, responsible for relations with local government.

Westminster's reserved responsibilities, exercised through the **Secretary of State for Scotland**, include: the UK constitution, foreign policy, Europe, defence, fiscal and economic policy, employment, benefits and pensions, transport safety, broadcasting policy, the national lottery.

Financial arrangements – Total budget is £27 billion in 2005–06, 90 per cent of which is funded by grant from Westminster, 7 per cent from business rates and 2 per cent from Europe. The Scottish Parliament can also choose to vary the basic rate of income tax for Scottish residents (the 'tartan tax') by up to 3p – equivalent to approx. £700 million, but so far has not done so.

Parliamentary committees – much of the Parliament's work is done through its committees, which are both more powerful – combining both legislative and scrutiny/investigative functions – and more proactive than Westminster's. Significantly, they can also initiate legislation. Committee chairs/convenerships are distributed according to the parties' shares of MSPs.

How is local government handled? It is part of the large portfolio of the interestingly entitled Minister for Finance and Public Service Reform (Tom McCabe in 2006). A parliamentary committee for Local Government and Transport can question the minister and scrutinise legislation.

Where is it? In a splendid, award-winning building adjacent to the Palace of Holyroodhouse. Though wildly over budget and less futuristic than Ken Livingstone's 'testicle' (see Exhibit 5.4), it is a modern, innovative showcase for many indigenous materials – Kemnay granite, Caithness flagstone, Scottish oak – and companies.

Exhibit 5.6 Devolved government in Wales

What is it? A form of executive and administrative devolution: UK Parliament retains, at least for the present, control over all primary legislation, but devolves to the Assembly the power to make secondary legislation on certain matters – similar to the Scottish list – in which, by convention, UK ministers will not involve themselves.

The National Assembly for Wales – 60 Assembly Members (AMs) elected, like Scottish MSPs, by the Additional Member System. 40 (67 per cent) represent individual constituencies; 20 represent five electoral regions. In the second set of elections in 2003 no party had an overall majority: 30 Labour (+2), 12 Plaid Cymru (Welsh Nationalist) (−5), 11 Conservatives (+2), 6 Liberal Democrats, 1 Independent/Other; 50 per cent of AMs are women – highest in the world in 2005 (Rwanda 49; Sweden 45), achieved by Labour's 'pairing' of constituencies and local activists sorting out m/f representation.

Welsh Assembly Government – unlike the UK Government and Parliament, the Assembly Cabinet is *part of* the Assembly, not separate from it. It comprises:

- The First Minister – elected by the whole Assembly and therefore usually the leader of the largest party. Rhodri Morgan (Labour), following the resignation of Alun Michael (February 2000).
- A Cabinet of 9 Assembly ministers, appointed by the First Minister. All Labour, following 2003 elections, as, technically, a minority administration. Exceptionally open, with publication of Cabinet minutes and advice papers to subject committees.
- An advisory civil service of approx. 3,500.

Financial arrangements – Westminster allocates a formula-based grant to the Assembly for all devolved services (£13 billion in 2005). The Assembly has no income tax-varying power.

Assembly committees – unusually inclusive: the minister is a member (but *not* chair) of the relevant subject committee, and non-executive AMs have more involvement with policy than do Westminster MPs. Main responsibilities of committees are policy development – jointly with the Cabinet – scrutiny of the work of the minister, and the monitoring of public bodies. All Assembly business is conducted bilingually, with most broadcast on a dedicated Assembly digital channel, S4C2.

How is local government handled? A Minister for Finance, Local Government and Public Services (Sue Essex in 2006), is a member of (and scrutinised by) the Local Government and Public Services Committee. Assembly works collectively with local government through a 25-member Partnership Council, comprising AMs and local government representatives.

Where is it? A state-of-the-art Assembly building on Cardiff Bay waterfront, designed by Richard Rogers – of Pompidou Centre and Millennium Dome fame. But Welsh AMs, less tolerant than Scottish MSPs of the massive budget over-run, sacked Rogers, then rehired him. Opened in early 2006.

Exhibit 5.7 Distinctive policies in Scotland and Wales

The Scottish Parliament

- Free long-term personal care for the elderly
- Abolition of 'up-front' student tuition fees for students in higher education
- Better pay and conditions for teachers
- Less restrictive Freedom of Information legislation
- Earlier abolition of fox-hunting
- Abolition of ban on 'promoting homosexuality in schools'
- Improved nutritional standards of school meals
- Prohibition of smoking in public places
- Proportional representation in local government elections.

The Assembly for Wales

- UK's first Children's Commissioner
- Creation of 22 Health Boards to work alongside Wales' 22 local authorities
- A Homelessness Commission, and extended support for the homeless
- Abolition of secondary school 'league tables'
- Free medical prescriptions for those under 25 and over 60
- Free bus travel for pensioners
- Free school milk for children under 7.

---

perhaps the most widely publicised being been the creation in 2001, following a harrowing inquiry into abuse in children's homes, of a Children's Commissioner, to champion children's rights, represent their interests, and, among other things, to try to ensure that future complaints of abuse are investigated thoroughly. Even though it required legislation by the Westminster Parliament, the idea appeared initially to be regarded in England as something of a curiosity – only for it to be copied four years later.

Northern Ireland – unplanned and interrupted devolution

There was no restructuring of local government in Northern Ireland during the 1990s corresponding to the spread of unitary councils in Scotland, Wales and parts of England. The position remained in 2006 as outlined in Chapter 4, with elected local government confined to 26 district councils, relatively small in British terms, and responsible for far fewer services than their counterparts elsewhere in the United Kingdom – see

Figure 5.6 *Northern Ireland's 26 district councils, 2006*

1 Belfast
2 Newtownabbey
3 Carrickfergus
4 North Down
5 Castlereagh

Figure 5.6. Most services affecting people's daily lives continue to be administered by appointed Area Boards – four for health and social services, five for education and public libraries – and almost countless numbers of other public bodies, from the Housing Executive to the Irish Medium Schools' Body.

It is true that the more proactive councils and the councillors themselves have often managed to make the most of their limited powers. In the years when there was no provincial elected assembly, they acted as an important debating forum for any key issue affecting Northern Ireland. They developed an important advocacy role, both for their own local areas and for helping individual residents, who turn out to vote in local elections in far greater numbers than on the mainland. In 1994, they were given the important power to spend money on economic development in return for Unionist support of the Major Government in the parliamentary vote on the Maastricht Treaty. Some of them also worked closely with councils on the other side of the Irish border, and were highly effective in negotiating European development funding. It had long been clear, though, that devolution of further significant powers was totally dependent on there being substantial and consolidated progress in the so-called peace process.

Yet, despite Labour's 1997 manifesto pledge in respect of Northern Ireland being much vaguer than for Scotland and Wales, it was in fact the Northern Ireland Assembly, following the intensive negotiations that culminated in the famous Belfast 'Good Friday' Agreement in April 1998, that was the first of the three devolved regional bodies to be elected. Within weeks, the Agreement had been endorsed in simultaneous referendums in both parts of Ireland, and barely one month later the Assembly was elected. Notwithstanding its title, the Assembly is an example of full executive and legislative devolution – very similar to the Scottish Parliament. It has authority for those matters previously within the remit of the Northern Ireland Office – agriculture, economic development, education, environment, finance, and personnel, health and social services. The most obvious omissions, compared to the Scottish Parliament, are security functions, policing and the courts.

The Assembly's 108 members are elected from Northern Ireland's 18 parliamentary constituencies by the Single Transferable Vote (STV) form of proportional representation (see pp. 231–3). STV has been used in all non-Westminster elections in Northern Ireland since 1973, specifically because it facilitates representation of the full range of opinions across the Catholic/Nationalist and Protestant/Loyalist communities – and prevents any single faction from gaining an overall Assembly majority. The second set of elections, held while the Assembly itself was suspended, were a predictable triumph for the 'hard-line' parties: the Revd Ian Paisley's Democratic Unionists (30) overtaking the official Ulster Unionists (27), and Sinn Fein (24), with its best ever result, outflanking the Social Democratic and Labour Party (18) (for full results, see Electoral Commission, 2003a).

Until the latest suspension of the Executive and Assembly in October 2002, it was these four parties that were represented on the 12-member power-sharing Executive Committee of Ministers that served as Northern Ireland's devolved government – four posts each for the Ulster Unionists and SDLP, two each for Sinn Fein and the Democratic Unionists. Local government was a responsibility of the Minister for the Environment, and it is the Department of the Environment – overseen during suspension by one of the UK Northern Ireland Ministers, Lord Rooker – that is formally responsible for policy in relation to local government. As in the other devolved bodies, though, it is the intention that Assembly members themselves, through departmental committees, play a greater role in both the development of policy and its scrutiny than do Westminster MPs.

As was noted in Exhibit 2.1, structural reform of local government continued to be debated, as part of the Executive's comprehensive Review of Public Administration (RPA). The Review proposed a two-tier model of public administration: a regional tier of the Assembly, Executive and central government departments, focusing on policy development and setting standards; and a sub-regional/local tier of organisations ideally sharing the same boundaries – a reduced number of stronger local councils, new health bodies, and the delivery units of regional bodies such as education. Councils would have 'a central role in developing and co-ordinating local policy on service delivery between major service providers within their council boundary'. If, as in 2006 seemed likely, the number of councils is reduced to the point where they serve populations of up to 400,000, they could be supported by more local 'civic councils', whose members would gather views to feed into their main council (RPA, 2005). As on the mainland, it would seem that reformers – if not the NI Local Government Association – have accepted the credo that local is parochial, and bigger somehow equals better.

English regional government – miscarried assemblies

If the 1997 Labour Government delivered promptly on most of its devolution commitments, the one area on which it arguably under-delivered was English regional government. The 1997 manifesto promised to:

> establish one-stop Regional Development Agencies (RDAs) to co-ordinate regional economic development, help small business and encourage inward investment. (p. 16)

These RDAs would be linked to appointed regional chambers, following which, if and where popular consent was established, arrangements would 'be made for elected regional assemblies' (pp. 34–5).

Eight *Regional Development Agencies (RDAs)* and associated *Regional Chambers* were duly set up following legislation in 1998, with an equivalent in London arriving with the new Greater London Authority two years later (see Figure 5.7). The RDAs are headed by ministerially appointed boards of between 8 and 15 members, including four from local government. Their purpose is to promote employment, investment, economic development and regeneration, and generally to improve the economic competitiveness and success of their regions, and they spend some £2 billion p.a. Some are known just as Development Agencies; others have opted for more macho names – Yorkshire Forward, Advantage West Midlands, for example – reflecting their predominantly male, business-led board memberships.

Regional Chambers are nominated bodies of local councillors and representatives of other relevant sectors: business, trade unions, education and training, and voluntary, cultural and environmental organisations. The chambers are consulted over their RDAs' preparation of their regional economic strategies, and they overview and scrutinise the RDAs' activities,

Figure 5.7   *The Regional Development Agencies: their names, headquarters and 2006–07 budgets*

but, in a crucial distinction, it is not to them that the RDAs are ultimately accountable, but to ministers and Parliament. Together with the Government Offices for the Regions (GOs) – the combined regional presence of domestic central government departments – each spending on average over £1 billion p.a., the RDAs and chambers form a not inexpensive tripartite structure, but with limited powers and confused accountabilities.

To extend these powers and unravel accountabilities was to be the function of directly elected regional assemblies, to replace the unelected chambers. In 2002, thanks almost entirely to the work and advocacy of the deputy prime minister, John Prescott, a delayed White Paper, *Your Region, Your Choice – Revitalising the English Regions*, outlined how it would be done. The assemblies or mini-Parliaments would have considerably less power than the Scottish Parliament or Welsh Assembly, but would be comparable in some ways to the Greater London Authority. They would not have the GLA's control over police and fire services, but would have responsibility for strategic planning, economic development, skills and employment, transport and housing strategy, public health, culture and tourism. They would also be able to levy a charge of 5p per week on the average council tax bill – in what the Conservatives, strongly opposed to the whole scheme, labelled a 'devolution tax'.

No region would be forced to have an elected assembly, but, where there was evidence of public support for one, people should have the chance to demonstrate it in a referendum – in which they would also vote for the structure of unitary local government they wanted. For – and here came the prime minister's contribution to the regionalism debate – no region could have more than one tier of sub-central government, lest Ministers be accused by their opponents of 'increasing bureaucracy'.

Prescott's initial hope was that three referendums would be held, in the North East, Yorkshire and the Humber, and the North West. In the event, faced with the scepticism of Cabinet and party colleagues, public indifference, and apprehension about the integrity of large-scale postal voting, he had to settle for one, held in the North East in November 2004, which produced a respectable response of 48 per cent, but a resounding and humiliating 78 per cent 'No' vote: 696,519 to 197,310. The exercise cost an estimated £10 million and, it hardly needs to be said, will not be repeated (see conference paper – Game, 2005 – on linked website).

But if *elective* and *democratically accountable* regionalism is dead, at least for the foreseeable future, *administrative* regionalism still thrives. As Tomaney (2004) notes, decisions made in the Government Offices for the Regions and in the RDAs, 'in policy fields such as economic development, housing and spatial planning' provide 'an increasingly important context for the actions of local authorities' (p. 180). But they constitute only a modest part of the total picture of regional governance, which must also include all those other agencies – Benefits, Child Support, Highways, Countryside, the Environment – and regional bodies for employment, the arts, sport, tourism, plus the health service, the prison service, and many more. A few years ago, an attempt to map 'the structure of governance in the West Midlands' identified some 50 public bodies responsible for a total annual expenditure of over £22 billion – all ultimately from national taxation, but none of it through elected bodies with direct democratic accountability (Ayres and Pearce, 2002, p. 16). By comparison, the 1,935 elected councillors in the region, or their 38 local authorities, were responsible for a combined budget of under £6 billion, some three-quarters of which was itself controlled by central government in the form of grants. And it would seem that the disparity is set to increase, as Labour's 2005 General Election Manifesto promised to 'devolve further responsibility to existing regional bodies in relation to planning, housing, economic development and transport' (p. 108).

Chapter 6

The Way It Is – Internal Structures

A political management 'revolution'

Radical and far-reaching as they have been, the recent external structural changes to the British local governmental system have been at least matched by those taking place within it – in particular, the advent of 'executive local government'. Indeed, 'reform' is probably too moderate a term for the changes in their day-to-day working practices that many councils have experienced over the past few years. In their comprehensive overthrow of almost two centuries of committee-based decision-making, the new mayoral and cabinet executives discussed in this chapter constitute almost a revolution.

Outlining and evaluating such change in a book of this nature, though, inevitably presents a problem, because, in order to appreciate the scale and significance of the new systems and institutions, you need first to understand what they replaced. It is therefore with councils' traditional institutions and operations that this chapter opens, before moving on to the changes resulting from the Local Government Act 2000.

Some explanations and clarifications

We start with a little more detail about some of the terms we have so far referred to in passing, but without further explanation: local authorities, councils, councillors, elected members, committees, departments and officers. In Chapter 2 we described a *local authority* as a semi-independent, politically decentralised, multifunctional body, created by and exercising responsibilities conferred by Parliament. The term is often used – and has already been used by us – interchangeably with *council*. Strictly speaking, though, the council is the legal embodiment of the local authority: the body of *elected councillors* who have collectively determined and are ultimately responsible for the policy and actions of the authority. In recognition of this legal responsibility, councillors are often referred to as the elected *members* of the authority, which distinguishes them from its paid employees, the *officers* (not 'civil servants', a term reserved in the UK for central government employees) and other administrative, professional, clerical and manual staff.

As already noted, British local authorities are generally very large organisations and, with the spread of unitary authorities, getting larger still: 468 for the 60 million population in the whole of the UK, or one for every 129,000 people. Several have more than 100 councillors, and larger county and metropolitan councils have tens of thousands of full-time and part-time staff. The councillors and staff make up the so-called 'two worlds' of local government. Decisions and policies emerge from the formal and informal interaction of these two worlds. In most authorities it would be neither possible nor desirable for councillors to take all necessary policy decisions in full council meetings, or for officers to manage and deliver the multitude of local government services, without some kind of internal structural divisions. The way in which local authorities in this country traditionally organised themselves, before the advent of political executives brought in by the 2000 Local Government Act, was through *committees* of councillors and professionally-based *departments*.

Councillors and committees

In a word association test, 'committee' would be the very first idea that many people would associate with local government – often negatively, but at least sometimes positively. The committee system was a key feature of 'the inherited world' of multi-functional authorities (Stewart, 2000, ch. 4) that enabled them to work effectively and at the same time democratically, without elected councillors handing over all policy-making to unelected officials. Committees were a council's workshops, where councillors' local knowledge and their political assessment of local needs were brought together with officers' professional and expert advice to produce, it was hoped, democratically responsive and implementable policy. They were where disagreements were thrashed out and where policy was *shaped*, though not literally determined, for neither the members of a committee nor even the chair had the executive authority actually to *take* decisions. That had to be done by all members of the council, gathered together in *full council* meetings.

Council committees, then, were composed of and chaired by elected councillors and advised by officers. A few, such as education and social services, were *statutory* for councils with these responsibilities. Most, though, were *permissive*, enabling councillors themselves to decide how to arrange and divide up their council's work. Different councils with exactly the same service responsibilities would therefore quite probably have very different committee and sub-committee structures. One or two small district councils in Scotland and Wales in fact chose to work entirely through full council meetings and had no committees at all. But the more common tendency was the reverse: for councils to acquire over time a proliferation of committees and sub-committees with correspondingly formidable numbers of meetings. The sense that such systems may duplicate discussion, complicate and slow down decision-making, and be generally too time-consuming, was one of the driving forces behind the recent reforms.

Committees, though, make easy targets for criticism, and, in their rush towards 'modernisation', some reformers possibly underrated the many positive features of committee practices that served local government well for most of its history. A modernised replacement for committees needs to try to recreate the opportunities they offered, or risk throwing the proverbial baby out with the bathwater. In brief, decision-making through committees can:

- enable councillors to acquire specialist knowledge in specific policy areas, thereby producing more informed decision-making;
- enable councillors to develop public speaking, chairing, and other potential leadership skills;
- allow decisions to be scrutinised publicly;
- allow opposition councillors to put forward alternative proposals;
- allow representations of special interests; and
- provide a forum for calling officers and contractors to account for their performance.

Of course, several of these positive features have their negative sides too. Councillors could over-specialise and become blinkered, failing to appreciate the work of the council as a whole. Committee meetings were often dominated by discussion of operational detail, at the expense of major policy issues, strategy, and the monitoring of service performance. Committees could also be excessively party political, creating a 'scrutiny shortfall' (Leach, 1999, p. 82), with majority party members being reluctant to criticise their own leadership publicly, and opposition members being in too small a minority to scrutinise effectively.

Perhaps most important of all for a multifunctional authority trying to present a coherent corporate image to the world, service-based or department-linked committees could become 'compartmentalised' and difficult to co-ordinate. Which is why almost all councils ultimately developed some kind of *central management committee,* known as Policy and Resources, Finance and Management, or some similar variant. The purpose of this committee, generally chaired by the Leader of the Council and containing some of its most experienced members, was to co-ordinate the work of specialist committees and provide the council with overall policy leadership. Some critics argued, however, that, in the absence of any *directly elected* individual leader, even the most coherent policy leadership was not able to impress itself upon local residents, service users and voters – which was part of the case for elected executive mayors put forward by the Labour government.

Officers, departments and directorates

The second of our complementary and interacting worlds of local government is that of the council employees, and particularly the 'white-collar' officers in their town hall and county hall departments. Traditionally, the arrangement and even the names of local authorities' *departments* would mirror closely their committees: quite large numbers, some providing services direct to the public – Education, Housing, Social Services, Libraries – some a servicing role for other departments – Finance (or Treasurer's), Personnel, Construction and Design – and each headed by a *chief officer* or *director*, who was a qualified *professional* and specialist in the functional area concerned.

Today, those 'matching' structures have entirely disappeared. Most policy committees have gone, and, with the development of a more strategic approach to service organisation, and the trend for councils to become 'enablers' or 'commissioners' rather than direct providers of services, departmental arrangements are unrecognisably different. For a start, terminology has changed – sometimes usefully and imaginatively, sometimes not: Personnel is Human Resources Management; Museums (and sometimes zoos) are part of Heritage; Housing may or may not be the Built Environment; Community is a near-universal default. And almost every council, it seems, wants its own unique management structure, increasingly headed by a dramatically slimmed down number of *directorates*, combining together several departments with linked interests. A typical county council today might have five directorates: Chief Executive's, Children's Services, Adult Social Services, Transport and Environment, and Corporate Services, each comprising several previously independent departments. So Transport and Environment, for example, might include Engineering, Highways, Waste Management, Environmental Health and Trading Standards.

Those heading these directorates – sometimes actually entitled Deputy Chief Executives, but more frequently Executive/Strategic/Corporate Directors, all of which, we suspect, signify the same thing – will have been appointed primarily for their *managerial* skills and experience. But they, like the probably two dozen or more *Principal or Chief Officers* that head the various services in their directorates, will still most probably be trained and qualified in one of the professions within their policy remit, as will many of the staff employed at lower levels in their respective departments.

Local authorities, then, have considerable discretion in the departmental structures they adopt and the officers they appoint – the only real constraint being occasional legislation requiring relevant local authorities to appoint certain chief officers – a Chief Education Officer, Chief Fire Officer or a Director of Social Services. Most recently, the Children Act 2004 requires councils to integrate key services for children by 2008, and to merge education and children's social services under a Director of Children's Services. Such statutorily imposed posts nevertheless remain the exception rather than the rule.

Directors and chief officers have overall responsibility for implementing council policies. Though highly trained, professionally qualified and, by most standards, extremely well paid, they are as much employees and 'servants' of *the council* as the most recently recruited manual worker. Unlike councillors – often much less formally educated and trained, and much less handsomely remunerated – officers have not been elected, and their role is to ensure that the policy laid down by the councillors is implemented, and that all their reasonable and lawful instructions are carried out. Note too the emphasis in the last sentence but one: in our traditional system, where policy was formally the responsibility of the whole council, officers' responsibility was naturally to the *whole* council, and *not* to any particular party, whether or not it happened to be in majority control. We shall see at the end of this chapter how these long-cherished principles of political neutrality and a unified officer structure are under some challenge with the arrival of executive government.

We have already referred to the post of *Chief Executive (CE)*. It is not a statutorily required appointment, and some councils nowadays, presumably wishing to emphasise their business-like culture, prefer managing director (MD) or borough director, while a smaller number tag 'town clerk' on to 'chief executive' as a reminder of pre-1970 times when the principal officer was a glorified legal adviser and record keeper. Over 90 per cent, though, opt for chief executives, and, while town clerk was an exclusively male profession, up to a fifth of present-day chief executives are women.

Whether CE or MD, the post-holder is the chief officer in overall charge of the council and its departments, or 'head of the paid service', as it tends to be known. An additional requirement since the Local Government and Housing Act 1989 has been that all councils have a 'monitoring officer', to check that the council is operating within the law. This role too is commonly taken by the chief executive. The chief executive is a kind of officers' team leader, and will generally chair some sort of directors/chief officers' management team, on which will sit most or all principal officers. Precise patterns obviously vary from authority to authority, but almost all have some such mechanism for ensuring effective liaison and policy co-ordination across departments.

Early approaches to internal management reform

The recent internal management reforms we referred to at the start of this chapter are all about the development of the institutions and processes of *executive local government*: cabinets, elected mayors, council managers, overview and scrutiny committees. The shape of reform has been determined almost entirely by the Local Government Act 2000, which itself was the product of a series of preliminary consultation papers from the 1997 Labour Government. But this was by no means the first attempt to restructure the internal management of local authorities. Several parts of the 'traditional' system – policy and resources committees, chief executives, officers' management teams – developed out of earlier governmental reports and inquiries, which we summarise below.

Maud 1967 – chief executives in, management boards out

The Committee on the Management of Local Government, chaired by Sir John Maud, later Lord Redcliffe-Maud, sat at the same time as the Redcliffe-Maud Royal Commission on reorganisation referred to in Chapter 4. It anticipated the criticisms about committees encouraging councillors to concern themselves too much with details of day-to-day administration, and not enough with broad policy and strategy. Its prescriptions were radical – too radical for many.

All but the smallest local authorities, Maud proposed, should have a *Management Board* of between five and nine senior councillors, with wide delegated powers. There should also be a radical pruning of committees and departments, and each authority should appoint a *chief executive officer* – not necessarily a lawyer, like the traditional town clerk – who would be the undisputed head of the authority's paid staff.

The instinctive response of most local authorities to the report was hostile. It was felt to be elitist, and just as in the recent moves towards executive government, many councillors were fearful of becoming second-class members of their councils, excluded from the management board, and with little or no policy influence. Nevertheless, Maud did serve as stimulus for change: many authorities did rationalise their committee systems and some appointed chief executives. The reform process was further encouraged by the broadly similar analyses in the early 1970s of the Bains Report (England and Wales) and the Paterson Report (Scotland).

Bains 1972 and Paterson 1973 – corporate icing, traditional cake

These two committees were set up to advise on internal management structures for the new local authorities being established under the Local

Government Acts of 1972 in England and Wales and 1973 in Scotland. Their reports received a far more favourable reaction than had Maud. Essentially, they argued that the traditional departmental attitude that permeated much of local government needed to give way to a broader corporate, or authority-wide, outlook. Maud's then controversial idea of an elite management board was left in the long grass.

Following the Bains/Paterson recommendations, the vast majority of the newly established authorities appointed *chief executives* and set up *policy and resources committees* and *senior officer management teams*, if these did not already exist. There was, therefore, in many authorities a good deal of internal *structural* change following Bains, although the effect on day-to-day working practices is more difficult to determine. Re-drawing organisation charts is comparatively easy; implanting lasting cultural changes in the way an organisation actually works is altogether harder. New and apparently more corporate *forms* of management emerged, but Bains' strong, co-ordinating chief executive remained the exception, with an ingrained departmentalist culture continuing to hold sway in most authorities.

Widdicombe 1986 – overdue recognition of party politics

The Widdicombe Committee was the Thatcher Government's response to its concern about the policies and campaigning activities of a number of urban Labour authorities, which came to be labelled the Municipal or New Urban Left, or the 'loony left' as such councils were known in the tabloid press. A mainly younger generation of Labour councillors in London and certain other cities came into office committed to using local councils as a testing ground for new radical, interventionist policies in economic development, housing, transport and planning, and to defending their communities against central government spending cuts.

The Maud, Bains and Paterson Committees had focused mainly on organisational structures, their managerial prescriptions largely ignoring the roles – indeed, almost the existence – of elected members and the increasingly prominent party political dimension of the country's local government. Widdicombe addressed these issues head-on. The spread of party politics in local government was acknowledged, investigated, and many of its positive features welcomed: more contested elections, clearer democratic choice, greater policy consistency, more direct accountability. At the same time, the Committee was concerned to safeguard the position of minority parties and of individual and non-party members.

The Widdicombe recommendations led, in the Local Government and Housing Act 1989, to the effective banning of one-party committees and sub-committees, and to senior officers being barred from all public political activity. Overall, the Committee's impact was to introduce a number of 'checks and balances', without seriously challenging the right of a majority party to determine and see implemented its policy proposals. It injected a new air of realism into discussions about local authority management, but full-scale recognition of the validity of majority party control would have to await a new millennium and a New Labour Government.

New Labour's 'modernisation' prescription – separate executives

The New Labour administration elected in May 1997 published its thinking about local government in a set of consultation papers in early 1998. The first of these, *Modernising Local Government: Local Democracy and Community Leadership* (DETR, 1998b), subsequently evolved into the Local Government Act 2000, but it is still a useful reminder of the Government's approach to reform. New Labour wanted to emphasise its belief in and commitment to democratic local government – in contrast, it claimed, to its Conservative predecessors. But it also saw the existing system 'falling short of its great potential':

> Turnout at local elections is on average around 40 per cent and sometimes much less. There is a culture of apathy about local democracy. The evidence is that councillors – hard-working and dedicated as they are – are overburdened, often unproductively, by committee meetings which focus on detailed issues rather than concentrating on essentials. The opportunity for councillors to have a stronger voice on behalf of local communities is being missed. (DETR, 1998b, para. 1.3)

Chapter 5 of the consultation paper spelled out the shortcomings of a system 'designed over a century ago for a bygone age' – its inefficiency, secrecy, opacity, and lack of accountability:

- Councillors spend too small a proportion of their time in their representational work directly with their community, which should be their most important role.
- They spend too much time inefficiently – particularly in preparing for, travelling to, and attending committee meetings, which may not be where the real decisions are made in any case. Rather, in most councils, those decisions are made in party group meetings, behind closed doors, beyond the reach of either public or opposition party scrutiny.
- Traditional committees are also a poor vehicle for developing and demonstrating community leadership and accountability. They confuse the executive (policy-making) and representational roles of councillors. It is not always clear who has actually taken a decision and therefore who can be held to account.

The consultation paper acknowledged that several more progressive councils had already developed innovative ways of rethinking their committee structures and involving the public in their decision-making, but far more comprehensive change was required. This change, in the government's view, had to be based on a *separation* of the executive and representative roles of councillors – a contentious departure from the prevailing culture that, formally at least, saw all councillors as equal. This role separation would produce greater clarity about where decisions are taken, and by whom, and therefore who is to be held accountable. It would also enable there to be sharper scrutiny of those decisions. Indeed, the greater the separation, the greater the likely benefits:

> The Government is therefore very attracted to the model of a strong executive directly elected mayor. Such a mayor would be a highly visible figure ... elected by the people, rather than by the council or party, [who] would therefore focus attention outwards rather than inwards towards fellow councillors. The mayor would be a strong political and community leader with whom the electorate could identify. Mayors will have to become well known to their electorate, which could help increase interest in and understanding of local government. (para. 5.14)

The choice is yours – from our three models

There were hints in the consultation paper that the government might allow councils to pilot a wide variety of managerial arrangements: cabinet systems, lead member systems, directly- and indirectly-elected mayors. The eventual legislation, however, was both narrower and more prescriptive. The Local Government Act 2000 required all major local authorities in England and Wales to choose one of just three specified forms of executive or propose some ministerially acceptable alternative arrangements, as summarised in Exhibit 6.1.

This restricted choice, plus its obvious predisposition towards the controversial directly elected mayor, led to the legislation being fiercely opposed in Parliament, and the Government was forced to make some concessions. One was that small shire districts – the approximately one-third under 85,000 – were allowed a fourth option of a 're-vamped' committee system, provided they had the backing of their local community. All other authorities in England and Wales were required to prepare plans for new structures based on one of the three executive models, to be submitted for ministerial approval in 2001 and in operation by 2002.

Scotland by now had its own Parliament and Executive and could go its own way. It also had a report – from the McIntosh Commission

Exhibit 6.1 The new 'separate executive' models of political management

The traditional committee-based structure

Council decisions could be delegated to officers, but *not* to individual councillors – not even to council leaders or committee chairs. Decisions not delegated had to be taken either in full council or by committees or sub-committees of councillors. *All* councillors, therefore, were legally part of the decision-making process.

The Local Government Act 2000 introduced, for the first time, a clear separation between the *making and execution* of council decisions and the *scrutiny* of those decisions. The council's policy framework and budget are agreed by the full council, following proposals from the executive. The executive is then charged with implementing the agreed policy framework.

3 (or more) possible forms of executive arrangements

All councils in England and Wales – except shire districts with populations of less than 85,000 – were required, after consulting their local residents, to choose one of three specified forms of executive or propose some ministerially acceptable alternative arrangements:

(1) **Mayor and cabinet executive** – a mayor directly elected by the whole electorate, who appoints an executive/cabinet of between 2 and 9 councillors.

(2) **Leader and cabinet executive** – an executive leader, elected by the full council (i.e. usually the leader of the largest party), plus between 2 and 9 councillors, either appointed by the leader or elected by the council.

(3) **Mayor and council manager** – a mayor directly elected by the whole electorate, providing the broad policy direction, with an officer of the authority appointed by the council as a day-to-day manager.

(4) **Alternative arrangements** – an alternative form of executive, approved by the Secretary of State as more suitable to the council's particular circumstances than any of the above models.

Smaller shire districts had an additional option open to them:

(5) **Alternative arrangements (not involving a separate executive)** – retention of the committee system, subject to the Secretary of State's approval that decisions would be taken in an efficient, transparent and accountable way, with acceptable provisions for overview and scrutiny.

Mayoral options could only be introduced after approval in an authority-wide referendum – triggered by the council itself, by a petition signed by 5 per cent of local electors, or by direction of the Secretary of State.

Overview and scrutiny committees

All councils operating executive arrangements must set up overview and scrutiny committees of non-executive members (and possibly non-member co-optees), in order to hold the executive to account. These committees may make reports and recommendations, either to the executive or the authority, on any aspect of council business or other matters that affect the authority's area or its inhabitants.

(McIntosh, 1999) – with some pertinent recommendations. McIntosh had been set up to look at the implications that the Scottish Parliament would have for Scottish local government. Its most publicised recommendation was for proportional representation for local elections. But it looked also at how councils organised their business and political decision-making, and proposed that each of the 32 councils should review its own management arrangements against stated criteria of openness and accountability.

Thus, while the Westminster Parliament was prescribing just three executive models for all but the smallest English and Welsh councils, the Scottish Executive explicitly rejected any 'central blueprint', preferring to encourage the emergence of a 'rich diversity of different models'. As a result, there are no directly elected Provosts (Scottish mayors), and only five of the 32 unitary councils opted for a leader/cabinet model, the remainder preferring streamlined, or in some cases not so streamlined, committee systems.

Where are the mayors?

Though John Prescott – deputy prime minister and Cabinet minister responsible for local government – was known to have reservations, the Government's official position was to do everything possible to get local authorities to adopt elected mayors, to the extent of weighting the three executive options (self-defeatingly, as we shall see) heavily in their favour. The public – as far as it was possible to tell from opinion polls asking them something that most had never even thought about – seemed broadly supportive of the principle. Elected mayors had also been a key recommendation of the independent Commission for Local Democracy (1995), with its chairman, Sir Simon Jenkins, a particularly ardent advocate and credited with winning over the prime minister to the cause.

Within local government, though, support was minimal and opposition fierce. Councillors were both critical and understandably concerned: critical of the concentration of power in the hands of a single individual, and concerned that, if they were not among the minority of executive councillors, they could find themselves excluded altogether from the policy making process. Much safer, surely, to go for the leader/cabinet model that, while still involving an executive/non-executive split, would be closer to what they were familiar with.

The mayor/council manager model suffered the double handicap of being based partly on an elected mayor and partly on another novelty in British local government, the council manager. Council or city manager systems are one of the most prevalent forms of urban government in the USA – in, among many other cities, Dallas, San Diego, Kansas City and

Phoenix. They are also found, in different forms, in Ireland and New Zealand. It is easy to appreciate their appeal, combining apparently the strong political and policy leadership of an elected mayor with the managerial expertise and experience of a professional manager, appointed by the council and responsible for day-to-day decision-making. On the other hand, giving a great deal of power to an appointed official was, if anything, even more disenchanting to serving councillors than handing it over to an elected mayor, and so far only one authority, Stoke-on-Trent, has taken this route.

With the 2000 Act passed, all major local authorities in England and Wales were required, following consultations with their local electorates, to select one of the three specified models. If they chose one of the two elected mayoral models, they would have to get the agreement of local voters in a referendum. They could also be *required* to hold a referendum, if (a) there was a petition in favour of an elected mayor, signed by more than 5 per cent of local electors; or (b) the Secretary of State concluded that, in opting for a non-mayoral system – the leader/cabinet model – a council was misrepresenting the views of local people. The consultation process required councils to produce some explanatory information, setting out in a balanced, supposedly unbiased way, the merits and drawbacks of each of the three models, as in Exhibit 6.2.

This is where ministers' keenness to steer councils towards a mayoral option proved to be self-defeating. Several councils – including some of the biggest, such as Birmingham and Bradford, which, had they opted for elected mayors, might have served as role models for others – found that, while a clear majority of their consulted electors were in favour of *one or other* of the mayoral systems, the *single* most popular option, though supported by a minority, was the leader/cabinet. This preference, therefore, was what they reported to the Secretary of State, who might have intervened and ordered a referendum, on the grounds of local opinion having been misrepresented, but in the event declined the challenge (Game, 2003, p. 20 – full article on linked website).

Berwick-upon-Tweed was the first authority to hold a mayoral referendum (on General Election day, 2001), triggered by a petition of electors, who nevertheless voted in the actual referendum decisively *against* having an elected mayor. This pattern has been repeated several times since, and in fact only four mayoral systems (Bedford, Mansfield, Stoke-on-Trent and, in 2005, Torbay) have originated in petitions – suggesting perhaps that at least some petitioners were, perfectly reasonably, signing up to the idea of having a say, rather than to having a mayor. These petition-prompted referendums, though, as can be seen in Exhibit 6.3, have been a minority of a minority. To ministers' obvious disappointment, in that initial selection of executive systems, just thirty mayoral referendums were held – equal to one authority in every thirteen – and only eleven

Exhibit 6.2 The three executive models – for and against

New Option 1 – Indirectly elected leader and cabinet

You would go to the polls as now and elect your city councillors, who in turn would select (and later vote out if they were unhappy with their performance) a few senior councillors to form a cabinet and elect one councillor to become council leader. Most of the present service committees would be abolished. The leader and cabinet between them would make big council decisions, and the remaining councillors would scrutinise and keep a watch on them. Each cabinet member would take responsibility for running a council service, such as education, housing or social services, and would be accountable for that service to the people of the city and other councillors.

Those who like this system say: it speeds up decision-making and improves accountability, as cabinet members would become well known locally; it retains important checks and balances on the exercise of power; non-Cabinet members would have more time to represent their wards.

Those who don't like it say: it's a fudge, and not a sufficient change from the system that supposedly needs reforming; people would not be any more interested or involved; decisions would not be taken as quickly as with an executive mayor.

New Option 2 – Directly elected mayor and cabinet

This new system would abolish most council committees and transfer most of their power into the hands of a mayor elected by all voters once every four years. The mayor will appoint a small Cabinet of councillors, each covering a major service area. The remaining councillors would perform the scrutiny role, vetting the decisions of the mayor and cabinet and representing their constituents.

Those who like this system say: a high-profile mayor will reinvigorate public interest in the council; decisions will be made more quickly and more accountably.

Those who don't like it say: it puts too much power in the hands of the mayor, who cannot be removed from office for four years; no strong decision-making role for other councillors; could lead to worse and less accountable decisions because so few people involved; no guarantee that it will increase people's interest or participation.

New Option 3 – Directly elected mayor and council manager

As in New Option 2, a mayor would be elected directly by the people. But in this model the council would appoint a council manager, and possibly other chief officers too, to run services on a day-to-day basis.

Those who like this system say: it has the advantages of Option 2 but, without a cabinet, decisions could be made even more quickly; with only two people responsible for policy-making, it would be easier for the public to know who to hold to account.

Those who don't like it say: it gives too much power to just two people, one completely unelected and neither of them directly accountable to councillors; it is anti-democratic and has few checks and balances on power; too many decisions would be made behind closed doors, rather than in open cabinet meetings.

Exhibit 6.3 Mayoral referendums, 2001–06

	2001	2002	2003	2004	2005/06	TOTAL
Total	16	14	0	1	2	33
How initiated						
Voluntarily by council	15	7	–	–	–	22
Following petition	1	6	–	1	2	10
Direction from Minister	–	1	–	–	–	1
Result						
Yes	6	5	–	–	1	12
No	10	9	–	1	1	21
Highest % turnout	64* Berwick-upon-Tweed 36 North Tyneside	42 West Devon	–	36 Ceredigion (Wales)	35 Crewe and Nantwich	
Lowest % turnout	10 Sunderland	11 Southwark	–	–	32 Torbay	
Highest % Yes vote	84 Middlesbrough	68 Newham	–	–	55 Torbay	
Highest % No vote	74 Berwick-upon-Tweed	77 West Devon	–	73 Ceredigion	61 Crewe and Nantwich	

Source: Original table, compiled by authors.

Notes: *Exceptionally high turnout due to referendum being held on same day as General Election.
For full details of all mayoral referendum results, see the Electoral Commission's website under 'Referendums'.

produced 'Yes' votes for having an elected mayor. These eleven comprised three unitary councils (Hartlepool, Middlesbrough, Stoke-on-Trent), two metropolitan boroughs (Doncaster, North Tyneside), three London boroughs (Hackney, Lewisham, Newham), and three districts (Bedford, Mansfield, Watford) – all significant and sizeable authorities, but hardly likely to cause the country's big city councils to feel compelled to follow their lead. The overwhelming majority of councils (316, or 81 per cent) opted, therefore, for the leader/cabinet model, and a further 69 (15 per cent) took advantage of the 'smaller council' concession of 'alternative arrangements' (see Exhibit 6.1).

The elections for the historic first generation of English executive mayors were held in May and October 2002, and they produced not only some remarkable results and some interesting winners (see Exhibit 6.4), but also worldwide media fascination. Of the eleven contests, five were won by Independents of varying descriptions, which, when Ken Livingstone was included, meant that half the popularly elected mayors in Britain's highly party politicised system of local government had won by *defeating* candidates of all the established national parties. Even six months before, you would have been offered extremely long odds by bookmakers against that outcome. As two years earlier in London, the party most damaged in this carnage was Labour. In Middlesbrough, their candidate lost to the populist ex-policeman, Ray Mallon. In North Tyneside, where Labour had controlled the council for 28 years, voters elected a Conservative. In Watford, the council's Labour leader was defeated by a Liberal Democrat schoolteacher, Dorothy Thornhill. In Stoke-on-Trent, Mike Wolfe, organiser of the petition that had instigated the election, was voted in as the country's first openly gay mayor. 'Who's Afraid of the Big Bad Wolf?' taunted his campaign slogan; Labour was – and in particular the defeated candidate, George Stevenson, one of Stoke's MPs.

And then there was Hartlepool, where, to the delight of the international media and cartoonists everywhere, they elected a monkey – or, rather, Hartlepool Football Club's mascot, H'Angus the Monkey, aka Stuart Drummond, who campaigned in full monkey costume under the slogan 'Vote H'Angus – he gives a monkey's'.

The message could hardly have been any shriller: voters wanted a change – almost any change – from the established coteries of local politicos who had been running their councils, worthily or otherwise, for what seemed too long. Even some of the successful Labour candidates – Martin Winter in corruption-ridden Doncaster, Jules Pipe in Hackney, a council so financially mismanaged that it was threatened with central government takeover – were elected in the hope of their being 'change agents', rather than 'consolidators' (Stoker, 2004b). But, emphatic as the message may have been, it was not exactly democratically weighty. Despite

Exhibit 6.4 Four mayors – elected to make a difference

Council MAYOR *Mayor's party;* *Council control*	*Mayor's thumbnail biography*
Doncaster MBC **MARTIN WINTER** *Lab;* *NOC (Lab)* *council (2006)* Re-elected 2005 with 8,400 majority over Independent	Ex-pro rugby league player, freelance sculptor, and management consultant. Elected 1999 to the reputedly most corrupt council in UK – 21 councillors imprisoned for expenses fiddles and planning fraud. As 'new broom' leader in 2000 and mayor since 2002, has headed council 'rebranding' and area's economic regeneration. Today: new international airport, redevelopment of racecourse, 'Doncaster Education City' and new university. One wish? 'Give me control of transport, the police and other public services – I believe I've been elected as mayor for the whole of Doncaster.'
Hartlepool BC *(Unitary)* **STUART DRUMMOND** *Indep;* *Lab council* *(2006)* Re-elected 2005 with 8,700 majority over Labour	Former credit controller in local call centre. Elected 2002, after standing 'for a laugh' as H'Angus the Monkey, the mascot of town's football club. Victory seen as ultimate rejection of conventional party politicians, who waited gleefully for him to fail. He refused to oblige: ditched monkey suit, cut down on US chat show appearances, formed cross-party cabinet, learned fast, took chairmanship of town's Community Safety Partnership, and instigated 'Operation Clean Sweep', in which neighbourhoods are singled out each month for intensive treatment – from street cleaning and anti-social behaviour crackdowns to health checks and healthy eating seminars (more than just bananas!). Finalist, with Livingstone, for title of World Mayor 2005.

an average of nearly seven candidates per contest, turnouts in these 2002 elections ranged from just over 40 per cent in North Tyneside and Middlesbrough to 19 per cent in Mansfield, which meant that Ray Mallon alone could claim to represent even a quarter of his *potential* electorate, while Mike Wolfe in Stoke was returned by under 7 per cent of his (Game, 2003, pp. 25–6). All in all, therefore, the elected mayoral element of Labour's new modernised world of executive local government had got off to what even one of its staunchest advocates conceded was 'an inauspicious launch' (Stoker, 2004b, p. 6). The intended policy flagship had turned out to be a pleasure boat, a mildly entertaining diversion for all those not directly involved.

This first generation of elected mayors came up for re-election in 2005 and 2006. In May 2005, Labour candidates, John Harrison and Mark Meredith respectively, took North Tyneside from the Conservatives and

Middlesbrough *(Unitary)* **RAY MALLON** *Indep; Lab council (2006)* Re-election 2007	Highest profile of non-London mayors. Joined police at 19, rising to Detective Superintendent in Cleveland and controversial ('Robocop') architect of 'zero tolerance policing' in UK. Captained GB water polo team. Elected 2002 on highest first ballot vote (63%) in the town most in favour of having an elected mayor. Has a cross-party, though predominantly Labour, cabinet. Quickly launched 'Raising Hope' initiative, and claimed to have cut crime by 18% in first year. With physical regeneration of town and creation of business-friendly enterprise culture, has vision of turning Middlesbrough into new Dubai – 'another desert development in another kind of desert'.
Watford DC **DOROTHY THORNHILL** *Lib Dem; LD council (2006)* Re-elected 2006 with 7,000 majority over Conservative	First woman elected mayor and first Lib Dem, who, like her party, was opposed to them in principle. Former assistant head of largest secondary school in Herts – and keen Corrie fan. Councillor for 10 years, and civic (ceremonial) Mayor, 1998/99. Elected Mayor 2002, defeating Labour leader in traditionally strong Labour town. Life easier since voters, including disaffected Muslim Labour supporters, returned first-ever Lib Dem majority council. Proud of having improved town's financial and service record while setting lowest council tax rates in the county; also of having introduced doorstep recycling.

Note: NOC (Lab) = No single party on council has overall control – i.e. more than 50 per cent of the council seats – but Labour is the largest party group.

Stoke-on-Trent from the Independent, Mike Wolfe. Martin Winter was re-elected in Doncaster, while in Hartlepool a now besuited Stuart Drummond won a second remarkable victory over assorted all-comers. It also being General Election day, turnouts were substantially up, but there were signs that many voters still did not realise that the Supplementary Vote system (see Chapter 11) used in these mayoral elections gave them, unlike in parliamentary elections, the opportunity to express a second preference, if they wished. In May 2006, all four incumbent mayors were re-elected: Jules Pipe in Hackney, Steve Bullock in Lewisham, Robin Wales in Newham (all Labour), and Dorothy Thornhill (LD) in Watford.

They may be few in number, but most, if not all, of these elected mayors have, in their own council areas, undoubtedly 'made a difference'. They are far better known than their predecessor council leaders ever were; they have raised their councils' profiles, and in several cases stimulated a change in their political complexion; and most are associated with a number of personal policy initiatives and campaigns. The idea of directly elected mayors, therefore, will certainly not go away, and indeed we already have the first of a new generation. In October 2005, following a successful petition-prompted referendum, local Conservative estate agent Nicholas Bye defeated his Liberal Democrat opponent plus eleven Independents and others, to become Mayor of Torbay.

The idea of the election of a Conservative mayor constituting encouragement for the Government is perhaps an odd one, but ministers have by no means abandoned their belief that more elected mayors would be a 'good thing' for local government. In *Vibrant Local Leadership* (2005h), one of a series of discussion documents setting out a 10-year vision for local government, the ODPM rehearsed the arguments for elected mayors and suggested that the requirement that a mayoral referendum be triggered by a petition signed by 5 per cent of local electors may be 'unnecessarily cumbersome' (p. 14). It continued: 'The Government is interested in views on whether there are more effective means of giving people the opportunity to express a view about whether they would like to have a directly elected mayor system of local leadership'. The Labour Party's 2005 General Election Manifesto, *Britain Forward Not Back,* echoed this idea, adding that: 'We will also consult with city councils on the powers needed for a new generation of city mayors' (p. 107).

Leaders and cabinets

We described mayors as having proved an entertaining diversion. What they tended to be a diversion from – for both the public and the local media – is the recognition that the 2000 legislation brought about major changes in *all* English and Welsh authorities, including the majority who never seriously considered having an elected mayor. The underlying objective of the Government's reform was to introduce executive-based policy-making and to require councillors to become *either* executive *or* non-executive members (see Exhibit 6.1). They could no longer be both. The leader/cabinet systems adopted by most councils have therefore meant almost as fundamental a role change for councillors and officers as have mayoral systems.

All (apart from exempted 'smaller districts') now have a fairly small cabinet or executive of, on average, nine members with personal policy portfolios, who individually and collectively are the policy makers for the authority. They operate within policy and budget frameworks approved by the whole council, but, in contrast to the previous committee system, this minority of executive members are clearly identifiable as the ones to hold to account for any particular decision. Clearly identifiable not least because all councils are required to publish, usually on their websites, a forward plan or forthcoming decision list, giving advance notice of key decisions to be made, when, and by which executive member(s), and a similar list of executive decisions taken. Those lists are as eloquent an indicator as any of the extent to which councils have had to change since the turn of the millennium, and of the increased transparency and accountability those changes were designed to bring.

There is, of course, one inherent difference between the mayor/cabinet and leader/cabinet models. A leader owes her or his position to the fellow councillors who elected them and can remove them – principally their party colleagues. Theirs is the support they must retain, whereas for mayors it is the support of the electorate, as the councillors alone cannot remove them. But, that distinction apart, the leader/cabinet model is just that: a model, that different councils have adapted in very different ways. The principal variable is the degree of personal authority that a council decides, through its constitution – another requirement of the 2000 Act – and its internal party rules, to allow the council leader. Early indications were that in only about a third of cases did leaders themselves select their cabinet members, and in only just over half did they even allocate portfolios (Gains *et al.*, 2004, p. 5). The personal power of Labour leaders is particularly limited, and one has to wonder how, say, Tony Blair would take to that kind of constraint. As at Westminster, though, cabinets develop different styles of working: some describable as 'leader-dominated', others operating largely collectively, as a team, while some allow individual portfolio holders a considerable degree of autonomy (Stoker *et al.*, 2004, ch. 2).

Leicestershire County Council offers an example of the leader/cabinet system (see Exhibit 6.5 and Figure 6.1). Leicestershire's new post-2000 constitution outlines, much more accessibly than in the past, just how the Council functions. Leicestershire's is no more or less typical of leader/cabinet systems than any other – it delegates little power to individual cabinet members, has no area committees, and its cabinet support members and Scrutiny Commission are both attempts to accommodate to a 'Leicestershire culture' – but it gives a useful insight into how the new executive-based system works. Figure 6.1 in particular can be compared to other councils' political management structures via their websites, and you might also contrast it with Leicestershire's very different 'pre-modernisation' committee structure (Wilson and Game, 1998, p. 72 plus Exhibit on linked website), with its Policy and Resources Committee, six main service committees, plus sub-committees and working groups too numerous to list – now virtually all swept away. In the context of UK local government, a break with the past on that scale – even without directly elected mayors – does qualify as near-revolutionary.

Exhibit 6.5 Leicestershire County Council's Leader/Cabinet system

The full County Council (55 members)

- Is collectively the Council's ultimate policy-making body;
- Is the only body able to adopt and change the Council's *Constitution*;
- Approves the Council's *Policy Framework*, comprising a series of major plans, and its budget;
- Approves or rejects any proposals from the Cabinet that are outside the approved policy framework or the budget;
- Receives reports from scrutiny bodies on activities of the Executive/cabinet.

The Council's executive role

- Is carried out under *delegated powers*, primarily through the 10-member Cabinet acting and chief officers;
- The *Executive* comprises the Leader of the Council – elected by the Council, and therefore usually the leader of the largest party – and a *Cabinet*. It is responsible for the more important executive decisions needed to implement the policy framework and budget approved by the Council;
- Cabinet members take *lead roles* on specific services; and exercise individual powers, if and as delegated to them through the full Council;
- Cabinet support members may be appointed by the Council to assist specific Cabinet members in their duties, but do not form part of the Cabinet;
- The Cabinet will refer to the full Council any proposal involving a significant departure from the policy framework or the budget;
- Any meeting of the Executive at which an executive decision is taken is held in public.

The Council's overview and scrutiny role

- Is directed and co-ordinated by a *Scrutiny Commission* – a politically balanced committee of *non-executive* members, chaired by the leader of the largest opposition group;
- Five standing *Overview and Scrutiny Committees* covering County Council functions – Education, Community Services, Social Care, Highways, Transportation and Waste Management, and Resources – also comprise only non-executive members, and have roles in relation to policy development and review, as well as scrutiny;
- They can review and scrutinise decisions made by the Executive and chief officers; they can question Cabinet members and chief officers about specific decisions, their views on issues and proposals, and their general performance; they can research and undertake in-depth analysis of policy issues and possible options; they can liaise with and scrutinise the performance of other public bodies in the area;
- The Scrutiny Commission can also appoint a number of small, 5-member, temporary *review panels* to carry out targeted reviews;

Exhibit 6.5 continued

- There is also a standing Health Overview and Scrutiny Committee responsible for scrutinising the 4 Primary Care Trusts in the area, and a joint committee with the Leicester City and Rutland Councils covering wider aspects of the health service.

The Council's regulatory role

- Regulation – of planning, health and safety, licensing, etc – is carried out by the Development Control and Regulatory Board.
- Other bodies with this role include:
  - a Standards Committee of at least two councillors and a voting member independent of the Council – to monitor standards of conduct of all elected members and officers;
  - an Employment Committee to deal with conditions of service issues;
  - a Constitution Committee to advise the Council on constitutional issues, electoral matters and members' allowances;
  - a Corporate Governance Committee to promote and maintain high standards in relation to the operation of the Council's Code of Corporate Governance.

Representational role of individual councillors

- To work to ensure the well-being of the community they represent;
- to bring constituents' views, concerns and grievances to the attention of the relevant bodies;
- to contribute to the overview and scrutiny of the Council's policy and performance; and
- to contribute to the development of corporate policies, and local initiatives.

Overview and scrutiny

Executive-based policy making necessarily involves two sets of bodies – executive and non-executive – and the overview and scrutiny (O & S) provisions in the Local Government Act 2000, which would hold executives to account, were as important as the choice of executive models themselves. Some went further still:

> Overview and scrutiny is potentially the most exciting and powerful element of the entire local government modernisation process. It places members at the heart of policy-making and ... is the mechanism by which councillors can become powerful and influential politicians. (Snape *et al.*, 2002, Executive Summary)

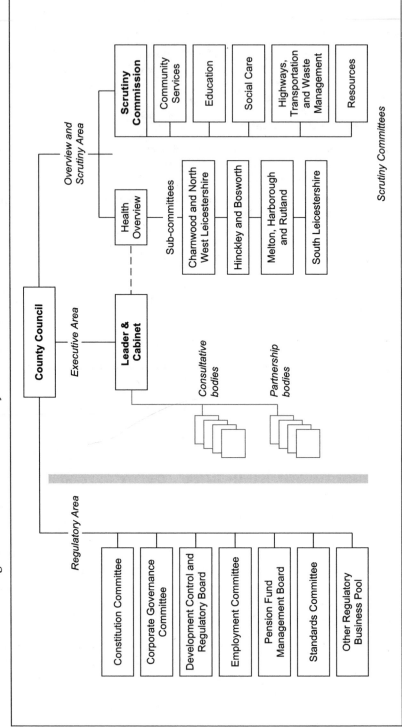

Figure 6.1 *Leicestershire County Council's Leader/Cabinet executive structure*

That at least was the theory. The practice, certainly in the early years, proved to be rather different, and it has undoubtedly been the hardest part of the modernisation package for councils and councillors to make work effectively. This is hardly surprising, since, as indicated in Exhibit 6.6, it involves ideas and ways of operating that were almost completely novel to those who for years had become used to decision-making by committee. Non-executive councillors, having been told that they were no longer policy *makers*, were inclined to suppose that that meant their being cut off from the policy process altogether, whereas potentially the reverse was true: they could have more influence on *shaping* policy or on evaluating its impact than many of them would ever have had under the committee system. If in some authorities O & S was seen as no more than 'a talking shop' which left non-executive councillors 'out of the loop' of real decision making (Fenwick *et al.*, 2003, pp. 29, 35), others were discovering that this need not necessarily be the case.

None of this is to deny that there are real hurdles to be overcome if O & S is generally to become as influential and powerful as its advocates envisaged – particularly in holding decision-makers to account. Undoubtedly, the main reason for the specifically scrutiny role (see Exhibit 6.6) proving so difficult is the dominant and entrenched nature of the political party system at local level. For entirely understandable reasons, councillors are reluctant to criticise, in a public setting and in front of their political opponents, senior members of their own party. It goes against both personal instinct and, quite possibly, party group rules.

If that weren't problematic enough, there is also the issue of adequate and appropriate officer support for the O & S role. Initially, many councils were slow to appreciate that, if a scrutiny committee is to investigate and question executive policy effectively, it will need something approaching the same quality of support that is available to the executive members themselves. A sizeable minority of councils now provide *specialist* support in the form of a dedicated Scrutiny Support Unit of officers working only to O & S committees. Rather more attempt a form of *integrated* support, with officers from a variety of departments across the council working partly for O & S and partly for the executive. Both practices have their advantages and disadvantages; what is indefensible is the *minimal* support still offered by at least some councils.

Two-hatted officers?

This reference to officer support enables us to emphasise something important but frequently overlooked: that these political management changes we have discussed primarily in terms of their impact on councillors have also had profound implications for officers. With separate mayoral and cabinet executives, local government has become much more

Exhibit 6.6 Overview and Scrutiny – what it is and how it's done

The key non-executive role

O & S is not the only role for non-executive councillors. They are also members of the full council, probably members of political groups, and may sit on various regulatory, appeals, area committees and outside bodies. But effective O & S is an essential part of the checks and balances necessary to hold the executive and other decision-makers to account.

It's not 'Overview'n'scrutiny'!

It was originally going to be just 'Scrutiny', but its revised form changes as well as extends the function. The two parts should be distinguished, however, and involve different skills and processes.

Scrutiny – the critical friend

Means holding the executive to account, by:

- scrutinising decisions *before* they are made or implemented – ideally through consultation with the executive, but if necessary through the use of 'call-in' powers, requiring the executive to reconsider its decision; and
- scrutinising decisions *after* implementation.

The aim is to be a 'critical friend' to the executive, but it's not an easy role. Be too adversarial, and executive members will be reluctant to co-operate; but too cosy and the whole purpose of the exercise is undermined.

Overview – you name it!

Can involve all kinds of different activities, including:

- *Policy development and review* – one of the most appealing additions to councillors' (and officers') roles, and can take many forms: contributing to the development of policy; examining a policy's implementation and impact, and whether it is achieving its intended outcomes; undertaking 'big picture' reviews of broad policy areas.
- *External scrutiny* – investigating the work of outside bodies on local communities: health service bodies, transport providers, utility providers, police, fire and rescue services, etc.

like central government, where senior civil servants' first duty is to their minister, not to Parliament as a whole or equally to all parties. Except that local government officers are now expected to try to do both: to wear, in effect, two hats. They must serve *both* executive and non-executive members, both the policy making process and the critical scrutiny of that process, with all the potential for role conflict that entails.

The reality is that the creation of separate executives has substantially challenged the principle that officers serve the whole council. The tendency, certainly in some authorities, is for officers to form a relationship with their corresponding portfolio holder 'akin to the relationship between minister and civil servant' (Gains, 2004, p. 97). As Stewart (2003, pp. 88–9) points out, 'If structures are adopted drawing on

- *Performance management and review* – assessing the council's performance against corporate priorities and targets, and ensuring its Best Value requirements are being met.

How it's organised

Almost all the legislation and ministerial guidance on O & S is pretty imprecise and flexible, including how councils should organise themselves. Different models include:

- several O & S committees or panels with, or without, a co-ordinating forum – e.g. a Scrutiny Management Board, Scrutiny Commission;
- a single standing Scrutiny Committee, undertaking both O & S work; somewhat similar to House of Commons Select Committees;
- different structures for different roles – e.g. a separate Scrutiny Committee and various policy review panels.

What can O & S members do?

Just about anything, preferably behaving as unlike a traditional committee as possible:

- interview and cross-examine executive members and officers;
- interview officers at their workplace;
- undertake/commission desk-based reviews of documentation;
- undertake site visits;
- interview expert witnesses, service users, citizens;
- commission external research;
- co-opt representatives of partner organisations, user groups, outside bodies;
- visit other authorities and organisations;
- organise workshops with user groups;
- hold public meetings;
- organise press releases and media launches;
- act as 'mystery shoppers' and test out council services; and
- produce member-led, and even member-written, reports for council and public discussion.

parliamentary models, it is no surprise if officers come to regard themselves as no more responsible to the whole council than civil servants are to Parliament.'

The mayoral authorities have faced the biggest upheavals, especially where the mayor has not been from the majority party group – for example, Hartlepool, North Tyneside, Bedford and Mansfield. 'The personal level of political legitimacy afforded to an elected mayor has altered relationships between all actors in those authorities, and has certainly created a clear line of authority for officers' (Gains, 2004, p. 98). By contrast, in the authorities with fewer than 85,000 population that opted for 'alternative arrangements', the traditional understanding that officers serve the whole council has been challenged far less.

Chapter 7

Changing Functions

A transformed role or the weakest link?

In Chapters 5 and 6 we outlined the structures of UK local government. The councillors and councils we elect and the officers who advise them and implement their policies, constitute 'the government' of Britain's cities, towns, counties or districts, in the same way that ministers and their civil servants constitute the government of the country. A fundamental historic difference, however, has been that national government is not, on the whole, a large-scale provider of services. There are some major exceptions – most obviously the Department for Work and Pensions and the Home Office – but generally, ministers and their Whitehall-based departments produce *policy*, *not services*. They decide, through legislation, what services to provide for citizens, by whom, and how they are to be financed. Others, in the main, do the providing itself, and throughout the twentieth century by far the biggest providers of local services were local councils.

This still remains the case today, although, as we have already seen in Chapter 2, this role has been and is continuing to be – to use the title of Stoker's interpretative book – 'transformed', decisively and maybe even terminally:

> There has been a decisive attempt to switch in Britain from a system dominated by elected local government to a system of local governance in which a wider range of institutions and actors are involved in local politics and service delivery. It may be that elected authorities are the weakest link in the chain of the new string of institutions of local governance and will eventually be asked to exit, or it may be that they will discover a new role as the lead organizations taking on the challenge of steering a complex set of managerial and democratic processes at the local level. (Stoker, 2004a, p. 3)

Councils have lost some of their responsibilities completely. Those retained are, almost without exception, exposed to private sector competition. We have already noted how some ministers and commentators see *the* key future role of local government as being the *commissioning*, rather than the direct provision, of services. Already, sometimes out of choice, sometimes not, councils are working alongside a wide range of other service-providing agencies in their localities. This is Stoker's 'new string of institutions of local governance', and nowadays they easily merit a chapter in their own right. First, though – and we feel the order is important – it must be recorded that, while service provision at local level is far more complex and diffuse than it once was, it remains a major role for local authorities, albeit not necessarily through direct employment and in-house management.

Still big business

It is a cliché, but true none the less, that local government in Britain, even after all the constraining legislation of recent years, the transfers of services to other agencies, the property sales and the enforced competition, is still very big business. On one estimate, local councils undertake, on their own or in partnership, over 700 different functions (LGA, 2005a). In Great Britain they employ well over 2.5 million people in over 400 occupations, and they spent £136 billion in 2005/06 – over a quarter of government spending and 10 per cent of the gross domestic product (GDP) (Treasury, 2005). If individual local authorities were listed by expenditure, almost a hundred would rank alongside the top 500 British companies. Kent County Council's 1.3 million population makes it larger than a quarter of the states in the United Nations, and its £1.9 billion budget is higher than that of almost a third of them.

County councils, such as Kent, are among the biggest of local government 'businesses', together with the metropolitan districts, London boroughs, and the larger unitaries. As can be seen in Exhibit 7.1, these are the authorities responsible for most of the council-provided services in their areas, or at least for the most labour-intensive and biggest spending ones: particularly education and social services.

It is important to understand the county/district division in non-metropolitan England. It is not a hierarchical relationship. Although in our organisation charts in Chapters 4 and 5 the counties and former Scottish regions appear above the districts, the two tiers should properly be seen as being equal in status, each responsible for the services felt to be provided most appropriately on either a relatively larger or a more localised scale. It is, however, a severely unbalanced division, with the cost of county-provided services likely to be four or five times that of district-provided services in any district area.

Unitary authorities in principle have responsibility for all those services in the parts of England that are not split into counties and districts. In practice, as we saw in Chapter 5, there is also a complex network of joint boards and committees – captured only partially in our deliberately simplified Exhibit 7.1 – contributing to service provision: bodies composed of councillors not directly elected to them but nominated by their respective councils.

Exhibit 7.1 Who does what? Main service responsibilities of UK local authorities

	Metropolitan/London authorities				Shire/Unitary authorities		
	Metropolitan districts	Joint authorities	London boroughs	GLA	County councils	District councils	Unitary authorities
Education including schools, youth service, adult education, under-5s	*		*		*		*
Housing including renovation, redevelopment, homeless persons	*		*			*	*
Social services including residential and community care	*		*		*		*
Highways including traffic regulation, road safety, on-street parking	*		*		*		*
Passenger transport	*	*	*	*	*		*
Strategic/structure planning	*		*	*	*		*
Local planning/development control	*		*			*	*
Fire and rescue including road accidents, safety inspection and certification		*		*	*		*
Libraries	*		*		*		*
Museums, galleries	*		*		*	*	*
Leisure/recreation including arts, leisure centres, playing fields, parks	*		*			*	*
Waste collection	*		*			*	*
Waste disposal	*	*	*	*	*		*
Consumer protection	*		*	*	*		*
Environmental health including food safety, pollution control, Agenda 21	*		*	*		*	*
Council tax collection	*		*			*	*

Cautionary note: This table is presented as a guide to usual practice. We have deliberately not complicated it with a string of detailed and technical footnotes. For details of how any particular service is provided in your area, go to the website(s) of your own council(s).

Then, in addition, there is the jigsaw of other 'local public spending bodies' that nowadays are involved in the governance of a locality: none directly elected, and many with no elective element at all. These too are very big business indeed and, even though their precise numbers are not easy to determine, their total spending on local service provision in any given area is likely to be around *three times* the total spent through elected councils (see, e.g., Ayres and Pearce, 2002). These bodies have changed the way in which local government services are managed and delivered, and Chapter 8 affords them separate treatment. First, though, we look, in the remainder of this chapter, at the services themselves.

A classification of services – Britain's particularity

We have noted how in Britain local government rests on a constitutionally weaker base than it does in many European countries; also that its scope and freedom of action have been reduced significantly in recent years as a result of national government policy. Just as important, however, is that Britain's local authorities are still unusually large, diverse organisations with large budgets and workforces, and responsibility for literally hundreds of different services.

As we shall show in more detail in Chapter 12 (Exhibit 12.3), Britain's local authorities are in fact much larger than those in virtually any other European country – larger in terms of their populations, but not necessarily so in the range of services they provide. It is better to see them simply as being different. British local authorities, for example, are unusual in *not* having direct responsibility for hospitals and preventive health services, which are, of course, provided through the entirely separate institutions of our National Health Service (NHS). In this respect, they keep company only with some of the smaller EU countries – Ireland, Greece and Portugal (John, 2001, p. 36). And most social assistance benefits are administered in Britain through the Department for Work and Pensions, rather than through local councils, as is the common European practice.

But, if our health and social services have been less institutionally integrated than in much of continental Europe, our education system has perhaps been more so. Education has been by far the biggest spender in British local government, because an education-administering local authority – known traditionally as a Local Education Authority (LEA) – has in fact provided almost all education services: from building schools and employing teachers to providing books and pencils. In much of southern and central Europe local authorities provide and maintain the school premises, but the national government employs the teachers. Frequently too, responsibility for primary and secondary, or at least higher secondary, schools is split between different tiers of local authorities. In the USA and Canada, many schools are run by elected special authorities or boards.

Another sphere in which Britain is now the exception is in the provision of 'public utilities'. In almost all other European countries, municipalities retain responsibility for providing one or more of the utilities – water, electricity and gas supply – all local government services in Britain until their nationalisation in the 1940s and privatisation in the 1980s. British policing, on the other hand, historically has been and remains, at least at the time of writing, more localised than in many countries. In Scandinavia, the Netherlands, Australia and New Zealand it is not a local function, whereas, even in the post-1995 independent police authorities, there is still majority local councillor representation.

These cross-national differences are worth keeping in mind as we deal briefly with the major local government services. We shall follow, partly for the sake of convenience, the fourfold classification summarised in Exhibit 7.2. This means starting with 'need services', which account in Britain for well over half of total net local government spending, reflecting the role of councils as deliverers of major parts of our welfare state. In other countries, 'amenity services', for example, might well feature more prominently.

Exhibit 7.2 A categorisation of local services

1. **Need services** – e.g. education, personal social services, housing benefit. Services provided for all, regardless of means, and which therefore contribute to the redistribution of resources within the community.

2. **Protective services** – e.g. policing and community safety, fire and rescue, emergency planning.
   Services provided for the security of people, to national guidelines. Access to them cannot be restricted, and use by one person does not affect availability to others.

3. **Amenity services** – e.g. highways, street cleansing, planning, parks and open spaces, environmental health, refuse disposal, consumer protection, economic development.
   Services provided largely to locally determined standards to meet the needs of each local community.

4. **Facility services** – e.g. housing, libraries, museums and art galleries, recreational centres, refuse collection, cemeteries and crematoria.
   Services for people to draw on if they wish, sometimes in competition with private sector provision.

Needs services – for all of us, regardless of means

Education – the declining role of the LEA

Education, of course, covers much more than compulsory schooling: early years development and nursery provision, youth and community education, adult and further education. But it was its responsibility for schools that gave an education department its *raison d'être* within a local authority, and it is this responsibility that over the years has been challenged and transformed.

The basis of our modern school system was the Education Act 1944, which set up precisely the functional split that we described in the opening paragraph of this chapter. Central government legislated and set the national policy framework – free compulsory schooling from the ages of 5 to 15 (later 16), every LEA to appoint a chief education officer, 'aided' or 'controlled' status for voluntary/church schools, free school milk. But the actual provision, staffing and running of schools were in the hands of local authorities. These LEAs decided for themselves how they organised their schools: selective or non-selective, primary/secondary or first/middle/junior high, grammar schools or sixth-form colleges. They had a similar discretion here as over most of the rest of their service provision – from adult education to play schemes and educational psychologists.

Since the 1980s, however, that central–local balance has changed so fundamentally that a recent commentator rhetorically entitled her analysis of the subject: 'Education: No Longer a Role for Local Government?' (Donnelly, 2004). The period of most dramatic change coincides with our 'funnel of discretion' (pp. 20–1), and the diminution of the A in the country's LEAs can be followed through the selection of Education Acts

---

Exhibit 7.3 Education – some key facts

- Education accounts for roughly 37 per cent of local council net current (day-to-day) spending – £35 billion in England in 2005–06.
- There were 25,400 schools in England in 2005, with 8.3 million pupils. 51 per cent of pupils attended the 70 per cent of primary schools, 40 per cent attended the 13 per cent of secondary schools, and 7 per cent attended the 9 per cent of independent schools.
- There were 431,000 full-time equivalent teachers in LEA schools in 2005 – 50 per cent secondary, 45 per cent nursery/primary, and 5 per cent in special schools and pupil referral units – plus 269,000 support staff (teaching assistants, administrative and technical staff).

Sources: Data from ODPM (2005a), LGA (2005a), DfES Education Statistics (2005)

included in the lower section of Figure 2.1. There was in fact an average of at least one Education Act each year during the 1980s and 1990s. Some removed LEAs' responsibilities altogether: for polytechnics, colleges and institutes of higher education, sixth-form and further education colleges, most of which became self-governing corporations. Other Acts reduced the authorities' role in schools management.

The keynote legislation was the Education Reform Act 1988. It brought in the national curriculum and 'key stage' or 'sats' tests, with results published in school performance league tables. It introduced local management of schools (LMS), requiring LEAs to pass on at least 85 per cent of their education budget to school governing bodies, who thus became responsible for overseeing the running of their own school and its financial operation. Even more controversially, it enabled schools, through parental ballots, to 'opt out' of the control of their LEA and be funded instead, as 'grant-maintained' (GM) schools, directly by central government, which then recharged the cost to the LEA.

These parental ballots failed to produce the full-scale educational revolution for which Conservative ministers had hoped, and by the time the incoming Labour Government abolished GM status in 1998, fewer than 5 per cent of state schools had in fact opted out. But, although LEAs continued to maintain the other 95 per cent, their involvement in day-to-day school management, already significantly reduced through LMS, was eroded further still under Labour. Ministers strengthened the regime of national regulation and inspection established under OFSTED (the Office for Standards in Education), increased the proportion of schools' funding that was 'ring-fenced' and thus beyond the discretion of the local authority, and in other ways too chose to bypass LEAs and deal directly with schools themselves.

Without the operational part of their role, LEAs are left with just strategy and support. Strategically, they are responsible for access – ensuring, through their management of admissions, appeals, parental advice, home to school transport, assessment of educational needs and free school meals eligibility, that there is a match between pupil requirements and available places. In terms of support, they offer educational welfare, catering, security, grounds maintenance, ICT support and cleaning services, but schools can, and are encouraged to, look for alternative cost-effective providers.

There is known to have been a notorious 'clause zero' in a draft Education Bill during the 1990s to sweep LEAs away altogether (Smith, 1999). In one sense, that looked in 2005 as if it was likely to happen. A highly controversial White Paper, *Higher Standards, Better Schools for All*, pronounced that, in recognition of the future institutional linkage between education and children's services more generally, the term 'local education authority' would be 'removed from the statute book' and replaced simply

Exhibit 7.4 New Labour's new schools – degrees of separation

The Labour Government's aim – to 'free' all schools from LEA control.

(City) Academies – divorced, at taxpayers' expense
Introduced in 2000 as a particular enthusiasm of Tony Blair. Publicly funded independent schools, intended to raise standards by replacing 'failing' schools in primarily inner city areas. A private sponsor – business interest, faith group, voluntary organisation, university – contributes up to £2 million, or 10 per cent, to the building or rebuilding of a school, with the remainder (up to £30 million) coming from the Government/taxpayer. The sponsor gains control of the governing body, including curriculum, staffing, assets and school 'ethos', plus complete freedom from the LEA.
Numbers: 2005 – 27; 2010 – 200(?).

Specialist schools – they've made the break
Originated as Thatcher-inspired city technology colleges, funded partly by central government and partly by private sponsors. The latter failed to enthuse, and only 14 CTCs survive.
Extended by Labour to ten possible specialisms, including arts, business, engineering, humanities, languages, maths, music, and sports. In addition to demonstrating a capability to meet learning targets, a school must raise £50,000 in private sponsorship, to which the Government/taxpayer adds £100,000 for a capital project in the area of specialism plus a recurrent fee of £129 per pupil p.a. Sponsorship earns operational independence from LEA – employment of staff, ownership of assets, and admission of up to 10 per cent of pupils not on 'ability' (which would be 'selection'), but on 'aptitude'.
Numbers: 2005 – 2,380 (75 per cent of all secondary schools); 2008 – 100 per cent(?).

Foundation schools – separate beds
Mainly schools that lost their grant-maintained status in 1998. Now receive funding from LEA, rather than direct from central government, but the governing body retains control over admissions, staff employment, land and buildings. Few new foundation schools created under Labour, but application process may become easier.

Community schools – happily married, but for how long?
What, before they were renamed in 1998, were county schools – wholly owned and maintained by the LEA, who, in traditional fashion, employ the school's staff, own the land and buildings, and act as admissions authority. Must be made to realise fidelity isn't everything.

by 'local authority'. However, as if in answer to the actual form in which Donnelly's question was posed (see p. 123), the White Paper identified *new* roles for local authorities (DfES, 2005, ch. 9). They would be 'commissioners of services and champions of users': promoting choice and diversity, ensuring access, monitoring and driving up standards, and mediating if necessary between schools and their parent and pupil 'consumers'. However, this commissioning role, the White Paper emphasised, is 'very different from acting as a direct provider of school places'. Had the White Paper been legislated without amendment, those days would effectively have been over – a point driven home by reference to 'Trust Schools': a yet further type of self-governing proto-academy to add to the list in Exhibit 7.4. In fact, the resulting Education and Inspections Act 2006, passed by Parliament only with the help of Conservative support, was extensively amended – with local authorities gaining the rights to bid for new community schools and take over under-performing Trust Schools, instead of being completely excluded from both.

Personal social services

The emphasis here is on *services*, because, as previously noted, most benefit and allowance payments are made not by local government, but through Jobcentre Plus and other local offices of the Department for Work and Pensions. Local authorities, frequently working nowadays through voluntary and private organisations, provide to a range of client groups services that include residential care, day care, help (such as meals, laundry, home modifications, practical aids) to enable people to remain in their own homes, counselling, fostering and adoption, and child protection.

The scale of activity is massive, and frequently very sensitive. Like teachers, social workers live with the continuous pressure both of new

---

Exhibit 7.5 Social services – some key facts

- Social services account for roughly 18 per cent of council net current spending – £17 billion in England in 2005–06. This spending figure had doubled in real terms over the previous 10 years.
- 15 per cent of this spending went on care assessment and management, with the remainder split almost equally between day and domiciliary provision (relatively increasing in recent years) and residential care (relatively decreasing).
- Principal client groups are older people (44 per cent of spending), children's and family services (24 per cent), learning disabled adults (15 per cent), and physically and mentally disabled adults (13 per cent).

Sources: Data from ODPM (2005a), LGA (2005a), Department of Health (2005a).

legislative demands and public expectations. Both groups too have become used to the exceptional case that propels one or two unfortunate individuals, a single institution or department, and indirectly the whole profession, into the glare of national media headlines. For social workers, this can be a tragic case involving the failure of child protection and the ensuing investigations into either inadequate or misguidedly zealous professional behaviour. Such cases are obviously atypical, which is why they attract the attention they do. But the very depth of their coverage, especially if they result in an official inquiry report, can reveal much about the day-to-day operations of the responsible council departments.

It was precisely one of the most shocking and distressing of these inquiry reports – by Lord Laming into the terrible death of 8 year old Victoria Climbié (Laming, 2003) – that led directly to the Children Act 2004, which, by imposing a number of new responsibilities on local authorities, sought to 'join up' or reintegrate a range of relevant children's services, some of which had in fact been at one time under the direct control of those selfsame councils. Among many other provisions, the Act required local social services authorities to appoint both a director of children's services and a lead member, to be responsible for, at a minimum, education and children's social services functions, plus any others – for example, housing, leisure – that the authority considered relevant. They also had to promote co-operation in order to improve children's well-being – by establishing Local Safeguarding Children Boards (LSCBs), comprising all agencies with responsibilities towards children, including strategic health authorities and primary care trusts, the police, probation service, youth offending teams, and governors of prisons or secure training centres.

In parallel, however, with these Labour Government initiatives to create 'seamless services' at the local level, there has been, as in education and health, 'a discernible policy drive in the opposite direction – that is, towards the pluralization of services' (Clarke and Harrison, 2004, p. 123). This 'mixed economy of care' started, Clarke and Harrison suggest, in the early 1990s, when the Conservative Government required social services authorities to spend a proportion of their expenditure on purchasing places in private residential and nursing homes, with the effect that:

> many voluntary sector organizations have effectively become providers of publicly-funded community care ... including 'Sure Start' projects in areas with high levels of children 'in need', and the 'Connexions' services for teenagers. (pp. 123–4)

The principle has been extended under Labour, with cash benefits offered to certain social care clients in lieu of publicly provided services. There is now the possibility, therefore, for older and disabled clients, and people with learning difficulties, to purchase services for themselves.

The mechanisms are different, but there are obviously similarities between the 'mixed economies' developing in the two big local authority service areas of education and social care. The terminology, though, isn't quite identical. Instead of 'commissioning', social workers tend to see (or fear) their future role becoming increasingly one of 'brokering': working across the fields of health and social care, carrying out assessments of clients' needs, and then, on the basis of the budget available, brokering a care package through a process of negotiation with a wide range of public, private and voluntary sector providers. What they see disappearing, like education officers' involvement in the day-to-day running of schools, is the 'face to face intervention' that often motivated them in the first place.

Protective services – for our security

Community safety and crime reduction

Until the 1990s, policing in the UK was very much a local authority service. Apart from London – where the Metropolitan Police reported directly to the Home Secretary before in 2000 becoming the responsibility of the new Greater London Authority (GLA) – chief constables were accountable to the police committees of county councils: in a similar way to other council committees, apart from their memberships, which comprised two-thirds councillors and one-third local magistrates.

The Police and Magistrates Courts Act 1994 changed the composition and role of police authorities by establishing them as independent authorities, with enhanced powers over their own service provision, and very much more independent of their respective councils. Their membership now comprises indirectly elected councillors, magistrates, and co-opted Home Office nominees – with a bare councillor majority – and the local government interest has become generally the weakest link in the 'tripartite structure' of central government, local government and chief constable. Police authorities still depend on local government for the collection of their revenue, and we shall see in Chapter 10 how they levy a 'precept', which councils must include in the council tax bills they send out to their residents. When determining their local policing objectives, though, it is consistency with the Home Secretary's national objectives that they will usually observe first, rather than conformity with policies of their local councils.

The likelihood is that, in the near future, this county-based structure will become much larger-scale, if not actually regionalized. From the local citizen's viewpoint, though, there are still plenty of signs of policing and community safety decisions being taken locally with apparently considerable local discretion. First, there are ASBOs (Anti-Social Behaviour Orders) introduced in the same Crime and Disorder Act 1998 that created CDRPs (see Exhibit 7.6). Over 5,500 were issued by the police between

---

Exhibit 7.6 Policing and community safety – some key facts

- Policing accounts for roughly 11 per cent of council net current spending – £10 billion in England and Wales in 2005–06.
- There were in 2005 43 police forces in England and Wales, 8 in Scotland, plus the Northern Ireland Policing Board. The 43 were based on counties, with smaller counties being part of joint forces; each force, therefore, was represented on several of the 376 Crime and Disorder Reduction Partnerships (CDRPs) that since 1998 have co-ordinated crime reduction strategy at local level.
- The 43 forces in 2005 employed 223,000 fte (full-time equivalent) staff: 64 per cent (143,000) police officers, 32 per cent civilian support staff, 3 per cent community support officers, and 1 per cent traffic wardens.
- 21 per cent of police officers were women, but only 10 per cent among Chief Inspectors and more senior ranks; 3.5 per cent of officers were from ethnic minorities.

Source: Data from Home Office (2005a).

1999 and 2005, the supposed intention being not so much to punish offenders but to stop various types of harassing or intimidating behaviour: verbal and racial abuse, vandalism, criminal damage, substance misuse, public drunkenness and the like. The inter-force variation, however, is substantial – with Greater Manchester accounting for 50 per cent more ASBOs than the whole of Greater London, and five times the number issued to what must be presumed to be the immensely more law-respecting citizens of Merseyside (Home Office, 2005b).

Second, there are the 500 or more warden schemes across the country, set up since 2000 under the ODPM's Neighbourhood and Street Warden Programme. Intended to provide a visible, trained and uniformed, semi-official presence on streets and estates, wardens work with the police and others in the locality to tackle anti-social behaviour. The wardens, though, are employed by local authorities; they are known variously as street, street crime, or neighbourhood wardens; they have varying powers, and distinctly varying relations with their respective police forces, who, initially at least, were seriously sceptical of these people, who seemed all too easy to confuse with their own community support officers.

A third area of local discretion will no doubt open up with the implementation of the Clean Neighbourhoods and Environment Act 2005, which gave councils significant new powers and penalties to deploy against those who litter, fly-tip, abandon vehicles, dogs or chewing gum, and in various other ways deface the local environment – powers that many overseas visitors would be amazed were not *already* available to these democratically elected and locally accountable bodies.

Fire, rescue and emergency planning

It was not until the late 1930s that all local authorities outside London were required to maintain fire services, and then these local brigades were amalgamated almost immediately into a National Fire Service during the Second World War. The Fire Services Act 1947 returned them to local control, and the present-day structure is not dissimilar to that of the police: 50 county-based or combined authorities in England and Wales (including the London Fire and Emergency Planning Authority), eight in Scotland, plus the single Northern Ireland Fire Brigade. The most notable difference is that fire authorities continue to consist entirely of councillors.

In complete contrast to the education world with its almost annual legislation, it took nearly fifty years for the 1947 Act to be updated in the Fire and Rescue Services Act 2004. The title extension reflects the way in which the service's work has evolved over the years – from fire-fighting to prevention and rescue. The Act introduced an explicit duty to promote fire safety and help create safer communities, and generally set a legislative framework in which fire authorities can be more proactive, work more closely with other bodies, and focus more on those responsibilities that were hardly envisaged in 1947: rescue from road traffic accidents, train and aircraft crashes, and dealing with chemical spillages, environmental and terrorist emergencies.

In addition to the London Authority's incorporation of 'Emergency Planning', six other authorities – those in the areas of the metropolitan county councils that were abolished in 1986 – are officially entitled Fire and Civil Defence Authorities, reminding us of another local government function that has changed dramatically in recent years. The Civil Defence Act 1948 gave certain local authorities powers – though very little financial assistance – to organise and protect their civilian populations from an emergency that was expected to take the form of either industrial and civil unrest or a nuclear attack from a hostile foreign nation. This civil defence responsibility became a regular butt of *Dad's Army* jokes and *Yes, Minister* storylines – unfairly perhaps, but understandably. It is difficult to plan in anything but fairly general terms for an emergency whose form, by definition, isn't known and when, in any case, the relevant legislation gives you powers, but without any actual *duty* to do anything.

The disaster of 9/11 and subsequent events, however, have obviously promoted emergency planning and what is now termed 'building resilience' from languishing in a backwater of local government to becoming a primary policy concern. Nationally, responsibility has moved from the Home Office to the Civil Contingencies Secretariat in the Cabinet Office, and it was this body that produced the Civil Contingencies Act 2004 – or 'Blair's Enabling Act', as it became known during its highly contentious passage through Parliament. As well as giving the Government very wide powers to declare a 'state of emergency' – the most controversial bit – the Act imposed several new emergency planning duties on 'Category 1 contingency response bodies' such as major local authorities. These duties include contingency planning, risk assessment and mitigation, warning and informing the public, promoting business continuity management, and strengthening co-operation between response bodies – specifically through a new framework for partnership working: local resilience forums, based on police force areas. With far more centralised direction of planning and response than previously, it is perhaps in theory a more subsidiary role than formerly, but one that is defined considerably more explicitly.

Amenity services – for our community needs

Highways, transportation and traffic management

This is perhaps the most shared of all public services, covering everything from motorways to bridleways, and involving all levels of government from the Department for Transport (DfT) to parish councils. The Secretary of State is responsible for trunk road and motorways, with decisions often being taken in the relevant regional office and most maintenance contracted out by the Highways Agency, an executive agency acting on the minister's behalf. The counties, unitaries and metropolitan districts, and in London the boroughs and the GLA, have responsibility for other primary and secondary roads. 'Responsibility' here includes the design of routes, taking into account cost, environmental impact, residential and industrial needs and safety; road building, improvement and maintenance; highway management, including parking restrictions, speed limits, street lighting, traffic signs, street cleaning and litter collection; winter maintenance and road safety. In practice, however, 'agency agreements' are common, and several of the above functions are likely in two-tier areas to be carried out by district councils. Local authorities also work with bus and rail companies to improve their local public transport networks, for that 14 per cent minority of the population who travel to work in this mode.

The Government's priority in its second term was to progress towards the elusive integrated and sustainable transport policy promised in its 1997 manifesto (Labour Party, 1997, p. 29), and particularly to increase the use of public transport. To this end, as in other policy areas, councils produce plans – in this instance, comprehensive 5-year Local Transport Plans (LTPs) that are submitted to the DfT, whose ministers and civil servants assess proposed schemes against various value-for-money criteria before deciding whether or not to approve them for funding. Probably the two most discussed issues in the first (2001) set of LTPs were how to reduce traffic congestion and improve passenger, and particularly bus, transport, and the most interesting and important transport initiatives of the early 2000s have surely been the efforts by pioneering local authorities to implement some of the more radical of these measures.

First, in 2002, came Durham City Council's rising bollards, restricting vehicle access to the city's historic centre through the country's first road-user charge. Between them, the bollards and the charge increased pedestrian usage and bus patronage, and greatly reduced traffic. The following February, Ken Livingstone introduced his electronic army of ANPR (Automatic Number Plate Recognition) cameras and the Central London congestion charge – with the same positive impact on bus usage and reduced congestion, plus enhanced journey reliability and a measurably more efficient distribution of goods and services. A similar scheme to Durham's was subsequently taken up by Cambridge, while in a 2005 referendum, Edinburgh residents rejected a camera-based experiment.

The wider importance of these schemes lies in their offering us our first experience of road pricing – attempting to control congestion not by the traditional, ineffectual and discriminatory means of taxing vehicle ownership (fuel duty, vehicle excise tax), but by pricing road use, enabling the driver to make a journey decision on the basis of knowing its true cost. If, as many experts think, road pricing in various forms is the long-term solution to traffic management, local authorities' role would seem to be almost indispensable – to pilot locally appropriate schemes, but also as the only bodies with the community leadership 'clout' to be able to ensure a balance between the pricing 'stick' and the imperative 'carrot' of having, as in both Durham and London, a visibly improved public transport system in place first (LGA, 2005b).

Planning and development

This is another responsibility shared between the different tiers of sub-central government – though not the same tiers today as in the recent past. There are in fact two principal planning functions: development control and forward or strategic planning. *Development control* is exercised by unitary, metropolitan and district councils, who respond, principally on the basis of local development plans, to applications for planning consent to change the use of existing land or buildings, or to carry out physical development, such as the construction, adaptation or demolition of buildings. Planning authorities are expected to respond to applications within two months, uncontentious cases normally being delegated to officers, with more controversial and complex developments being determined by the council's planning committee – one of the 'regulatory' committees that have continued to exist even after the adoption by councils of executive arrangements. Various responses are available to the council – from unconditional consent, through conditional or outline consent, to refusal – and a disappointed applicant has the right of appeal to a planning inspector appointed by the Secretary of State, and ultimately to the High Court.

Strategic planning is the process by which these development plans, with which planning applications are expected to conform, are determined – how, in other words, planning authorities decide how they would like their area as a whole to develop over, say, the following fifteen years. Until recently, *structure plans* were drawn up, after extensive consultations, by county councils, and local plans by district councils, while in unitary authorities the two were combined in a unitary plan. These plans would allocate areas of land for future housing, industrial, commercial and leisure developments, taking into account national and local policies for protecting the environment. Housing allocations tend to be especially contentious, with developers wanting more generous provision of green-field sites, and councils, backed by local residential and environmental pressure groups, usually preferring more 'brown-field' redevelopment. Governments have their own, not always consistent, views on these matters, and the Secretary of State had the power to 'call-in' a structure plan for modification or rejection.

The Planning and Compulsory Purchase Act 2004 changed this system, principally by 'regionalising' county councils' traditional statutory planning powers – perhaps in the anticipation, since unrealised, that elected regional assemblies would take over from the counties as the upper tier of English sub-central government. As it is, the still unelected assemblies, with their memberships of predominantly nominated councillors from the region's authorities, are the new regional planning bodies, with responsibility for preparing *regional spatial strategies* (except in London, where it is the Mayor's Spatial Development Strategy). These strategy documents then become the framework within which unitary and local councils produce their local plans, known now as 'local development frameworks'. The 2004 Act contained other commendable measures, aimed at speeding up the planning process and introducing sustainable development as an explicit objective of the planning system, but, in respect of the actual planning process, it has apparently brought another move away from local democratic accountability.

Environmental and public health

This is one of the oldest local government services, in that today's borough and district councils grew out of the local boards of health and sanitary authorities set up under the Public Health Acts of the 1870s. Victorian local government pioneered the provision of clean water, decent public housing, food inspection, and the treatment of infectious diseases; yet, in creating a National Health Service in the 1940s, the Labour Government opted for what in effect was a free-standing 'national sickness service', controlled by and answerable to ministers – rather than a comprehensive *health care* service, integrated with linked functions such as social care, housing, education and the environment, both responsive and accountable to elected local councils. Local government thus lost most of its health functions in 1948 and 1974, leaving it with 'only' environmental health, although this responsibility still gives councils – as employers, service providers, regulators, and community leaders – far greater health promotion and disease prevention potential than any other institution, including the NHS itself.

So extensive are councils' environmental health and consumer protection responsibilities that in the second edition of this book we produced an A–Z of these services alone – from abandoned vehicles via dog fouling and tree preservation to zoo licensing (Wilson and Game, 1998, p. 26 plus Exhibit on linked website). The full list involves all those functions of inspection, regulation, registration, licensing and certification that tend to be relatively unnoticed until there is a food contamination crisis, a dangerous dogs scare, a massage parlour scandal, or a threatened avian flu pandemic.

Also, notwithstanding the funding prioritisation of the NHS under the Labour Government, there has been a growing acknowledgement that health should be seen as a public, as well as a private, good. This in turn has contributed to there being at the time of writing far closer institutional links and joint working arrangements between local authorities and health bodies than at any time in the history of the NHS. Some of these developments – pooled budgets and joint investment plans, the health scrutiny role given to councils under the Health and Social Care Act 2001 – pre-dated the Government's development of its health inequalities and improvement agenda. But the priorities of this agenda as set out in the 2004 public health White Paper, *Choosing Health: Making Healthy Choices Easier* – reducing smoking, increasing exercise, reducing obesity and improving diet, encouraging sensible drinking, and improving sexual and mental health – all involve significant roles for local authorities, both on their own, as service providers and regulators, and in partnership with primary care trusts and other organisations.

Economic development and regeneration

Look at some councils' websites and you could almost get the impression that – with their business parks and industrial estates, commercial property files, relocation grants, advisory and investment services – economic development and business promotion are their principal activities. Their importance would seem to be confirmed by councils' recently acquired well-being power – to promote the *economic*, social and environmental well-being of their area. In fact, statutory recognition of councils' key role in economic development dates back only to the Local Government and Housing Act 1989, and in another sense too it is a modern role, involving as it does almost necessarily working closely in partnership with both the private sector and other bodies – for example, Regional Development Agencies, Learning and Skills Councils, Chambers of Commerce and Trade. It remains, however, essentially a permissive or discretionary responsibility, rather than mandatory, and there are vastly different patterns and intensities of activity across Britain.

Facility services – for all of us, if we wish

Housing – the last chapter?

If we were dealing with services not by function but in order of their historic importance to local government, housing would have featured pages ago. In terms of its future importance, however, towards the end of the list may well be the most appropriate place, for some housing experts predict that the council home – one of the integral features of Britain's post-war welfare state – will have virtually disappeared by about 2015. Two major government policies will have been responsible for this development: the Conservatives' 'Right to Buy' legislation in the 1980s,

---

Exhibit 7.7 Housing – some key facts

- Housing accounts for roughly 14 per cent of council net current expenditure – £15 billion in England in 2005–06. This figure excludes Housing Revenue Accounts – self-contained accounts that councils are required to keep that cover all income (mainly rents) and expenditure (management and maintenance costs) relating to their own housing stock.
- Of the UK's 2004 housing stock of 26 million dwellings, 70.5 per cent were owner-occupied, 11.5 per cent rented from local authorities (compared to 29 per cent in 1981, when 'Right to Buy' was first introduced), 8 per cent were rented from registered social landlords (mainly housing associations), and 10 per cent rented privately.
- Of 190,000 new dwellings completed in the UK in 2003–04, 90 per cent were built privately, 10 per cent by registered social landlords, and just 207 by local authorities. By comparison, there were 252,000 completions in 1979, and a record 426,000 in 1968, of which over 40 per cent were built by local authorities.

Sources: Data from ODPM (2005a), ODPM Housing Statistics (2005d).

Exhibit 7.8 LSVTs and ALMOs – the end of council housing?

LSVTs – what are they?

Large-scale voluntary transfers: they allow councils to transfer ownership and control of their homes to 'registered social landlords' (RSLs) – mainly housing associations – provided their tenants vote in favour.

Why are even Labour councils willing to transfer their housing stocks?

To raise the capital needed for a national repairs and renovation backlog of over £20 billion. Successive governments have prohibited councils from borrowing money to undertake necessary repairs and maintenance, and RSLs are one of the few alternatives. Instead of relaxing borrowing restrictions, the 1997 Labour Government actively encouraged wholesale transfers by writing off the accumulated housing debts of poor boroughs.

So everybody does it?

Yes and no. Initially, it was mainly Conservative councils, but by 2001 more than 100 councils of all political colours had sold off nearly 600,000 homes under stock transfers. Most were to housing associations set up by the councils themselves – emphasising the 'voluntary' nature of the process – often with councillors making up a third of the new management board.

   Then the biggest council landlords of all became involved – Glasgow (94,000 homes and a £1.2 billion repairs backlog), Birmingham (88,000 and £1 billion), Bradford, Liverpool, Sheffield – and tenant opposition began to increase. Transfer ballots, it was argued, presented a choice weighted against staying with the council, while RSLs are in effect unaccountable private companies, likely to raise rents and reduce security of tenure. Despite the pressure to vote for transfer, several big ballots were lost – in Birmingham, Dudley, Southwark.

and the large-scale housing transfers initiated by the Conservatives but accelerated by New Labour.

   The 1957 Housing Act placed a duty on local authorities to consider local housing conditions and provide any further housing required – either building it themselves or buying, converting and improving existing properties. Two decades later, the nation's council housing stock comprised nearly 7 million dwellings. Then in 1980 the incoming Thatcher Government's Housing Act gave council tenants the right to buy their homes at discounts of up to 70 per cent, depending on their length of tenancy. Labour councils sought to resist the policy, concerned at the reduced housing stock that would be left available for people unable to rent privately, but they could be forced to comply. If the Secretary of State

Presumably the Government's had to think again?

Yes. Local authorities now have three optional means of meeting the Government's target of getting all social housing up to its Decent Homes Standard by 2010 – all three, though, involving some form of switch away from council housing:

- Transfer to **housing associations**;
- Use of the controversial **Private Finance Initiative (PFI)** – the council retains ownership, but private consortia of contractors raise the money to undertake required improvements and are repaid, typically over 30 years, with additional money from the Government; or
- **ALMOs (arm's length management organisations)** – the council retains ownership, but contracts a separate not-for-profit company to improve and manage its housing stock on its behalf, through a management board comprising council representatives and tenants.

Despite pressure from councils, unions and Labour Party members, the Government insists there is no fourth option. 'Tenants' choice' does not include the choice of continuing to have their homes managed by the council.

So what's happening?

Standoff. RSLs are unpopular, and PFI even more so: expensive, complicated, risky, and exploits public housing for private profit. ALMOs are the least unpopular, but the Government will only give extra resources to ALMOs assessed as good or excellent by the Audit Commission. Transfer rate has dropped to well below Government's target of 200,000 homes p.a. RSL homes will soon outnumber those under council control, but the latter may not disappear quite as quickly or completely as once seemed possible.

believed a council was restricting tenants' statutory right to buy their homes, a housing commissioner could be sent in – as happened in Clay Cross, Derbyshire – to take over the sales process and charge the cost to the council.

With nearly 2 million one-time council properties in private hands by 1997, the new Labour Government declined to abolish an obviously popular policy. Despite its clearly exacerbating the incipient housing crisis, and evidence of abuse by property developers who paid tenants to buy their homes in order to let them out at market rents, ministers would go no further than to reduce the maximum discounts available. A further 500,000 sales were therefore completed by 2004, and the remaining stock fell below 3 million dwellings for the first time since the 1950s (see Exhibit 7.7).

Even a declining housing stock, though, has to be maintained, and, as governments increasingly restricted both the revenue spending and capital borrowing of local authorities, large backlogs of repairs began to build up. Rather than allowing councils to borrow the funding required to deal with these backlogs themselves, governments preferred the transfer approach (see Exhibit 7.8). The Housing Act 1988 introduced 'tenants' choice', allowing new landlords – notably housing associations who were permitted, unlike councils, to raise private finance – to take over council housing following a ballot of tenants: a ballot whose rules were weighted heavily against the local authority. On a larger scale, the Secretary of State had powers to designate an area as a Housing Action Trust (HAT) – for example, Castle Vale in Birmingham; Stonebridge in Brent – provided again that a majority of tenants voted to opt-out of local authority ownership and management. Six of these HATs were set up: quangos that took over the local authority's housing and its accompanying repair and management functions.

Some 250,000 council homes were transferred to housing associations in the decade to 1997, and they quickly became the main providers of new housing for rent. New Labour ministers, faced with the choice of ending councils' borrowing restrictions or ending completely their traditional housing management role, opted firmly for the latter. As we saw in relation to schools, there is still in principle a significant strategic role – reviewing current housing conditions and identifying future needs in relation to provision, repairs, slum clearance, grants for improvements and repairs, consulting with housing consumers and other agencies – but, compared to education, the legislative basis of such a role remains at present rather underdeveloped.

Libraries – a quiet revolution?

Public libraries have been provided by local councils for over 150 years – although not until 1919 were they permitted to spend significant amounts of money to fill them with books. In recent years, ironically, there has been no statutory limit on spending, but at a time when the limits on council budgets for a largely discretionary service can seldom have been tighter. Libraries have been closed, opening hours cut, book funds slashed, and, not surprisingly, usage of libraries and borrowing from them has correspondingly declined.

Against this background, however, parts of the library system at least have been undergoing a 'quiet revolution' (MLAC, 2004), a result in large part of outside funding. The catalyst was the £120 million from the National Lottery's New Opportunities Fund (NOF) that in 2000 launched 'The People's Network', which has connected almost every public library to the Internet, by broadband and increasingly by wi-fi hotspots. That was

---

Exhibit 7.9 Libraries – some key facts

- There are roughly 3,700 public libraries in England: 3,200 'static' – of which just over half are 'full-time', opening more than 30 hours per week – and 500 mobile. They contained in 2005 over 325 million items, of which a quarter were books.
- Among UK residents, 60 per cent have a public library ticket and in 2003–04 they made more than 300 million library visits – more than to either the cinema or to football matches.
- In 2005, public libraries in England were providing 70 million hours of computer use through 'The People's Network', almost all of it free.

Source: Data from Department for Culture, Media and Sport website www.culture.gov.uk.

---

followed by a further £140 million from NOF's successor, the Big Lottery Fund, for a community learning project aimed at fostering community libraries and family learning. Reinforced by some outstandingly designed new buildings – in Brighton, Bournemouth, Norwich and Peckham, for example – these initiatives have led the way to a broadening of the libraries' user base, better physical access, accessibility and layout, and (gradually) a culture that endeavours to appeal to, rather than overawe and 'hush', children and young people.

Labelled 'street corner universities' by Labour's first Culture Secretary, Chris Smith, rejuvenated libraries have a contribution to make to several key government objectives: lifelong learning, delivering public services online, neighbourhood renewal, combating social exclusion, and increasing online access to the treasures of national and international museums. Book-lending will remain important, but alongside their expanding roles as information, reference and resource centres, as specialist service providers for schools, the blind and partially sighted, hospitals, ethnic minorities, and as community cultural and arts centres. They will also, it is worth noting, continue to receive and display details of council services, copies of agendas and reports, information on council meeting times, and contact numbers and addresses for councillors.

Leisure, arts and recreation

Perhaps appropriately, these last services are the most discretionary of those we have addressed. All the others have discretionary aspects to them – different councils according them differing priorities, providing services in differing ways, with differing standards of efficiency. But most of the legislation concerning leisure and recreation is *empowering* rather than mandatory. Councils *may* provide museums and art galleries; they *may* contribute to provision by other authorities; they *may* establish orchestras, concert halls, promote tourism, and provide all manner of sports and leisure facilities (see Gray, 2002). Increasingly, virtually all new initiatives in culture, recreation and the arts are carried out in partnerships with other agencies, for example, the Arts Council, the RDA or the Sports Council. As a citizen this discretion can prove frustrating if you happen to live in an authority with relatively modest standards of provision, or one that imposes high charges for the use of its facilities. As a student of local government, however, you can learn a great deal about a council's political, social and cultural values from the scale and patterns of its leisure expenditure.

Conclusion – more sharing of the local turf

This inevitably somewhat breathless overview of local authority services rounds off aptly, we feel, a chapter that began with our emphasising councils' continuing role as large-scale service providers, despite increasing collaboration with partners. Almost all the services we have mentioned have undergone significant transformation during the past few years and, in an increasing number of cases, the council's former largely exclusive role is being shared with a range of other providers. But while, as Davis puts it, the balance and much of the detail have changed and will certainly change further, the 'traditional' picture is still recognisable:

> it has never been the case that local authorities have exercised all governmental powers in any particular locality. Others have always been involved but, in the past, local authorities confidently saw themselves as the rightful and undisputed leaders of their communities. Now their position is under challenge as they find themselves sharing the local 'turf' with a whole range of bodies also exercising governmental powers at the local level. (Davis, 1996, p. 1)

Chapter 8

Governance and Partnership

Introduction – a crowded pitch, but it's not all over

In the course of Chapter 7 – one focused specifically on elected local authorities as direct service providers – we also had cause to mention a whole raft of other organisations: foundation schools, city academies, learning and skills councils, police and health authorities, registered social landlords, housing action trusts, primary care trusts, plus partnerships at almost every turn. There could be no clearer demonstration of how the 'established ways of doing local government are giving way to new, as yet not fully formed, governance alternatives' (Stoker, 2004a, p. 9). Elected local government today is just one – albeit unique – part of what is now widely termed 'local governance': a complex mosaic of organisations, none of the rest of which are directly elected and thereby electorally accountable. Davis (1996 – quoted on p. 140 above) used the metaphor of elected local authorities getting used to 'sharing the turf'. Tony Blair's image, perhaps with the private sector more prominently in mind, is a bit more aggressive (Blair, 1998, p. 10): 'There are all sorts of players on the local pitch jostling for position where previously the local council was the main game in town.' Unlike the conclusion of Kenneth Wolstenholme's immortal 1966 World Cup Final commentary, however, this pitch invasion does not signal that 'it's all over' for elected local government – simply that there have been some extensive changes in the rules of engagement. This chapter will map and evaluate these changing rules, the world of partnerships, and the ubiquitous quango.

What is local governance?

What exactly is local governance? Until quite recently the term 'governance' carried no great theoretical meaning; if used at all, it was as a synonym for government. The 1990s, however, saw an explosion of interest in governance as a concept – initially in Britain (see, e.g., Rhodes, 1997, 1999a, 1999b; Stoker, 1999a; Leach and Percy-Smith, 2001), but subsequently across Europe (see John, 2001, Denters and Rose, 2005). It is particularly valuable as an organising framework that enables us to better understand the *processes of governing*. Local governance brings together governmental and non-governmental agencies in flexible partnerships to deal with different problems by using different strategies. It is not based on a single authority, the provision of a specialised service, or a new set of structures, but on a *fusion* of different styles and different working relationships. Flexibility of approach is central; given that the boundaries between public and private sectors have become increasingly blurred, the traditional hierarchical and bureaucratic styles of governing are no longer appropriate. The key features and emphases that an appreciation of governance brings to the study of government are summarised in Exhibit 8.1.

Those who hoped that a new Labour government, critical in opposition of the 'quango state' being created by the Conservatives, would bring a swift reduction in central intervention, with councils regaining some of

---

Exhibit 8.1 'Government' and 'Governance' – differing emphases

Government	Governance
Is concerned primarily with the INSTITUTIONS of the STATE	Is concerned more with the PROCESSES of GOVERNING and with the many NON-STATE ACTORS and AGENCIES involved
Is primarily about what happens in the PUBLIC SECTOR	Is much more INCLUSIVE, recognising that policy-making, service provision, and problem-solving nowadays involve ALL SECTORS of society – private, voluntary, community, as well as public
Focuses mainly on STRUCTURES	Is concerned more with POLICIES, OUTPUTS and OUTCOMES
Organisations are characterised by BUREAUCRATIC HIERARCHIES, AUTHORITY RELATIONS and CLEAR lines of ACCOUNTABILITY	Is about NETWORKS and PARTNERSHIPS, BARGAINING and EXCHANGE RELATIONS between individuals and organisations, and inevitably BLURRED ACCOUNTABILITY
Is about PROVIDING, DIRECTING and 'ROWING' (Osborne and Gaebler, 1992)	Is about broader, but less involved, roles of government – ENABLING, FACILITATING, and 'STEERING'

Source: Information from Leach and Percy-Smith (2001, pp. 2–5).

their lost responsibilities, soon realised it was not about to materialise. There would be no return to local authorities being near-monopolistic service providers; provision would continue to be shared with a range of partners. In fact, drawing on US experience, Labour made its own contribution to the lexicon of public administration with its introduction of *zones*. The advent from 1999 of Employment Zones, Health Action Zones and Education Action Zones clearly demonstrated the new Government's commitment to working through the same mixed economy of local provision that had characterised the previous decade. Likewise, the New Deal for Communities (NDC) programme for the regeneration of some of the country's poorest housing estates, and the Sure Start project, designed to support pre-school children and their families. These and similar initiatives were early demonstrations of the Labour Government's intention to embrace collaboration between agencies as a way of joining up hitherto fragmented services to meet community needs more effectively. Indeed, the development of 'joined up', more integrated government was a central theme of the 1999 White Paper, *Modernising Government* (Cabinet Office, 1999).

In the age of governance, then, elected local government is just one of a multiplicity of bodies involved in local service delivery. No longer, even in a city such as Birmingham with a so-called unitary council, is the organisation of government relatively straightforward and comprehensible. For, in addition to the City Council, you now have to take into account, among numerous others: the separate police authority, several joint boards, eight NHS hospital and health care trusts, four primary care trusts, a learning and skills council, regeneration partnerships and task forces, boards of further education colleges and foundation schools, housing associations, the Housing Corporation, Jobcentre Plus, Connexions, Sure Start, the Regional Development Agency, and a regional Government Office. The city council is involved in or with all of these bodies, but it no longer has control over, or direct responsibility for, the service delivery it once had.

The local quangocracy – mapping the five thousand

The Conservative years saw not only a reduction in the number of elected local authorities, but also the rapid growth of non-elected or indirectly elected bodies at the expense of directly elected councils. Weir and Beetham (1999) in their 'democratic audit of Great Britain' outline the nature of Labour's inheritance in 1997 (pp. 251–2):

> The local quango state is now extensive and has taken over or usurped the role of local authorities in providing many services. In social housing, the Housing Corporation has taken control of most new

housing investment from local authorities. It also oversees the local housing associations which have become the main channel for investment in new social housing programmes locally ... A handful of housing action trusts have replaced local housing department management on some public housing estates. In education, grant-maintained schools have been removed from local authority control ... all further education colleges, formerly run by local authorities, have been merged and transformed into quangos; polytechnics have moved from local authority control to become universities within the province of the Higher Education Funding Council; the school careers service has been taken out of local government and passed on to private companies. In planning, 12 urban development corporations were created in England to take over planning in inner-city areas ... Employment services were developed outside local authority control, through training and enterprise councils (TECs) and their Scottish equivalents, local enterprise companies (LECs) ... Local authorities lost their representatives on health authority boards; and their role on the new police authorities was further diminished.

These new associations, councils, companies, corporations, boards and trusts are all structured differently and have different working practices. But they are all bodies appointed directly or indirectly by central government, performing functions and providing services that were, until quite recently, provided mainly or exclusively by local authorities. They thus bypass local authorities and may well come into conflict with them. They add greatly to the complexity of sub-central government, as well as increasing the influence of their respective 'sponsoring' departments at local level – especially useful if local political control happens to differ from that at the centre. They are, in a sense, agents for the centre, or, as Weir and Beetham (1999) describe them, 'government's flexible friends' (p. 196). Collectively, they came to be known as 'the local quango state'.

'Quango' is the acronym for quasi-autonomous non-governmental organisation, but that is about the limit of agreement on the subject. It is a slippery term, definable in a multitude of ways, depending on whether the political objective is to minimise or to maximise the count. Governments are minimisers, especially if they come into power like New Labour, vacuously promising 'to sweep away the quango state' (Skelcher *et al.*, 2000, p. 13). Auditors of democracy tend to be maximisers (Lewis, 2005). Oddly, the Government, having for years run a 'quango website' and offered a definition – a body with a role in the processes of government that operates at arm's length from ministers – has decided presumably that this is potentially too expansive and now declares rather pompously that it 'does not use the term'. For our purposes of mapping the 'local quango

Exhibit 8.2 The local quango state in Great Britain, April 2000

Further education institutions	511
Foundation schools (ex-GM and voluntary-aided schools)	877
City technology colleges	15
Learning and skills councils (replaced TECs in 2000)	47
Local enterprise and careers service companies (Scotland)	39
Registered social landlords	2,421
Housing action trusts	4
Police authorities	49
Health authorities/boards	114
NHS trusts	387
Primary care groups/trusts	488
Total	**4,952**

Source: Information from House of Commons Select Committee on Public Administration, Fifth Report, 2000/01: Mapping the Quango State, Table 6.

state', Charter 88's simple and unambiguous definition will do nicely: 'unelected bodies spending public money'.

Such a definition would at any time since the mid-1990s have produced a rough total of around 5,000 local quangos in the United Kingdom. The most systematic attempt at mapping them all has been that of the House of Commons Public Administration Select Committee, whose chairman is in the privileged position of being able to fill in any gaps by putting Parliamentary Questions to ministers. Even the Committee in places confused its boards, councils and companies, but Exhibit 8.2, summarising the Committee's findings, is probably our most accurate depiction of the local quango state.

The 5,000 or so local quangos are run by well over 60,000 mainly ministerially appointed or self-appointed 'quangocrats', making almost three quangocrats for every councillor. Earlier Democratic Audit reports had expressed concern at the scale of this new 'local magistracy', at the arbitrary and partisan way in which quango board members were appointed, and at the serious deficiencies in the accountability and openness of many boards. The Major Government established the Nolan Committee on Standards in Public Life and set in motion a gradual reform process. But, as noted above, New Labour promised to go much further and unleash a 'quango cull'. In fact, no cull ever materialised. Within a year the goal was modified to one of 'keeping the number to the minimum necessary' (Cabinet Office, 1998), and by 2005 at least 111 completely new quangos had apparently proved to be necessary – not least the English Regional Development Agencies and new Welsh and Scottish bodies following devolution (Lewis, 2005).

Ministers know not what they do, Skelcher *et al.* (2000) concluded charitably, in their evaluation of the local dimension of these developments, for the consequences may be profound (p. 5):

> We suspect that ministers do not appreciate the consequences for local democracy and elected government at local level of this expansion of quasi-governance ... But the cumulative effects are draining away the powers and functions of elected local government and vastly complicating its ability to co-ordinate the delivery of public services locally. For local communities and citizens, for whom the local town hall is the natural focus for inquiries, requests, complaints or demands concerning public services and duties, the unco-ordinated plethora of public bodies are in effect out of reach.

No one would seriously dispute that quangos perform important functions and can do so effectively. They can bring valuable experience and expertise into government, including sections of society under-represented through the local electoral system. They may be able to bring objectivity and a non-partisan perspective to the discussion of sensitive issues. Democrats would argue, though, that taking over whole areas of policy making and service delivery from elected and accountable local authorities runs the risk of opening up a serious democratic deficit.

In addition to their members being elected, and thereby knowable by name and readily accessible to their constituents, local authorities conduct their business relatively openly and transparently. They produce annual reports, have their accounts audited annually, advertise their meetings, publish agendas, minutes and background papers, report their major decisions, invite complaints, and keep registers of members' interests. They are also subject to extensive central direction, inspection and regulation. Many quangos, as the Commons Public Administration Select Committee found, are required and choose to do none of these things (House of Commons, 2001, table 11). About half of their 5,000 local quangos did in fact publish annual reports, and agendas and minutes of their committee meetings. But only a fifth, for example, admitted the public to those meetings, or conformed to the Government code of practice on access to information, or consulted with their local authorities regarding their plans and policies.

None of these democratic practices in themselves – not even direct election – guarantee efficient services. They are, however, rather more likely to produce effective, responsive and improvable services than other bodies, some of whose members, when interviewed by Skelcher and Davis (1996), seemed uncertain as to whom they even represented:

[Long pause] I've never actually been asked who I'm responsible to. [Long pause] It's an interesting question. [Pause] The community probably. [Pause] The people of the area. I do feel I'm trying to do something for them. Also, of course, I represent my company.

Partnerships – the new paradigm

There is an almost inevitable resentment felt by local authorities at their loss of powers and the fragmentation of their previously direct service provision. But this did not prevent many of them – even before the government increasingly required it – working closely and productively in partnership with some of the new quangos, and with private sector and voluntary organisations in their localities. 'Community leadership' as a key future role for local authorities made its first major appearance in 1998 in the title of the Labour Government's first local government consultation paper (DETR, 1998a). Yet, as Stoker noted (1999a, p. 15), during a period in which local authorities had faced serious financial and other legislative constraints, many had already begun to assume, much more proactively than in the past, a broader leadership role in the community. Economic development, urban regeneration, environmental protection, community safety and anti-crime measures, anti-poverty initiatives, preventative health care schemes and anti-domestic violence projects were all areas where local authorities had taken forward the vision of community governance. The Labour Government's particular contribution was to introduce a whole series of funding schemes that variously encouraged and required such initiatives and programmes to be undertaken through formal partnerships – indeed, to promote partnerships as the new 'paradigm' for policy making and service delivery (Lowndes and Sullivan, 2004, p. 52).

The paradigm was outlined by the prime minister himself in the early days of the new Labour Government (Blair, 1998, p. 13):

> The days of the all-purpose [local] authority that planned and delivered everything are gone. They are finished. It is in partnership with others ... that local government's future lies. Local authorities will deliver some services but their distinctive leadership role will be to weave and knit together the contribution of the various local stakeholders.

Such partnerships are seen by the Government as a crucial vehicle for 'addressing successfully those endemic social ills of society: low educational standards, social exclusion, poor health and poverty. No one agency could tackle such obdurate problems; these "wicked issues" cross organisational boundaries and require collaborative solutions' (Snape

Exhibit 8.3 The labyrinthine world of zones and partnerships

The future is bright – if the future is partnerships

The Blair Government made it clear from the outset that local government's future lay in partnership working with other public, private and community organisations, rather than as a sole service provider. The resulting explosion of local partnerships was included by the House of Commons Public Administration Committee in its attempt at 'mapping the quango state'. The following selection of 2,393 – and it is only a selection – all involve local authority officers (and sometimes councillors) from the relevant departments, representatives of other public bodies, local voluntary and community groups, and usually also private sector and business organisations.

113   **Education Action Zones** – clusters of schools working with local organisations to raise attainment and overcome barriers to learning in areas of high deprivation.

 26   **Health Action Zones** – to tackle health inequalities and key priorities – for example, mental health, teenage pregnancy, drug abuse – through health and social care programmes.

 15   **Employment Action Zones** – to help the long-term unemployed to improve their employability through individual action plans and 'personal job accounts'.

 12   **Sport Action Zones** – networks of schools, sports clubs and other bodies working to enhance the social and economic contribution of sport in deprived areas.

 22   **New Commitment to Regeneration Partnerships** – to improve the quality of life and governance across a wide area, and provide a framework within which other, more specific, local partnerships can operate.

and Taylor, 2003, p .1). This meant, at the local level, partnerships that brought together public bodies, private firms, community and voluntary groups, and, to ensure that the point was understood, central government funding became increasingly contingent on the establishment of multi-agency partnerships.

The resulting partnership explosion has been documented by Sullivan and Skelcher (2002, pp. 24–7) who found at least 5,500 local partnerships, spending some £4.3 billion a year and involving 75,000 people as partnership board members. They vary in every conceivable way – by size, function and service area; they include the statutory and voluntary, executive and non-executive, strategic and operational, limited companies and charitable trusts. The list in Exhibit 8.3 is a selection of under half the

39 **New Deal for Communities Partnerships** – to narrow gaps in housing, crime, educational attainment, health and employment prospects between deprived neighbourhoods and the rest of the country.

900 **Single Regeneration Budget (SRB) Partnerships** – to address the regeneration objectives of the several government departments contributing to the SRB.

285 **Local Agenda 21 Partnerships** – to advance the principles of sustainable development, environmental conservation and preservation agreed at the 1992 Rio 'Earth Summit'.

47 **Connexions Partnerships** – to advance the goals of the Connexions Service, of delivering comprehensive support for 13–19 year olds.

150 **Early Years Development and Child Care Partnerships** – to co-ordinate the Government's commitment to good quality, affordable and accessible child care.

100 **Learning Partnerships** – to improve the planning, coherence and standards of post-16 learning, and to widen participation.

139 **Sure Start Partnerships** – to improve prospects for disadvantaged pre-school children.

16 **Creative Partnerships** – to offer young people opportunities to enhance their arts and cultural education outside schools.

376 **Crime and Disorder Reduction Partnerships** – to co-ordinate action to tackle crime and crime-related issues at the local level.

153 **Community Legal Service Partnerships** – to improve access to and the delivery of legal and advice services.

Source: Information from House of Commons (2001) *Select Committee on Public Administration, Fifth Report, 2000/01: Mapping the Quango State*, Table 7.

total, but it does include most of the large, multi-agency partnerships in which all local authorities with responsibilities in the relevant service areas will have leading roles. The other half of Sullivan and Skelcher's 5,500 are likely to be smaller and more localised partnerships, like those in which a district council such as Guildford – *not* directly responsible for key partnership services such as education, social services and the police, nor an area of severe deprivation – might be involved (see Exhibit 8.4). Then, overseeing and attempting to co-ordinate these different thematic partnerships, there are, as you might by now expect, local strategic partnerships (see Exhibit 8.5), with their responsibility for producing and implementing community plans and leading the negotiation of local area agreements (see Chapter 17, especially Exhibit 17.6).

Exhibit 8.4 A good partner – one council's partnerships

All local authorities nowadays are necessarily at least formally involved, through their local strategic partnerships, with many other service-providing bodies and agencies, and a large unitary urban council's links would run into the hundreds. It is perhaps more insightful, therefore, to see how a district council, directly responsible for only a limited range of services, mapped its partnership working. Guildford Borough Council is one of 11 district councils in Surrey, and its partnerships in 2005 included:

- **Multi-agency partnerships**
  Crime and Disorder Reduction
  Early Years Development and Child Care

- **Partnerships with other local authorities**
  Joint Municipal Waste Management Strategy – with Surrey County Council (SCC) and Surrey district councils
  Waste Awareness Campaign – with Waverley BC
  Very sheltered housing provision – with Surrey CC
  On-street parking management – with Surrey CC

- **Partnerships with other public bodies**
  Surrey Scholar programme – with University of Surrey: sponsored research into links between transport, pollution and health in Guildford
  Single assessment process for older people – with Guildford and Waverley Primary Care Trust (PCT) and Surrey CC
  Walking for Health programme – with Guildford and Waverley PCT, the Healthy Living Centre, West Surrey NHS Health Promotion Service, Age Concern Surrey, and University of Surrey
  Live and Direct project to develop skills of young musicians – with Youth Music (charity), Surrey Youth Development Service, Arts Partnership Surrey, and Rhythmix youth music project

- **Partnerships with the private sector**
  Comatco Ltd – catering franchise at Guildford Spectrum Leisure Complex
  Tunstall Telecom Ltd – building of 'Smart' demonstration house, showing how to support people in their own homes using assistive technology
  Aldershot Car Spares – free-of-charge, 24-hour removal of abandoned cars

Source:　Information from Audit Commission (2005a), pp. 22–3.

Added value or scary big numbers?

Even without the stick of central government and the carrot of financial incentives, it is easy to appreciate the added value that local authorities might see resulting from partnership working. Partnerships can overcome the limitations of separately run services in meeting the needs of some of the most vulnerable groups in British society – children, older people, those with mental health problems, for example. Partnerships can attempt to address these complex 'cross-cutting' or holistic issues, and problems that affect whole communities and are beyond the scope of even multi-functional local authorities – poverty, urban regeneration, community safety, preventative health care, environmental protection. Partnerships may be able increase citizen participation and community engagement more effectively than democratic local government has been able to.

There are, however, counter-arguments. Skelcher (2004a) has described the recent rush to partnership working as a challenge to the 'functional sovereignty' of local authorities, undermining their political authority 'as the democratic voice of the community' (p. 35). The LSP, for example, can become a forum for bargaining amongst the leaderships of the constituent bodies, with the public interest becoming marginalised. Then there are the costs, as emphasised, appropriately, by the Audit Commission (2005a, p. 25):

> Partnership working incurs costs. If partnerships spend too much time in meetings discussing process issues instead of focusing on achieving their objectives, the costs can outweigh the benefits.

It does not require any very penetrating reading between the lines of its 2005 report to conclude that the Commission feels that the Government's uncritical enthusiasm for partnerships may have gone too far, too fast. 'Is it possible to manage all these collaborations successfully to produce benefits that public bodies could not achieve by other means?', it asks rhetorically (p. 5), and then makes very clear its doubts. Few of the organisations in the Commission's study even knew the number of partnerships they were involved in, and 'almost none ... had tried to calculate the total cost involved in working in partnership', one admitting that 'We've never looked in detail at inputs, outputs and outcomes, and would find this damned scary, since it would clock up big numbers' (2005a, p. 25).

If, for understandable reasons, these accounting issues in multi-agency partnerships are difficult, accountability is necessarily weakened. It is impossible to claim effective use and management of resources, and

---

Exhibit 8.5 Local Strategic Partnerships (LSPs)

What is an LSP?

A single, non-statutory, multi-agency body, which matches local authority boundaries and brings together at the local level representatives of the public, private, voluntary and community sectors plus local residents. The LSP's initial aim was to prepare, implement and monitor a *Community Plan* or *Strategy* to promote the economic, social and environmental well-being of the area and its residents, and, by working in partnership, to increase co-ordination of service delivery.

Where did they come from?

From the Local Government Act 2000, and partly from a 2001 strategy document from the Cabinet Office's Social Exclusion Unit, which spelled out the Government's *New Commitment to Neighbourhood Renewal*: to raise living standards in England's most deprived neighbourhoods by tackling their deep-rooted and multi-faceted problems – industrial decline, unemployment, entrenched poverty, failing public services, crime, vandalism, drug-dealing and family breakdown. LSPs are not, however, confined only to these deprived areas; all English authorities are involved, individually and/or jointly.

So how many are there?

There are two groups:

- 88 'NRF LSPs' in the most deprived local authority areas, containing over 80 per cent of the poorest electoral ward areas in the country. These LSPs receive additional funding from the Government's Neighbourhood Renewal Fund.
- 288 Non-NRF LSPs in the remaining local authority areas, based on either single authorities or a county council plus its districts. These are funded usually by their local authorities and other public sector organisations.

---

impossible to demonstrate quantitatively either benefits achieved or value for money. The Commission's main conclusion is that nothing like the same standards of scrutiny and performance measurement are brought to bear on partnerships as on the non-partnership work of the bodies involved, with the result that partnerships regularly break down, many others experience significant problems – sometimes acknowledged, sometimes not – while the effectiveness of the remainder is unassessable. 'Local public bodies', the Commission advises, 'should be much more constructively critical about this form of working: it may not be the best solution in every case' (2005a, p. 2).

In both cases, they are most commonly chaired by the Leader of the principal council.

Who are the partners?

They are quite large bodies, simply because of the range of interests – several represented by 'umbrella groups' – that they have to seek to include. Leicestershire LSP's membership is typical:

- Leicestershire County Council – councillors and officers
- 7 Leicestershire District LSPs
- Association of Parish Councils
- Shire Economic Partnership
- Business Link
- Connexions
- Learning and Skills Council
- City Learning Partnership
- Rural Partnership
- 4 Primary Care Trusts
- 2 NHS Trusts
- Strategic Health Authority
- Environmental Partnership
- Cultural Strategy Forum
- Police authority
- Racial Equality Council
- Combined fire authorities
- Council for Voluntary Service Community Partnership
- Business community representatives
- Jobcentre Plus
- Faith community representatives.

What do they do?

Early on, probably more discussion than action – about membership of the LSP, developing structures and processes, agreeing shared objectives and so on. In most cases action or thematic groups were set up to consult with relevant interests and service users, and produce programmes, projects, targets and timetables that feed into the overall Community Plan. Now, as key bodies responsible for negotiating and implementing Local Area Agreements (see Exhibit 17.6), they are set to become major drivers and co-ordinators of local service delivery.

The Private Finance Initiative (PFI)

Many of the cross-sectoral bodies referred to in the past few pages could be described as public/private partnerships (PPPs). The PFI, however, is a particularly important, and controversial, form of partnership and warrants a section of its own. It originated in the early 1990s, when the Conservative Government was continuing its long-term policy of reducing public spending, but also facing the political consequences of years of under-investment in schools, hospitals, transportation and other parts of the nation's economic and social infrastructure. It was a new way of enabling the public sector to afford capital-intensive projects (buildings, roads, plant, apparatus, vehicles) without inflating the government's public expenditure figures, while at the same time extending the 'privatisation' of public services.

Instead of the Government borrowing from the private sector to finance these capital projects and then owning and operating them itself, the private sector would be invited not only to finance the construction, but also provide some or all of the *services* associated with the project. In return, the Government would pay for the *use* of the asset and its associated services over a period of time – perhaps 20 or 30 years – with these fees to include the costs and compensation of risk associated with the capital investment. There are several varieties of PFI schemes, some in which the entire asset and service provision is undertaken by the private sector, others involving a mix of public and private funding, and still others involving leasing arrangements.

PFI was slow to take off, but it gradually spread from large-scale transport projects – such as the Channel Tunnel Rail Link and the Jubilee Line extension – to hospitals, prisons, roads, and new teaching and residential accommodation in further and higher educational institutions (Unison, 2002). For local government, though, the first PFI projects did not even start until 1996/97 – largely because of the tight legal and financial constraints under which British local government finance has to operate. It is the Blair Administration, therefore, that has been largely responsible for local authorities' now extensive use of PFI.

Many PFI projects are 'financially free-standing' in the sense of their not needing central government revenue support – in which case they do not require endorsement by the relevant government department. For most major local authority projects, however, government backing is essential, and between 1997 and 2005 some 300 PFI projects and £12 billions of funding were endorsed by different central government departments (ODPM, 2005c). Schemes have included a wide range of services, as illustrated in Exhibit 8.6, the most popular being education (44 per cent of funding), transport (15 per cent), and housing (12 per cent).

PFI has obvious attractions to central governments, even ones less predisposed towards the private sector than recent UK governments have been. Most obviously, it shifts the immediate burden of government expenditure from capital spending today to current spending in the future. Proponents would also point out the advantages of transferring the risks involved in the design, building, financing and operation of the asset to the private sector, and of having private sector management skills contributing towards the enhancement of service quality and efficiency (see, for example, ODPM, 2005c). Critics, on the other hand, argue that 'such

---

Exhibit 8.6 A selection of local government PFI projects

Leeds Supertram – a new 'Supertram' to boost local transport services and help regenerate some of the run-down areas of the city.

From schools to learning centres in Knowsley – all 11 secondary schools in the Merseyside borough to be replaced by 8 new learning centres.

Social housing in Kirklees – provision of 550 units of affordable housing, replacing 650 old units that are uneconomic to refurbish to the Government's Decent Homes standard.

New street lighting in Derby – City Council to replace 17,000 street light columns (lamp posts to most of us) and 2,700 illuminated traffic signs, bollards and beacons.

One-stop library for Lewisham – an integrated library, leisure and health facility, including two GP practices, their primary care teams, district nurses and health visitors.

Waste management in Cambridgeshire – provision of long-term waste management facilities to promote waste minimisation, maximise recycling and composting, and divert bio-degradable waste currently sent to landfill sites.

Source: Data from ODPM Endorsed Project list – www.local.odpm.gov.uk/pfi/endorsed.xls

---

advantages may be offset ... by the concessions that may have to be made to attract private contractors' (Gray and Jenkins, 1998, p. 352), or by having to play down environmental and other concerns, as Heald and Geaughan suggest happened with the Skye Bridge project in Scotland (1999).

The most serious criticisms, though, as set out in Exhibit 8.7, centre on costs. While PFI enables projects to go ahead that a resource-strapped public sector could not afford, in practice what is being achieved is an expensive accountancy trick – simply a delay in the cost to the public purse, not a saving; in fact, quite the reverse (see, e.g., Challis, 2000, Ch. 11; Pollock and Price, 2004).

Despite such reservations, PFI remains an important element of the Labour government's infrastructure planning, and therefore central to many of the governance and partnership initiatives taking place at local level – even when, as with social housing, its deficiencies are acknowledged by ministers themselves. The attractions to a local authority in need of capital investment are obvious. PFI appears to offer good value for money

Exhibit 8.7 The costs of PFI

Criticisms of PFI range from the ideological to the alleged absence of any evidence base for its claimed benefits. Most serious, however, are those relating to its excessive cost to public bodies, such as local authorities, for whom there are few alternative sources of capital finance available. PFI projects, it is argued, are likely to cost more because:

- the private sector cannot borrow at the lower interest rates available to the government;
- the private sector always needs to make a rate of return for shareholders that is not required by the public sector;
- this rate of return is greatly exaggerated by comparison with any transferred risks, which are treated as if they were spread over the length of the contract, instead of in fact being concentrated during the construction phase and largely disappearing thereafter;
- there are high 'set up' costs arising out of PFI process itself and the need for both sides to employ usually expensive lawyers and consultants;
- there may be no 'public asset' at the end of the process;
- negotiations at the end of the contract period may result in additional costs owing to the monopoly position of the private sector supplier;
- far from assuming risk for project failure or default, when big or high profile PFI deals run into financial trouble, they are likely to bailed out by the public purse.

compared to the traditional option of buying the asset and being responsible for running and maintaining it – even in the unlikely event of that option being affordable. The private sector's assumption of risk should in principle make cost overruns less likely, and should lead to savings in both building and running costs. And, because the authority will pay on a performance-related basis for the use of the asset, there is an additional incentive for the contractor to build it to a high standard and maintain it in good condition.

All of this, however, is ultimately secondary to the fact that PFI was and continues to be driven less by a government commitment to the quality of local service provision than by the Treasury's concern to keep borrowing off the nation's public sector balance sheet. For as long as this is the case, it will continue to be promoted by central government – and utilised extensively, if not always enthusiastically, by local government.

Chapter 9

Central–Local Government Relations

Introduction – letting go or hypercentralisation?

You could be forgiven for thinking that a good part of this book has already been taken up with central–local government relations. In Chapter 2 we noted the statutory and financial constraints that limit local government's operational discretion; in Chapter 4, the successive 'top-down' restructurings that have produced its present-day shape and scale; and in Chapters 7 and 8, local government's loss of power to quangos and central government's insistence on partnership working. You would be right in thinking so, and indeed most of the remaining chapters will also refer to the topic. The fact is that an account of local government in a unitary state such as the UK must necessarily also be an account of its central–local government relations. The latter provide the backdrop, the stage, the direction, and much of the script, for the former, and it is appropriate that, in this pivotal central chapter in the book, we bring the various strands of the subject together.

We do so at what might prove to be a particularly critical time for the future of British local government. Talk abounds of a 'new localism' – a notion espoused, in albeit rather vague and differing ways, by all political parties. The Government, shortly before the 2005 Election, published a '10-Year Vision' (ODPM, 2005c), with the development of a new central–local settlement as one of its major aims. We shall return to these matters in our final chapter. Yet, while some parts of the centre, notably sections in the Office of the Deputy Prime Minister (ODPM), talked of 'letting go' and of more 'freedoms and flexibilities' for local authorities, other ministers and departments in the same government were giving out patently different behavioural messages.

That there is room for some fairly extensive 'letting go' cannot seriously be questioned. The UK is an already highly centralised – even 'hyper-centralised' (Loughlin, 2001, ch. 2) – governmental system, becoming even more centralised, with its reduction in the numbers and powers of elected local authorities and its tight central controls on all elements of local finance. In this chapter, dealing successively with the formal framework of central–local relations, the dynamics of the relationship, key institutions, and some theoretical perspectives, we shall endeavour to provide the material to foster an understanding and permit an evaluation of one of the most important and disputed topics in contemporary British government.

The formal framework: controls and constraints

We begin with a review of some of the main instruments that are available, principally to ministers and their departments, to control and direct local authorities and generally keep local government in its constitutionally subordinate place.

Legislation

Legislation is the most direct instrument of central control of local authorities, and one used in recent years with unprecedented frequency and impact. The Conservative Governments from 1979 to 1997 produced well over 200 Acts of Parliament affecting local government, at least a third of them in major and far-reaching ways. In the Queen's Speech following the 2005 general election, at least 20 of its 50 bills contained what the Local Government Association felt were 'important implications for local government' – from animal welfare, child care, education, and election administration through to road safety and violent crime (LGA, 2005c).

In Chapter 2 we used the term 'partial autonomy' to describe the constitutional status of British local government, and we indicated the constraints imposed by the *ultra vires* doctrine. National governments can, through legislation, create, abolish, restructure and amend the powers of local authorities as and when they determine. Local authorities, for their part, are authorised to provide or secure the provision of certain services, but only within a framework of national legislation. The new 'well-being power' (see Exhibit 9.1) significantly qualifies this traditional position, but does not overturn it. It genuinely extends local authorities' powers and links directly into the implementation of their community plans and strategies, but it is not unlimited and it cannot change their constitutional position as 'creatures of statute'.

The same is true of local authorities' powers to initiate private legislation and make by-laws. Both powers are important and probably unwarrantedly neglected by commentators (Jones and Stewart, 2004, p. 24). *Private legislation* – giving the promoting body powers *over and above* the existing law – was used extensively during the nineteenth Century, not least by local authorities, for the construction of railways and tramways, gas and water systems. Private bills, however, are both procedurally complex and comparatively easily blockable either by government departments or by other affected interests, and have become rarities in modern times. *By-laws*,

Exhibit 9.1 The power of well-being

This power – enabling local authorities 'to promote the economic, social and environmental well-being of their area' – was introduced in the Local Government Act 2000 as an important part of the Government's modernisation agenda for local government. Though not unlimited, and subject to ministerial interpretation, it significantly extends in particular local authorities' trading and commercial powers, and enables them to 'improve the quality of life, opportunity and health of their communities by undertaking both new and traditional activities in innovative ways' (LGA, 2003, p. 5). Examples of initiatives that would previously have been potentially or actually *ultra vires* include:

- **Torbay's development partnership**
  Torbay Council formed a public–private Development Agency with private sector business interests, to identify ways of boosting the area's economy, exploiting its harbours for regeneration, and developing tourism opportunities.
- **Temping in Greenwich**
  The London Borough of Greenwich established a 'not for distributable profit' employment agency, Gateway Employment Ltd, to supply temporary staff to the council and other employers, with profits going to local arts and cultural projects.
- **Hastings' own suntan lotion**
  Hastings Council entered into a partnership with a local toiletries manufacturer to market their own suntan lotion at half the price of branded lotions, profits going towards funding the council's 'safer sunbathing' campaign.
- **Norfolk's mobile post offices**
  Norfolk County Council, in partnership with the Rural Shops Alliance, the Post Office, and the Countryside Agency, examined how its mobile libraries and school-based computer network might be used to provide PO services in rural areas.

Source: Data from LGA (2003).

in contrast, are to be seen all over the place – hanging from lamp posts, displayed inside taxis, pinned on public notice boards. They are a form of delegated legislation, which permits local authorities and other bodies to make regulations *within* existing law that relate to a specified area – regarding, typically, the use of recreation grounds, swimming baths or libraries, the control of dogs, skateboarding, or ball games. Neither power alters local government's subordinate position in the central–local relationship, but, as councils recognise them increasingly as part of their community leadership armoury, and several city authorities test out both procedures in attempts, for example, to prohibit smoking and drinking in public places, we may well hear more of them.

Statutory instruments

Acts of Parliament, as we noted in Chapter 5, are often termed 'primary legislation'. Many Acts, however, require detailed 'secondary legislation' or clarifying regulations before they can properly be implemented. This secondary legislation comprises in the main Statutory Instruments, which, even though they escape full parliamentary debate, are generally seen as a regrettable but relatively harmless inevitability of modern-day life. Sometimes, however, they take the form of so-called 'Henry VIII clauses', allowing ministers – following the Tudor monarch's practice of legislating by decree – effectively to amend or even repeal primary legislation.

Even the administratively necessary variety of Statutory Instruments, though, constitutes a significant means by which ministers can 'flesh out'

Exhibit 9.2 Statutory Instruments: secondary but still significant

A small selection of the more than 3,500 Statutory Instruments that passed through Parliament in 2005:

SI 52   **Education (Student Support) Regulations.** These define the precise eligibility for financial support of different categories of students taking designated higher education courses in the 2005/06 academic year.

SI 221   **Greater London Authority (Allocation of Grants for Precept Calculations) Regulations.** They detail the amounts of council tax the GLA will receive from the 33 London boroughs for its provision of police services through the Metropolitan Police Authority.

SI 345   **Education (Budget Statements) (England) Regulations.** These regulations specify, in exhaustive detail, the precise form in which local education authority budget statements must be prepared and published.

SI 694   **Local Authorities (Categorisation) (England) Order.** This assigns all 387 English local authorities into five categories – Excellent, Good, Fair, Weak or Poor – according to their performance as assessed under the Government's Comprehensive Performance Assessment (CPA) procedure (see Exhibit 9.3).

SI 2114   **Civil Partnership Act 2004 (Amendments to Subordinate Legislation) Order.** This order brings some 85 pieces of subordinate legislation into line with the policy of enabling same-sex couples to form civil partnerships, by replacing the words 'wife or husband' with 'spouse or civil partner', etc.

Source: Information from Office of Public Sector Information (Cabinet Office), UK Statutory Instruments – www.opsi.gov.uk/stat.htm.

their own legislation and thereby strengthen, if they choose, their control over local authorities' actions and activities. Our minute selection of SIs in Exhibit 9.2 ranges from the official confirmation of the results of one of the Government's most contentious policies (694), through the determination and communication of vital administrative information (52, 221), to what might be considered a not atypical example of central government micro-management: does a *Local* Education *Authority* really require 11 pages of regulatory instructions on how to prepare a budget?

Circulars and guidance

In addition to statutory instruments, government departments will also issue circulars to local authorities containing 'advice' and 'guidance' on how they should exercise their various responsibilities. Such circulars are often perceived as further vehicles for central direction, and indeed they can be. But not all circulars are directive, and some are the product of genuine negotiation with local authority interests and contain useful practical advice. Even when benign, however, their sheer volume makes them a powerful and continuous reminder of central government's presence. Planners alone, for example, checking out the DCLG's website, would find that, in addition to conventional departmental circulars, they should be acquainted with nineteen planning policy and sixteen mineral policy guidance notes, and seventy guidance, advice and information papers, plus, of course, ministers' latest pronouncements in the form of parliamentary answers and statements.

Judicial review

British local government, then, operates within a complex and often subtle legal framework. Central government, through Parliament, has ultimate authority as well as extensive powers of direction and supervision. But local authorities too have substantial powers of discretion, promotion and experimentation in relation to their service-providing responsibilities. When the priorities and policies of a local council clash with those of central government, or of any other organisation, the disputes may have to be settled in court by a process known as judicial review – something that happened with increasingly frequency in the period from 1979 onwards. In 1974, leave for judicial review was sought 160 times. By 1995, this figure had increased to 4,400.

Loughlin (1996b, p. 61) emphasised the significance of this massive expansion of the formal legal dimension of central–local relations, arguing that the contemporary period was 'one in which both Parliament and the courts have been brought back into the central–local relationship'. Indeed, following an analysis of some of the most important cases of the period, Loughlin (1996a) identified 'a remarkable pattern ... so marked that it may even be expressed in the form of a law: the further up the court hierarchy the dispute progresses, the greater the likelihood of a principle restrictive of local authority action being enunciated' (p. 408). We summarised in the previous edition of this book (Wilson and Game, 2002, p. 154, plus Exhibit on linked website) two such cases where the House of Lords, the highest court in the land, ruled in favour of ministers against local authorities. Nottinghamshire County Council failed in 1986 to prove that it had been discriminated against in the Government's grant distribution formula, and Leicester City Council in 1985 was deemed to have acted illegally in banning the city's rugby club from using a council-owned pitch, on the grounds that the club supported sporting apartheid in South Africa.

Ministers don't always win though, and, while they can try to persuade Parliament quickly to make legal what has just been pronounced illegal, in the short term an adverse judgement can prove to be both embarrassing and a policy setback for a government. We summarised a couple of these cases too: the Lords' 1977 ruling that a Labour Education Secretary had acted illegally in trying to force a comprehensive schools policy on Conservative Tameside Council in Greater Manchester, and the over-turning in 1994 of the Conservative Environment Secretary's attempt to influence the recommendations of the Local Government Reorganisation Commission against the interests of Derbyshire and Lancashire County Councils.

The local ombudsman

These high profile cases are exceptional, in having implications extending beyond the cases themselves, and involving organisations rather than individuals. Many local government judicial review cases, however, involve individuals challenging decisions of a local authority and *choosing* to pursue their grievances through the courts – 'choosing', because they are likely also to have had open to them an alternative means of seeking redress: through their local ombudsman or, to give the office its official title, the Commission for Local Administration (CLA).

The CLA and the separate commissions in Wales and Scotland were established in 1974, following the creation of a national ombudsman, the Parliamentary Commissioner for Administration, in 1967 – just 158 years after Sweden created its first Ombudsman or 'agent of the people'. The public sector appointments proved to be trendsetters, as in the following two decades there sprang up private sector 'ombudspersons' for everything from insurance, banks and estate agents to the removals industry and funeral services. On the other hand, it is arguable that neither Parliamentary nor Local Commissioners have had as high profile an impact on either the country's Government or its citizens' consciousness as have several of their European, and especially Scandinavian, counterparts. Even so, the three English local ombudsmen alone deal nowadays with nearly 19,000 cases a year, which, in their absence, would constitute a great deal of unhealthily pent-up suspicion of council maladministration.

That is what Britain's local ombudsmen mainly do: they investigate written complaints from the public about injustice caused by *maladministration* on the part of their local councils, and the police and fire authorities, joint boards, education appeals panels, and (concerning admissions practices) school governing bodies. They do not initiate their own investigations, although they have in recent years taken up what might be termed 'class actions' arising out of individual cases – as with over 5,000 mental health patients wrongly charged for aftercare by social services authorities, and who are likely to receive total reimbursements of around £87 million (CLA, 2005, p. 4). Nor do they deal with complaints about the actual policy of a council. They are concerned solely with the way in which policy is administered – for example, the speed, efficiency, fairness and propriety with which it was implemented.

The ombudsmen will accept such complaints either from aggrieved citizens themselves or via their local councillor. If the complaint is one of the roughly 45 per cent that qualifies for investigation, the ombudsmen will normally get the local authority concerned to respond in detail and, if there seems to have been maladministration, do everything possible to bring about some local settlement – successfully in around a third of the cases they take on. In only a small minority of cases will a much more exhaustive investigation be required, resulting in a final report and published judgement of whether or not maladministration and injustice have been found. If so, the ombudsman will look to the local authority for some form of satisfactory action: an apology, financial compensation, or a change of procedure in dealing with future cases. Usually acceptable action is forthcoming, but on occasion a council will continue to dispute the ombudsman's judgement, whereupon the latter is left with little sanction beyond the production of a second critical public report.

The inability of the CLA to enforce compliance has sometimes led to the suggestion that what we have is more of an 'ombudsmouse', but the accusation depends on more weight being attached to the exceptional case than to the generality. It can hardly be disputed that the CLA does valuable work. In 2004/05 it received 18,700 complaints, principal topic areas being housing and housing benefit (32 per cent), planning (23 per cent), highways and parking (10 per cent and growing), and social services (8 per cent). For complainants, it is a free, accessible and generally informal service that leaves untouched their right to take their case to court, if they choose, and that over the years has dealt with increasing numbers of cases at, in real terms, falling costs per case.

It is also, however, an institution employing over 200 staff at a cost of nearly £12 million, which after thirty years in operation is unknown to more than half the English adult population (MORI, 2003, p. 6), which finds maladministration with injustice in only 2 per cent of the cases it takes on, and even then cannot enforce any redress. Alternative and more streamlined procedures have been proposed, on the grounds that, since 1974, councils' own internal complaints systems and their general customer orientation have improved immeasurably, and that an ombudsman-quality sledgehammer is no longer required to crack these proverbial nuts of alleged maladministration. Better, perhaps, to have a more localised procedure of investigation, based on councils' own complaints systems and overseen by council-funded but genuinely independent local adjudicators, with a much smaller-scale Commission acting as a central monitoring body.

This is not, however, what will happen. In Scotland and Wales, the respective devolved administrations have introduced combined Public Services Ombudsmen offices, bringing together the parliamentary and health service, local government and housing association ombudsmen. A similar proposal was made for England in 2001, snappily followed just four years later by a Cabinet Office consultation paper, which stopped short of such revolutionary change, but proposed instead that the three ombudsmen for central government, local government and the NHS might in future like to work more 'collaboratively on cases and issues that are relevant to more than one of their individual jurisdictions' (Cabinet Office, 2005) – as in fact they already do.

Default, engagement and intervention

Legislation sometimes confers default powers on ministers, so that a minister dissatisfied with the way an authority is providing a particular service can, as a final resort, step in and take it over, or transfer responsibility to another local authority or special body. Until quite recently the invariably cited example of default powers being exercised was that of Clay Cross, Derbyshire, when the Labour council refused to increase its council house rents to the 'fair rent' level defined in the Housing Finance Act 1972. The Conservative Government sent in a housing commissioner to take over the council's housing responsibilities, and 11 Clay Cross councillors were disqualified from holding public office and surcharged £63,000 (roughly £500,000 at 2005 prices) for the money lost through the Act not being implemented.

The sheer practical difficulties involved in government-appointed officials taking over the running of a whole council service, quite apart from the political and personal animosity provoked, meant that such default powers used to be exercised only very rarely. In recent years, though, specific powers of ministerial intervention have been written into all kinds of legislation – from planning and environmental protection to, rather extraordinarily, public libraries and museums (ODPM, 2004a, Annex A), and, prompted by the arrival of Comprehensive Performance Assessment (CPA – see Exhibit 9.3 and Chapter 17), there is now a subtle distinction drawn between 'intervention' and mere 'engagement'. Both happen a great deal more frequently than ever before, and, as a council on the receiving end, one or more of whose services are causing ministers 'serious concern', it must sometimes seem a distinction without a difference. 'Engagement', however, should be seen as a kind of comradely non-statutory intrusion, undertaken prior to and in the hope of preventing the necessity for an armed statutory intervention by the relevant Secretary of State (ODPM, 2004a, Annex E).

As might perhaps be expected, the services in respect of which statutory intervention has become most prevalent – indeed, a key policy instrument – in recent years are education and (especially children's) social services. The School Standards and Framework Act 1998 gave Labour's instinctively 'hands-on' Education Secretary, David Blunkett, powers to intervene in Local Education Authorities to secure higher standards, and, if necessary, to require them to contract out some or all of their functions. Adopting over the years a more graduated and less confrontational approach than at first seemed likely, the Department for Education and Skills' Standards and Effectiveness Unit (SEU) claimed by 2005 to have closed or successfully 'turned round' over 1,300 schools identified by the schools inspectorate, OFSTED, as needing the application of 'special measures'.

Where failure has been judged to be at the level of the whole education authority, rather than the individual school, more radical 'remedial action' has been required. In a few cases, this has taken the form of 'pairing' the failing authority with a more successful one – for example, Rochdale and Blackburn with Darwen. Much more frequently, though, ministers have looked to the private sector, and at least a dozen authorities, following adverse OFSTED inspections, have had to 'outsource' some or all of their education services to private companies: Capita, Nord Anglia, Cambridge Education Associates, and, most notoriously, W. S. Atkins, the international engineers, whose failing takeover of Southwark's schools had itself to be prematurely ended by a further ministerial intervention.

The Blair Government's readiness to 'name and shame' and then intervene extends, though, far beyond education and social services departments. In September 2001, DTLR Secretary of State, Stephen Byers, used for the first time new powers under the Local Government Act 1999 to intervene in Hackney in order to 'protect and improve the key services and ensure the council tackles its budget deficit'. For a time the whole

---

Exhibit 9.3 Comprehensive Performance Assessment (CPA)

What is it?

Part of the Government's agenda for continuously improving public services. Developed out of the Best Value regime, in which external inspectors assessed *individual* council services on two 4-point scales: quality of service (0 to 3 stars) and prospects for improvement (no, unlikely, probably, yes). CPA is similar, but assesses the performance of the *whole council*. Through external inspections and other evidence, all 388 English councils are allocated into one of just 5 categories: from 2002–4, Excellent, Good, Fair, Weak, Poor; from 2005, 4 stars to 0 stars.

Top performing (4- and 3-star) councils are 'rewarded' with various 'freedoms and flexibilities', while 0- and 1-star councils receive external 'engagement' – ministerially appointed officials overseeing and assisting the wayward authority in formulating and implementing a recovery plan.

How are the assessments actually determined?

Three main elements of a council's activities are assessed and allocated scores:

- Its **core service performance**, covering six key service areas: children and young people, social care (adults), housing, environment, culture, benefits. These services are judged on various evidence, including inspection and audit reports, and the council's own service plans.
- Its **use of resources** – financial and strategic management, including its achievement of value-for-money.
- Its **ability to improve** – arrangements for securing continuous improvement. Judgement is by a corporate self-assessment and follow-up external assessment by a small team assembled by the Audit Commission – the body responsible for conducting the whole CPA process.

---

hapless – though since recovered – London borough was in effect run from Whitehall, with no fewer than five central government departments issuing 'Directions' detailing required service improvements in education, social services, waste management and housing benefits, plus action to establish a new system of financial management.

Inspection

If the Thatcher Governments brought a mushrooming of judicial reviews, the Blair Governments' equivalent contribution has been inspections. External regulation of local service providers is hardly new, with schools and police inspectors dating back to the mid-nineteenth century, but in recent years a seriously expensive inspection *industry* has sprung up.

Isn't giving a large, multi-service organisation a single adjectival or star rating a bit crude?

Not 'a bit' – extremely! Even a generally excellent organisation has its known weaknesses, and, more important still, even under-performing organisations have areas of strength and good practice. Inner city authorities representing areas of multiple deprivation felt – with some justification – that they in particular would lose out in any national scoring system.

So how good really is English local government?

Almost too good! Between the first CPA scores – for the 150 single-tier and county councils – in December 2002 and CPA 3 in 2004, Excellent and Good authorities had risen from 51 per cent to 67 per cent, while Weak and Poor authorities had halved, from 23 per cent to 11 per cent. The first assessments of the 238 district councils showed a similarly positive picture, three times as many being classified as Excellent (28) and Good (86) as were Weak (29) and Poor (9).

That's the difficulty with a system required to demonstrate 'continuous improvement' to sceptical local authorities and critical local media: in this case, sooner rather than later, almost everyone becomes at least good, with few left needing major improvement. In 2005, therefore, the Government and Audit Commission changed the scoring system and introduced literally 'a harder test' (Audit Commission, 2005b; also Figure 9.1), with tougher assessment criteria, greater focus on user experience and value-for-money, and the star-based categorisation – plus a '**direction of travel**' label, indicating progress made towards achieving improvement.

There was the same need, though, to avoid showing councils' performance officially worsening, so, contrary to local government apprehensions, 68 per cent of the 150 were still rated 3- or 4-star performers, with over 70 per cent improving strongly or well.

OFSTED, already mentioned, now inspects education authorities as well as schools. Similarly, the Commission for Social Care Inspection examines both council departments and private providers. And there is a large handful of other inspectorates that can descend on a unitary or county authority – covering adult learning, benefit fraud, the fire service, housing, court services, probation, the police, not to mention the inspector-in-chief, the Audit Commission.

Even the Government has acknowledged that the 'architecture' of inspection has got out of hand. In his 2005 Budget the Chancellor of the Exchequer, Gordon Brown, announced a cut in the number of inspectorates by the year 2008 from eleven to four – with single inspectorates for children and learners; health and adult social care; justice and community safety; and local services, this latter bringing together functions of the Audit Commission and the Benefit Fraud Inspectorate. The message is that fewer inspectorates should mean significantly fewer inspections. Meanwhile, Comprehensive Performance Assessment (CPA) will continue until at least 2008 as the focus of the Government's inspection regime – albeit in a revised and more testing form (see Exhibit 9.3 and Figure 9.1).

There is obvious potential value, as most people in local government will concede, in having independent and impartial inspection of public services. It provides external challenge and assurance, and can be an important stimulus to improvement. That recognition, however, is accompanied by almost unanimous criticism of the scale, the overlap, the inflexibility, the overwhelming centralism, and, above all, the phenomenal cost and burden of the present regime. A 2004 survey of county councils found that each county 'was spending almost £500,000 a year and an average of 2,555 days handling inspections, the equivalent of 12 full-time staff'. Across all 36 counties, that equated to well over 400 (mainly senior) staff working full-time on inspection at a cost of £15.7 million (Marinko, 2004, p. 5). The whole inspection industry is estimated to cost over £600 million (Hetherington, 2004) – which, a sceptic might think, is rather a lot to divert from serving the local public to serving national inspectors, especially when a principal outcome of all this diverted time and energy can be damaging to staff morale.

Figure 9.1   *Cartoon – CPA: the harder test*

Source: Local Government Chronicle, 16 June 2005.

It looks, at the very least, illogical to subject high- and low-performing authorities to the same inspection regimes, when the former 'will have already demonstrated they can use external challenge and scrutiny effectively to drive their own continuous improvement' (LGA, 2004a, p. 2). There is, therefore, a strong case indeed for inspection becoming more 'risk-based, proportionate, and effective' (ODPM, 2005e, p. 3); also for some inspection functions being carried out by other means – through peer/partner review, local authorities' own scrutiny arrangements, customer/user mechanisms.

Statutory appeals

Inspectors act at arm's length from their respective departments. In some circumstances, though, ministers may be keen to be seen acting more personally as arbitrators or defenders of the rights of local citizens. Since many local authority powers can adversely affect the interests of individual citizens – for example, the closure of a school, the issue of a compulsory purchase or clearance order, the granting of licences, the refusal of planning permission – they may require ministerial confirmation or approval before they can be implemented, as well as offering aggrieved citizens a statutory right of appeal to the minister and ultimately to the courts.

Finance

Chapter 10 is devoted entirely to finance. Here, therefore, we simply note in passing that additional means available to a central government wishing to control local authorities are through, first, regulating the amount of money they can spend locally and, second, scrutinising the way in which that money is spent. The government – by, for example, effectively capping local budgets and closely controlling capital investment – can and does tightly restrict local spending.

There are countless examples of central government in effect bullying or blackmailing local authorities into doing what it wants – refusing them cash for school repairs, for example, if they refuse to consider establishing city academies. Our concern here, though, is with macro-management, not micro-meddling, and there has been no more macro influence on local authority finances in recent years than 'Gershon' – Sir Peter Gershon's 2004 review of national and local government efficiency, *Releasing Resources to the Front Line*. Gershon required £21 billions of efficiency savings by the public sector by 2007/08, with local government, including police authorities, responsible for delivering £6.45 billion. At least half of these savings were to be 'cashable', releasing resources that can be recycled into frontline service delivery.

In practical terms, each council had to identify its own ways of achieving efficiency gains over three years equivalent to some 2.5 per cent of its revenue budget. Early reactions tended to be that figures on this scale were, as the parliamentary Urban Affairs Select Committee put it, an 'unachievable dream'. In 2005, however, although the efficiency drive was already 'beginning to bite' (*Local Government Chronicle*, 26 May, p. 4), most councils were on course to meet their targets, with the largest savings coming from corporate or 'back office' services – finance, legal, human resources, ICT, asset and estate management – followed by adult social care and procurement, the latter an area where collaboration between several local authorities and other public bodies can yield both swift and almost painless savings. Whether this response says more about authorities' present efficiency or their previous inefficiency is unclear.

Financial scrutiny is exercised principally through the *Audit Commission* in England, and in Scotland, Wales and Northern Ireland through their own audit offices. The Audit Commission was established in 1982 as an executive quango, appointed by what is now the Department for Communities and Local Government, and responsible for ensuring that public money is spent properly within the areas of local government, housing, the criminal justice services, and the fire and rescue services. The Commission appoints external auditors for these bodies, either from its own staff of 'district auditors' or from private accounting firms of accountants such as PricewaterhouseCoopers, Deloitte and Touche, and KPMG.

External auditors traditionally have checked an authority's accounts to satisfy themselves that its (or our) money has been spent legally and reasonably. Nowadays they must also audit for value-for-money (VFM), to confirm that the council is securing the '3Es' – economy, efficiency and effectiveness – in its use of resources. Following this process, the auditors will send an Audit and Inspection Letter to the authority, summarising their views and identifying key issues arising. These letters should be available on councils' own websites, and they are all published on the Audit Commission's site, as are all CPA reports, prepared in its more recently acquired capacity as inspector of local authority service performance.

Though established by a government anxious to impose a tough scrutiny regime on what it saw as financially irresponsible local authorities, the Audit Commission has never been central government's poodle. It has been outspokenly critical of government policy when it has deemed it appropriate, and on occasion strongly supportive of individual councils' spending priorities, when it has judged them to reflect the preferences of the local population. Inevitably, however, it remains a creature of central government and is perhaps seen as rather more so today, with its responsibility for CPA and performance 'league tables'.

Working relationships – the full complexity of sub-central government

We have dealt so far with what bondage magazines might describe as the instruments of control in the relationship – in this case between central and local government: the various means of imposing their will that are available principally to ministers and central departments as a consequence of their superior constitutional and legal status. We now move beyond these formal legalities and look at actual working relationships. The centre, as we have seen, has plenty of capacity to legislate, regulate, direct and exhort,

> but it does so in the context of a system of sub-central government in which day-to-day control and the scope for innovation are in the hands of a range of other elected representatives, appointees and full-time officials and managers. The centre may seek to control, but its influence is limited by the scale and fragmented character of the governmental system it oversees. (Stoker, 1990, p. 127)

Working relationships, then, are complicated. They vary over time, from authority to authority, and from one service area to another. Moreover, local government has *its* resources too. You should by now have come to expect local authorities to differ from one another: to have their own political outlooks and policy agendas, their own service or spending priorities, histories and traditions. The constant danger of seeking to say anything universally generalisable about 'local government' is that there is bound, somewhere, to be an exception.

It is equally important to recognise that, despite the UK's centralist political culture, central government itself is not a single uniform entity either. There are, of course, far fewer central government departments than local authorities, but they too have their own traditions, cultures and ways of working, as well as fundamentally different – and sometimes directly conflicting – approaches to local government. As Lowndes puts it (2002, p. 145): 'The "centre" is not joined-up and local councils experience a myriad of different cross-cutting and often contradictory relationships with central government departments and agencies.'

As local government's 'sponsoring' department, the Department for Communities and Local Government (DCLG) [until May 2006, the Office of the Deputy Prime Minister (ODPM)] would be hoped to be tolerably supportive, but, as Nick Raynsford indicated in an interview towards the end of his four years as Minister for Local Government, other ministers and their departments can need almost constant cultivation:

> He admitted 'there was a genuine anxiety among some ministers about local government. One of my tasks has been to build confidence about

its capacity to deliver.' He said there had been 'a significant change of attitude' at both the Home Office and the Treasury, with both co-operating in recent ODPM reports respectively on neighbourhoods and performance. He remained tactfully tight-lipped about the DfES [Department for Education and Schools]. (Burton, 2005, p. 12)

For their part, those in local government are likely to feel more predisposed towards the DCLG, and even the Treasury – departments that deal with local government 'in the round' – than towards the DfES, the Department of Health and the Home Office, for whom local government can seem merely an inconvenient means to an end.

The reality, in truth, is complex indeed. Not only is there a multiplicity of local authorities, a diversity of central government departments and policy areas, and a constantly changing party political dimension to consider. Account must be taken too of the many other appointed agencies and partnerships that go to make up anything approaching a full picture of what is sometimes usefully labelled '*sub-central government*'. It is a term particularly associated with Rhodes (1988), who adopted it as the sub-title of his comprehensive analysis of government *Beyond Westminster and Whitehall*, if only, as he put it, to draw attention to the fact that links between the centre and sub-central units of government are *not* restricted to the relationship between central departments and local authorities (p. 13). Skelcher (2004b) provides a contemporary illustration (p. 58):

Connexions, Sure Start and a number of other partnerships are essentially the local delivery arms of national ministries. Connexions, for example, delivers the Secretary of State for Education's targets for training and employment of 16 to 19 year olds. In the words that used to be used of education, these are 'national services, locally administered'. As more government initiatives are delivered through local partnerships, so we need to reconceptualise the centre-local relationship.

Our own 'sketch map' in Figure 9.2 is inevitably a brutal simplification. For a start, it omits, purely for reasons of space, much of the regional tier of governance noted in Chapter 5. It does, however, incorporate some of the many other public, private and voluntary sector organisations that now make up the world of *local governance,* and it should convey some impression of just how fragmented both 'central' and 'local government' really are. We have resisted, however, the temptation to relabel it a map of 'inter-governmental relations' for the same reason that we have retained 'local government' for the book's title. It is *primarily* a map of the links between central government departments and local authorities. The broken lines of communication symbolise the myriad relationships that can in theory exist between each local authority and a range of central

Figure 9.2 *Central–local government networks: a sketch map*

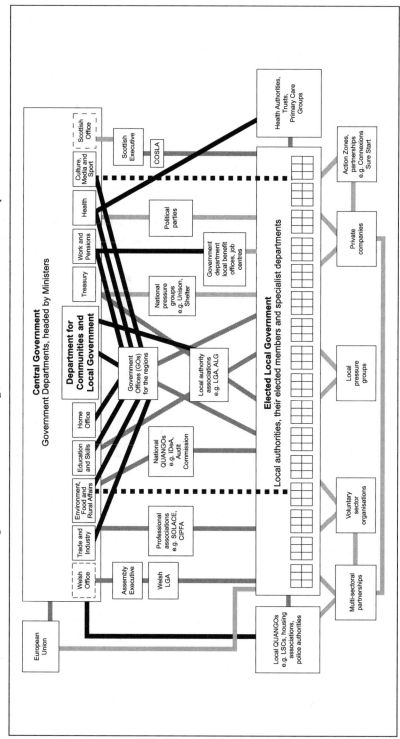

government departments. The unbroken lines signify that in practice much of this contact and attempted influence is necessarily channelled through 'umbrella' organisations and other agencies.

Interpreting central–local relations – a study of mixed messages

In principle, the *scale* of central intervention in local authorities' affairs could be quantified. We could add up all the relevant Acts of Parliament, the plethora of regulations, circulars, guidance notes and statutory instruments emerging from Whitehall and doubtless conclude that the scale of intervention is massive. It is, however, far more difficult to assess the *nature* of the central–local relationship – partly because it changes over time, but mainly because even a 'freeze frame' at a particular point in time will contain, on detailed examination, more complexity than is initially apparent.

In previous editions of this book we ourselves identified five distinguishable C-initialled phases of central–local relations since the 1960s (Wilson and Game, 2002, p. 163, plus Exhibit on linked website). The period until the mid-1970s we characterised as 'Consultative': growing local service spending, much of it centrally financed, with local authorities generally left to their own devices. Accelerating economic decline brought phases of 'Corporatism' – with Labour governments trying to incorporate local authority representatives in securing voluntary expenditure restraint – followed in the 1980s by the 'Confrontation' and 'Control' that were the successive approaches of the Thatcher Administrations, captured in part in our 'Funnel of local authority discretion' (Figure 2.1). Persuasion hadn't worked, so ministers legislated themselves total control over local spending. Authorities that challenged them, like the GLC, were abolished, while the remainder were required to sell off their assets or invite the private sector to bid to take them over. With central financial control established, the Major Administrations ushered in a period of less overt aggression and more 'Conciliation', which in 1997 was inherited by New Labour.

New Labour came into power with high expectations on the part of an unprecedently Labour-dominated local government. The party's parliamentary and local politicians had both opposed, from their differing vantage points, the depredations of the Conservative years, and the latter, while recognising that a partnership of equals was constitutionally impossible, hoped at least for a partnership of spirit and like-mindedness. In practice, although eventually the funding of local services was greatly increased and their improvement became a major government priority, there was no 'step change' reduction (as the deputy prime minister would certainly have put it, had there been) in the central control and direction to which local authorities were subject. The outcome, as in other areas of government policy, was to create among some observers an embittered disillusionment, and, as Stoker noted (2002, p. 430), it is easy to find Labour's approach to central–local relations dismissed as 'a classic example of a hierarchist approach, or in the more common parlance of some newspapers, "control freakery gone mad"'.

We have tried to suggest, in the shaping of our funnel of discretion and also in Exhibit 9.4, that the true picture is rather more ambiguous – indeed, that it has been the Government's policy to convey a deliberately mixed message. Certainly, there is no shortage of ammunition for the 'hierarchists'. Council tax remained unreformed, and the massive central–local imbalance in revenue funding virtually unchanged, with three-quarters coming from the centre and just a quarter from local taxpayers. Despite the party's vehement opposition to the very principle of tax- and expenditure-capping when introduced by the Conservatives in the 1980s, Labour ministers both retained the powers and, from 2004 onwards, used them. Compulsory Competitive Tendering (CCT) was abolished, but was replaced by the equally centralist and far more interventionist regimes of Best Value and CPA. Targets and inspections, as we saw earlier, have gone beyond anything that Conservative Governments ever contemplated.

There is, then, as Stoker concedes (2002, p. 430), 'no point in denying that there are hierarchist facets to New Labour's approach to public service reform at the local level'. The Government believed central prescription was required in order to bring about change. Yet at the same time there has been a localist dimension to Labour's agenda. For example, while the Local Government Act 2000 was highly prescriptive in its regulations about new executive forms of political management, there was more scope for operational distinctiveness than some councils initially appreciated. The same Act also gave local authorities new powers: a new community leadership role, backed by the well-being power, and a duty to prepare community strategies with other local partners. The Health and Social Care Act 2001 gave overview and scrutiny committees of unitary and county councils the power to scrutinize publicly NHS bodies. The Local Government Act 2003 introduced several significant financial flexibilities, most notably the 'prudential' capital regime described in Chapter 10. These and similar developments indicate that a *purely* 'top-down' interpretation of Labour's period in office is simplistic – even if, as Pratchett and Leach suggest (2004, p. 378), it is sometimes necessary to delve beneath the surface:

> Despite a whole range of constraints, choice is a reality ... and extends across a whole range of policy areas. Often it lies in the detail of implementation rather than in wider strategic direction.

Exhibit 9.4 Labour's central–local relations balance sheet

Localist	Centralist/Non-localist
Increased 'real terms' funding for local services, particularly from 2000	Local authorities increasingly 'commissioners', rather than providers, of several major services
'Crude and universal' capping of spending and council tax levels abolished	Selective capping retained, unlike in Scotland, and revived by Labour ministers in 2004
Some relaxation of capital funding controls	No major reappraisal of the role of local government and local democracy
Compulsory Competitive Tendering (CCT) abolished, and priority given to continuous improvement in service quality	No major reform even of local finance, despite repeated promises; no re-localisaton of business rates, or increase in percentage of revenue raised locally; no reform of council tax
Some 'freedoms and flexibilities' for high performing councils – reduction in grant 'ring-fencing', relaxation of inspection and plan requirements	Grant funding increasingly 'ring-fenced' – directed specifically towards ministers' priorities – for example, schools
Introduction of power to promote 'well-being'	CCT replaced by Best Value regime – more bureaucratic, more interventionist – and by centralist, as well as comprehensive, CPA
Restoration of democratic government in Greater London	Discretion has to be 'earned', and in practice is only discretion to do what central government wants and approves
Attempt to establish elected regional assemblies in England	Ever more targets, league tables, inspection and monitoring regimes, plus government insistence on partnership working
Strengthening of local government's community leadership role through political management reforms, including mayoral referendums and overview/scrutiny procedures	Planning responsibilities of English county councils given to unelected regional bodies
Introduction of local public service and local area agreements	Continued restrictions on capital funding force councils to transfer homes
Establishment of Central–Local Partnership – regular meetings of senior ministers and LGA leaders.	Imposition of three restrictive models of executive management, and insistence on mayoral referendums
	Little done to increase accountability of local quangos
	Undisguised contempt for local government from prime minister and other key ministers and departments

The same authors also draw a distinction between the government's major policy priority areas, such as education, and the wide range of other local authority functions: 'There is much greater discretion outside the priority areas' (p. 378); blanket generalisations are dangerous.

The Government's intendedly mixed message on these matters was picked up early by the *Local Government Chronicle*'s cartoonist (see Figure 9.3). It took the form of the carrot and stick – or, as it sometimes seemed, carrot and Semtex. The incoming government wanted to emphasise that it was far more supportive of the principle of local self-government than the outgoing Conservatives had been. However, the present state of local government was unsatisfactory in various ways and in urgent need of reform – not just generally, but in the ways identified in the Government's 'modernisation agenda'. Those councils that accepted this diagnosis and adopted the Government's prescriptions enthusiastically would be rewarded with the metaphorical carrots that later became known as 'freedoms and flexibilities'. Any that mulishly resisted, though – as some had tried to thwart Conservative policies – would be sharply reminded by the bludgeon-brandishing deputy PM, John Prescott, that the national government had both the superior mandate and the greater power. If necessary, ministers could and would intervene, impose their policies, and ultimately hand over the management of the recalcitrant department or authority to another agency.

Figure 9.3 *Cartoon – Carrots and Semtex: New Labour's agenda for British local government*

Source: Local Government Chronicle, 15 August 1997.

The Government's mixed messages have continued into its third term – not surprisingly, given their roots at the heart of New Labour's whole ambivalent view of the public sector: extolling the services it provides but deeply distrustful of the providers. A major example is the mixed giving and taking away of LEA powers in the 2005 Schools White Paper (see Chapter 7). Minor by comparison but very typical are the alcohol licensing powers that local authorities have taken over from magistrates, which specify in immense detail the procedures they are to follow, yet prohibit them from setting fees to reflect their local circumstances or even to cover their costs.

The ODPM and the ministerial odd couple

Local authority working relationships with central government focused in the first, agenda-defining year of the Labour Government's third term on the Office of the Deputy Prime Minister (ODPM) – in previous incarnations the Department for Environment, Transport and the Regions (DETR) from 1997 to 2001, and the Department for Transport, Local Government and the Regions (DTLR) from May 2001 to May 2002. With the creation in 2002 of a separate Department for Transport, the ODPM was not even then – before its mutation in May 2006 into the Department for Communities and Local Government – one of the larger departments. But its responsibilities, and now those of the DCLG, cover a wide range of functions, including – in addition to local government and the regions – housing and planning, homelessness and social exclusion, urban policy and regeneration, fire and resilience, women and equality. With devolution, these 'domestic' functions, and particularly relations with local government, are in Scotland, Wales and Northern Ireland very largely the responsibility of the respective Executives and assemblies.

Following the 2005 General Election, the department's six-member ministerial team was headed, unusually, by two Cabinet ministers: the deputy PM, John Prescott, with overall responsibility for the whole department, and David Miliband, the country's first ever Minister of Communities and Local Government. Intentionally or not, the new ministerial title seemed unusually revealing, both in its ordering and *per se*, as Simon Jenkins (2005) immediately noted:

> These two responsibilities would be considered the same in any normal country. The trouble for Miliband is that his boss regards them as complete opposites. To Blair "community" is sugar and spice and all things nice, pink, soft and politically neutered. Local government is snips and snails and puppy dogs' tails. It is sweaty civic rooms and Old Labour councillors, the hoodies of the public sector. It is where people

like John Prescott have punch-ups. Thus Miliband's task is to promote community but suppress local government … a paradox that [he] cannot possibly resolve.

As things turned out, he didn't have to, for he was suddenly and prematurely replaced, along with Prescott, by Ruth Kelly in the Prime Minister's 'musical chairs' reshuffle of ministers immediately following the May 2006 local elections. Until that reshuffle, though, the contrast in the two ministers' backgrounds – Prescott the Welsh-born, northern-adopted, proudly working-class, 'Old Labour' trade unionist; Miliband the Oxford- and US-educated, academic Blairite son of a Marxist intellectual – was so dramatic that they were inevitably tagged 'the odd couple' (see Figure 9.4), and Miliband's role in particular, like his detailed views, remained somewhat unclear. He was, however, the minister who had publicly to take responsibility in September 2005 for the Government's deeply embarrassing U-turn in postponing indefinitely council tax revaluation, and would have led its response to the delayed Lyons review of the future

Figure 9.4 *Cartoon – The ministerial odd couple*

Source: 'Teal', *Local Government Chronicle*, 26 May 2005.

role and funding of local government, expected in late 2006 (see Exhibit 10.6). More day-to-day ministerial links with the world of local government are maintained by the actual minister for local government – in 2005/06 the unshuffled Phil Woolas, as it happens, the only male in the DCLG's six-minister team.

Considering its range of responsibilities, the DCLG's core London-based staff of around 2,500 may sound modest, and certainly it is a small fraction of the size of big service-providing departments such as Work and Pensions. Unlike the DWP, the DCLG is not a direct service-provider; rather, as Hennessy (1990) described the old Department of the Environment, 'a bit like a Whitehall holding company in the range of activities it supervises to a greater or lesser extent at arm's length' (pp. 439–40). The Department's 2005/06 budget of some £57 billion (ODPM, 2005f, p. 116) put it quite high in the Whitehall league table, but £51 billion of that total was passed on to and spent by local authorities and the Regional Development Agencies, and most of the rest either by its executive agencies – like the Planning Inspectorate – or through the kinds of quangos and partnerships encountered in Chapter 8: the Audit Commission, the Housing Corporation, Housing Action Trusts.

The DCLG has several London addresses, but its centre of operations is the glass-fronted Eland House in Bressenden Place, near Victoria Station, where Ruth Kelly and most of the department's civil servants are based. Staff include economists, statisticians, lawyers and researchers, as well as general administrators and managers, and they are involved in all aspects of policy and legislation, from the modernisation of councils' powers and constitutions to electronic service delivery, from European relations to by-laws for public conveniences.

The DCLG is at the centre of extensive formal and informal communications networks in Whitehall, dealing with any and all local government matters, or, as we phrased it earlier, with local government in the round. Numerous other departments (for example, Education and Skills, Home Office, Health) have their own specific dealings with local authorities, which are handled through formal and informal civil service meetings, various *ad hoc* groups and committees. While the DCLG communicates directly with local authorities through directives and guidance, it spends much time consulting with broader representative bodies, chief among which is the Local Government Association (LGA).

The LGA – local government's national voice

Prior to 1997 there were three major English and Welsh local authority associations representing the three main classes of authority: county councils, metropolitan authorities and district councils. In 1997, after much agonising, it was decided that unification offered local government the best chance of making any political impression on national policy making, and a unified LGA was created. Scotland already had a single association, the Convention of Scottish Local Authorities (COSLA), there is a Welsh LGA, as well as a separate Association of London Government (ALG).

The LGA has had its critics, not least those who would have liked it, despite (or, indeed, because of) its being Labour-led until 2004, to oppose more vigorously some of the Government's centralist record in Exhibit 9.4. But few would deny that, speaking as it can claim to on behalf of its nearly 500 member authorities (including police, fire and transport authorities), it is a significantly more influential 'umbrella' organisation for local government than its predecessors. Like its member councils, the LGA is naturally a party political body. In 2006, therefore, with the Conservatives

---

Exhibit 9.5 The work of the LGA: a national voice for local government

Some of what the LGA was up to in early 2005:

- **Opposing** the Education Secretary's announced intention to introduce three-year ring-fenced budgets for schools, on the grounds that it would further centralise the education system and undermine democratic accountability.
- **Working** closely with the Departments of Transport and Education and Skills to finalise details in the School Transport Bill facilitating new approaches to the provision of school transport.
- **Lobbying** the Government to ensure that local authorities' new powers in the Clean Neighbourhoods and Environment Bill would be backed by adequate financial support and national education campaigns to tackle public attitudes and behaviour.
- **Launching** a paper, *Stronger political leadership, better local government*, arguing that a 'one size fits all' approach to local government will not work, and calling for greater freedom for councils to determine what arrangements best suit local circumstances.
- **Organising** a major conference on youth homelessness, to link in with new legislation requiring local authorities to treat 16 to 18 year olds presenting themselves as homeless as a priority.
- **Financing** a Parliamentary Monitoring and Intelligence Service (PAMIS) to provide specialist online coverage of the activities of Parliament as they affect local government.
- **Criticising** aspects of the Government's identity card scheme: although supportive, in principle, of the idea of a population register, the LGA was concerned to ensure sufficient safeguards to protect personal data privacy.

controlling comfortably the largest number of councils across the country, they led the LGA, under the chairmanship of Kent County Council's Sir Sandy Bruce-Lockhart with a majority of seats on the Executive and on most of the six policy boards that steer the Association's work. An indication of the *way* it seeks to serve as a constant two-way channel of communication between local and central government can be seen in Exhibit 9.5, which lists a small sample of its activities early in 2005.

Government Offices for the Regions

If the LGA is the national voice of local government, the nine Government Offices (GOs) – co-ordinated by a Regional Co-ordination Unit (RCU) in the DCLG – are the regional voice of central government. Set up in 1994 and extended greatly under Labour since 1997, they bring together the regional services of the nine departments shown in Figure 9.1 plus the Cabinet Office. They are the third main institutional arm – with Regional Development Agencies and Assemblies – in the regional tier of governance described in Chapter 5, and work increasingly closely with local authorities.

With a 2005/06 budget of around £10 billion, GOs are the principal channel through which much government policy is delivered nowadays, particularly cross-cutting projects in areas such as regional economic performance, environmental improvement, transport, health and education. They manage spending programmes directly on behalf of departments, monitor and give feedback on the effectiveness of these programmes, link departmental policies, and, particularly through the RCU, provide a previously largely absent regional voice in national policy formulation. They obviously play a vital role in the Labour Government's aim of reducing disparities between and within regions, and, with their responsibility for negotiating and overseeing local area agreements (see Exhibit 17.6), they will be leaders too in the drive towards more 'joined-up' government.

Some conceptual models

In the final section of this chapter we outline some of the models that have been applied to the study and interpretation of central–local relations. You should think and make use of these models in much the same way – to use Loughlin's analogy (1996b, p. 53) – as you would maps. For, like maps, they are deliberate simplifications of the real world that should enable us to understand its complexities and find our way through them a little more easily.

Agency model

The agency model sees local authorities as having a completely subordinate relationship to central government: as arms or agents of the centre, with little or no discretion in the task of implementing national policies. From our accounts of the increasing by-passing of elected local government and the growing dominance of the centre, it might be supposed that the agency model is nowadays an accurate characterisation of reality. Such an interpretation, though, ignores the substantial policy diversity that manifestly still exists among our local authorities. Central government does exercise tight financial control, but that control does not produce anything approaching uniform expenditure patterns or service performance. This can be demonstrated in many ways, but one of the most insightful is to compare – and then try to explain – the financial and other statistics compiled each year by CIPFA (the Chartered Institute of Public Finance and Accountancy). All councils are required to produce such statistics, enabling their service figures to be compared with those of other councils of the same type – as in Exhibit 9.6.

Far more fun – sorry, informative – but difficult to demonstrate here because of limitations of space is to do the same kind of exercise using the DCLG's excellent Local Government Performance website (Googleable, of course). The site enables you to compare your own or any other authority with any selection of others, on dozens of *Best Value Performance Indicators* (BVPIs). These PIs are mainly produced by central government departments, and each year councils have to publish locally – as, perhaps, a double-page spread in the local paper or in their own free newspaper – their audited performance measures against these indicators, drawing attention no doubt to what they are shown to be doing well, what services they are prioritising, and even why on some PIs they appear to be lagging behind other councils of the same type. All PIs and all council performance measures are accessible on the DCLG site (see also Exhibit 17.2), which also enables you to draw charts, plotting performances on different indicators against each other.

These comparisons can be fascinatingly revealing in themselves, but, particularly if you're using your own local authority and area, you may feel you can begin to explain, or at least speculate about, the variations you will undoubtedly find. Many factors may suggest themselves: political control, pressure group activity, differences in the geography, economy and socio-economic character of the area, but *not* population size, since all these statistics are *per capita* or the equivalent. You should also remember that expenditure statistics, like those in Exhibit 9.6, are not performance measures; they tell us simply what is being put into the provision of a service, which may or may not relate to the quality of that service or to the value for money being received by local users and taxpayers. PIs obviously

Exhibit 9.6 Local authority service statistics, 2002/2003: some comparisons

| | SECONDARY EDUCATION | | SOCIAL SERVICES | LIBRARIES | RECREATION | ECONOMIC DEVELOPMENT |
	Spending per pupil (£)	Pupils per qualified teacher	Net cost per capita (£)	Net cost per capita (£)	Net cost per capita (£)	Net cost per capita (£)
A. UNITARY AUTHORITIES						
Bracknell Forest	3,550	15.6	216.66	20.69	44.40	0.33
Hartlepool	3,873	16.5	n/a	52.29	70.38	21.74
Kingston-upon-Hull	4,019	16.1	336.10	20.21	87.00	21.47
Leicester	3,679	9.7	276.84	17.84	68.10	11.70
Middlesbrough	4,204	n/a	291.47	18.03	77.42	50.46
Nottingham	4,354	11.7	n/a	17.09	n/a	n/a
Rutland	3,706	19.2	156.24	n/a	n/a	6.13
South Gloucestershire	3,562	16.5	169.20	9.64	10.37	3.38
Swindon	3,139	n/a	213.45	n/a	66.90	n/a
Southampton	3,266	19.3	260.46	20.14	68.68	26.60
All English Unitaries	3,597	16.1	246.82	16.33	50.01	12.36
Percentage variation between highest and lowest	39	99	115	442	739	15,191

B. ENGLISH COUNTIES

Devon	3,394	16.7	247.77	11.71	n/a	2.43
Durham	3,530	19.9	n/a	14.51	7.93	11.61
Hampshire	3,390	13.2	174.41	14.02	11.43	1.69
Hertfordshire	3,526	16.6	222.82	17.35	0.92	0.82
Leicestershire	3,381	16.1	166.81	14.58	10.84	2.71
Lincolnshire	3,564	16.3	198.82	11.10	5.31	7.80
Northumberland	3,335	15.5	n/a	13.98	2.99	14.28
Suffolk	3,233	17.2	210.77	11.68	3.16	5.16
Surrey	3,375	16.4	217.79	13.89	3.38	0.69
Worcestershire	4,802	18.0	n/a	n/a	n/a	2.23
All English counties	**3,469**	**16.7**	**211.40**	**13.96**	**4.21**	**3.44**
Percentage variation between highest and lowest	49	51	49	56	1142	1970

Notes: ▢ signifies highest figure; ◯ signifies lowest figure; n/a = not available.

Source: Data from CIPFA, *Local Government Comparative Statistics, 2003* (CIPFA, 2004), pp. 64–71.

should be performance measures, but some you will find, though interesting, are simply descriptive statistics and tell you little, if anything, about the performance of the council.

Trying to explain even input differences can be a hazardous exercise and one we do not intend to attempt here. Our main aim in introducing these comparative measures is to question the agency model by highlighting the apparent extent of budgetary and policy discretion that exists among councils with exactly the same formal responsibilities. Even in a largely statutory service such as school education, the percentage variations may strike you as being significant. But at the mainly or entirely discretionary end of the service spectrum, the recreation and economic development expenditure differences and some of the performance variations become massive. Councils clearly do vary in efficiency and in the priority they give to different aspects of their service provision. They have, in other words, a degree of *choice*, which is why we suggest that, on its own, the agency model is a less than fully satisfactory representation of the central–local relationship.

Power-dependence model

This is an elaboration of the *partnership model,* which sees central government and local authorities as more or less equal partners. The partnership model itself is unsatisfactory in at least two respects. The concept of partnership tends to be left vague and imprecisely defined. It also disregards the constitutional difficulty of Britain being a unitary state, and local government being necessarily, therefore, a subordinate creation of the national Parliament. To circumvent these criticisms academics developed an alternative power-dependence model. This model postulates that both central departments and local authorities have *resources* - legal, financial, political, informational, and so on – that each can use against the other, and against other organisations (see Exhibit 9.7).

The model thus sees power in relative terms, hingeing on a process of bargaining and exchange. The central–local relationship certainly isn't evenly balanced, but councils do have significant assets of their own that they can exploit: local knowledge and professional expertise, their networking and negotiating skills, and above all their position as the elected and concerned representatives of their communities. Its obvious appeal is that neither central nor local government are depicted as monolithic blocs. This is also, though, one of its alleged weaknesses, for it has regularly been criticised (see, e.g., Houlihan, 1988, p. 70; Cochrane, 1993, p. 25) for understating the superior power of central government. It is said to pay insufficient attention to the internal politics of organisations, and insufficient consideration to the broader (capitalist) economic and political system within which these inter-governmental relations take

---

Exhibit 9.7 The resources of central and local government

CENTRAL GOVERNMENT	LOCAL GOVERNMENT
• Controls legislation and delegated powers	• Employs all personnel in local services, far outnumbering civil servants
• Provides and controls the largest proportion of local authorities' current expenditure through the Revenue Support Grant (RSG)	• Has, through both councillors and officers, detailed local knowledge and expertise
• Controls individual authorities' total expenditure and taxation levels by 'capping'	• Controls the implementation of policy
• Controls the largest proportion of local capital expenditure	• Has limited powers to raise own taxes and set own service charges
• Sets standards for and inspects some services	• Can decide own political priorities and most service standards, and how money should be distributed among services
• Has national electoral mandate.	• Has local electoral mandate.

Source: Based on Rhodes (1988), Figure 2.2, p. 42.

---

place. Such points should not be disregarded; nor are they by Rhodes (1986b), progenitor of the model, who saw it and the conceptual debate it generated of sufficient 'continuing relevance' to justify a 'revisit' (Rhodes, 1999b, esp. chs 5 and 6).

Policy communities and networks

A limitation of both the agency and power-dependence models is that they are essentially 'bilateral', and therefore fail to embrace the complexities of inter-governmental relations which, as we have seen in Chapters 7 and 8, are far wider than a simple central government–local authority axis. Both models focus on *institutional* or organisational relationships – at the inevitable expense of policy systems, policy communities and policy networks. The main point of studying political and governmental institutions should be to understand better how they inter-relate to make and implement policies.

Our local authorities are multi-service organisations and 'local authority policy-making', even in the age of cross-sectoral partnerships, still takes

---

Exhibit 9.8 Policy communities

Characteristics of policy communities include:

- A limited number of participants with some groups consciously excluded.
- A dominant economic or professional interest.
- Frequent interaction between all members of the community on all matters related to the policy issues.
- Consistency in values, membership and policy outcomes over time.
- Consensus, with the ideology, values and broad policy preferences shared by all participants.
- Exchange relationships, with all members of the policy community having some resources.
- Bargaining between members with resources.
- The hierarchical distribution of resources within the participating organisations, so that the leaders can guarantee the compliance of their members.

Source: Based on Rhodes (1999b), p. 143.

---

place for the most part within service-specific 'policy communities' based on education, social services, planning and so on. The power-dependence model could be said to concentrate on the 'national community for local government', while substantially ignoring the multiplicity of other functional policy communities and policy networks.

Policy communities, as defined by Rhodes and Marsh, have the characteristics listed in Exhibit 9.8 (Rhodes, 1999b, p. 143). It is easy to see from this listing the thematic continuity with the power-dependence model, and, with its emphasis on professional interests, a direct applicability to the profession-based world of British local government. Policy communities, in short, seem to have a closer congruence than superficially neater models with the complex and sheer messy reality of local governance that we encountered in Chapter 8.

Chapter 10

Local Finance

Lady Godiva and other myths

One of many myths about local finance concerns Lady Godiva, whose husband Leofric, Earl of Mercia, agreed to abolish the Heregeld tax on the local peasantry if she rode naked on a white horse through the streets of eleventh-century Coventry. Sadly, killjoy historians reckon that, real persons though they both were, the equestrian bit – and presumably the tax cut – was invented by medieval tourist development officers to attract pilgrims to the city. A more contemporary myth is the one that emerges whenever people are asked in opinion polls what proportion of council services are paid for by their council tax. Typically, the guess – and it almost always is a guess – is between 70 and 80 per cent, with 20 to 30 per cent coming from central government (ODPM, 2003, p. 3). Key purposes of this chapter are to emphasise how the truth is *precisely the reverse* (see Figure 10.4), to indicate the consequences of what, from local government's perspective, is a debilitatingly adverse balance of funding, and to reduce the necessity for some of that guesswork.

The first part of the chapter outlines and illustrates the basic elements of local government finance and budget-making – from the reader's perspective: that of an aware, service-using, and probably tax-paying citizen. Specifically, we seek to arm readers with the information necessary to interpret their own council tax demand and understand the main decisions that produced it. Later, we provide some recent historical and comparative context, not least to enable us to appreciate why, as noted at the start of Chapter 9, a body such as the Congress of Local and Regional Authorities of Europe (CLRAE) should see the system and process we have been describing as undemocratically centralist.

Your own tax bill

We start with the council tax, introduced by the Major Government in April 1993 as a politically necessary replacement for the poll tax or community charge – of which more later. Specifically, we suggest readers look at their own council tax bills and at the accompanying explanatory information sent out by their local council – particularly the details of the council's budget. If, perhaps as a student, you have no personal tax bill, try to borrow one, or go to the Budget, Accounts and Council Tax pages of your council's website and look for the Budget or Council Tax Leaflet or a Summary Statement of Accounts. With luck, other goodies will be found there, such as a glossary or jargon-buster, and a reader-friendly description of the council's approach to budgeting.

At the foot of your tax bill – the bottom-line figure – will be the amount that you or your household are required to pay. We shall explain, using Birmingham City Council's 2005/06 budget for illustration, how that bottom line figure was calculated. Your council will, though, have provided its own explanation, in the various additional leaflets it sent out with the bill. These may include:

- The budget and spending plans of the *billing authority* that sent the bill – your district, borough or unitary council;
- The separate budgets and spending plans of *precepting authorities* entitled to have tax known as a 'precept' collected by the billing authority on their behalf – county and possibly parish, town and community councils, and police and fire authorities;
- Explanatory Notes from the Treasurer's or Finance Department of the billing authority, detailing possible methods of payment, appeal procedures, discounts and benefit entitlements – often translated into relevant languages.

This information is one of the many ways in which local authorities are considerably more open and accountable than central government chooses to be. The Inland Revenue provides no such literature about central government's spending plans when it sends out tax returns for taxpayers to complete.

Capital and current spending

If we turn first not to the tax bill itself but to the accompanying budget or council tax leaflet, it will be clear that we need to start with some basic definitions.

> *BUDGET* – a statement defining a council's policies over a specified period of time in terms of finance.

The 'specified period of time' is obviously crucial. Instinctively, we think of budgets as annual events, but a local authority, spending perhaps several hundred million pounds each year, cannot possibly afford to think only of the short term. It will try to forecast the future and plan at least three years ahead. The first noteworthy feature, therefore, of any council's budget is its division into *current* and *capital* expenditure.

CURRENT (also known as REVENUE) EXPENDITURE - the day-to-day spending needed to keep services running: staff wages and salaries, books for schools, office equipment, petrol for refuse collection vehicles, heating bills in children's homes, and so on.

CAPITAL EXPENDITURE – spending which produces longer-term assets, often expensive, but whose benefits will last beyond the next financial year: purchase of land, construction of buildings and roads, major items of equipment.

Far more of local government's spending nowadays goes on current running costs than on capital investment, as shown in Exhibit 10.1. But it was not always so. The capital:current spending ratio increased massively over recent decades, from 1:2 in the 1960s to 1:6 in the 1980s to over 1:11 in 1998/99 (Wilson and Game, 2002, p. 181), largely because of central governments' relentless pressure on local authorities to limit their capital spending. This trend has been reversed under Labour, and the 2003/04 ratio was 1:9, but an impression of how comparatively small a step that reversal represents can perhaps be gained from Derek Wanless's (2002) study for the Treasury of the long-term financial needs of the NHS. Wanless calculated that the cumulative under-investment in the health service between 1972 and 1998, compared to the European average, had

---

Exhibit 10.1 Local authority spending, England 2003/04 – current vs capital

	Current (%)	Capital (%)	Total £ billion	Total %
Education	35	23	37.8	34
Social services	19	2	18.8	17
Housing (excl. Housing Revenue Account)	10	28	12.9	17
Police and courts	10	5	10.9	10
Local environmental services (LES)*	9	16	9.2	8
Highways and transport	7	21	9.1	8
Culture, sports and recreation	4	4	4.3	4
Fire	2	1	2.0	2
Central and other services	6	1	6.2	6
Total (£ bn)	**98.9**	**12.3**	**111.2**	

Note: * LES include refuse collection and disposal, environmental health, planning, economic development, etc.

Source: Data from ODPM (2005g), Tables 3.2a and 4.1c, pp. 62, 90

been an almost incredible £267 billion (p. 37). We know of no comparable figures for local government services, but capital under-investment was by no means limited to the NHS.

The total expenditure figures at the foot of Exhibit 10.1 indicate the scale and national economic significance of local government in Britain. Local government today accounts for about a quarter of all government spending, and about 10 per cent of the country's gross domestic product (GDP) of £455 billion in 2003/04, representing some £1,900 for every single resident (ODPM, 2005g, p. 9). In Scotland especially (and in Wales), that last *per capita* figure would be even higher.

The percentage figures in Exhibit 10.1 demonstrate the still-prominent positions of education, in particular, and housing in the authorities with responsibility for these services, notwithstanding the great changes in the nature of those responsibilities that we noted in Chapter 7. The contrasting character of these two major services can be seen in the first two columns of the Exhibit. Education, like social services, is labour-intensive; housing, like highways and transport, highly capital-intensive.

The current spending of local authorities understandably receives the bulk of both councillors' and citizens' attention. It will be our chief concern too, but we should look first at councils' capital spending programmes, because they are the embodiment of any council's longer-term political and strategic objectives. They have to be financed in very different ways from current spending; and, once started, they can have major implications for subsequent years' current budgets.

Financing capital spending – major reform

We noted how central governments have sought continuously to regulate local authorities' capital spending. In recent years that regulation was based on the Local Government and Housing Act 1989, which gave central government effective control over three of the four main methods of capital financing: borrowing (32 per cent of the total in 2003/04), capital receipts (16 per cent), and capital grants (28 per cent). These capital constraints were resented by local government quite as much as the comparably tight controls over current spending, and their substantial relaxation in April 2004 was the most important local finance reform since the abolition of the poll tax.

Borrowing – welcome to Prudence

Until 2004, if a council wanted to borrow to finance any project whose cost would be spread over several years, it had to get ministerial approval. Each year, the Government gave every local council a *Basic Credit Approval*, reinforced perhaps by *Supplementary Credit Approvals* for particular projects, which specified the maximum sums it could borrow for investment purposes – not the maximum sum of a government interest-free loan or any other kind of loan, but the maximum that this elected and publicly accountable body was permitted to borrow at competitive interest rates on the open market.

It took a little time, but by 2000 the Labour Government acknowledged in a Green Paper that 'the present capital control system blurs accountability, limits local financial freedom, and has become an obstacle to effective capital investment' (DETR, 2000, para. 4.4). Outlined in that Green Paper and introduced in the Local Government Act 2003 was the *Prudential system*, the essence of which is to treat local authorities a little less like irresponsible children and, provided they could afford to service the debt without extra government support, permit them to borrow up to a level that they themselves calculate they can afford, using the Prudential Code drawn up by CIPFA (the Chartered Institute of Public Finance and Accountancy). If they require government assistance to cover the borrowing costs, that is available as before, up to a specified limit, and known as *Supported Capital Expenditure (Revenue)* or 'supported borrowing' in Scotland.

Inevitably, the prudential regime is reinforced by a government reserve power to impose borrowing and credit ceilings, both nationally and on individual councils, but in fact the system itself encourages responsibility by forcing a council to consider value for money, its future revenue streams and council tax implications at the time of borrowing in a way that Credit Approvals did not.

There are several benefits to local authorities in prudential borrowing. They can focus on outcomes – what they want to achieve, rather than on inputs – what they were told they could afford. They can undertake self-financing investment – such as the extension of a leisure centre that will earn additional income, as well as create local employment. And it offers an alternative to councils who are wary, for whatever reason, of PFI deals with the private sector (see Chapter 8). Larger authorities in particular were quick to seize this new opportunity. Birmingham is modernising its National Exhibition Centre and improving its housing stock to the national Decent Homes Standard. Other councils were renovating or building new schools and residential homes, constructing car parks, refurbishing libraries, and, in the case of Cornwall, replacing three Torpoint ferries (LGA, 2005d). The biggest project by far, though, is Transport for London's £2.9 billion bond issue to finance station and line improvements, which sounds great unless you are cynical enough to see it also as a rather effective way of shifting some of the massive pre-Olympic transport investment costs from the Treasury on to London taxpayers and farepayers (Gosling, 2004).

Using capital receipts

A second way for councils to finance capital spending is by using money raised by selling assets such as land, buildings and housing. Again, though, until 2004, governments had set limits on the proportions of these receipts that were 'usable' to fund new capital spending. For most of the 1990s, councils could use for new investment a maximum of 25 per cent of receipts from housing sales, and 50 per cent of receipts from the disposal of other assets. Remaining receipts, said the Conservative Government, should go to paying off outstanding debts. The Labour Government relaxed these limits in 1998, but the 'set aside' in relation to housing receipts continued until 2004. Now no part of a receipt needs to be set aside, although instead there is a new *pooling system*, requiring local authorities to pay the Government a proportion of the capital receipts from asset sales. As the saying goes: what the right hand giveth, the left hand taketh away.

Capital grants

The Government, through the Single Regeneration Budget or programmes such as Sure Start and New Deal for Communities (see Chapters 7 and 8), makes capital grants to local authorities, usually for specific purposes. So too does the National Lottery, and also the European Union, both through its structural funds, such as the European Regional Development Fund (ERDF) and the European Social Fund (ESF), and through more focused initiatives. These grants can be substantial and crucial to the viability of major developments – such as Birmingham's £180 million International Convention Centre and Symphony Hall, some £50 million of which came from the European Union. Here too the Local Government Act 2003 relaxed previous constraints a little, and grants can now be given by government departments for a wider range of purposes.

Using current (revenue) income

The one source of capital finance available to a council that, even in the 1990s, was not subject to direct government control was its own revenue income – from local taxes, rents and other charges. But in a period of financial constraint, that freedom may seem like the freedom we all have to dine at the Ritz: the many more immediate calls on a council's government-capped revenue budget are likely to appear more practically and politically insistent.

The capital budget

We saw in Exhibit 10.1 that, nationally, the services with the biggest capital budgets are housing, education, highways and transportation. Among individual councils, though, capital budget profiles will vary considerably, both according to the range of their responsibilities and from one year to another. Details of your own council's main capital projects should be itemised in its budget; also its principal sources of capital finance. So you should be able to see, for example, whether your council is undertaking any prudential or unsupported borrowing, as well as its capital:current spending ratio.

Birmingham's 2005/06 capital budget was, as it happened, utterly exceptional – partly because, as the country's largest urban authority, it always is, but mainly because of the distorting effect of the Council's one-off £215 million bond issue to finance the upgrading and refurbishment of the National Exhibition Centre referred to above. That bond issue inflated the capital budget to £552 million and produced what by contemporary standards was an extraordinary capital:current ratio of 1:6 – but one projected to return to a more normal 1:9 in 2007/08. Of the remainder of the city's capital budget, over half went to housing and redevelopment, including £58 million on heating, insulating, re-roofing and rewiring its 80,000 housing stock; £67 million was invested in education, mainly through capital grants from the Government – £15 million from the New Opportunities Fund to improve schools' PE and sports facilities, £15 million from the Sure Start programme to create 2,226 child care places in Children's Centres; £52 million went to transportation, and smaller capital projects included the restoration of Handsworth's Victorian park, the extension of Saltley Leisure Centre, upgrading car park security, and, like almost all local authorities, improving access to council buildings and services to comply with the Disability Discrimination Act.

Current or revenue spending

How much is to be spent? On what? Where is the money coming from? The three fundamental questions we have just asked of our council's capital budget are similarly applicable to its considerably larger revenue budget. In fact, the answers should be more easily obtainable, as the main purpose of the tax demand literature is to present and explain the council's revenue budget: its planned expenditure on the day-to-day provision of services for the coming financial year. With luck, yours may be one of the enterprising councils that seek to convey such information in as eye-catching a manner as possible, with imaginative use of illustrative diagrams and graphics.

Exhibit 10.2 Birmingham City Council's revenue budget, 2005/06

MAJOR SERVICES (by Cabinet portfolio/committee)
Leader's Budget incl. NEC, Convention Centre, Indoor Arena, cabinet office
Deputy Leader's Budget Rent allowances and rebates, council tax benefit, benefit service, markets
Education and Lifelong Learning
Social Care and Health
Transportation and Street Services incl. highway maintenance, traffic management, refuse collection and disposal
Leisure, Sport and Culture incl. libraries, parks, nature conservation, museums, support for the arts
Housing
Regeneration incl. economic development, employment creation, business support
Local Services and Community Safety incl. neighbourhood renewal, community development and safety
District and Constituency Committees
Regulatory Committees Planning, Licensing, Public Protection
Other Services (incl. Equalities and human resources)
Total Portfolio/Committee Council expenditure
Less: Capital receipts
Plus: Contingencies
Total Council expenditure
Plus: Contribution to reserves
COUNCIL'S NET BUDGET REQUIREMENT

Note: * = under 0.5.
Source: Data from Birmingham City Council, *Budget 2005/06*.

Gross expenditure		Income from charges and specific grants (£ m)	Net expenditure		
2005/06 (£ m)	% of total		2005/06 (£ m)	Change from 2004/05 (£ m)	% of total
168	6	101	67	−2	4
434	16	408	26	+1	2
973	35	205	768	+50	50
451	16	106	345	+44	23
127	5	37	90	+6	6
56	2	11	45	+4	3
324	12	285	39	+5	3
76	3	55	21	+2	1
29	1	24	5	=	*
111	4	14	97	−2	6
30	1	15	15	−1	1
11	*	*	11	=	1
2,790	100	1,261	1,529	+107	100
(85)			(85)		
7			7		
2,712			1,451		
			1		
			1,452		

But, in whatever way they are presented, you should encounter some figures set out under service or cabinet portfolio headings that will resemble those of Birmingham City Council in Exhibit 10.2, even if the figures themselves are on a very different scale. In order to interpret them, two further definitions are required:

GROSS SPENDING – the total cost of providing the council's services, *before* taking into account rents, fees and charges for services, and income from government grants.

NET SPENDING – gross spending *minus* income from rents, fees and charges and from *specific* government grants for particular projects or services – for example, towards rent rebates and allowances, council tax benefits, Learning and Skills Councils.

We see from the first column of Exhibit 10.2 that Birmingham City Council proposed to spend a total of nearly £2.8 billion on its day-to-day service provision in 2005/06. Even after the transfer of further education and sixth form colleges out of local authority control and the opting-out of some of its secondary schools, a third of the council's gross spending and half its net spending goes on education, with roughly 60 per cent of that sum on teachers' salaries. The next biggest net spender, similarly labour intensive, is social services, with a clientele in Birmingham of over 50,000 children, elderly and disabled people. These services meet, respectively, about a fifth and a quarter of their expenditure through income from service charges and specific grants for designated purposes, such as nursery and child care, special education, children leaving care, asylum seekers, and the treatment of mental illness.

By comparison, nearly 90 per cent of Birmingham's housing expenditure is met by income, much of it from rents on the council's still huge housing stock of around 70,000 dwellings. Since 1990, Housing Revenue Accounts (HRAs) have been 'ring-fenced'. Not only must they be kept separately, but no transfers are permitted between HRAs and a council's General Fund, to subsidise either tenants or council tax payers. There is a housing subsidy scheme, but no longer subject to the political discretion of local authorities. They now receive a formula-defined specific grant from the government to administer on its behalf – in Birmingham's case, through the Deputy Leader's budget. The arrangement is similar to the one-time provision of LEA mandatory student grants, though here the payment takes the form of rent rebates and allowances to low-income tenants. As a result of these two major sources of income – rents and government subsidies – Birmingham's *net* revenue spending on housing is lower than might be expected of what once proclaimed itself Western Europe's largest landlord.

The Leader's and Deputy Leader's budgets are, of course, a consequence of the move to executive-based local government, as is the whole presentation of the budget by cabinet portfolio. The number, titles and responsibilities of portfolios will vary from council to council – Birmingham's District and Constituency Committees being an interesting example. In 2003, Birmingham embarked on a radical 'Going Local' policy of devolving some of its powers to 11 constituency-based District Committees comprising the elected councillors in the area, with services such as street cleaning, refuse collection, libraries, sports and leisure facilities organised in local district offices. As shown in Exhibit 10.2, by 2005/06 these District Committees were administering a combined budget of over £100 million – money previously controlled by councillors and officers in the Council's city centre headquarters.

Levies and precepts

Identifying the council's net spending requirements is just the first step in the determination of an individual's local tax bill. To the council-provided services listed in Exhibit 10.2 must be added the services provided for Birmingham residents by bodies that cannot themselves directly demand and collect local taxes. In Birmingham – and the other six West Midlands Metropolitan districts – there are four such bodies:

1. *The West Midlands Police Authority* - formerly a joint board, but now a separate Authority, half of whose members are councillors nominated by the West Midlands district councils and the other half local magistrates and the Home Secretary's nominees. Like all police authorities, it receives a direct central government grant equivalent to half of its net revenue expenditure.
2. *The West Midlands Fire and Civil Defence Authority* - still a joint board of nominated district councillors.
3. *The West Midlands Passenger Transport Authority* - another joint board, the largest slice of whose revenue budget provides free bus and rail travel for senior citizens and concessionary fares for children and school students.
4. *The Environment Agency* – a quango that maintains flood defences and water resources, through a Midlands Region Flood Defence Committee.

Just like the City Council, all these bodies have their own capital and revenue budgets, funded in part through a combination of loans, grants, capital receipts and revenue income. But they also finance some of their revenue expenditure by means of a *precept* or *levy* on their tax-collecting district authorities, divided among them according to their population size. These latter councils are therefore required to collect from their local taxpayers, in addition to their own tax demands, these other monies, and then hand them straight over to the various precepting and levying authorities.

Birmingham's *total* net revenue requirement thus included in 2005/06 over £80 million that it had to collect, but over which it had no direct control. As may be imagined, this obligation can be distinctly irritating to city councillors, who have to take the political responsibility and blame for a tax level, part of which they can have hardly any influence over, even indirectly. But their irritation is mild compared to that of some of their shire district council colleagues. For they have to collect a county council precept that may amount to almost 90 per cent of their total tax demands, plus, in some cases, an additional few pounds in parish council precepts which, just to add to their frustration, are not even capped.

One of the tensions in the two-tier parts of our local government system is that in non-metropolitan England it is not the counties – with their bigger spending education, social services and transport responsibilities – that are designated billing and tax-collecting authorities. The council tax is a property tax, and therefore most obviously collected by the local housing authorities, the much smaller and inevitably lower spending district councils (see Exhibit 7.1). This position, you may be sure, will be emphasised by district councils in their explanatory budget literature. Just look, they will say, at all the housing, leisure, environmental and community services we provide to enhance your quality of life, and all for less than the cost of a weekly pint of beer.

Financing current spending

There are two final 'technical' adjustments to be made to the spending side of our council's current account. It has to be decided how much to set aside for any unforeseen items of expenditure, known as 'contingencies', and how much to keep as balances or reserves. With those adjustments made, Birmingham City Council's *total net spending requirement* for 2005/06 amounted to a formidable £1,452 million, or about £1,450 per resident. The obvious next question is: how is it to be found?

There is a certain symmetry to British local government finance. There are four main methods of raising capital finance, and four main ways of funding revenue spending.

Charges

Local authorities have always set fees and charges for the use of some of their services – passenger transport, car parks, home helps, school meals, swimming baths and other leisure facilities. They also collect council rents. In Birmingham's case, these charges collectively meet 16 per cent of the council's gross current expenditure. Since the Local Government and Housing Act 1989, councils have been able to charge for any of their services except education, the police and fire services, elections, and library book borrowing. This extension of charging was part of the Conservatives' programme to increase local accountability by making consumers more directly aware of the cost and value of the services they receive.

Most charges are discretionary, councils deciding for themselves what they wish to charge, or what they feel the market will bear. They can try to encourage the use of a service, such as adult education classes or day nurseries, by setting a *social* charge, below the full cost of provision. They can *just* cover the provision cost; impose a *means-related* charge based on ability to pay, as for some residential homes; or a *market* charge to maximise profit. Finally, they can try to limit the use of certain services, such as city centre car parks or cemetery burials, by imposing a *deterrent* charge.

Such decisions – whether or not to subsidise a particular service, by how much and in what way, or whether to try to maximise profit – raise most fundamental political questions. Quite properly, they offer councillors a ready-made subject for debate whenever charges and a council's charging policy come up for review. Different economic, social and political objectives will be argued, and sometimes intriguing policy decisions taken – which is what makes your council's Fees and Charges booklet one of its few publications you might just possibly contemplate for bedside reading.

Even the charges for standard services – car parking, leisure centres, refuse collection, public conveniences – can raise interesting issues, especially if you know the area or can make comparisons with other councils. Why do some councils encourage their senior citizens to swim, while others extort as much as possible from them? Does your council charge for children's burials? Are there 'deterrent' burial rates for non-residents? Why are allotments about the only things still measured in rods? More recondite services can be even more fascinating. Do the car boot sale charges include the use of mobile toilets, or are they, as it were, a hidden extra? Why is the treatment of bedbugs and cockroaches, even during standard hours, more expensive than wasp and hornet nests out of hours? Does your council's dangerous wild animals licensing policy differentiate discriminatorily between vertebrates and invertebrates? However you answer such questions, it is difficult to argue, after even a brief perusal of their charging practices, that councils have been stripped of all their powers of decision and discretion.

Government grants

Grants, like charges, have long been an integral feature of local government finance, although their nature, role and scale have all changed significantly in recent years. Focusing on the budget process, we shall concentrate mainly on one particular grant: the Revenue Support Grant (RSG). There are, however, numerous other grants paid by central government to local authorities, and many different reasons for paying them. The two most fundamental purposes of grants, though, are compensation and persuasion.

Compensation takes various forms: one form being compensation to local councils for providing certain necessary services – for example, for disabled children, carers, or asylum seekers – that are acknowledged to be in the public interest and for which, therefore, local taxpayers should not have to foot the whole bill. Councils may be compensated too for their varying spending needs and taxable resources. The rationale behind the RSG is that local authorities should be able (and be given grant incentives) to provide a common standard of service at broadly the same cost to local taxpayers across the whole country.

The *persuasion* motive for grants can be seen as a straightforward wish by central government to influence some aspect of local spending: those who pay the piper expect to call the tune. Grants can be used to promote spending on certain services, to enforce minimum standards, to encourage councils to implement central government policy initiatives, and generally to push them in directions in which they otherwise might not go.

It should be that the principal purpose of a grant will suggest its most efficient form, and that a grant's form will imply its purpose. We must distinguish therefore between the two basic forms of grant – specific and general – to match our two fundamental purposes.

SPECIFIC GRANTS (also known as ring-fenced, selective or hypothe-cated grants) – government grants to local authorities that must be spent on some specified project or service – for example, Nursery Education Grant for 3 year olds, AIDS/HIV Support Grant, Rural Bus Service Grant. As can be seen from Figure 10.3 on p. 218, specific grants have steadily increased as a proportion of total central government's contribution to local government.

GENERAL GRANTS (also known as non-selective or unhypothecated grants) – grants that may be spent at the discretion of the grantees, the local councils themselves. The general grant to local government – the RSG – still accounts for the biggest single slice of central government support.

The distinction between the two grant forms is important, to both central government grantor and local authority recipient. If persuasion and influence are the government's objectives, it will presumably opt for a specific grant, and define its purpose as precisely as possible. If compensation is the objective, or the retention of the maximum degree of local financial discretion, then a general grant is the logical choice. The specific:general grant ratio can thus serve as a rough and ready indicator of central government financial control. The trend towards specific grants, from a 1:4 ratio in the early 1970s to the point where collectively they now exceed the Revenue Support Grant, is in no way accidental.

You will recall from Exhibit 10.2 that, together with its income from fees and charges, the *specific* grants received by Birmingham City Council – £721 million in 2005/06, or 27 per cent of its gross current income – were taken into account in translating that gross spending to a net spending requirement. We come now, therefore, to the council's single largest source of current income – its 'general' *Revenue Support Grant (RSG)* of £835 million (31 per cent).

The annual RSG distribution process takes the public form of a series of government announcements, concentrated in the late autumn, or less than six months before the start of the new financial year. First, the government decides how much money in total that local authorities will be permitted to spend during the coming year – their *Total Assumed Spending* (TAS). Secondly, it declares the proportion of that total spending – around 80 per cent in recent years – that it will finance through national taxation, or *Aggregate External Finance* (AEF). The difference between the two figures – just over 20 per cent – is the proportion that local authorities collectively will have to find for themselves: the reverse of the commonly held impression, as noted in the opening paragraph of this chapter.

The government then moves from the aggregate to the individual authority level. It produces an assessment of what *it* feels each authority needs to spend – both in total and in each of seven service blocks – in order to provide what it defines as a 'standard level of service'. These figures constitute a council's *Formula Spending Share (FSS)* and are absolutely critical in determining the level of grant it will receive. The government bases its calculations on a range of indicators, such as the council's total residential population, the number of over-65s living alone, kilometres of road. If it over-estimates a council's spending needs, the council will receive in effect a grant subsidy; if it under-estimates, council tax bills must rise, or services be cut.

From the council's total FSS, two deductions are made. The first is for the total income the government estimates the authority should receive, were it to set its council tax at a specified standard level – the *Assumed National Council Tax (ANCT)*. The second is for the income it will receive from the government-set *National Non-Domestic Rate* (NNDR). A council's RSG is the figure remaining after these deductions.

Expressed as a formula, we have:

$$RSG = FSS - (ANCT + NNDR)$$

where   FSS   is the government's aggregated assessment of a council's spending needs;

ANCT   is the government's assessment of a council's income from its council tax payers at a specified standard tax level; and

NNDR   is a council's population-based income from its national non-domestic ratepayers at a government-set rate.

Clearly, this grant distribution process incorporates both fundamental purposes of grants. It seeks to compensate authorities with above-average spending needs, but within a system based on the government imposing its judgement of what these authorities ought to be doing, and how much of it they should be doing.

For their part, local authorities – of all political complexions – protest and plead. They protest at the presumption of ministers and their Whitehall civil servants claiming to know better than they themselves and their local electorates what should be spent on different services. They protest at the government's methodology – its choice of indicators, its use of unreliable and outdated information – and at the consequential anomalies. Thus Gateshead, to take one recent example, will complain that, while the FSS formula has a built-in element for road repairs, it doesn't take into account the maintenance of back lanes between terraces, of which Gateshead has over 70 kilometres.

Councils protest too at the distribution of grant: that the total is inadequate and fails fully to take into account the prevailing inflation rate; that the whole process is political; and that the wrong authorities have gained and lost. And they will plead – though rarely with marked success – their exceptional local circumstances which, they claim, the government's formulas fail to recognise, and which merit special treatment.

National Non-Domestic Rate/Uniform Business Rate

The third source of councils' current income is one we just touched on in describing the calculation of grant: the *National Non-Domestic Rate (NNDR)* or, as it is also known, the *Uniform (not* Unified, Unitary or Universal!) *Business Rate (UBR)*. This came into operation at the same time as the community charge, though with nothing like the same public outcry, despite being arguably the more constitutionally significant of the two tax reforms.

For almost 400 years prior to 1989/90, the one local tax available to UK local authorities was a property tax, known as *the rates*. Its principles were administratively simple, which is one reason why a property tax of some kind is to be found in most developed systems of local government (see Exhibit 10.5). Every property in the area – houses, flats, shops, offices and factories – was given a valuation: its *rateable value*. Each year, the local council would calculate how much, in addition to the grant it would receive, it needed to collect to pay for the services it wished to provide, and would set an appropriate *rate poundage*: so much to be paid per £1 of each property's rateable value. Domestic ratepayers paid a slightly lower rate poundage than non-domestic or business ratepayers, because the government would pay a compensating subsidy to the local council.

In 1989 in Scotland and 1990 in England and Wales this whole system changed. Domestic rates were abolished, to be replaced by the community charge. Northern Ireland alone retained its rating system, no doubt to many people's relief – in both senses of the word, since, as formerly in Great Britain, a large proportion of the population is entitled to rate rebates.

The non-domestic rate was not abolished, but nationalised: hence the *National* Non-Domestic Rate. In future, central government would each year set a standard or uniform rate poundage for *all* non-domestic properties in England and Wales – though not in Scotland, where existing rate poundages were retained. Local councils continue to send out the bills and collect the rates, but these are now paid into a national fund and redistributed back to the councils in proportion to their populations. The NNDR has become, in effect, part of the central government general grant – its more than £21 billion in 2005/06 amounting to nearly a fifth of total central government support. Former local ratepayers have become national taxpayers, and there is no longer any direct tax link between local authorities and the businesses in their area.

In 1989/90, non-domestic rates had provided over a quarter of local government current income: more than that from domestic rates (see Figure 10.3 (b)). At a stroke, therefore, local councils saw the proportion of their income that they themselves controlled fall from over a half to barely a quarter: a fraction that, as we shall see, was to decline even further.

Local taxation

It will be obvious by now that the final source of local authorities' current income is their own local taxation: traditionally, the rates, then the community charge, and since 1993 the council tax. We shall deal towards the end of this chapter with the respective merits and deficiencies of these

Exhibit 10.3 The council tax: key features

What is it?	A *tax on domestic property*, not people, but with a personal element. There is *one bill per household*, with a 25 per cent discount for single-person households and certain other property.
How much?	Will depend first on the *Inland Revenue's valuation of your property*. All domestic properties were placed in 1993 in one of 8 bands, A to H, which are in a fixed proportional relationship with each other – e.g. A:D:H = 2:3:6. Band A, the bottom band, is for properties valued *in 1993* at under £40,000 in England, under £27,000 in Scotland, and under £30,000 in Wales. Band H, the top band, is for properties over £320,000 (England), £212,000 (Scotland), and £240,000 (Wales).
Who sets it?	*Each local authority*, though in two-tier non-metropolitan England, billing and collection are the responsibility of the district alone.
Exemptions?	Apply only to property, mostly if unoccupied. Additions to property *types* previously exempt from community charge: halls of residence, flats/houses occupied solely by students.
Discounts?	Relate to types of people occupying the property, *not* to ability to pay: 25 per cent discounts for all single householders; 50 per cent for under-18s, full-time students, the 'severely mentally impaired', some carers for disabled people. Most controversially, second-home owners: 10–50 per cent discount at the council's discretion.
Rebates?	*Up to 100 per cent* for taxpayers on low incomes.
Students?	*Do not* pay, if they are full-time students in a hall of residence, hostel, or other *exclusively* student accommodation.
Who is liable?	The resident, over 18, with the strongest legal interest in the property.
Non-payment?	Dealt with like poll tax non-payment: appearance in magistrates' court, liability order issued by court, attempted recovery of money by council, imprisonment for up to 3 months (except in Scotland).
Registers?	Unlike poll tax, no specific register required.
Capping?	Capping powers *retained* by Labour and reactivated from 2004/05.
Non-domestic rates?	Still the 'nationalised' system introduced in 1989/90. Labour's pledge to re-localise reversed when in government.
Is it fair?	No – and it gets unfairer by the year. Inherently regressive: those in lower bands pay far higher % of their income than those in higher bands. Especially tough on those on fixed incomes, like pensioners. Valuations massively outdated – *average* London property price in 2006 was £300,000.
The future?	Who knows? Promised 2007 revaluation postponed indefinitely. Sir Michael Lyons' 2004 local government funding inquiry extended to late 2006, thereby ruling out even those minor reforms – e.g., splitting the top band, extending the ratio between Bands A and H from 1:3 to 1:7, abolishing discounts – requiring only Parliamentary Orders.

Figure 10.1   *Cartoon – council tax assessment*

Source: Local Government Information Unit, *LGIU Briefing*, No. 55, December 1991.

and other possible local taxes. For the present, we need only to remind ourselves that, whereas rates were a tax on property, the community charge/poll tax was a tax on the individual: a flat-rate tax payable by most adults over the age of 18. The council tax combines the two (see Exhibit 10.3). It is a domestic property tax, but with the size of the bill depending in part on the number of residents as well as on the property's value, since taxpayers living alone get at least a 25 per cent reduction, regardless of their income. It is also very different from the old rating system, with each home assigned to one of eight property bands (Figure 10.1).

As a policy failure, the Thatcher Government's introduction of the poll tax in 1989/90 was the domestic equivalent of the invasion of Iraq. It had huge and mainly damaging effects on many people's personal finances, and brought not one but two major administrative upheavals for those council officers responsible for its administration and collection, with the number of tax bills sent out being first doubled and then halved. But purely from the narrow viewpoint of those involved in a council's annual budget process – which is our perspective here – the key decisions remained essentially the same throughout all the changes.

The tax levied is still the final residual outcome of a process in which all the other elements are now known: your own council's spending plans, those of any precepting authorities, the amount you will receive in specific grants, fees and charges, the income you will get from the NNDR pool, your RSG. The sum still outstanding has to come from the council's own local council taxpayers since, unlike their counterparts in most other countries, British local authorities have access to only the one local tax.

The last point is important, especially when considering the budgetary discretion of local authorities. Common sense suggests that an authority with access to several different local taxes, paid by different groups of taxpayers, has more options at its disposal than one forced to rely on a single tax and a single group of taxpayers. In most developed countries that is precisely what happens. Japanese prefectures and municipalities, for example, have taxes on residents, consumption (sales), enterprise (businesses), automobiles and their purchase, tobacco, property purchase, light oil delivery, mini-cars and motorcycles, and, if they have them, hot springs. New York's mayor has four major taxes – on property, personal income and general sales, plus a general corporation tax – and a fistful of minor ones, including a hotel tax, utility tax, commercial rent tax and property transfer tax. It may be, as Hambleton suggests (2005, p. 23), that such lists offer 'too many tax options for local politicians', but he is emphatic that this situation is greatly preferable to ours:

> Compare this with the UK, where the council has only one tax – generating a small fraction of revenue spending. And, incredibly, even that is subject to capping by central government. Effective local leadership cannot be expected to prosper in such a constrained setting.

Capping

Picking up Hambleton's observation, it could be argued that significant local tax choice has in recent years been removed completely from British councils. Since the Rates Act 1984, local authorities' previously limited discretion has been curtailed still further through the process known as *capping*. The term tends to be used slightly misleadingly: 'rate-capping' and 'council tax-capping', instead of the strictly more accurate *budget-capping*. Since 1984, successive ministers – in 2006, the Secretary of State for Communities and Local Government – have had the power to cap, or impose a statutory ceiling on, the planned budget of any local authority that is, in their view, excessive. The effect is essentially the same as placing the cap directly on the council tax. For, with only the one local tax, that tax has to be reduced on a pound-for-pound basis to reflect the spending cut demanded.

Initially, Conservative ministers used their new power *selectively*, devising criteria each year that enabled them to pick out usually between 12 and 20 councils – almost all of them Labour – whose proposed budgets and rates they would then reduce. With the advent of the poll tax, though, capping rapidly moved from being selective to being *universal*, applying to all councils except parishes. If the system sounds centralist and dictatorial, that is because it was designed to be so. It is also quite simple to understand. The coming financial year's capping criteria – maximum percentage budget increases – were announced in November along with the other RSG details. Each council thus knew, before it made any of its key budget decisions, exactly how much it would be permitted to spend and to raise from its own local residents in tax. Many (indeed most) then used these figures in effect as guidelines, and spent and taxed at their government-determined levels.

To local authorities of all political colours, if not to the general public, this practice of universal capping was probably more offensive than was the imposition of the community charge/poll tax itself. It amounted to the Government setting a spending ceiling for every council in the country, leaving locally elected politicians in the position of having the framework of their budgets, if not their detailed content, determined for them.

Labour, in its 1997 election manifesto, promised that this 'crude and universal capping should go' – but not completely. It would be replaced by what presumably has to be described as discriminating and selective capping, as Labour ministers would 'retain reserve powers to control excessive council tax increases' – increases, that is, that they, rather than locally elected councillors (or local taxpayers and voters), judge to be excessive.

This legislative change was introduced in the Local Government Act 1999, and relatively little notice was paid to it until, in Spring 2004, ministers announced that they would protect the taxpayers of five councils by capping what they decreed – without having previously announced any criteria of acceptability – were 'unacceptable' tax increases being proposed by their councils. The following year's tax announcements coincided with the run-up to the 2005 General and county council elections, and, in what certainly smacked of party electioneering, ministers announced that this year they would be capping the budgets and tax increases of eight councils – none of them with any 'previous' of wanton extravagance, and seven of whom just happened to be Conservative: Aylesbury Vale, Daventry, Hambleton (North Yorkshire), Huntingdonshire, Mid-Bedfordshire, North Dorset and Runnymede (Surrey).

More significantly, even though these councils' 'headline' tax rises breached the Government's declared threshold of 5 per cent, they were all district councils, all therefore had relatively small budgets, and most, even with their new tax yields, would still have had spending and tax levels below the national average. Ministers, however, had spoken, and the councils were consequently – not to say nonsensically – forced to spend *additional* tens of thousands of pounds mailing out new tax bills and dealing with the associated administration, for what in one case was a 'saving' of under 10p per household per week.

The eighth council, South Cambridgeshire, was so incensed that it applied for judicial review (see pp. 161–2) on various grounds, including that the tax increase was the Council's first for three years, that its spending and tax levels would still be below the national average, that 60 per cent of respondents to a Council survey had supported the tax increase, and that the same Government department that was capping its spending was also telling the Council to plan for a 33 per cent population increase over the coming ten years. Not unexpectedly, the application was denied, despite the High Court judge expressing his personal sympathy and pronouncing that the Council 'is not profligate. It is low spending and has given cogent reasons for the proposed increase in council tax'. The law permitted ministers to act in the way they had – the law that is part of the framework of the most centrally dictated local financial system in Western Europe.

Budget setting – managing the margins

Local budgeting, from the perspective of the local councillors and officers involved, has inevitably become an exercise in 'managing the margins', to quote the sub-title of an account of the subject (Elcock *et al.*, 1989). In fact, the sub-title is intended to emphasise the almost inevitable *incremental* or marginal nature of most local budgetary decisions: adding relatively small increments to, or cutting them from, a largely unchallenged and untouched budgetary base. But it could equally suggest the management of the very tightly defined and delimited margins left to local councils' discretion, once government ministers have taken and announced all the major decisions on total spending, grant distribution, the NNDR poundage, and possible capping criteria.

Either way, there may be the temptation to see the role of 'managing the margins' as being insignificant, even demeaning. The temptation should be resisted, by those in local government and by citizens as observers. As we emphasise throughout this book, the size, employing and spending power of local authorities are such that even their marginal budgetary decisions can have an important local impact. The government may define, and tightly, the budgetary framework, but there is still scope *within* that framework – albeit less than might be desirable democratically – for councils to respond to particular local needs and for councillors to pursue their political objectives.

To illustrate, we return to Birmingham's 2005/06 revenue budget, as set out in Exhibit 10.2, and complete the story of the setting of the city's council tax. As noted before, while the scale of Birmingham's budget may be exceptional, the basic decisions underpinning it are essentially similar and comparable to those required of your own council.

The effective starting point in both cases would have been the Government's announcement in early December 2004 of its proposed RSG Settlement. The vital data for Birmingham in that announcement were the details of its Formula Spending Share (FSS) – what the Government felt the council should be spending in total (£1,445 million – up 6.4 per cent from 2004/05), and specifically on education (£699 million – up 7.4 per cent), social services (£358 million – up 5.9 per cent), and so on, in order to provide a standard level of service. Those FSSs determined the RSG Birmingham would receive, even if, like most councils, it spent above the figures calculated by the Government.

As noted above, the common response from local authorities to the RSG settlement has been one of almost ritualised outrage. Council leaders are interviewed by their local media, protesting at how the government has seriously under-assessed their council's spending needs, and that major service cuts, tax increases, or both, will be required – for which, of course, Government ministers, not councillors, must take the responsibility and blame. The Labour Government has, with some effect, sought to disarm such protests by announcing three-year spending plans, but in December 2004 the far more critical factor was the anticipated General Election the following May.

If governments seek to control local government spending almost totally, they, not surprisingly, take much of the public blame for council tax increases. Anxious, therefore, not to face an electorate angry at what would have been a second successive year of average council tax rises of over 10 per cent, the Government – and specifically Gordon Brown's Treasury – ensured that the increase in total grant funding (the Aggregate External Finance figure) was, at 6.2 per cent, substantially above the rate of inflation – generous enough, threatened Local Government Minister, Nick Raynsford, for all authorities to keep their tax rises below 5 per cent or face the prospect of capping.

Service cuts and Gershon efficiency savings (see pp. 169–70) would still have to be found, but the overall settlement for 2005/06 was as well received by most authorities, including Birmingham, as any in recent years.

Councillors, therefore – in particular the service portfolio holders in the Conservative-Liberal Democrat 'partnership' cabinet – set about addressing the key policy questions:

- Which services should be prioritised, protected from cuts, and allocated extra resources, and which service areas should we look to for savings?
- What percentage tax increase should we aim for, bearing in mind the prevailing inflation rate of 2–3 per cent and the (Labour) Minister's indicated 5 per cent capping threshold?

Increasingly, councils endeavour to consult their own local taxpayers and service users about *their* priorities. Public meetings of residents, because of generally poor and unrepresentative attendances, have tended to be displaced by a variety of other methods: smaller focus groups or 'deliberative workshops' comprising representatives of the public and/or business and community group interests; online leaflets and questionnaires; telephone hotlines. Several councils have consulted at least once through postal referendums – Bristol, Croydon, Milton Keynes – the latter perhaps confirming most interestingly the experience of tax referendums in other countries that the low-tax option doesn't *always* win. Birmingham in 2005/06 undertook no particularly notable external consultations, and the most difficult discussions would have been those in private between the leaderships of the two administration parties concerning how to square the very different sets of policies on which they had contested the previous elections. Eventually, however, agreement was hammered out, in the form of the decisions that headlined in the local media and took pride of place in the Council's Budget leaflet:

- The increased FSS allocations for education and social services to be passed on in their entirety, producing £39.4 million (6.6 per cent) more for schools, £6 million to help develop children's services in schools and extended schools, and £20 million more for social care, directed particularly at replacing children's homes and modernising services for vulnerable children and older adults;
- £13 million to help relieve pressures on services – e.g., the loss of grant for housing benefits, higher electricity bills for street lighting, an increased payment to the Passenger Transport Authority for concessionary fares;
- £6 million for council members' priorities – e.g., community safety improvements, development of apprenticeships and vocational training, investment in libraries;
- £23.5 million in efficiency savings – from better procurement (purchasing) practices, reduced debt financing costs, targeted efficiency reviews.

Exhibit 10.4 Birmingham's council tax, 2005/06

	£ millions	
City Council's 2005/06 net budget requirement (set at limit to be approved by government)	1,452	
Less: Revenue Support Grant (determined by government)	835	= 57.5%
Less: Redistributed National Non-Domestic Rate (collected at uniform poundage set by government)	330	= 22.7%
Leaves: Budget Requirement to be financed by Council Tax	287	= 19.8%
Which represents for a Birmingham property in Band D a council tax of	1,013.64	= +2.8%
Plus: Police Authority precept	83.68	
Plus: Fire Service precept	41.21	
Equals: Total Band D council tax	1,138.53	= +2.99%
Which equals: 3/2 of the tax for a Band A property	759.02	
And: Half of the tax for a Band H property	2,027.28	

Source: Data from Birmingham City Council, *Budget 2005/06*.

These decisions, and dozens of similar ones, were brought together in the budget that was formally approved by the full City Council on 22 February 2005 (see Exhibit 10.4). They amounted to a net revenue spending increase of 6.6 per cent, producing a council tax rise for a Band D property of 2.8 per cent for the Council's own services and an obviously symbolically significant overall increase of 2.99 per cent. Band D is commonly quoted for comparative purposes as representing the average property value across the country, although the majority of Birmingham properties are in Bands A and B – another fact to be taken into account when setting the tax rate. It was Birmingham's Band D rate of £1,138.53, therefore, that the Council's leaders quoted when emphasising that it was lower than that of most other 'core cities' – Manchester, Sheffield, Liverpool, Bristol, Nottingham and Newcastle (though not Leeds), and than most West Midlands districts – Coventry, Sandwell, Wolverhampton and Walsall.

There is a sense, perhaps, in which such policy decisions, made nowadays primarily individually and collectively by cabinet members, can be regarded as 'marginal'. The most prioritised services had budget increases of only a few percentage points. No department, in this year at least, faced major, let alone enforced, redundancies. The overwhelming bulk of the council's budget and all its major services remained intact.

Marginal they may have been; trivial they were not. All these decisions had costs and consequences for those involved in and affected by them. They were not inevitable; they were not wholly determined by central government; they were politically, even socially, contentious, and were the subject of much political debate, both across and within the parties represented on the Council.

The fact remains, however, that it was not these policy decisions by locally elected politicians that played the crucial part in determining Birmingham's *overall* level of spending and service provision, or its overall level of council tax. These decisions, once the responsibility of local councillors and their electorates, were in 2005/06 very substantially determined by national politicians and civil servants in London. As can be seen in Exhibit 10.4, local taxpayers in Birmingham – as across the country – now contribute only about a fifth of their council's net expenditure. Such a situation blurs accountability, in that voters remain uncertain as to who is in fact responsible for any tax change for which they are asked to pay or vote. A 'gearing effect' also acts as a big disincentive for any local authority proposing to increase its net spending, because, with central government controlling all other sources of funding – grants and the NNDR – a 1 per cent budget increase will require a 4 per cent to 5 per cent rise in council tax. It was not always like this; nor, as we shall see, is it how most other countries organise their local finances.

How other countries do things

In commenting on Exhibit 10.1, we noted that local government accounted for a quarter of the country's total government spending, and about 10 per cent of the gross domestic product (GDP). It sounds – and obviously is – a lot, and it explains why, in any local authority area, the council itself will be among the largest employers, spenders and purchasers, and frequently *the* largest.

Compared with other Western local government systems, however, the UK, in football parlance, would barely make the Championship. The 'Sub-central Premiership' would be headed by Denmark, with a local government sector contributing over 30 per cent of GDP, followed by Sweden (24 per cent) and the federal systems of Canada (28 per cent), the USA, Belgium, Germany and Austria (all around 20 per cent) (UNPAN, 2005, tables A2 and A6). In tax terms, the distinctions are even more striking. As we can see from Figure 10.2, British local government contributes a very small slice to a not particularly large national cake. We are, no matter what we may believe or are told, a comparatively modestly taxed country, and, of every £1 of tax we pay, less than 5p goes direct to our local councils.

Figure 10.2 *Britain's council tax – a small slice of a modest cake, 2003/04*

The Cake	Under 5%	5%–25%	Over 25% **The Slice**
Over 40%		Austria (43, 18) Finland (44, 21) France (44,10) Norway (45, 15) Italy (42, 17)	Sweden (51, 33) Denmark (50, 36) Belgium (46, 29)
30–40%	Netherlands (39,4) **UK (36, 4.8)** Greece (36, 1) Ireland (30, 2)	Portugal (37, 6) New Zealand (35, 6)	Germany* (35, 28) Spain (35, 28) Canada* (33, 47) Australia* (32, 32)
Under 30%			USA* (25, 35) Japan (25, 26) Switzerland* (29, 40)

Total tax revenue as a percentage of GDP

Local/state taxes as a percentage of total tax revenue

Notes: The first figure for each country is the tax revenue as a percentage of GDP; the second is local tax as a percentage of total tax revenue. For federal countries (*) the second figure = state + local taxes.
Source: Data from OECD (2005) *Revenue Statistics of OECD Member Countries, 1965–2004* (Paris: OECD).

It is true that some of Britain's other EU partners have markedly smaller local government sectors than we do – notably those countries in which teachers are employed by central, rather than local, government. But, following the introduction of capping and the 1989–93 tax changes noted above – particularly the 'nationalisation' of business rates – there are no longer many Western countries in which local government has apparently got less financial discretion. The key to that situation lies, we suggest, in Exhibit 10.5.

The detailed figures in Exhibit 10.5 are in some ways less important than the evident message:

- In very few Western countries are local authorities forced to rely on only one source of local taxation.
- In most countries, local authorities can levy a variety of taxes on different groups of taxpayers and service users.
- The few exceptions are those mainly Scandinavian countries that rely very heavily on a broad-based and progressive direct tax: a local income tax.
- Britain has been unique in placing such a concentrated burden on *either* a property tax *or* a flat-rate personal tax.

Exhibit 10.5 Composition of state/local tax revenues, 2003 (%)

		Income and profits	Property	Goods and services	Other
Federal countries					
Canada	State	43	5	40	12
	Local	–	94	2	4
USA	State	39	3	58	–
	Local	5	73	22	–
Belgium	State	46	12	42	–
	Local	87	–	13	–
Germany	State	50	5	45	–
	Local	75	19	6	–
Unitary countries					
Denmark		93	7	–	–
Finland		95	5	–	–
France		–	54	11	35
Italy		22	15	23	40
Japan		45	32	22	1
Netherlands		–	57	42	–
Norway		89	9	2	–
Spain		24	26	49	1
Sweden		100	–	–	–
UK pre-1989		–	100	–	–
1990–1993		–	–	–	100
1993–		–	100	–	–

Source: Data from OECD (2005) *Revenue Statistics of OECD Member Countries, 1965–2004* (Paris: OECD), Tables 132, 138.

The burden of a single local tax

Taxes, pronounced economist John Maynard Keynes, are the membership fee we pay to live in a civilised society: not inherently a 'bad' thing, as many politicians would have us believe, but a force for good, funding things we value, such as universal education, social services and public transport. It is when tax liabilities are inadequately or inappropriately shared that they come to seem burdensome. For British local authorities, the enforced reliance on a single local tax is burdensome in two senses: on the system itself and on those liable to pay it. As a local authority's responsibilities increase, more money is required from the same group of taxpayers, whose readiness to pay, and eventually ability to do so, is finite. When, in addition, the single tax is either a flat-rate one or related only loosely to a taxpayer's changing income and wealth, problems are magnified. That, in essence, has been the story of post-war British local government.

The longstanding local rating system described above had been effective, but, in the postwar years, as councils took on more and more services, its limitations became manifest. As a property tax, rates were 'regressive' – not directly related to any ability to pay either of a head of a household or of its members. Domestic rates were efficient, predictable, relatively cheap and easy to collect, and difficult to evade. But during the 1970s, as they increased year by year, and householders saw other service-users apparently 'freeloading', accusations of unfairness multiplied. The Conservatives, or more precisely the Opposition environment spokesperson – one Margaret Thatcher – produced a 1974 manifesto pledge to 'abolish the rating system within the lifetime of a Parliament and replace it by taxes more broadly based and *related to people's ability to pay*' (emphasis ours).

Of that four-part pledge, half was eventually achieved, and half was not. Domestic rates were abolished, but after three Parliaments, not one. The replacement community charge – or 'poll tax' as it became known almost universally – was certainly more broadly based, being a completely flat-rate tax payable by almost everyone; but it was emphatically not related to ability to pay. The story of its introduction is a fascinating one (see Butler *et al.*, 1994; Wilson and Game, 1998, ch. 10), not least for the sheer chutzpah of ministers – and particularly the prime minister – in attempting to finance a large part of a large-scale local government system through a personal tax that was unique in the Western democratic world.

The reason rating reform took a Conservative government ten years to introduce was that it had tried and finally run out of other means of controlling local spending. The Thatcher Government came to power in what we termed the 'corporatist' phase of central–local relations (see p. 174), and inherited Labour's policy of seeking to constrain local expenditure by reductions in local government's *total* annual Rate Support Grant. This policy was ratcheted up in the Local Government Planning and Land Act 1980 by the quite unprecedented introduction of spending 'targets' and grant penalties for *every individual council*. If a council's spending exceeded significantly its supposedly 'guideline' target, its grant, far from being increased, would be cut. In the mid-1970s, Rate Support Grant had funded over half of English local authorities' net spending (see Figure 10.3(a)), leaving councils themselves having to find only about a third (35 per cent) through their locally set domestic and business/non-domestic rates. But year by year, as their grant fell, many councils, rather than cut services, made up their income deficit by raising rates, often by formidable percentages – 27 per cent on average in 1980/81 and 19.4 per cent in 1981/82.

Figure 10.3 *The changing composition of funding for English local authority net expenditure, 1975–2006*

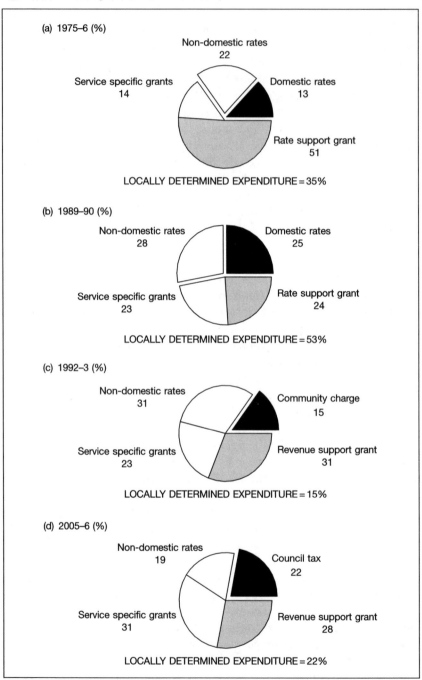

(a) 1975–6 (%)

Non-domestic rates
22

Service specific grants
14

Domestic rates
13

Rate support grant
51

LOCALLY DETERMINED EXPENDITURE = 35%

(b) 1989–90 (%)

Non-domestic rates
28

Domestic rates
25

Service specific grants
23

Rate support grant
24

LOCALLY DETERMINED EXPENDITURE = 53%

(c) 1992–3 (%)

Non-domestic rates
31

Community charge
15

Service specific grants
23

Revenue support grant
31

LOCALLY DETERMINED EXPENDITURE = 15%

(d) 2005–6 (%)

Non-domestic rates
19

Council tax
22

Service specific grants
31

Revenue support grant
28

LOCALLY DETERMINED EXPENDITURE = 22%

Source: Data from ODPM (2005g) and similar earlier sources.

The Government's response was threefold. First, a Green Paper examined a wide range of possible *Alternatives to Domestic Rates* (DoE, 1981) – local sales taxes; petrol, alcohol and tobacco duties; a local payroll tax; local income tax – and then rejected most of them, including a poll tax, on the grounds of their impracticability. Second, and consequently, 'rate-capping' was introduced – in 1982 in Scotland and 1984 in England and Wales. The Rates Act gave central government complete control for the first time over the spending and taxing policies of some, and eventually all, local authorities – a constitutional development arguably more fundamental than the third strand of the Government's action: the abolition in 1985 of the 'excessively' high-spending and -taxing GLC and Metropolitan County Councils.

Poll tax – a short-lived policy disaster

There had been no mention of the rating abolition pledge in the Conservatives' 1983 manifesto. But, as the Government continued to cut its general grant funding, ratepayers' proportion of the local government spending 'pie' inevitably increased (see Figure 10.3(b)). It was time for another – this time uncompromising – Green Paper, *Paying for Local Government,* which outlined 'proposals for the most radical reform of local government finance in Britain this century' (DoE, 1986, p. 76). It was not exaggerating.

There were two main strands to the reform:

- *Domestic rates* would be abolished, to be replaced by a Community Charge – a flat-rate payment by all adults aged 18 and over at a level set by individual local authorities; and
- *Non-domestic rates* would be 'nationalised' – that is, set in future by *central* government at a uniform rate across the whole country.

The protests against the inequity of the Community Charge/poll tax were widespread, passionate and aggressive. The warnings about its operational difficulties – the compilation and maintenance of a rolling register and the problems of enforcement – were legion. Even ministers acknowledged that this Thatcherite 'flagship' policy would hardly be universally popular, but that merely persuaded them to introduce it 'at a single stroke', rather than, as previously planned, phased in gradually as the rates were phased out. Accordingly, 'the most celebrated disaster in post-war British politics' (Butler *et al.,* 1994) was launched – on 1 April 1989 in Scotland and 1 April 1990 in England and Wales.

The average poll tax bill for 1990/91 – £363 per adult – was some 14 times higher than the figure envisaged in the 1981 Green Paper. There were at least three times as many 'losers' as 'gainers', and the heaviest losers were those, such as pensioners and single-parent families, in the smallest properties and with the most modest incomes. Protests and demonstrations turned into riots. Tens of thousands of people were criminalised for the first time in their lives because of their inability or refusal to pay, and non-collection rates rocketed. The unpopular tax was proving unacceptable in practice. In November 1990, Mrs Thatcher lost the Conservative leadership, at least partly as a result of the damage the poll tax was doing to the party. The new prime minister, John Major, despite his collective ministerial responsibility for the tax, was committed to its abolition, but first he had to neutralise it. This was achieved in Chancellor of the Exchequer Norman Lamont's budget in March 1991, in which he raised Value Added Tax (VAT) from 15 per cent to 17.5 per cent to finance a cut of £140 in the poll tax bill of every adult in the country.

Exhibit 10.6 Balance of funding reform: nothing happens, twice

What balance?

Actually the *imbalance* – between the national and local funding of local government's revenue spending, roughly 75:25 in recent years. This imbalance distorts accountability through the 'gearing effect' – meaning that a 1 per cent spending increase requires a 4 per cent council tax rise – thereby confusing local taxpayers and electors, who see no clear relationship between local taxes paid and services received.

Chronology of non-reform

2001 – White Paper promises 'high-level working group' review of all aspects of balance of funding (DTLR, 2001, para. 6.7).

2003 – *Balance of Funding Review* starts work, chaired by Local Government Minister, Nick Raynsford.

2004 – July: Review produces ultra-bland report: an unoriginal overview of options, albeit with a few interesting research reports (see DCLG website). Non-conclusion: only way to achieve major shift in the balance of funding is to supplement a reformed council tax with relocalised business rates and/or a local income tax.

Nothing happens once: minister announces further *Inquiry into Local Government Funding*, led by Sir Michael Lyons, ex-Chief Executive, Birmingham City Council. Inquiry to examine detailed case for change and how best to reform council tax, reporting by December 2005.

2005 – September: Nothing happens twice – new Local Government Minister, David Miliband, announces a presumably prime ministerial electorally-driven decision to postpone indefinitely the 2007 revaluation of domestic property in England. Also extends Lyons' terms of reference to cover the future function and role of local government, postponing final report until December 2006.

Two days later, Environment Secretary Michael Heseltine announced the abolition of the poll tax and its replacement from 1993 by the council tax.

The financial, fiscal, economic and employment costs of the community charge/poll tax, massive as they were, can at least be estimated (Wilson and Game, 1998, Exhibit 10.5). The longer-term social and community costs, and the irreparable damage done to local government, are inestimable. The effects are still in evidence – in people's resistance to registration and census completion, in their disengagement from local government, and in the reluctance of some to pay even the initially obviously fairer council tax. Even more damaging to local government, though, was the two-stage switch – first the uniform business rate, then the VAT increase – from local taxation funding over half of net local expenditure to its funding only one-sixth (see Figure 10.3(b) and (c)). In the

How to judge Lyons – the localist benchmark

Most prominent reform package proposed is the LGA's 'Combination Option' (LGA, 2004b; Travers and Esposito, 2004b). Containing most of the proposals on which Lyons would have to form some view, it is a scoresheet against which to mark the Inquiry's eventual recommendations.

The LGA would *reverse* the present 75:25 central:local balance, and improve the gearing ratio from 4:1 to 1.5:1, while still equalising across local authorities for their differing needs and resources. The combination package could include:

- **A more equitable property/council tax** (producing, at 2003/04 prices, £18 billion) – involving a revaluation, and maybe more bands, steeper ratios, regional bandings;
- **Relocalisation of business rates** (£15.6 billion);
- **Transfer of a proportion of national income tax to fund local government directly** (£18 billion) – ideally through a progressive Locally Variable Income Tax;
- **Commensurate reduction in Revenue Support Grant** (from £40 billion to £18 billion);
- **A basket of supplementary smaller taxes or charges – for example:**
  - Localised vehicle excise duty – councils allowed to retain receipts;
  - Local sales taxes – on retail prices of certain goods or services;
  - Localised Stamp Duty – on property transfers;
  - Land value taxes – based on land ownership, not property occupation;
  - Tourist/bed taxes;
  - Charges for utilities' street works;
  - Town/city centre congestion charges;
  - Green/environmental taxes – fuel tax, plastic bag tax, household waste generation charges.

ensuing decade, the proportion of locally determined expenditure crept up to around a fifth. But, as we have noted, that is a much lower figure than in most other Western European countries, and too low, many observers would feel, to support a financially robust local democracy.

Indefinitely postponed reform

The most obvious legacy of the post-1988 tax reforms is that British local authorities are still in the almost unique position of having access to just one source of local taxation – a property tax that is neither big enough nor buoyant enough, that does not necessarily reflect ability to pay, that discriminates against those on low and fixed incomes, and that can still be almost arbitrarily capped by central government. For a self-proclaimed modernising and devolutionist Government well into its third term, the story summarised in Exhibit 10.6 ought to be at least a cause of considerable embarrassment to Tony Blair.

The keys to reform – the damaging imbalance in central–local funding and the increasingly inadequate and regressive council tax – were acknowledged explicitly by the Government in 2001. Ministers then spent two and a half years producing a report for themselves that added nothing either substantive or analytical to the far more comprehensive and challenging work of the Layfield Committee in the 1970s. Then, in a way that even *Yes, Minister*'s Sir Humphrey Appleby might have found a touch audacious, they appointed another inquiry, and, as it approached completion, extended its terms of reference and pushed it back yet another year – to the point at which it becomes unlikely that legislation will be enacted before a 2009/10 General Election, when council tax valuations will be 18 years out of date. Understandably, the sorry saga reminded one commentator of Samuel Beckett's play, *Waiting for Godot* – partly because Godot never actually appears, partly too because of a famous review in which it was described as a play in which nothing happens, twice (Grant, 2005, p. 14).

If, on this occasion, life deviates from art and a Lyons Report does materialise, local council Pollyannas will hope that its delineation of local government's future role is sufficiently robust to persuade the Government that its funding requires a radical localist reform package along the lines of that in Exhibit 10.6. Eeyores, on the other hand, will suspect that, almost regardless of Lyons' analysis, the Government is more likely to opt for a different radical prescription – in which the big and financially troublesome social services and education become fully centrally funded, leaving a slimline local government to fund what would be a respectable 60 per cent or so of its remaining services from a modestly reformed council tax (Travers, 2005a, p. 28). Not a very glorious solution, but one that many would feel makes more sense than what we have now.

Part 2

The Politics and People of Local Government

Chapter 11

Local Elections – Christmas Tree Lights?

Introduction

We noted in Chapter 2 several characteristics that distinguish local authorities from other institutions of public administration. One – the most fundamental – is the fact of their election, aspects of which provide the content of the next two chapters. Chapter 12 focuses on the products of the electoral process: the councillors. This chapter deals with local elections themselves – how they are conducted, who votes in them, and how those votes are cast. They have been tagged 'the Christmas tree lights of British politics – one has to have them every year and they undoubtedly add colour to the scene, but are rarely that illuminating' (*The Times*, 3 May 2003, editorial). We shall try to show that their candlepower is underrated – and that the metaphor itself is incidentally *very* illuminating, of how the national media typically disparage our local democracy.

But why are we bothering?

It is easy to follow *The Times*' reasoning. Everyone knows that far fewer people vote in council elections than in even the 2001 and 2005 General Elections, with their record low turnouts of around 60 per cent. Are not government ministers – real, as well as fictitious ones like *Yes, Minister's* Jim Hacker – right when they suggest that:

> Local democracy is a farce ... Most people don't even vote in local elections, and the ones who do just treat it as a popularity poll on government in Westminster. (Lynn and Jay, 1983, p. 45)

Certainly, local elections are not accorded much importance in Britain's national political life. Their results are analysed mainly for what they would mean *if* they had been produced in a General Election, rather than for what they *actually* mean: namely, councils changing political control, policies altering, councillors winning and losing seats.

So why are we bothering to devote a whole chapter to them? The answer is simple. We do not believe that – even when, as in 1979, 1997, 2001 and 2005, they are held on the same day – local elections should be dismissed as merely a General Election writ small. They are much more complex, and

225

much more important, than a national popularity poll, or, as Margaret Thatcher seemed to regard them in 1983 and 1987 and Tony Blair in 2001 and 2005, a handy aid for prime ministers seeking tactically advantageous election dates. Our view of what local elections are and are not about can be summed up in the kind of 'before and after' editorials regularly produced by our more serious national newspapers – such as *The Times*. On an earlier polling day, Thursday 3 May 1990, editorial readers were instructed:

> Today's local elections are about the running of Britain's cities, towns and county districts. They are not a public opinion poll. They are not meant to be a judgement on Mrs Thatcher, on her government at Westminster, or on the vexed matter of the poll tax. They are to select the men and women who are to run local administration. Those of all political persuasions who treat local elections as surrogate General Elections are merely playing the centralist game. They are enemies of local democracy.

Odd, then, and disappointing, that just two days later, the same paper's editorial should choose to play its own 'centralist game':

> Yesterday's election results showed, as predicted, that the public does not like the poll tax ... The swing to Labour on a high turnout would be enough to give Mr Kinnock a good parliamentary majority.

Setting aside the fact that many voters demonstrably *did* like the poll tax, benefited from it, and voted accordingly, what happened to all those councillors running our cities, towns and county districts? The writer's assumption is that national and local elections are interchangeable. A principal message of this chapter is that *they are not*. Local elections are local political events, and a great many voters, if not political commentators, clearly treat them as such. Far fewer actually use their votes than in parliamentary elections, but many of those doing so *consistently vote differently* in the two types of election.

They will vote on the basis of local, rather than national issues, and for or against the records or personalities of particular candidates, regardless of their party. We shall introduce some specific examples later in the chapter, but first we must outline how British local elections are in fact conducted – see Exhibit 11.1.

The case for whole council elections and individual registration

Undeniably, some aspects of local electoral arrangements at the time of writing – most notably, when they are held and how we register – are confusing and unsatisfactory. If you happen to live in non-metropolitan England, you may well have to contact your district council's electoral registration office to find out whether yours are 'all out' or 'partial' elections, and when you therefore have your next chance to vote. Should it be the former, you may feel not just confused but also discriminated against, in having fewer opportunities to vote and influence the political composition of your council than your friend in a neighbouring district. While in many areas of life variety of local practice is commendable, it is not self-evident that the organisation of elections should be one of them. The Electoral Commission and the Widdicombe Committee before it (Widdicombe Report, 1986a, para. 7.15) were surely right in arguing for a uniform system, with as many voters as possible turning out on the same 'Local Election Day'.

There are arguments for and against 'whole council' elections. By giving councils a clear breathing space between elections, they may encourage policy consistency, forward planning, and reduce the temptation to defer politically difficult decisions: such as school closures, tax increases or the siting of roads. On the other hand, they can lead to dramatic changes in political control, producing large and sudden influxes of inexperienced councillors. Opponents declare that they dilute the political accountability that comes from politicians having to explain and justify their policies regularly to the electorate. But the harder and, for many, the clinching evidence is that turnouts are generally at least a few percentage points higher in whole council elections (Rallings and Thrasher, 2003; see also Exhibit 11.4 below), when, if you're really dissatisfied with your council's performance, you can 'vote the rascals out' in one go.

Just as the merits of local diversity can be exaggerated, so too can those of tradition. Unsecured electoral registration by household may have made sense when the Victorians had a property qualification for voters, and there was a significant adult illiteracy rate. Today it seems fundamentally wrong in principle, and democratically undermining in practice, for voters not to take responsibility for their own registration. Operated in conjunction with postal voting on demand – introduced in 2000 – it means that there is no effective check on who is applying for or receiving ballot papers, who is completing them, and under what kind of duress. It is an open invitation to widespread, systematic and organised fraud – as revealed in the Birmingham election trial (British Helsinki Human Rights Group, 2005; Parris, 2005), in which Labour candidates and their supporters were found guilty of having 'stolen' the 2004 council elections in two inner city wards by exploiting the many loopholes in the existing system.

Northern Ireland had already introduced individual registration in 2002, with voters having to provide personal identification information in the form of their date of birth, national insurance number and signature, as

Exhibit 11.1 The who, when, how and why of local elections

1. **When are local elections held?**
   Every May, normally the first Thursday of the month. *Not*, as in many countries, at weekends or on a public holiday.

2. **Can I vote?**
   Almost certainly – if you are 18 or over, a citizen of Britain, Ireland or the Commonwealth, and not a convicted prisoner. Also EU citizens, peers and peeresses, ineligible in parliamentary elections.

3. **Must I register first?**
   Yes, as for parliamentary elections. Since 2001, the UK has had a continuously maintained, or rolling, electoral register – administered by your local district or unitary council, and specifically by the Electoral Registration Officer, who should require you to complete a registration form confirming *your residence in the electoral area*. Primitively and patently abusably, though, the registration form is completed not by the individual voter, but by the head of household. Despite the known non-registration of 8–9 per cent of the eligible population (3.5 million + in 2000) (Electoral Commisson, 2005a), it is an offence and, as former East 17 singer and Epping Forest resident Brian Harvey discovered, can lead to a fine of up to £1,000.

4. **Isn't there also a property qualification?**
   Not any longer. Non-residents used to be able to vote if they occupied land or property in an area, but this plural voting was abolished in 1969, except in the City of London.

5. **So can I vote every year?**
   Easy question, ludicrously complex answer: it depends entirely on where you live. Most local authorities have *'whole council'* or *'all out'* elections every 4 years, though not on the same day, for example:

   > English Counties (2005, 2009)
   > London Boroughs (2006, 2010)
   > Greater London Authority (2004, 2008)
   > Scottish Unitaries (2003, 2007)
   > Welsh Unitaries (2004, 2008)
   > Northern Ireland Districts (2005).

   But Metropolitan Districts have *'partial'* or *'by thirds'* elections – one-third of councillors standing for re-election in each non-county year: 2004, 2006, 2007, 2008, 2010.
   Some – English Unitaries and Non-metropolitan Districts – may *choose*. About a third of mainly more urban authorities have elections by thirds, most of the rest have whole council elections every four years (2003, 2007), and 7 have elections by halves (2006, 2008).

6. **Whom do I elect?**
   The councillor(s) representing the particular area in which you live. All councils are divided into single- or multi-member electoral *divisions* (counties) or *wards* (districts, boroughs, and unitaries), each returning 1, 2 or 3 councillors for *4-year terms* of office. Until the London Mayor was elected in 2000, there were no directly elected political executives in British local government. The first mayoral elections outside London were in May 2002.

7. **When and where do I do it?**
   Traditionally, *on election day itself*, in your designated local polling station. Remarkably, you just turn up – no ID needed (outside Northern Ireland), not even the polling card you should have received. In 2000, *postal voting on demand*

was introduced, leading to some increase in response and, in a few notorious cases, also in fraud. Several all-postal votes have been held, notably in mayoral and regional assembly referendums, and several e-voting methods have been piloted – internet, touch phone, SMS, interactive digital TV – with a view to eventual *multi-channel elections*.

8. **Is voting easy?**
    Yes – completing the ballot paper could hardly be easier. In Great Britain we have used the same *plurality* or *first-past-the-post* system as in Parliamentary elections. You simply mark X against your preferred candidate (or candidates in a multi-member ward), and whoever gets the most votes is elected. Only in Northern Ireland – and, from 2007, in Scotland – is there a more voter-friendly opportunity to rank candidates in order of preference through the more proportional *Single Transferable Vote* system.

    Counting the votes is similarly straightforward, and councils' complete results are often available nowadays within a couple of hours of the polls closing.

9. **Will I recognise the candidates' names?**
    Not necessarily – though you may recognise your existing councillor if s/he is standing for re-election. Your ward may consist of between 1,000 and 20,000 registered electors, so even the most diligent candidate may not have got round to visiting you in person. But candidates can have delivered free to your residence at least a brief, probably illustrated, 'election address', describing themselves and the policies they support. They may also describe themselves, in up to six words, on the ballot paper itself, which will usually consist of their party affiliation.

10. **Could I stand as a candidate?**
    Probably – provided you are aged 18 or over (lowered from 21 in the Electoral Administration Act 2006), a British, Commonwealth or EU citizen, and have lived or worked in the council area for at least 12 months prior to your nomination. But there are disqualifications – for convictions, bankruptcy, etc. – the most important and controversial being that, if you are a paid employee of a local authority, you cannot also be elected to it, though you may be eligible to stand for a different authority. The latter disqualification was extended in 1989 to prevent senior local government officers and those in 'politically sensitive' posts from standing for election at all.

11. **Would I have to be nominated?**
    Yes, again as for parliamentary elections – by 10 electors for the ward concerned.

12. **Is it expensive?**
    Not terribly. It is cheaper to do badly than in parliamentary elections, since no forfeitable deposit is required. There is also an enforced limit on each candidate's expenditure – £600 plus 5p for each registered elector in 2006 – though few report spending anywhere near their permitted limit.

13. **Why is the system unnecessarily complicated?**
    Good question. It's simply historical accident, but it is, as the Electoral Commission have forcefully argued (2004), disjointed, discriminatory, confusing and effectively disenfranchising, since many electors simply don't know when 'their' elections are taking place.

    The Commissioners felt the case for simplification outweighed the merits for local diversity that we as authors favour in most other contexts. They recommended that all local electors in England elect all members of their district, borough or unitary councils simultaneously every 4 years, with county councils elected at the mid-point in that 4-year cycle. We agree.

well as some form of photographic ID at the polling station. However, in the face of the advice of almost all those professionally – as opposed to politically – concerned about the integrity of the electoral system, the Electoral Administration Act 2006, while creating new offences of electoral fraud, stopped short of reforming the registration system in the obvious practical way that would largely prevent it.

The electoral system – should England follow Scotland?

This casual abandonment of the principle of the privacy of the ballot is a constitutionally important, but recent, concern, arising out of the Government's rush to postal voting as a means of raising election turnouts. Even today, though, the greater controversy about current electoral practice is generated by the system itself: the *plurality* or *first-past-the-post* (FPTP) method of election. It is a well-tested and easily understood system, familiar to almost everyone through its long-standing use in all governmental elections in mainland Britain. Yet there is also widespread resentment of its obvious deficiencies and biases and, as all of the newly devolved institutions – the Scottish Parliament, the Welsh, Northern Ireland and London Assemblies – have adopted more proportional methods, electoral reform for local government has inevitably become part of any constitutional reform agenda. The main arguments for and against the existing system are summarised in Exhibit 11.2.

We do not intend to add greatly to the extensive literature on electoral reform, but it is appropriate, given the confusion that manifestly exists about one of those citizenship subjects of which we should all have a basic understanding, to make a few key points. First, it must be emphasised forcefully that the choice of electoral systems, locally or nationally, is not simply between *either* FPTP *or* proportional representation (PR). It is probably most useful to think of there being four basic *types* of system, as outlined in Exhibit 11.3.

Second, by far the most common local electoral system in Western Europe is the party list – but *not* the closed, depersonalised, unalterable list system UK voters were required to use in the 1999 and 2004 European Parliamentary elections. Most countries use either unblocked lists, enabling voters to express personal preferences for individual candidates, or an 'unordered' list, as in Finland, where, by voting directly for candidates, it is the electorate, and not the party 'selectorate', that determines the order in which parties fill their quotas of seats, and therefore who represents them.

Exhibit 11.2 The case for and against 'first-past-the-post' (FPTP) in local elections

For FPTP

- *Maximises the chance of a decisive electoral outcome*, with a single party having full power to carry out its programme. Conversely, minimises the likelihood of a coalition or minority government, and of protracted post-election inter-party bargaining.
- *Provides for a direct and personal councillor-constituent relationship*, unlike some systems of proportional representation in which representatives may not be linked directly to any geographical constituency.
- *Encourages parties to be broad-based, tolerant and moderate*, and discourages the creation and proliferation of new parties to represent new interests and arguments.
- *Reduces the impact of extremist parties and views.*
- *Is the easiest system*, both to understand and to administer.
- *There is no alternative system* on which there is widespread agreement.

Against FPTP

- *Distorts*, often grossly and even more than in Parliamentary elections, the relationship between votes cast and seats won. Parties regularly win overwhelming control of councils on either a bare majority, or even a minority, of votes. In other instances, a party gaining most votes may win fewer seats than rival parties with fewer votes.
- *Can effectively eliminate opposition*, producing councils on which opposition representation is either non-existent or too small perhaps even to be able to fill available committee places.
- *Wastes more votes* – in the sense of their going either to losing candidates or to build up needlessly large winning majorities – than almost any other system.
- *Reduces incentive to vote*, by reducing the proportion of potential voters who feel they can affect the result, either in their own ward or in the council as a whole.
- *Undermines perceived legitimacy of councillors*, since many, like MPs, are elected on minority votes – and usually on smaller turnouts than MPs.
- *Is electorally inefficient*, using only voters' first preferences and giving them no opportunity to express their political opinions in greater detail.
- *Is socially and geographically divisive*, benefiting the two major parties in areas in which they are already strong.
- *Is politically divisive*, encouraging adversarial politics, with more attention being given to demolishing the opposition than to fostering inter-party understanding. Can make post-election negotiation and co-operation on a hung council even more difficult than it would have been in any case.
- *May discriminate against women and ethnic minorities*, by making it harder for them to be selected and thus elected, though in fact female representation in British local government is higher than in at least some countries with PR systems.

Exhibit 11.3 Basic types of electoral system

1. *Plurality (or first-past-the-post, FPTP) systems*
   Vote for one candidate only, and the candidate with most votes (a plurality, not necessarily a majority) wins.
2. *Majority/majoritarian systems* – e.g., Alternative Vote (AV), Supplementary Vote (SV), double ballot
   These are *preferential* systems, usually in single-member wards/constituencies – including council-wide constituencies for mayoral elections. The main aim is not proportionality, but to eliminate, through the counting, if necessary, of voters' second and subsequent preferences, the possibility of a candidate being elected on a minority vote – as, for example, two-thirds of all MPs were in the 2005 General Election.
3. *Proportional systems*
   Any system, *necessarily* based on multi-member constituencies, which has as its aim the achievement of proportionality between votes cast and seats won.
   There are two main sub-types of proportional system:

   (a) *Party List systems* – which aim to represent *parties* in relation to their popular support, and in which any vote for an individual candidate is, at best, secondary to the vote for the party.
   (b) *The Single Transferable Vote (STV)* – preferential voting in multi-member constituencies, the key objective being to provide voters with a choice of candidates *within* as well as between parties.

4. *Additional Member Systems (AMS) – aka Top-up or Mixed Member Proportional (MMP) systems*
   Hybrid systems, combining single-member constituencies and party lists, 'additional' or 'top up' members being added to constituency members to achieve party proportionality in the elected body as a whole.

Third, notwithstanding its international popularity, no version of the list system *per se* is likely to feature prominently in any debate on the virtues of PR in British local elections. For us the principal choice would probably be between STV and some version of the Additional Member System (AMS), the latter, of course, incorporating a party list vote as part of its hybridity. STV, in use for many years in Northern Ireland, is the PR system chosen for Scottish local elections from 2007 (though rejected by the Welsh Assembly), and could be introduced comparatively easily in England, where there are already many multi-member wards and divisions.

In principle, it ought to appeal to those of all political persuasions who advocate maximum consumer choice.

AMS, however, is a form of election with which we are becoming increasingly familiar, and was the model advocated by the Jenkins Commission for the House of Commons, before the Labour Government reneged on its 1997 manifesto commitment to put the issue to a national referendum. It is also favoured by the LGA, whose Local Government Additional Member System (LGAMS) would have two-thirds of councillors directly elected by first-past-the-post as ward representatives, with the remaining third chosen from open party lists of 'top-up' members (LGA, 2001). Advantages over STV are felt to be that ward sizes could be kept smaller, and that, if allocated on an authority-wide basis (as for the London Assembly), top-up members would have the distinctive and useful role of representing the council area as a whole.

Both systems could give independent and minority party members a better chance of election, and both would certainly increase substantially the already sizeable proportion of hung or 'balanced' councils: 33 per cent, or 147 out of Great Britain's 441 in 2006/07 (see Exhibit 14.3). Neither would result, as the FPTP system does, in many of the country's biggest and most important councils *never* changing political control, and in three-quarters of London boroughs (12 Labour, 12 Conservative) and half of all metropolitan boroughs (18 – all Labour) having experienced periods of single-party control of at least twenty years, mainly on the basis of only minority votes for the controlling party (Game, 2004). Whether such outcomes are considered desirable depends on your personal political views. There is, however, plenty of evidence that hung councils can work eminently satisfactorily and may 'foster a more open and democratic form of local government than that typically found in majority controlled authorities' (Leach and Game, 1992, p. 152; also Leach and Stewart, 1992; Temple, 1996; Game, 2004).

Turnout – the British cultural disinclination to vote

The one thing that everyone thinks they know about local elections is that most people don't vote in them. They are right. Britain's 61.4 per cent in the 2005 General Election put us last among the 'original' fifteen EU countries in a listing of turnouts in most recent parliamentary elections (ERS, 2005, p. 5). But that figure was roughly double the recent average for English local elections, and in that league table we are and have long been indisputably at the bottom, as shown in Exhibit 11.4.

Exhibit 11.4 excludes the compulsory voting countries – Belgium, Luxembourg and Greece. Even so, the average turnout in most recent

Exhibit 11.4 Turnout in local elections: the UK and Western Europe

	Typical/averaged turnout		Percentage change pre-1995 to post-1995	Most recent General Election turnout
	1980–94 (%) (n)	1995– (%) (n/date)		(%) (date)
ENGLAND				61.3 (2005)
London boroughs[wc]	46 (4)	33 (2)	−13	
Metrop. boroughs[P]	40 (11)	31 (8)	−9	
County councils[wc]	40 (4)	*		
Shire districts[wc]	46 (4)	34 (2)	−12	
Shire districts[P]	41 (8)	33 (5)	−8	
SCOTLAND	44 (4)	45 (1995)*	+1	60.8 (2005)
WALES	50 (4)	42 (2004)*	−8	62.6 (2005)
N. IRELAND	55 (1)	55 (1997)*	=	62.9 (2005)
Austria	82 (1)	76 (2)	−6	84 (2002)
Denmark	80	69 (2005)*	−11	85 (2005)
Finland	73 (4)	59 (3)	−14	67 (2003)
France	68	65 (2)	−3	64 (2002)
Germany	71 (1)	58 (1999)	−13	79 (2002)
Ireland	60 (1)	54 (1999)*	−6	63 (2002)
Italy	85	75 (1999)	−10	81 (2001)
Netherlands	67 (3)	58 (2)	−9	80 (2003)
Norway	67 (1)	62 (3)	−5	77 (2005)
Portugal	65 (4)	60 (2)	−5	65 (2005)
Spain	63 (1)	67 (3)	+4	77 (2004)
Sweden	85 (3)	82 (3)	−3	80 (2002)

Notes: n = number of elections on which an averaged turnout figure is based; [wc] = whole council elections; [P] = partial, usually one-third of seats only. * indicates where sets of local turnout figures have been omitted on the grounds of elections having, exceptionally, taken place on the same day as national parliamentary, assembly or European Parliamentary elections.

Sources: Data from European Union, Committee of the Regions (1999); Rallings *et al.*, 2000, ch. 4; individual countries' statistical offices, etc.

European local elections, though frequently significantly lower than in earlier years, was between 65 per cent and 70 per cent – or roughly double most UK figures, except when local elections happened to coincide with either parliamentary or national assembly elections. In almost all countries fewer voters turn out for what are sometimes termed 'second-order' elections, for local councils and the European Parliament, but in England the local–national gap at the time of writing is between about 33 per cent and 60 per cent, whereas in Western Europe generally it is between about 63 per cent and 80 per cent.

What the UK figures in Exhibit 11.4 at least hint at is that, while voting in local elections clearly has declined in recent years, by comparison with continental Europe, it *always was* a minority pastime. This upsets those who argue that today's low figures represent either a conscious or subconscious response of electors to the undermining and enfeeblement of local councils by successive central governments. Back in the days when, say, a city council such as Birmingham's ran everything from education and trams to the gas and water supply, with its own municipal bank thrown in, *then* voters could see the point of voting and turned out in their droves – or so the argument goes. Well, not in Birmingham they didn't, as Exhibit 11.5 clearly shows.

Exhibit 11.5 What golden age? Birmingham local elections, 1920–2004

	Number of elections	Average turnout in contested seats (%)	Uncontested seats (%)	Candidates per vacancy
1920–29	10	42	17.7	2.1
1930–38	9	36	17.7	2.0
1945–50	5	44.4	0.5	2.2
1951–60	10	39.2	–	2.4
1961–72	12	32.4	–	2.9
1973–80[†]	7	36.1*	–	3.3
1981–90	8	41.2	–	3.6
1991–2000	8	33.0	–	3.8
2001–04	3	33.0	–	3.9

Notes: [†] 1972–74: Reorganisation of local government in England.
*Excluding 1979, when General and local elections were held on the same day.
Source: Data from Phillips, 2000, p.xxviii

The city may have had a golden age of municipal government, but, unless you count 1950, when, for the only time since 1918, local turnout touched a hardly awesome 50 per cent, it never experienced a golden age of local electoral democracy. Nor, in all probability, did most other towns and cities. In Birmingham's inter-war years, more than one council seat in six went totally uncontested – a proportion that would have been much higher still in more rural and less party-politicised parts of the country – and those elections that did take place were mostly straight fights between Conservatives and Labour. Indeed, by that contestation measure, local democracy's heyday is right now. The numbers of uncontested seats, certainly in England (less so in Wales) are minimal by comparison with even 30 years ago, and in many authorities, as in Birmingham, there are more minority party and independent candidates challenging for each seat than ever before (see Exhibit 11.9).

These two measures of electoral vitality – supply of candidates and voter turnout – need to be considered carefully by those keen to increase our involvement in local governance by increasing our voting opportunities. There are very few signs that people disinclined either to stand or vote in elections for councils responsible for setting local taxes and running a whole panoply of services – or, indeed, in parent governor elections at their own children's schools – are suddenly going to be enthused by elections for a police, social services or parks board. At best, the evidence in Exhibit 11.6 from elections to existing special-purpose bodies, is ambiguous.

A few of the early turnouts in New Deal for Communities (NDC) board elections – in Bristol, Sheffield and Newcastle – were certainly striking in what are by definition some of the most deprived localities of the country. But these owed much to their being small-scale, intensively publicised postal votes, often over two days, with well-known local candidates (identified by personal photographs), and with voters having a very personal financial stake in the outcome. *Average* turnouts have been below the figures expected in local elections in the same areas (Rallings *et al.*, 2004).

With Foundation Trust Hospital elections, it is the franchise itself that raises questions. In a high turnout election a few thousand voters will attempt to select up to 20 names from a list of several dozen, few, if any, of which they will recognise. Those elected, with perhaps no more than a large handful of first-preference votes, will then endeavour to represent the hospital's 'public', more than 99 per cent of whom have not taken the minimum step necessary even to register as trust members. To strip councils of still further responsibilities in the cause of single-purpose 'participatory democracy' of this nature would seem, on the face of it, bizarre.

Returning to council elections, it was those in 1990 that produced the most recent peak in local turnout: 46 per cent in Birmingham and over

Exhibit 11.6 Elections to single-purpose bodies

Americanisation or community control?

US local government is characterised both by its exceptional number of governmental units, and by the service fragmentation that results. The Census Bureau's 2002 *Census of Governments* recorded 88,000 local governments: 39,000 (44 per cent) General Purpose (counties, municipalities, townships), and the remaining 49,000 Special Purpose.

These *Special Purpose authorities* are largely independent of their respective General Purpose governments. Best known are the 13,500 school districts, responsible not least for curriculum content. Others include local single-purpose bodies for drainage and flood control, housing and community development, cemeteries, libraries, parks and recreation. Their board or commission members are in many, though not all, cases directly elected.

In recent years, we too have seen elections to single- or special-purpose bodies, as well as suggestions from different political perspectives for their spread to more policy areas. Both Labour and the Conservatives have supported wholly or partially elected police boards and/or police commissioners, and Labour Minister, Hazel Blears, wants 'community control' of a wide range of separate services run by locally elected Stakeholder Boards (Blears, 2003).

New Deal for Communities (NDC) boards

NDC is the Government's flagship strategy to renew and regenerate 39 of the country's most deprived neighbourhoods. Through the investment of some £50 million (£2 billion in all) over 10 years, these NDC areas are empowered to tackle problems of under-employment, crime, educational under-achievement, poor health, and housing. Strategic direction is provided by a board elected by and from local residents.

Early elections attracted the interest of both participants and observers, who saw the turnouts of 50 per cent in some places as pointing the way to a new 'distinctively local brand of politics' (Shaw and Davidson, 2002, p. 5). These figures, though, were the exception: turnouts have averaged less than 24 per cent (Rallings *et al.*, 2004), notwithstanding the novelty, the exceptionally local scale, and voters' personal stake in the project.

Foundation Hospital Trust Boards

Foundation hospitals are a controversial form of hospital introduced by the Government, intended to encourage a new spirit of enterprise and efficiency within the NHS. They are independent, member-owned legal entities, with greater financial discretion than traditional NHS hospitals. They are controlled by boards of guardians elected by their 3 constituencies of members: staff, patients and, most contentiously, the public – namely, individuals who live in the electoral area specified in the trust's constitution.

Staff and patient memberships are frequently 'opt out': people are registered and therefore able to vote unless they opt out. Public membership, potentially millions in some cases, is 'opt in', which means that the high and 'satisfactory' turnout figures of up to 70 per cent reported by the trusts themselves and the independent regulator (www.monitor-nhsft.gov.uk) are in fact percentages of perhaps 1 per cent of the public supposedly served by the hospital (www.epolitix.com/EN/MPWebsites/Frank + Dobson/Articles).

50 per cent in many districts across the country. Those figures, and the fact that they resulted very largely from people's infuriation over their poll tax bills, offer us an interesting insight into local voting behaviour. If and when people feel that what their council is doing really can make a difference – particularly to their local tax bills – more of them will vote. But, even at a time of almost unprecedented hostility between local and central government, a time of protest marches, demonstrations, riots, regularly disrupted council meetings, and widespread civil disobedience, it was still only *a few* more – and nowhere near the numbers in most other European countries in normal years. As Britain's General Election turnouts consistently show, the country's national political culture does not lead to the populace being particularly dedicated voters in any form of election, and any search, therefore, for some magic key to increase local turnout *substantially* is likely to be in vain.

Three ways to increase turnout

The absence of a single magic key, though, does not mean that nothing can be done. There are three types of reform that, certainly between them, would surely both increase interest and turnout in local elections: reform of local taxation, the electoral system, and voting methods.

In one important respect, Mrs Thatcher was right about the community charge/poll tax. If, through paying local taxes, people felt that they had a stake in their community and could see a clear relationship between the tax they paid and the services their council provided, more of them would be inclined to vote. Where she was wrong was in making her flat-rate personal tax the *only* local tax available to councils. If, however, as outlined in Exhibit 10.6, the present central:local balance of funding were reversed in local government's favour, and councils could call on a raft of different local taxes, payable by different groups of taxpayers, the conditions would exist for a repeat of the poll tax effect. A council's budget and any changes in its principal tax levels would be tied closely to proposed improvements or cuts in services, competing parties could put forward alternative budget and service plans, and voters would have a meaningful choice to make.

That choice, though, is only truly meaningful, if voters see themselves as having at least a fighting chance of replacing a council whose policies they dislike with one they prefer, which brings us back to the electoral system. In the 2005 General Election, in addition to the nearly 10 per cent of eligible voters who failed to register and the 38 per cent of registered electors who stayed at home, 70 per cent of those who did cast votes in effect 'wasted' them – either by voting for a losing candidate or contributing to an unnecessary surplus for the winner (Electoral Reform Society, 2005, p. 8).

Local elections, using the same plurality electoral system, are very similar. Millions of potential voters know that they live in wards and/or in council areas that are almost certainly 'safe' for one party or another: however they vote, or even if they don't bother, that party's candidate will win, and control of the council will remain unchanged. As has already been noted, more proportional electoral systems would do two things. First, they would take more account of an individual's vote preferences – either through a party vote as well as a candidate vote with the Additional Member System, or by considering their second and additional preferences with STV. Second, they would eliminate most wards and councils that are currently safe for any single party, making results and outcomes much less certain and reducing the perception of any individual vote being a waste of time.

Bringing as it would these increased incentives to vote, a PR electoral system in local government would almost certainly raise turnout a little, as happens elsewhere. Blais and Carty (1990, p. 179) studied over 500 national elections in 20 countries and found that:

> Everything else being equal, turnout is seven percentage points lower in a plurality system, and five percentage points lower in a majority system, compared with PR.

The Blair Governments' refusal even to examine the case for local electoral reform has at least had the merit of consistency – perhaps not surprisingly, considering that their power has been derived very largely from the FPTP system's ability to turn minority votes into massively inflated parliamentary majorities. The disingenuous dismissal from the outset has been that the Government 'does not view changes to the voting system as a panacea for the current weaknesses in local government' (DETR, 1998d, para. 4.26) – as if anyone were seriously suggesting that they were.

Consequently, when driven by the embarrassing collapse of the 2001 General Election turnout to consider ways of getting more of the population to vote, Ministers turned not to the electoral system itself – nor, indeed, to compulsory voting, as practised in Australia, Belgium, Greece, Turkey and in all about a sixth of the world's democracies – but to the administration of elections and *methods* of voting. At each annual set of local elections, apart from the General Election years of 2001 and 2005, the Electoral Commission organised and evaluated an extensive programme of pilot schemes, ranging from postal and different forms of electronic voting to the replacement of ballot paper serial numbers with barcodes. While barcodes in themselves are not great vote motivators, the

Exhibit 11.7 The shape of future elections

Piloting of alternative voting methods

Between 2000 and 2004, the Electoral Commission (EC) evaluated 130 pilot schemes, mainly by individual local authorities, testing out various innovations in the electoral process. The majority of these pilots were of different voting methods – by post or electronically; by touchtone telephone; the internet; digital television; and SMS text messaging; but they also included electronic counting, extended voting hours and non-traditional voting locations.

Impact on turnout

The Government's main concern in initiating this pilot programme was to raise voting turnout.

Postal voting was found to be the most effective – all-postal voting in pilot areas in the 2003 local elections appearing to raise turnouts on average by 15 per cent, from 34 per cent at the previous election to 49 per cent (Electoral Commission, 2003b). In the four all-postal pilot regions at the 2004 European Parliamentary and local elections, turnout was on average 5 per cent higher than in non-pilot regions.

Electronic voting, whether by electronic kiosks based in polling stations or remotely, was generally well received by voters, who appreciated the additional choice, but in most cases it made no significant difference to turnout.

The way forward to multi-channel elections

Both the EC and the Government are committed to the principle of multi-channel or e-enabled elections, including an e-enabled General Election sometime after 2006. Progress towards that goal includes:

- *Continued choice* of voting methods. *All-postal voting*, certainly in the EC's view, should *not* be used in future statutory elections or referendums.
- *Postal voting on demand* should continue, *but* with the necessary safeguards to improve security and reliability, and retain/regain public confidence.
- The EC argues that these safeguards should include:
  o the replacement of household registration with *individual registration*, with electors being required to provide individual identification details – e.g. signature, date of birth;
  o voters being asked to confirm their date of birth against the information held on the register; and
  o all postal and proxy vote applications to include the personal identification details collected at registration.
- *Electronic voting schemes* will require further technical piloting, and the consideration of issues such as vote-selling. These are not a high priority, at least until after the implementaton of the Electoral Administration Act 2006.
- There should be a Great Britain-wide electronic register, compiled locally, to enable people to vote at any polling station in the country.

pilots suggested that postal voting definitely could be (see Exhibit 11.7), and it quickly became a widely used option in all major elections, accounting for 15 per cent of the votes cast in the 2005 General Election (Electoral Commission, 2005b, p. 47).

To judge from the 2004 local elections, postal voting, at least until the novelty wears off, may provide the kind of 'quick fix' solution to plummeting turnouts that the Government was apparently looking for. Nothing changed overnight about the quality of either the government or the services that councils were providing, yet the overall 41 per cent turnouts for both the metropolitan boroughs and the shire district councils were the highest since the 1990 poll tax elections (Rallings and Thrasher, 2004, p. xv). No form of e-voting has yet shown anything like the same impact on turnout, and, while it will undoubtedly be a key element in full-scale multi-channel elections in the future, it was not in 2005/06 being accorded any governmental priority.

Local votes

As we saw when discussing the Single Transferable Vote, certain types of reformed electoral system could have the effect of increasing the 'localism' of local elections. Independent, local or minority party candidacies can be encouraged, and electors given more opportunity to vote on local issues, on the merits or otherwise of the candidates, and generally to play a more involved part in influencing election outcomes. But, while an extension of these practices would be welcomed by many, they do all in fact happen *already*. Many voters require no reminders from the editor of *The Times* (see p. 226) of the importance of treating local elections as genuinely local events.

Local issues, local candidates

This section of the chapter returns to our starting point by introducing some actual illustrations of local voting behaviour. A comprehensive study of the subject, Miller's provocatively entitled *Irrelevant Elections?* (1988), found, even in the 1980s, when more of the populace identified strongly with political parties than they do today, that a great many voters treated local elections very much as *local* events:

- 56 per cent of respondents claimed to be influenced in local elections *more by local than by national issues*;
- 39 per cent claimed to vote *more for the individual candidate* in a local election than for the party; and

- 20 per cent had *local party preferences different* from their current national party identification.

In summary, up to one-fifth of electors reported voting for *candidates of different parties* in local and parliamentary elections. To this figure, moreover, should be added the many more who supported candidates of the same party in the two sets of elections, but on the basis of different considerations.

Split-voting evidence

A certain proportion of this differential voting behaviour will inevitably be self-cancelling, with some voters preferring Party A's candidate locally and Party B's nationally, while others do precisely the reverse. There has, though, been a perceptible bias in recent years towards the Conservatives in parliamentary elections and to non-Conservative parties locally, with the Liberal Democrats especially polling consistently higher locally than nationally.

The most conclusive evidence of people's readiness to vote differently in parliamentary and local elections is that provided fortuitously in the 'synchro-elections' in 1979, 1997, 2001 and 2005, when prime ministers Callaghan, Major and Blair, respectively, were forced or chose to call General Elections on a day already fixed for the year's local elections. Millions of voters found themselves with two votes to cast: one for their MP and one for a local – usually county – councillor.

Exhibit 11.8 indicates the extent to which such people chose to split their votes in two recent instances, supporting candidates of different parties in the two different elections. The 33 constituencies were deliberately selected *not* for any exceptional evidence they showed of split-voting, but because their local and parliamentary boundaries coincided precisely, and because each major party fielded a candidate in every council contest. Typically, in both years the turnouts in the two sets of elections were almost identical, but actual voting behaviour was not. Tens of thousands of these roughly 1.5 million electors must have split their parliamentary and local votes in each election year. How many in total we cannot know, but even the *net* effect of their actions meant that both the Conservative and Labour parties fared considerably better in the General Elections, while the Liberal Democrats did very much better locally.

We do not in fact need synchro-elections, however; there is plenty of evidence to be found of the impact of local electoral influences through the study of almost any set of local results. Start digging beneath the headlines and the aggregated figures, and you will be struck almost immediately by the diversity and apparent inconsistency of the detailed ward-by-ward

Exhibit 11.8 Split-voting, 1997 and 2001

33 English constituencies with 'perfect' competition

	Con (%)	Lab (%)	LD (%)	Other (%)	Turnout (%)
General Election, June 2001	38.8	38.3	19.2	3.8	61.7
Local (county council) elections	37.0	34.3	26.3	2.3	61.0
Difference: General minus local	+1.8	+4.0	−7.1	+1.5	+0.7
Difference in 1997	+2.0	+4.4	−8.5	+2.1	+0.6

Source: Data from Rallings and Thrasher (2001, p. 12)

results. One ward is gained by the Conservative candidate, while an adjacent, previously Conservative-held ward is lost. Labour win control of one council but lose control of several others. Third and minority party candidates and Independents win seats and even whole councils against all other parties (see Exhibit 11.9).

The June 2004 elections – baths and bus routes as well as Baghdad

For our illustrations of local electoral influences at work we have chosen what should have been a particularly difficult year – 2004. The local elections – for all metropolitan and 108 English unitary and district councils, Welsh unitary councils, the London Mayor and Assembly – were postponed from May, because of the earlier foot-and-mouth disease outbreak, to coincide with the June European Parliamentary elections. The delay, though, was immaterial, because, as the electorate was told repeatedly by the national media, these elections would be all about the Government's participation in the invasion of Iraq and associated issues, and, if not, then about opposition to the EU and its proposed constitution. Any local factors would be submerged in what would be in effect a national opinion poll, the anticipated outcome being a heavy defeat for Labour councils and councillors, swept out of office on what would in reality be an anti-Government or anti-Blair vote.

The post-election media headlines suggested that this is exactly what did happen. Labour's results were among its worst ever. Its 26 per cent share of the national vote was below that of both the Conservatives and the Liberal

Exhibit 11.9 The Idle Toad and friends

A few of the many minority parties contesting, and winning, recent local elections

IDLE TOAD – one of the growing number of local community parties. Based in South Ribble, Lancs, where they have 4 district councillors and a county councillor – the 'IT' himself, Tom Sharratt. A fee-less, whip-less party with a constitutional aim borrowed from Labour's old Clause IV. Check out their website, newsletters and useful 'Guide for Young Voters'.

LIBERAL PARTY – *not* the Lib Dems, but the rump of the historic Liberal Party who opposed the party's 1988 merger with the Social Democratic Party. 30+ councillors, many elected against Lib Dem opposition.

GREEN PARTY – evolved from the Ecology Party (1975–85). Peaked in 1989 with 15 per cent of the vote in Euro-elections and nearly 9 per cent in locals, but has gradually extended representation from rural and university town base (Stroud, Oxford) into urban areas – Kirklees, Bradford, Leeds, Hackney. 90+ councillors in 2006, including 2 London Assembly members.

MEBYON KERNOW – 'Sons of Cornwall' or, more prosaically, 'The Party for Cornwall'. Left of centre and decentralist, rather than separatist. For a better deal for a neglected county – a Cornish Assembly, university, EU funding recognition. Members on three of the six districts.

BRITISH NATIONAL PARTY – Formed out of National Front (NF) in 1982, though NF still in existence. Under Nick Griffin's 'respectable' leadership, has exchanged its racism for 'ethno-nationalism' and a populist programme aimed at those disaffected by either New Labour or Cameronian Conservatism. Attracted massive alarmist publicity at 2006 local elections and reached total of 46 councillors.

HEALTH CONCERN – the ultimate single-issue party, with its own MP since 2001, Dr Richard Taylor. Campaign launched in 1998 to stop downgrading of Kidderminster hospital and demand reopening of its A and E department. Deprived Labour of overall control of Wyre Forest Council in 1999, became largest group in 2000 and for a time part of an anti-Labour governing coalition.

PEOPLE'S JUSTICE PARTY – also started as a single-issue campaign to free two Pakistani Kashmiri separatists jailed for killing an Indian diplomat. Took council seats from Labour in inner city Birmingham, and changed its name to appeal to all sections of the community in these deprived areas.

RESIDENTS' AND RATEPAYERS' ASSOCIATIONS – long-standing alternatives to parties as a form of representative democracy. Strongholds in suburban Surrey – Epsom and Ewell, run by RAs since 1936, and Elmbridge – and East London/Essex – Epping Forest, Barking, and especially Havering, where they have been part of power-sharing administrations.

PEOPLE AGAINST BUREAUCRACY GROUP – founded in 1976 to reduce bureaucracy in and keep party politics out of local government, particularly in Cheltenham, where they have 5 borough and 2 county councillors. Other concerns: underground parking, residential area speed zones, firework sales.

Democrats, it lost a total of 545 seats and its former control on 16 councils, including Newcastle and Doncaster – both for the first time in 30 years – Leeds, Burnley, Ipswich, Oxford, Cardiff and Swansea. The Lib Dems took Newcastle and Pendle (Lancs) and gained 239 seats. The Conservatives gained 315 seats and 12 councils, including Dudley, Trafford and Walsall metropolitan boroughs and Eastbourne from the Lib Dems.

If these elections had been fought and won entirely on national issues, that would have been the end of the story. Scratch beneath these surface figures, though, and you quickly come across some apparent anomalies. Among all their losses, Labour in fact *gained* 84 seats and as many as 7 new councils – including Hartlepool and Stoke-on-Trent, both led at the time by Independent elected mayors. Similarly, the Lib Dems' victories were qualified by the *loss* of 110 seats and 4 councils. Even the Conservatives lost 56 seats, including that of their group leader on the London Assembly, and, more significantly, they failed to prevent Ken Livingstone's re-election as London mayor.

As indicated in Chapter 5, Livingstone's win owed almost everything to his unique public profile and the well regarded record of his first term of office, but, on a necessarily smaller scale, there will have been comparable 'local' factors of some sort at play in all the other results that deviated in any way from the national trend. In Swansea, for example, voters were certainly disaffected, but more by the Labour council's closure of civic swimming baths than by the fate of Baghdad, while in Redditch it was voters' opposition not to Saddam that swept Labour back to power, but to the Conservatives' plans to abolish concessionary bus fares for the elderly and vulnerable. In other places the story was sheer hard work by local party activists, as one Labour councillor in Birmingham defeated by a Lib Dem ruefully acknowledged (Coulson, 2005):

> [It was] the culmination for them of ten years of serious leafleting, six or seven leaflets to each house ahead of each election, the quality of the leaflets greatly improved by the use of desktop publishing and fast Xerox copying.

The point about all these local factors – let alone the micro-local issues, such as the number 14 bus route and new dog mess bins that a Milton Keynes candidate, Liz Campbell, found raised when she canvassed on doorsteps (Campbell, 2004) – is that they are completely unknown to national journalists and election 'pundits', who will therefore dismiss as 'freak' or 'maverick' any result that doesn't fit into their own national picture of what the elections were about. But, of course, they are not freak; simply the visible and perfectly rational products of voters' recognition that, on this occasion, it was not an MP they were being asked to elect, or a national government, but, rather, a local councillor and council to carry out local policies and provide local services. It is to these councillors that we shall turn in Chapter 12.

Councillors – The Voice of Choice

Introduction – counterbalancing a bad press

The Local Government Association once lobbied hard to get an informative and sympathetic local government storyline into ITV's North Yorkshire soap, *Emmerdale*. It is not hard to see why. The image of councillors conveyed to TV viewers – even before *Dr Who*'s alien, flatulent and definitely unelected Lord Mayor of Cardiff and her city centre nuclear power station scheme – has been not so much bad as awful. *Coronation Street*'s Councillor Audrey Roberts, handicapped by having to be unconvincingly scripted as an Independent on what in reality would be a totally party-dominated council, was self-important and manipulable. *Eastenders*' Ian Beale, in his brief membership of Walford Council, operated entirely self-interestedly and quite possibly corruptly. And the two outstanding 'state of the nation' drama serials of the 1990s – Alan Bleasdale's *GBH* with Robert Lindsay, and Peter Flannery's *Our Friends in the North* with Christopher Eccleston (again) – both had councillors' abuse of power and corruptibility running through their storylines (see Brooke, 2005; Mahony, 2005).

This chapter explores – with a bit more information and balance – who councillors really are, what they do, and why they do it. Don't rely wholly on us, though. Try to talk to one or two of your own councillors. Find out at first hand how they spend their time and how they justify their elective existences. They will not be 'typical', but a key message of this chapter is the unhelpfulness of thinking exclusively of typical roles and behaviour. Others may generalise, whether or not for dramatic effect. You should aim for a little more subtlety in your own analysis, and you will probably find that your councillors differ one from another just as much as do our own small castlist, which we shall now introduce.

Five pen portraits

Maureen

Maureen has been a councillor for some twenty years, and today is an executive member on the Labour-controlled unitary council of a

Lancashire textile town. She is a single parent who has brought up three now teenage children. From a Labour-voting family, she joined the party soon after leaving school and worked her way steadily up through its local hierarchy.

Once elected, she was quickly rewarded with the 'apprentice' post (long disappeared) of Vice-Chair of the Allotments Sub-Committee. She later served for several years as Chair of Housing, politically responsible for the council's stock of 12,000 houses and flats. Long before the advent of executive local government, she became effectively a full-time councillor, living off income support, spending most evenings as well as daytimes at the town hall, conscious that she was seeing less of her children, and 'bribing them' with money for chips. She then started some employment training, of which she disapproved politically but it brought in an extra £10 a week. It also meant, however, that she had to fit as much of her council work as possible into her lunch hour –'when officers are never available, unless I absolutely insist on it'.

As Housing Chair, she saw through to completion a large town centre clearance programme, negotiated with a housing association for the provision of good quality rented housing, and reduced the council's empty properties and rent arrears significantly. But

> the single most important policy I delivered, believe it or not, was to allow our tenants the choice of colour of their front door. I could remember, as a tenant myself, the people from the council going down the street on our estate, and they used to have so many colours which they used in turn. One of the colours in my particular street was a purple and I remember counting the houses and being relieved that I just missed getting this awful purple. I didn't want the yellow I got, but I really hated that purple. So, when I was Chair, I said to officers that they had to give a choice of colour. They couldn't understand at first the importance of going to someone's door and asking them what colour, of having contact with them *as tenants*, and *not* because they'd done something wrong. It's a small thing, but it gives everyone a good feeling.

Simon

Like Maureen – indeed, like most councillors – Simon's membership of a West Midlands city council has involved some tricky time management, though in rather different circumstances. He was one of several young Conservatives whose election in 2000 reduced the council's average age considerably, as well as enabling his party to take at least minority control from Labour for the first time in 20 years. This was obviously exciting. However, at just 23, Simon found his chief qualification – a recently completed Politics degree – was scant preparation for the initial demands of council life in the pre-executive era:

> I remember our first [party] group meeting following the election, and the process of allocating committee places. Not that any of us 'new boys' knew what we were volunteering for, as there seemed very little explanation about what the different committees actually did. I just liked the sound of Leisure Services – it tied in well with my experience at the time as a manager of a local nightclub riverboat firm.

A problem with riverboat nightclubs, though, is their tendency to operate in the evenings, coinciding with council committees, and Simon admits he depended greatly on 'an understanding boss who was very supportive of my political foray'. Fortunately, his natural self-confidence enabled him to cope with the 'shoved in at the deep end approach', as the council provided no formal training for new councillors:

> The formal members' induction was a wine and nibbles evening with the chief officers. The guided tour consisted of a brief description of the rooms in the Guildhall that we needed to know about: the committee admin, post room, where the chief executive lived. We were also told how the 'yellow peril' system worked – a form for submitting enquiries or requests for action to the departmental chief officers. Evidently, modern forms of communication such as the telephone or email were frowned upon, as this would mean members might contact other officers without going through the chief officer – something that would clearly cause a mutiny.

Simon, a 'big C' rather than a 'small c' Conservative, resolved to cause or, if necessary, lead such a mutiny and shake up this seemingly laid-back, officer-dominated culture as soon as he was in a position to do so – which proved to be sooner than even he had imagined. By 2004, the Conservatives had achieved majority control, and Simon was deputy leader of the party group, and thereby of the Council:

> We now have a member training champion who, with our training officer, has put together a comprehensive induction programme. New members will now be mentored by an experienced colleague. The Council also provides a home PC to any member needing one, and pays for an internet subscription, so that members can either email or talk directly to the officer best placed to answer a query.

As deputy leader, Simon is portfolio holder for what on this council is known not as 'finance and the budget', but 'Financial Prudence and Value for Money', and, as if that were not time-consuming enough, in 2005 he became a 'dual member' and very much a 'professional councillor', winning a seat on his county council.

Afzal

Afzal's council career, like Simon's, advanced swiftly following his first election in 2000, but in his case his 'overnight' success in becoming in 2005 the first Asian, and first Muslim, Lord Mayor of Manchester, took more than half of his 47-year lifetime (see Hammond, 2005).

Mohammad Afzal Khan was born in Pakistan, the son of a British Indian army officer. When aged 12, he was 'adopted' by his uncle, came to England, settled in a Lancashire cotton mill town – and, hardly surprisingly with his almost complete lack of English, struggled. Leaving school without qualifications, he worked in the mill, progressing to become a weaver, until he experienced 'a life-changing moment – I just said to myself: "No, I'm not staying here" '.

He took O-levels in his spare time, then, by now married to his younger cousin, studied for A-levels at the local college, becoming student president and founding Asian and Muslim groups. Reversing the convention in many Asian families, he took a succession of jobs as bus driver, youth worker and policeman, to enable his wife to qualify as a dentist. Today she has her own NHS practice. Afzal's own professional qualification came later, after rejecting his superintendent's advice and leaving the police to study for a law degree, eventually becoming a partner in a thriving solicitor's practice. Once more, though, he changed his life:

> I was drawn more and more to public service and, given my background, I was attracted naturally to the Labour Party because of its tradition of fighting for social justice and helping the disadvantaged.

His first term as a Labour councillor was inevitably a difficult one. Afzal was opposed to and spoke out against the invasion of Iraq by his own party's Government, and had to become a kind of public spokesperson for his religion:

> Contrary to how it is sometimes seen, Islam is a very generous religion. I do not see it as proscriptive at all. In fact, it is very open and pluralistic, quite happy to tolerate the existence of other creeds.

Which is why during his year of office as (ceremonial) Lord Mayor, he appointed not the traditional single chaplain from his own religion, but a team of chaplains, representing the various religions in the city: 'That I can embrace Manchester and Manchester can embrace me exposes the lie of the racists; it proves that different races, religions and cultures can happily co-exist.'

Joyce

Joyce too came relatively late to party politics. Her first significant contact with her West Midlands metropolitan council, though, was as a protester.

Indeed, before being elected, she had never attended a council meeting. Like many future councillors, she was activated by a public issue with a personal impact: the threatened closure of her daughter's primary school by the Labour-controlled council. She tried to galvanise other parents into action, but without success: the school was closed.

Soon afterwards she was contacted by the local Liberal Democrat leader, who said how impressed he had been with her activity, and would she consider standing as the party's ward candidate at the following May elections? While previously a Lib Dem voter, she had never contemplated becoming a councillor. But, having given up her career as a civil servant and with her children now at school, she agreed and was elected with a large majority.

From Joyce's viewpoint, her Lib Dem ward seemed like a small yellow island in an otherwise largely red Labour sea. She feels fortunate in having been mainly on committees (and now Cabinet Advisory teams and scrutiny panels) in which she is genuinely interested – education, schools and environment – but gets frustrated at always being in a very small minority. Almost inevitably, therefore, she spends a great deal of her time on the representational or ward-based part of her councillor role: dealing with electors' problems.

Keith

There are thousands of councillors who could identify with both the positive and negative aspects of Joyce's position, but none better than Keith, as, at one time, that was precisely his position; same council, same ward and same minority party.

Keith was similarly approached about standing as a Lib Dem candidate after playing a leading role in a community protest: against the council's erection of an unwanted fence around a local housing estate. He, like Joyce a few years later, was elected at his first attempt. But, with his business background, disillusion swiftly set in:

> I was naive. I thought that, being a councillor, I could actually assist people in my area ... but not as a Liberal Democrat I couldn't. My time is precious. If I was going to put 100 per cent effort in, I wanted to see results.

That, he concluded, on his perpetually Labour council, meant switching parties. So he left the Lib Dems, first becoming an Independent, and then 'crossing the floor' to join the Labour group. He was, hardly surprisingly, viewed with much suspicion, but was 'rewarded' at the next Annual Meeting with the Chair of Further Education, 'which sounds exalted, but in fact no one else wanted it'.

With his sole GCE O-level in Biology, his knowledge of FE was minimal – though, as he says, 'that's what the officers are there for'. What he knew about and was genuinely interested in was the youth and community part of his committee's responsibilities. So, for three years he threw himself into the job. He was heavily involved in the council's planned reorganisation of secondary education, and was able, at the same time, to do something for his own ward: bringing together all the local voluntary organisations and forming a community association with its own Community Centre ... in the very building that used to be Joyce's daughter's school!

Here, then, is our own small cast, to which you may be able to add one or two of your own pen portraits. Three women, two men; a unitary councillor, one shire and three metropolitan district councillors; one Conservative, two Labour, one Liberal Democrat, and one Lib Dem–Lab switcher; three currently in powerful policy-making positions, one very active ward representative, and one major community figurehead. Plenty of labels and contrasts, but what do they have in common – among themselves and with the other 22,000 councillors across the country?

Elected local politicians – the voice of choice

To start with – and it is not quite such an obvious statement as it may appear – they are, all 22,000 of them, elected local politicians. Let us examine briefly the three parts of that description in turn.

There was a time, before the 1970s' reorganisation of local government, when the majority of members on many councils were unelected. Part of the reason was *aldermen*: usually senior and experienced councillors, who were appointed by the elected councillors to bolster their numbers by up to an additional third, and to add expertise and continuity. Their appointments were for six years – compared to councillors' then three-year term of office (now four years); they tended to take disproportionate numbers of committee chairs and vice-chairs; and they never had to seek the support of, or face possible defeat from, a fickle electorate. They were undemocratic, but they unaccountably – in all senses – lived on until, apart from in Northern Ireland and the City of London, they and their Scottish near-equivalents, *bailies*, were finally abolished in the 1970s.

These unelected aldermen would have seemed even more anachronistic, had not many councillors themselves also never had to face an election, because, as noted in Chapter 11, the sorry truth is that, throughout most of the history of UK local government, thousands of council seats at each year's elections were filled by unopposed returns, 40 per cent or more councillors by the 1960s winning or retaining their council memberships unchallenged.

There thus existed a kind of double democratic deficit – up to a quarter of council members who did not have to be elected and large numbers who should have been but were not. This is one local government deficit that has, since the 1972–4 reorganisation, been virtually eliminated. With over 95 per cent of seats in most parts of the country now being contested by more candidates than at any time previously, councillors, both individually and collectively, can claim with far greater legitimacy to be speaking as their community's 'voice of choice'. They are the instruments through which the residents of a particular geographical area have expressed their preferences for one set of candidates, policies, service standards and tax levels, rather than another.

Politicians all

Choice, preference, priorities ... they are the currency of politics, and those who translate them into practical policies are politicians. The third attribute of all our councillors – in addition to being at least nominally elected and representing specific geographical localities – is that they are politicians. All of them – even the small minority of self-styled 'non-partisans' and 'independents' – perform what Sir Lawrence Boyle, a key member of the Widdicombe Committee, termed the 'political function':

> all governments, be they central or local, have a two-fold function to perform. They have the *service function* and the political function. The service function consists of the provision of those goods and services which for one reason or another are supplied through the public sector. The political function, on the other hand, is the management and reduction of the conflict which arises out of the issues involved in the public provision of goods and services. It embraces such questions as *the scope, the scale and the quality of the public services and the manner in which their costs should be met.* And it should be noted that it is easier in fact to remove the service function from local government than it is to remove the political function. Because the service function, as we know, can always be privatised, but *the political function cannot and should not be delegated. If the political function is removed from local government, it ceases to be local government.* (Boyle, 1986, p. 33, emphases ours)

That, surely, is what we expect of our elected representatives, national and local alike: that they debate and determine *themselves* – not delegate to unelected officials – the distribution of our society's resources. The electorate delegates the political function to them: to take on their behalf decisions about the building of houses, schools and roads, about levels of service provision and rates of taxation. That is their role and responsibility, whether or not they happen to have been elected under a party label. Most are; and we shall see in Chapter 14 how that party identity shapes almost every aspect of their work.

Representatives, not reflections

Councillors, then, are all local elected politicians. But what *kinds* of people are they, who have the apparent arrogance to wish to exercise *their* political will on the behalf of others, yet who are, at the same time, prepared to plead for the electorate's votes and to risk ridicule and rejection? How like their own electors are they, or how different? The standard response to this question tends to detail councillors' personal and socioeconomic characteristics, as in Exhibit 12.1. There is nothing intrinsically wrong with such data. They are relatively easily collected and categorised – in fact, there are nowadays regular councillor 'censuses' – and they furnish us with measures of over- or under-representation of particular attributes in the population of councillors.

It is, for example, worth knowing – as opposed to merely suspecting – that there are fewer women councillors than there are councillors over conventional retirement age; that the number of black and minority ethnic (BME) councillors has declined since Labour came into office in 1997; and that the proportion of councillors with current responsibility for dependent children is under half that for adults generally.

Such data, though, have their limitations. They can prompt unwarranted and misleading generalisations. They may obscure significant contrasts among councillors in different parts of the country, on different types of councils, and from different parties. They can also seem to imply that 'representative government' is more about trying to produce, like President Clinton's first 'Mirror on America' Cabinet, a socioeconomic reflection of the electorate than about the representation of ideas and ideals. With these reservations in mind, we draw out a few key distinctions and implications – in the hope of *discouraging* the idea that there is a 'typical councillor'.

Gender

Most readers will surely find the gender figures in Exhibit 12.1 dispiriting, even if the proportion of women councillors has increased by about a half since the 1980s and, as ever, is substantially higher than that of women MPs (19.7 per cent in 2005). There are also more women *councillors* in the most senior positions in local government than there are women officers:

more women leaders and deputy leaders (16 per cent) than chief executives, more women cabinet members (26 per cent) than chief officers (EO/IDeA, 2005). Perhaps more surprisingly, though lagging far behind Sweden and Norway (42 and 37 per cent) and our own PR-elected Scottish Parliament and Welsh Assembly (40 per cent and 50 per cent), Britain has more women councillors than many European countries (CEMR, 2000). France, however, leads the way with 48 per cent, following its controversial Parity Act 2000, requiring political parties to nominate equal numbers of men and women as prospective *commune* candidates: an example for those who favour quota systems as the only effective way of changing biases in electoral representation.

Does such gender distortion matter, or make a difference? Inevitably, yes. Councils on which 75 per cent of members are men simply do not pursue the same priorities and arrive in the same way at the same decisions as would councils with even 40 per cent, let alone 75 per cent, of women members. The cliché illustration is that more women would mean better child care facilities and fewer municipal golf courses. But there is much more to it than that. Women are the main users of council services. They make three-quarters of all calls to council departments. They are the majority of tenants, the family members who make most use of swimming pools and libraries, who are most likely to put the bins out for collection, and who are most affected by the quality of the local environment – inadequate street cleansing, poor lighting, dog fouling, pot-holed roads and pavements, inadequate public transport, and street crime. They are likely to have distinctive priorities and agendas.

If you still have doubts, try two simple questions. Why do most public buildings have far fewer female than male toilets, instead of recognising, like the rebuilt Royal Opera House – a noteworthy exception to the rule – that roughly three times as much space should properly be allowed for women as for men? And why, as a Birmingham overview and scrutiny committee discovered, are there almost no workplace policies in public sector organisations covering the specific needs of breast-feeding mothers returning to work?

Ethnic minorities

An equivalent argument applies to the under-representation of ethnic minorities – 3.5 per cent compared with 8.4 per cent of all adults. These groups also fare a little better locally than nationally (2.3 per cent of MPs in 2005) and – while, as in Exhibit 12.1, their presence is still recorded more meaningfully in absolute numbers than percentages – the election of black and Asian councillors especially has increased markedly in recent years.

Exhibit 12.1 Personal characteristics of councillors – England, 2004

Party (percentage of total)	All councillors (%)	Conservative (39%) (%)	Labour (29%) (%)	Lib Dem (23%) (%)	Indep. (8%) (%)
GENDER					
Male	71	73	71	65	77
Female	29	27	29	35	28
ETHNIC MINORITY	3.5	1.4	7.2	2.1	0.7
Black (total numbers)	(85)	(6)	(62)	(15)	(0)
Indian	(184)	(26)	(140)	(15)	(3)
Pakistani	(119)	(25)	(64)	(28)	(2)
Other, including mixed	(230)	(44)	(135)	(41)	(6)
Total	(618)	(101)	(401)	(99)	(11)
AGE					
Under 25	*	*	1	*	*
25–34	4	3	4	4	1
35–44	9	8	10	10	6
45–54	20	16	26	21	17
55–64	37	36	36	42	38
65–69	16	18	14	13	19
70 and over	14	18	10	11	19
Average	58	59	56	57	61
HAVE CHILDREN UNDER 16	13	15	14	15	9

EDUCATION – HIGHEST QUALIFICATION					
Degree or equivalent (NVQ 4/5, HNC, HND)	50	48	51	61	38
GCE A-level or equivalent (NVQ 3, ONC, OND)	12	14	10	11	11
GCE O-level or equivalent (NVQ 2, School Cert)	13	16	9	11	16
Trade apprenticeship	6	5	7	4	8
Other	5	5	6	4	5
No formal qualifications	14	12	17	9	22
EMPLOYMENT STATUS					
Full-time paid employment	25	21	32	26	16
Part-time paid employment	11	9	13	12	9
Self-employed	16	22	8	14	25
Unemployed	2	1	3	2	1
Retired	39	41	36	37	41
Looking after home and family	3	3	2	5	3
Other (incl. disabled, full-time education)	4	3	6	4	5
CURRENT OCCUPATION (excl. council work)					
Managerial/executive	37	46	29	30	37
Professional/technical	28	26	30	31	26
Teacher/lecturer/researcher	9	5	13	14	5
Admin/clerical/secretarial/sales	14	13	14	15	14
Manual/craft	14	10	14	10	19
TIME SPENT ON COUNCIL WORK					
(average hours per week)	(21.5)	(20)	(24)	(21)	(20)
DUAL MEMBERSHIP					
(of more than one principal council)	8	9	8	9	7

Notes: * = less than 1 per cent | . | = significantly higher than for adult population   ( ) = actual number, not percentage

Source: Data from EO/IDeA (2005).

But any national figures in this instance are particularly misleading. What matter are the levels and details of representation in those areas with sizeable ethnic minority populations. In Birmingham, for example, there are more than 20 ethnic minority members on the 120-seat City Council. Nearly 20 per cent might seem like a tolerable representation of the city's 30 per cent ethnic minority population – until you consider the sheer diversity of that population: the African-Caribbeans; the Kashmiri restaurant owners, taxi drivers and textile industry outworkers; the Punjabi Sikhs, with their prominent role in the local economy; the small-business-owning Gujuratis from both India and East Africa; the Bangladeshis; the Yemenis; the Chinese and Vietnamese, and all the newer refugees – the Somalis, Sudanese, Afghans, Bosnians, ethnic Albanians, Kurds, Iranians, Iraqis, and the many more identifiable 'communities' in the city. Most of these groups are bound to feel unrepresented – not merely under-represented – on the City Council in any direct racial, religious or cultural sense, and if this is true in Birmingham, it is even more so in most other towns and cities.

Age

If age really did bring wisdom, our local government could compete with the Chinese gerontocracy, for the world of councillors is an increasingly middle-aged and elderly one. Simon and his fellow young Conservatives are, today at least, very much the exceptions. In the 1985 Widdicombe Committee survey reported in this book's early editions, over a quarter of all councillors were under the age of 45, including a third of Labour members and nearly a half of the then Liberals. At the time of writing, the proportion of under-45s – 13 per cent, compared with 46 per cent of all adults – is much lower than even the 21 per cent in 1964 (Wilson and Game, 1998, p. 221) – which means that nearly 30 per cent of all today's councillors are aged over 65. Labour and the Lib Dems are the 'youthful' parties in modern-day local government, but they have age averages of 56/57 – about six years higher than those of MPs. In Scotland, the average age is slightly lower, but it is higher for English counties and was for Welsh councils until the Assembly approved a 'past service award scheme' of severance payments of up to £20,000 for older councillors, to encourage them to retire. Few councils, though, are anything other than visibly venerable, as Joyce recalls thinking at her first council meeting:

> I was really surprised by the number of elderly gentlemen. There were only about five councillors in my age group [mid-30s], and I'm the only lady councillor with young children. I'm probably the only one who has to organise arrangements for looking after their children while they're at council meetings.

Regrettable, it might be felt, for a council whose responsibilities include childminding, children's centres, crèches, day nurseries, play centres, parent and toddler groups, pre-school playgroups, toy libraries and nursery schools.

Education

Partly as a result of their age profile, councillors as a whole are both better and no better educated than their constituents. Returning again to the 1985 Widdicombe survey, the proportion of councillors with no formal qualifications (23 per cent) was half that among the adult population as a whole. Today there is virtually no difference. There are still differences, though, in levels of qualifications, with 50.2 per cent of councillors having NVQ 4 or above, compared with under a quarter of the general population. While such qualifications are not in themselves, of course, any measure of fitness or aptitude for government, education is presumably one characteristic on which most of us would be happy to see our elected representatives not perfectly reflective of the population at large.

Employment

Given the long-standing tradition of council membership being a voluntary and part-time activity, it is striking that only 41 per cent of today's councillors are in full-time paid employment – a figure that varies in total very little across the parties, although the employed/self-employed balance predictably does. Part of the explanation of the major decline from 65 per cent in 1976 and 54 per cent in 1985 is obviously the fact that almost as many (39 per cent) are now retired, compared to just 16 per cent in 1976 (Gyford *et al.*, 1989, p. 51). The other key factor, as we shall see, is that councillors' allowances have increased significantly and are just reaching the levels that can support, albeit modestly, a life-style as a full-time councillor. In the past, few councillors openly admitted to being 'full-time', no matter how many hours a week they put into the job; in the 2001 councillor census, over 30 per cent did so, and the number will surely continue to grow almost by the year.

With their higher educational qualifications, it is not surprising to find councillors coming disproportionately from non-manual backgrounds in general, and from professional and managerial groups in particular. There is a correspondingly low proportion of manual workers: 14 per cent of employed councillors or 7 per cent of the total, compared with nearly 30 per cent of the adult population. The manual proportion of Labour councillors in particular has fallen, from 35 per cent in 1985, and in 2004, for the first time, it was no higher than that for all councillors.

Councillors' jobs and roles

We now know something about who councillors are. They can and do come from all kinds of backgrounds and walks of life. It is neither easy nor helpful to talk of there being a 'typical' councillor. So does it follow that there is no such thing as a typical councillor's job? Yes, it does. Different councillors will have their differing interests, motivations, skills, aptitudes and opportunities, and they will at least endeavour to spend their inevitably limited time in differing ways.

There is nowadays, unlike in the past, at least some guidance in most councils' constitutions (usually Part 2, Article 2) as to councillors' 'Roles and Functions', swiftly followed by their 'Rights and Duties'. These are of limited assistance, partly because of their blandness, but mainly because they are aimed consciously at 'all councillors', which, in our new regime of executive-based local government, means that they cannot provide more than a very incomplete picture. With that proviso, however, we can construct out of these role lists a kind of composite starting description, as in Exhibit 12.2, not so much of the councillor's job, but of the job of councillors.

Exhibit 12.2 The job of (all) councillors

- To represent, be accountable to, and an advocate for, all their electors ...
- in formulating policies and practices for the local authority ...
- monitoring their effectiveness ...
- and providing leadership for the community ...
- while (of course) maintaining the highest standards of conduct and ethics.

To balance its limitations, this kind of starting description has three considerable virtues. First, it is a neat distillation of what might otherwise be a lengthy catalogue of more specific councillor duties and responsibilities.

Second, it takes us far beyond the traditional and apparently almost unthinking textbook distinctions that used to be made between 'policy' and 'administration': that councillors made policy and officers implemented and administered it, and ne'er the twain should meet. The sheer lack of realism underpinning this 'formal model', as we term it in Chapter 15, grated most with local government practitioners. Was it seriously imagined, on the one hand, that a small group of part-time, amateur councillors had the capacity – or even the inclination – to produce a 'policy' for every aspect of every council service *without* there being a necessarily substantial contribution from the numerous highly trained, experienced and generally well-paid officers whom they themselves employed? Similarly, were councillors really supposed, having delivered their policy pronouncements like proverbial tablets of stone, to stand aside and pay no attention as to how the policy was delivered and to its impact on their own local residents and electors? As Maureen might say, that is a recipe for loathsome purple doors!

This thought brings us to the third virtue of our starting definition, which is its expression in language that makes sense to councillors themselves. Councillor roles and 'role orientations' have long been a favourite topic of academic investigation, and some insightful studies have resulted (Lee, 1963; Heclo, 1969; Hampton, 1970; Budge *et al.*, 1972; Dearlove, 1973; Jones, 1973; Corina, 1974; Newton, 1976; Jennings, 1982; Gyford, 1984). But so too has a positive lexicon of role labels: politico, delegate, trustee, representative, broad policy-maker, tribune, statesman, ministerialist, parochial, people's agent, policy advocate, policy spokesman, policy broker, party politician, ideologist, partyist, facilitator, resister, politico-administrator, communicator, populist, conventional politician, community politician.

For the reader, such a proliferation of labels can produce confusion as well as enlightenment. From most councillors, though, the more likely response would be cynicism. Even if they recognised the actual words, they would not naturally think of using most of them to describe the behaviour of either themselves or their councillor colleagues. They would, on the other hand, recognise and identify with the language of representation and accountability, policy formulation, performance monitoring and community leadership.

The councillor's 'traditional' job description thus embraces a wide variety of potential roles and responsibilities – as representative, policy-maker, scrutineer, and community leader. Today, without further qualification, that simply will not do. With executive-based policy making, and councillors having to be either part of their council's executive or not, some of these roles and responsibilities continue to be shared by all councillors, and all are exercised by some. But, for the first time, not all councillors are able even to claim that they have all roles. To explain, we shall examine each in turn.

Representative – on the grand scale

We start with the most fundamental role of all, yet sometimes the most overlooked. Under our system of local government every councillor is elected by, and is accountable to, the residents of a defined geographical area, known as an electoral *ward* or *division* - 'constituency' being primarily a parliamentary term. With the exceptional scale of UK local government, these local electorates can be dauntingly large from the viewpoint of councillors trying to represent them.

Exhibit 12.3 lists only the 'old' EU countries, but its underlying message would hold, no matter how many other countries were added. We have proportionately fewer and much larger 'local' authorities than almost any other Western country, and they will be even fewer and larger, if the anticipated restructurings in Northern Ireland, Scotland and non-metropolitan England go ahead. Corollaries of this scale of 'local' government are that – with the single exception of Ireland, the most centrally administered governmental system in Western Europe – we citizens have fewer councillors to represent us, and inevitably we are less likely to know or be known by them. If anything, the figures in the final columns of Exhibit 12.3 understate the scale of the councillor's task. When many districts' multi-member wards are taken into account, an average English district councillor has an *electorate* of between 3,000 and 5,000, a county councillor one of up to 10,000, and a metropolitan district, unitary or London borough councillor one larger still. Multiply these figures by, say, 1.5 for total residential populations, and the reality is that in large city and unitary authorities councillors may represent wards of up to 25,000 people.

As with other aspects of the job, councillors themselves decide how much energy they put into the representation of their electorate. They do not *have* to hold surgeries or advice bureaux, or publicise – preferably nowadays through the council's internet – their availability to deal with constituents' problems, complaints, queries and opinions. Most council-lors, though, do choose to do these things, and much more besides. In which case, they are likely to find themselves acting in several distinct representational 'sub-roles', in addition to case-worker and individual problem-solver: as listener, advocate, ring-holder, facilitator and empow-erer (Goss and Corrigan, 1999, pp. 13 ff.).

They *listen*, and talk of course, when they meet the various groups, organisations and individuals within their wards: tenants' and residents' associations, community groups, housing associations, youth clubs, local fêtes, health and police authorities, local business people and journalists. They act as *advocates* in ensuring that the views, needs and problems of local people, particularly those likely to experience access difficulties, reach the appropriate sections of the council. Sooner or later they will be required to act as *ring-holder* in some dispute between individuals or groups, each convinced of the validity and justice of their case. They will go further and *facilitate*, by working with excluded, aggrieved or factionalised groups, bringing people together to discuss problems and jointly agree solutions. And on occasions they may *empower*, assisting local groups to organise, prepare and resource themselves in order to manage some council project or take over responsibility for a service.

All these 'external' activities are capable of bringing relatively swift and positive outcomes and, at least very occasionally, an expression of

Exhibit 12.3 Britain's large-scale local government – by population per council

	Population (millions)	Number of lower tier (most local) principal councils	Average population per council	Total number of councillors	Persons per councillor
France	60.7	36,782 Communes	1,650	515,000	118
Austria	8.2	2,380 Gemeinden	3,440	40,570	201
Spain	40.3	8,108 Municipios	4,970	65,000	623
Germany	82.4	12,434 Gemeinden	6,630	198,000	418
Italy	58.1	8,101 Comuni	7,170	97,000	597
Greece	10.7	1,033 Dimoi, Kinotites	10,360	18,600	573
Finland	5.2	444 Kunta	11,710	12,400	418
Belgium	10.4	589 Communes	17,660	13,000	800
Denmark	5.4	271 Kommuner (until 2007 → c.100)	19,930	4,700	1,161
Sweden	9.0	290 Kommuner	31,000	46,240*	195*
Portugal	10.6	309 Municipios	34,300	9,000	1,200
Netherlands	16.4	467 Gemeenten	35,120	9,600	1,713
Ireland	4.0	85 Cities, boroughs, towns	47,000	874	4,576
UK	60.4	434 Unitaries, districts	139,000	19,999	3,020
UK	60.4	468 ALL principal councils	129,000	22,268	2,712

Note: * includes deputies, elected at the same time. To enable the most realistic cross-national comparisons, these figures exclude tiers of councils that, like the UK's parish, town and community councils, have only very limited service responsibilities and/or are not universal.
Sources: Data from The Local Channel (2005), pp. 4 and 7; individual countries' sources.

gratitude from those benefiting. The rewards of 'internal' town hall or county hall work, especially for a non-executive member, may seem more diffuse, and it is easy to understand why many councillors find that their representational work is what brings them the greater satisfaction (Barron *et al.*, 1987, pp. 73 ff.). Intriguing (in all senses) as he sometimes found meetings in Lambeth town hall, Jonathan Myerson, a member of the council's Labour minority from 2002 to 2006, was probably one of those. Certainly, there has been no better contemporary insight into the councillor's representative role than that provided by his monthly column in *Society Guardian*, to be preserved eventually in book form, one hopes.

For other first-hand accounts, several authorities, including Brent, Kirklees, Stockport and Tameside, have developed the useful practice of having their councillors produce regular reports for their personal websites detailing what they have been doing, and what they feel they have achieved. There are also councillors' weblogs, still (in 2005) relatively few in number, but bound to grow, particularly with clearer Government guidance on the distinction between informing the public and political campaigning. Stuart Bruce (Labour, Leeds) was the acknowledged first councillor blogger, and, in the interests of party balance, honourable mentions go also to Lynne Featherstone (Lib Dem, Haringey) and Kevin Davis (Conservative, Kingston upon Thames).

Policy maker

The mention of town halls brings us to the policy role of councillors – traditionally their work in committees, sub-committees and panels in developing policy, both for the authority as a whole and for particular services. They are assisted, informed, advised, and perhaps even steered, by their officers, but constitutionally they have the responsibility for giving strategic direction to the authority and for determining its policy priorities.

In the past, this policy or executive role, like that of representative, was shared by all councillors, though again the nature and impact of their contribution varied enormously. A committee might be chaired by a long-serving member, seemingly as conversant with the technical details of departmental policy as most of the professional officers, but include also a neophyte and perhaps minority party backbencher, still struggling to follow the procedure of the committee, let alone its agenda. All councils, though, organised their work through committees, and all councillors would find themselves appointed to at least one or two. All councillors could thus quite properly regard themselves as contributing to policy-making in at least some of their council's service areas, and all were collectively responsible for its policy as a whole. All too were potentially liable to be individually surcharged for supporting unlawful local expenditure, even when they themselves had received no personal benefit from the decision – quite unlike, say, a government minister who is demonstrably responsible for a major and horrendously costly policy failure. The personal surcharge was finally abolished in the Local Government Act 2000, but, as recently as the rate-capping battles of the mid-1980s, 78 Labour councillors in Liverpool and Lambeth were surcharged a total, with costs, of over £600,000 and consequently bankrupted (Taafe and Mulhearn, 1988).

The far more comprehensive change introduced by the 2000 Act, though, was the executive/non-executive split in councillors' roles described in Chapter 6. From 2001/02 councillors on most authorities became *either* executive *or* non-executive members. With most authorities adopting either mayor/cabinet or leader/cabinet models (see Exhibit 6.1), the small minority of cabinet or executive board members usually have responsibility for a specific service portfolio. But even if that portfolio closely resembles the title of a committee they formerly chaired, being a cabinet member is very different from being a committee chair. The key point of the executive/non-executive split is to clarify publicly who is responsible for making any particular policy decisions, and that is what executive members do: they make decisions and take public responsibility for them through the process of scrutiny by non-executive members. Some of these decisions will be taken collectively, by the cabinet as a whole, but others will be taken *individually* - in a way that previously was not legally permitted for even the most powerful committee chair or council leader.

Executive members, then, are now the key *policy makers*, but that does not mean that non-executive members no longer have a policy role. They do, in several distinct ways. First, as ward representatives and perhaps members of area committees, they see and hear how the policies of the council and other bodies have an impact on their own electors and localities. If a policy is not working in the way intended, or if service delivery is unsatisfactory, they are likely to be the first to receive complaints, and repeated complaints should feed into the process of policy evaluation and review.

Second, they are members of the *full council*, which, like councillors themselves, has a much changed and potentially enhanced role under executive government. The executive leads the preparation of the local authority's policies and budget, but the policy and budget frameworks have to be agreed formally by the full council. The full council has similarly to agree the many policy plans and strategies that authorities are now required to produce: the best value and performance plan, children's services plan, community care plan, crime and disorder reduction strategy, and so on. Executive members take 'in-year' decisions on resources and priorities to implement agreed policies, but decisions not in accordance with the policy or budget framework, or that are not constitutionally the executive's responsibility, go to full council. The council also receives and debates all overview and scrutiny reports, which brings us to councillors' third main role, that of scrutineer.

Scrutineer

The policy process is best visualised as a continuous cycle – from initiation, through formulation, enactment and implementation, with the cycle completed by evaluation, the outcome of which may lead in turn to a further policy initiative or adaptation (see Figure 12.1). The cycle does not stop with legislation or enactment, and nor do councillors' policy responsibilities. As John Stewart emphasises (1990, p. 27):

> Councillors are concerned not merely with policy, but with how policy is carried out, for in implementation policy succeeds or fails. Policy and implementation can never be completely separated. Policy is made and re-made in implementation.

The overview and scrutiny (O & S) function is *the* key non-executive role in the Government's 'modernisation' of councils' political management, and its effective operation is arguably the real determinant of whether the executive/non-executive split is judged a success. The good news, therefore, is that it was given a considerably broader interpretation than at first seemed likely, and introduced into local government something that clearly ought to have existed previously but, by almost universal admission, did not. The bad news is that it is the aspect of the new arrangements that councils and the non-executive councillors most affected have found it hardest to get working productively (see, e.g., Rao, 2005).

Under the committee system, there had long been something called 'performance review', but it was almost invariably reactive and superficial

Figure 12.1   *The policy cycle*

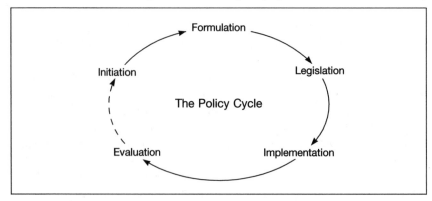

– often delegated to a single sub-committee with responsibility for monitoring the council's performance across any and all service areas. O & S can and should be unrecognisably different: expansive rather than delimited, pro-active rather than reactive, prospective as well as retrospective, creative and constructive as well as critical and blame-seeking (Audit Commission, 2001, p. 9; see also Exhibit 6.6 above).

Quite properly, councils themselves decide how to organise the O & S function. There are thus differing configurations of committees and panels, of differing sizes, and with differing terms of reference. Some councils, commendably, have chairs and vice-chairs from minority parties, and some do not. Some invite community representatives to participate as non-voting co-opted members, others do not. All, however, *must* reflect the political balance of the council, must meet in public, and must review all matters that are the responsibility of the executive, no members of which can be members of a scrutiny committee.

In so far as the council's constitution permits, scrutiny committees set their own agendas. They can require members of the executive and council officers to attend their meetings and be questioned about what they are planning to do (policy review), what they are doing ('call-in'), what they have done (*ex post* scrutiny), and how effective it has been (service review). If unsatisfied, they can make recommendations for further action or amendments to either the executive or the full council. They can invite evidence from other individuals and organisations. They can, if they wish, investigate the performance of other organisations and partnerships in local governance – the health service, the police authority, registered social landlords, a PFI project, even the local university.

As will be apparent, the ultimate effectiveness of scrutiny and overview involves non-executive councillors challenging not just the executive, but also their own party identities and loyalties. Majority party members have to work with colleagues from *other* parties in scrutinising and perhaps criticising publicly the performance of senior executive members of their *own* party. But, to vie for the place of the 'party loyalist' role, other specifically scrutiny-related 'sub-roles' have emerged: lobbyist, policy analyst, challenger (Snape and Dobbs, 2003). All of which emphasises just how novel and alien O & S have been found to be by those familiar with, and perhaps skilled at, working the committee system. They *are* different; they are *not* easy, they almost certainly *do* require training and the development of new skills – and that, precisely, is their importance.

Community leader – or champion?

It is striking that not one of the role labels listed at the start of this section included the word 'leadership', and it is a role that many councillors may not embrace readily. It is, though, one that is being pressed on councillors at precisely the time that councils no longer have the service-providing dominance in their areas that they once had. As service provision has become more fragmented and councils work in partnership with other organisations in a network of community governance, councillors stand out increasingly as the only democratically elected pieces in the ever more complex jigsaw. They are the ones in closest touch with the electorate and service users; they are the ones likely to have to field inquiries about non-council service providers – health authorities, housing associations, primary care groups. If their particular local community is going to have leadership, over and above mere representation, where else is it going to come from?

The Government's answer, to encourage councillors to embrace this new responsibility, is through their becoming 'community champions' (ODPM, 2005h, ch. 4) – in much the same way that they can boost their scrutineer role by becoming 'champions' of special interests, such as the elderly, the under-5s or the disabled. Or through reinventing the wheel, as Myerson (2005, p. 11) more or less put it, in his gentle mocking of the idea:

Does John Prescott not realise that councillors are already champions? When you walk into a room and the officer has to address you as 'Councillor', that is accountability. It is not power, but it is championing with consequences.

Of course, champions for disabled or older people are important, but *councillors champion everyone*. So maybe it does make sense to replace local councils with champions. But here is my idea: let's replace them with people called councillors. (emphasis ours)

A split, but not a chasm

With community leadership, we have come full circle – back to one of what we described as jobs for all councillors. With the executive/non-executive split of councillors' roles, policy making and scrutiny can no longer be so described, but a key message of the past few pages is that this is as far as the split should go – it is not a chasm. If you list, as in Exhibit 12.4, the principal council arenas or councillors' potential roles, you will see that, numerically, most are still shared by executive and non-executive members alike. Moreover, given what we have argued about the inter-dependence of policy and implementation, and the policy development role of scrutiny, even the big arenas – cabinet, overview and scrutiny – should not be seen as entirely separate worlds. For either to function to optimum effect, collaboration is required. It may, for perfectly understandable reasons, be hard to cultivate, but it has to be sought.

Exhibit 12.4 Roles for all

Council arenas	Executive members	Non-executive members
ALL MEMBERS – SAME ROLES		
Representation of ward and constituents	✔	✔
Area committees – various devolved functions	✔	✔
Regulatory committees – e.g. planning, licensing	✔	✔
Standards Committee – to oversee standards of conduct	✔	✔
Appeals panels – e.g. on school admissions and exclusions	✔	✔
Appointments to outside bodies	✔	✔
Community 'champions'	✔	✔
Political groups	✔	✔
ALL MEMBERS – DISTINCTIVE ROLES		
Full council – debating and approving council's budget and policy framework	✔	✔
Full council – questioning and holding executive members to account	Being questioned	Questioning
EXECUTIVE MEMBERS ONLY		
Cabinet/executive	✔	
NON-EXECUTIVE MEMBERS ONLY		
Council Chair and Vice-Chair		✔
Overview and scrutiny	Attending when invited	✔
Supporting the executive – e.g. policy forums, cabinet advisory panels		✔

Source: Information from LGA (2000a).

The workload

It is clear that, with more than 2,700 of us to every one of them, the job of a UK councillor in either a committee or an executive system is both multi-faceted and potentially extremely demanding. So how much time does it all take?

There is no simple answer. Like an MP, a councillor could 'get away with' doing an absolute minimum: attending the occasional council and scrutiny committee meeting and avoiding, as far as possible, all contact with constituents. Evidence suggests, however, that there are few such councillors nowadays, and that the more frequent behavioural pattern adopted is a maximalist and proactive one. That was certainly the impression formed by the authors of a study of councillors and their partners entitled *Married to the Council?* (Barron *et al.*, 1987, 1991). Their albeit limited sample of county councillors were spending between about 20 and 35 hours *per week* on their council duties.

Other studies, using different methods of recall and recording, have produced slightly lower figures. But there has been sufficient consistency across national surveys over the years for us to have confidence in the latest councillor census figures given in Exhibit 12.1, showing that the time spent by members of *all types* of authority on their council and related political work is around 86 hours per 'typical' month, or just over 20 hours per week (Robinson Committee, 1977; Widdicombe Committee, 1986b; Rao, 1994, 2005). Such averages, though, must be read with care. Figures for executive members (113 hours per month – Rao, 2005) and for most on urban and unitary authorities – including those in Scotland and Wales – would be much higher; and those for 'backbench' shire district councillors rather lower.

It seemed that up to two-thirds of councillors' time in the 1980s and 1990s was in some way meetings-related: attending them, preparing for them, and travelling to and from them. By comparison, constituency and community business occupied only about a fifth of their time – an imbalance that was one consideration behind the Government's political management reforms, aimed at enhancing members' representational roles and reducing the time spent relatively non-participatively in committee meetings. The councillor census figures suggest there has been less change in this pattern than had been hoped for by the Government. Constituency work now occupies on average just under 5 hours per week (23 per cent), while the combination of council, party, external meetings and travel amounts to nearly 12 hours (56 per cent).

Financial compensation

The jobs of councillor and MP may be similar in their open-endedness. In their financial rewards, though, they are emphatically different. MPs have index-linked salaries of £59,095 (2005), as part of an annual pay and allowances package totalling, for the *average* backbencher, over £180,000 – a sum that would cover what many shire district councils pay out to *all* their members in the form not of salaries, index-linked or otherwise, but allowances. Yet ironically, of the two groups, it is councillors, even under the traditional committee system, that have by far the greater and more immediate personal power – in the sense of contributing directly to decisions to spend budgets and allocate contracts of hundreds of millions of pounds. MPs can merely question, scrutinise, approve or disapprove the spending decisions of Government ministers.

Times, however, are changing fast. With the arrival of executive councillors have come, on a modest scale at least, UK local government's first executive salaries – or, strictly speaking, 'pensionable remuneration', to emphasise that pensionable allowances do not make executive members employees of the authority. In earlier editions of this book we equated the annual allowances that most councillors received to the then maximum undergraduate student grant of under £2,500. Though there are plenty of authorities where basic allowances are still well under £2,500 (£50 per week), a more accurate comparison nowadays is with the maximum student loan of £4,195, or £5,175 with the London allowance (2005/06). As shown in Exhibit 12.5, the average basic allowance for all councillors in England in 2004 was £5,187, ranging from under £1,700 in Cambridge and Great Yarmouth shire districts to £12,600 in Manchester and £14,000 (£280 per week) in Birmingham. In Scotland the average was £7,000, with the prospect, though delayed at least temporarily by the Scottish Executive, of a rise to £20,000 after the 2007 local elections.

Unlike the situation prior to 1995, English local authorities are now entirely responsible for determining their own structures and rates of allowances, acting on the advice and recommendations of a local independent remuneration panel. It is these panels, therefore, who should take most of the responsibility for the rising national averages, their aim presumably being – like that of the Government – to acknowledge the demanding nature of councillors' work, to attract a more diverse range of quality candidates, secure adequate support and training budgets, and assist family members with child care. Then, of course, there is the additional issue of recognising the greatly extended personal responsibilities of the leaders and executive members of particularly large urban and unitary councils and determining the appropriate remuneration of what are in some cases more than full-time posts.

So why do they do it?

The Government hoped this new system of allowances would address some of the existing disincentives to serving in local politics, while recognising that 'people do not enter public service to make their fortune' (DETR, 1998a). The latter 'recognition' hardly needed stating. Few councillors would claim that a desire for financial reward was their prime

Exhibit 12.5 Councillors' remuneration – England 2004

HISTORY

1972   Attendance Allowances first introduced – £10 per day maximum

1980   Special Responsibility Allowances payable to leaders, committee chairs, etc.

1991   Three allowances available to every local authority, within limits defined by the Minister:
(a) Basic flat-rate Annual Allowance;
(b) Special Responsibility Allowances;
(c) Attendance Allowance

1995   Government-imposed limits removed. Councils built *job description* for each councillor in line with their responsibilities and payable at rate of the average non-manual wage.

THE PRESENT SYSTEM – from 2001

Individual authorities continue to decide their own allowances. The Local Government Act 2000 requires all principal councils to establish and maintain an *independent remuneration panel* of at least 3 persons to advise the council on: its scheme of allowances; the amounts to be paid; and the pensionability of executive members' allowances.

Allowances *no longer* to be paid:

● *Attendance Allowance* – abolished 2001: encouraged an 'attendance culture'.

Allowances that *must* be paid:

● *Basic Allowance* – flat-rate allowance paid to all council members in recognition of their time commitments in attending council and party group meetings, meeting officers and constituents, and their incidental costs – use of home, private telephone, etc.

Allowances that *may* be paid:

● *Special Responsibility Allowance* – for executive members and other councillors with significant additional responsibilities, including at least one minority party member
● *Childcare and Dependent Carers' Allowance* – new allowance payable to councillors who incur expenditure for care of dependent relatives or children while undertaking 'approved council duties'
● *Travel and Subsistence Allowance* – payable if felt not to be adequately covered in basic allowance
● *Meetings Allowance* – payable to non-elected members co-opted or appointed to certain council committees and panels (eg scrutiny committees, school exclusion appeals panels)

THE THREE ELEMENTS OF BASIC ALLOWANCES

1. Estimate of hours required to perform the tasks expected of a non-executive member of the council.
2. Decision on the appropriate hourly/daily rate to be paid (e.g. median male full-time earnings: £25,100 pa/£471.50 per week (2005) – often adjusted to compare with local pay rates).
3. Decision on size of Public Service Discount: in recognition of the principle of council work as voluntary service, some proportion of hours should *not* be remunerated – usually between 20 and 50 per cent.

AVERAGE ALLOWANCES – SOME EXAMPLES, 2004

	Basic	Lowest	Highest	Exec. member	Leader
All authorities	**£5,187**	**£1,666** (Cambridge)	**£14,000** (Birmingham)	**£7,782**	**£14,571**
London boroughs	8,084	5,000 (Kingston upon Thames)	10,490 (Croydon)	14,929	26,742
Metropolitan districts	8,700	6,000 (Dudley)	14,000 (Birmingham)	11,377	24,420
Shire counties	8,091	5,400 (Cambridgeshire)	11,300 (Kent)	12,195	21,724
Shire districts	3,396	1,666 (Cambridge)	8,445 (Bolsover)	4,732	9,363
Unitaries	6,493	2,097 (Windsor/ Maidenhead)	10,195 (Brighton/ Hove)	8,528	17,089
London Assembly (2005)	49,266	n/a	n/a	n/a	see below

SOME HIGHER PAID LEADERS, 2004

Greater London Authority	Ken Livingstone (Mayor)	£134,000 (2005)
Newham LBC	Sir Robin Wales (Mayor)	£68,000
Hackney LBC	Jules Pipe (Mayor)	£65,000
Stoke-on-Trent Unitary C	Mike Wolfe (Mayor)	£62,000
Hartlepool Unitary C	Stuart Drummond (Mayor)	£50,200
Birmingham City C	Mike Whitby (Leader)	£48,000
Islington LBC	Steve Hitchins (Leader)	£45,000

Source: Data from IDeA (2005).

motivating force in becoming a councillor, and even the figures in Exhibit 12.5 are hardly beyond the dreams of avarice. So what are councillors' motives? What drives them to put in these large numbers of hours for distinctly modest compensation and apparently little public recognition?

Power, status, self-aggrandisement, ambition, compensation for personal insecurity, or even sexual inadequacy … the drives and motives attributed to politicians are legion, and mostly unflattering. They are not to be ridiculed or lightly dismissed, but this is not the place in which to speculate about councillors' essentially private motivations. Our intention is to conclude this chapter in the way we started: with our own small castlist of members, to see what we can conclude about *their* motivations.

Our first observation must be the apparent lack in most of their pre-local government careers of any deep-rooted or single-minded wish to become councillors. Maureen's original candidacy was a natural progression from her increasingly active involvement in her local party, and her wish to further its policies and goals. Afzal's spur was somewhat similar, though considerably later in life. For Joyce and Keith, 'events' were really the key recruiting agent, since neither were even party members before being asked to consider standing.

Far from it being carefully planned, most of our members found themselves projected almost unpreparedly into council membership. They were not exactly 'reluctants', but neither can they be seen as very driven 'self-starters', actively seeking and scheming for an additional career. They were working full-time, bringing up young children, looking after elderly relations, or all three. As a result, the almost insatiably time-demanding nature of council work has involved for them, as for most councillors, potentially costly occupational choices, and at least some sacrifice of home and family life – Simon perhaps being the exception, having arrived at a time when becoming a full-time councillor was just about financially feasible.

If they have a 'lust for power', most of our five manage to keep it fairly well concealed. They do, however, seek *influence* and *involvement*: in the planning and development of their local environment, in getting a better deal for their constituents and local community, in furthering a particular cause or, more generally, the policies of their parties: activities that may bring them more direct satisfaction and sense of achievement than their day-to-day jobs. Similarly, they value being in or close to the places where decisions are taken, and the quality of people's lives are determined.

They also appreciate the company of their fellow councillors, the shared interests and experience, and the gossip-laced conversations and negotiations – including those (initially unexpected) across the political divide. As Maureen recalls:

At first, I didn't understand why we even sat in the same room as these Tories. But they're mostly quite helpful, and I find that most councillors are fully committed to what's good for the borough. Often you walk out of a meeting and they'll tell you privately they agree with you. These are the things nobody ever told you – that you could and do co-operate.

With executive government and the development of all-party scrutiny procedures, it was never more important for her to be right.

Chapter 13

The Local Government Workforce

Beware (again) of generalisations – look around you

A key message in Chapter 12 was that there is no such person as a 'typical councillor', and that we should avoid making unthinking generalisations as if there were. There are well over a hundred times as many employees of councils as there are elected members – so it is at least as important to avoid a similar trap with them. There is a potential trap, just as with councillors. Ask, say, a class of students what ideas they immediately associate with a career in local government, and their replies are likely to include things like: office work, meetings, routine, bureaucracy, nine-to-five, red tape, more meetings, job security – and, possibly nowadays, the 85-year pension rule. The reality is far more complex.

As we noted in Chapter 12, the democratic scale of our so-called 'local' government system is so large that most people do not personally know their own councillors, or, in many cases, any councillors at all. Statistically, this is highly unlikely to be true of employees of councils. If

Figure 13.1   *Cartoon – The emotional frontline*

Source: Harry Venning (*The Guardian*).

you know 20 employed adults, the chances are that one or more will work full-time or part-time for a council. The chances are at least equally high, though, that they will not describe themselves as council *officers,* which is one reason why this chapter is entitled as it is, rather than being headed 'local government officers' or even 'the professionals'. When it comes to the making of policy or interacting with councillors, we shall have plenty to add to what we have already said about the role of professional officers. We start, though, with a much wider look at the whole local government workforce. It covers over 500 different occupational areas and more than 3,000 job titles, which means that many employees are *not* based in offices, or even indoors, do not have their lives governed by meetings, and would not remotely conceive of themselves as bureaucrats.

Our own favourite council employee is Harry Venning's *Society Guardian* cartoon strip star, *Clare in the Community* (Wednesdays, along with the public service job adverts), now in her own award-winning radio series, played by *Smack the Pony*'s Sally Phillips. Clare would certainly never call herself an officer, but might well hit you if you questioned her professionalism. She is a college-educated, professionally trained and professionally responsible social worker, with all the compassion, care and conscience that such training imbues. She spends her days, and frequently evenings too, doing 'society's dirty work', confronting life on the 'Emotional Frontline'. She rarely sees a councillor or goes near her council's town or county hall, but works, probably from an outlying district office, as part of a five-member social work team. The team is mixed-gender and a real source of mutual support – even when managed, to the chagrin of Clare and her friend Megan, by a man. We encountered one of Clare's constant frustrations – shortage of resources – in Chapter 10,

and she needs no *Local Government Employment Digest* statistics to tell her that social workers and care assistants are among the occupations that councils have long found it hardest to recruit and retain. She agonises regularly over the conflicting pressures facing the 'caring professions': the demands of her individual clients against those of the community, the battle between the requirements of care and of control. It is hardly surprising that, as in Figure 13.1, she sometimes finds it difficult to 'switch off'!

Other council jobs inevitably involve completely different concerns and modes of working, as is revealed by our own small selection here. Steve is a 'manager' – a Sports Marketing and Promotions Manager in the Arts and Leisure department of a large city council. His role is to ensure that the city's residents have easy access to as wide a range of sports as possible, thereby enhancing their overall physical and mental health. Steve himself does not put it quite like this, but his job is a kind of twenty-first-century extension of one of his council's earliest nineteenth-century responsibilities: public health. Much of his work entails talking with sports facility managers and others responsible for actually running sporting activities and events and then overseeing their marketing and promotion. A 'typical day', therefore, might include having a meeting with sports development officers to discuss 'Awards for All' promotions; checking that a Special Events Guide contains full details of disabled sports activities and minority ethnic community festival events; meeting with potential event sponsors and charity fundraisers; and providing some 'anti-racist' material for a local football club's annual report.

Ron too has a job title with distinct hints of the private sector about it. He is the sales and marketing manager of Shelforce, a company with a multi-million pound turnover that is also part of his council's Social Services Department. The company started in 1838 as a workshop for the blind, and today is a successful business employing several dozen workers, over two-thirds with a severe disability. Shelforce makes PVCu windows and doors, most of which it sells to the council's housing department, and beds, made from scratch on the premises and sold both to the hotel trade and the general public. Ron is keen to dispel the common image that 'people who are disabled aren't capable of producing a quality product. We are proud that everything we make conforms to the relevant British Standard and that we have been an outright winner in the Glassex Industry Awards'.

Marcia is a Housing Support Officer with specific responsibility for settling asylum seekers – most recently from Iraq, Albania, Iran and Somalia – into temporary accommodation while they wait to hear whether they can stay in the country permanently. She gets angry at the media's portrayal of her clients, pointing out not just the council's legal obligation to provide basic accommodation, but also the 'catalogue of torture' that may have driven them to leave their homes for an alien country. 'One man was forced to drink battery acid, made to eat broken glass – how can we begrudge these people a home here?' Part of her job is 'planned' – 'sorting out English classes or whatever', and part 'unplanned' – 'when I have to deal with problems as they crop up – trying to locate an interpreter or someone to fix a front door!'

Andrew is neither a manager nor an officer, but a ranger: an Urban Park Ranger. His responsibilities cover the sixty or more parks and open spaces in the south of his council's area, and his own base is an office in one of those parks. He is part of a team whose function is to develop the council's parks and open spaces to their full potential, make them safer, and encourage families in particular to make more use of them. Most days are split between office duties and work outdoors. The former might involve answering a written complaint about the state of public toilets, designing leaflets and posters, taking bookings, and arranging for dog bins to be installed. The latter, on the day we met Andrew, had included a meeting with the gardeners in one of his larger parks, attending a consultative meeting with park users, and running a tennis session for 8 to 14 year olds.

If space permitted, we could continue indefinitely – with accounts of a job share pensions and payments assistant, a Sheltered Housing Scheme residential warden, a part-time school caretaker, a library website editor, a crèche worker, an engineering services inspector (gas), a social work assistant (Cantonese/Hakka speaking), and dozens more besides. We have now, though, to turn from the trees to the wood, and impose some structure on all this diversity. In the remainder of this chapter, therefore, we first identify some facts and features of local government employment. We then turn to the roles of senior managers and the importance of professional bodies, and conclude by examining the adoption of more flexible employment practices and what employees themselves feel about working for local government.

Local authority employment – some quick facts and figures

Local authorities are, by any standards, major employers. They are highly labour-intensive, up to half their total expenditure going on staff costs. The chances are that your local council is, or is close to being, the largest single employer in your area. Birmingham City Council certainly is, employing over 52,000 staff, or 37,000 'full-time equivalents' (FTEs); Glasgow, Scotland's largest authority, employs 36,000. The UK workforce in 2005 numbered 28.7 million, of whom over 2.6 million worked in local government. In other words, nearly 10 per cent of the UK's full-time and part-time jobs are provided by local authorities.

Exhibit 13.1 Local government employment – Great Britain, 2004

	Full-time (000s)	Part-time (000s)	Total (000s)	Percentage of total	Average per authority	Part-time (%)	Female (%)	Part-time female (%)
Education – teachers	429	187	616	24		30	75	27
Education – other employees	199	625	824	32		76	87	70
Social services	182	191	373	14		51	83	46
Services direct to the public	361	209	570	22		37	51	30
Corporate functions	156	54	210	8		26	60	22
Total (GB)	**1,327**	**1,275**	**2,602**			**49**	**74**	**44**
Type of Authority								
Counties (34)	320	463	783	30	23,000	59	80	53
Shire districts (238)	99	45	144	6	600	31	52	26
Metropolitan districts (36)	293	253	546	21	15,200	46	73	41
London boroughs (33)	150	103	253	10	7,700	41	71	35
English unitaries (46)	188	207	395	15	8,600	53	75	46
Welsh unitaries (22)	85	79	164	6	7,500	48	71	41
Scottish unitaries (32)	192	126	318	12	10,000	40	67	36

Notes: **Services direct to the public include:** housing and construction, libraries, museums and galleries, leisure and recreation, environmental health, refuse, recycling and cleansing, planning and economic development, engineering and technical services.
Corporate functions include: central administration and secretarial, personnel, and central management services.
Total local government employment in Northern Ireland is approximately 10,000.

Sources: Data from Employers' Organisation, *Local Government Employment Survey, 2004;* Scottish Executive, *Joint Staffing Watch Survey, December 2004.*

Contrasts with the private sector

Even in extreme summary form, as in Exhibit 13.1, the statistical profile of local government employment today is dramatically different from that of the private sector, or even of the workforce as a whole (see *Labour Force Survey*, 2005). Nationally, roughly three-quarters of all jobs are full-time; but in local government almost half are part-time. In the private sector the male:female ratio is 60:40; local government's is 26:74. Nationally, full-time male employment constitutes 48 per cent of the total, as in local government in the 1950s; in today's local government it is less than 20 per cent. Nationally, part-time women workers are 20 per cent of the total; in local government, 44 per cent – many of them doing at least three of women's traditional 4Cs – caring, cleaning, catering and cash registers – that, precisely because of relative job segregation, have continued, notwithstanding Equal Pay legislation, to be literally undervalued and underpaid.

Because of this high level of part-time employment, care is constantly needed, as advised in Chapter 7, in noting whether statistics are *gross*, as in Exhibit 13.1, or *FTE* (full-time equivalent). The UK's 2004 FTE figure was almost exactly 2 million. Accounting for nearly two-thirds of part-time employment, and well over half the total, is, as you will have come to expect by now, education – which explains too the big range in average employment per authority. If you are responsible for education, and therefore also for social services, your employment is necessarily going to run into several thousands. Which is why under 40 per cent of councils employ over three-quarters of the local government workforce.

Changing numbers

The major growth in local authority employment came in the 1960s and early 1970s. From 1979 until the late 1980s, numbers remained fairly static at around 3 million – the steady reduction in numbers of manual workers during this period being largely cancelled out by the increase in non-manuals. The biggest losses resulted from the abolition of the GLC and metropolitan county councils in 1986, and the transfer of polytechnics and higher education institutions out of LEA control in 1989.

The overall decline in numbers came in the early 1990s, particularly following the LEAs' loss of control of further education institutions in 1993 and the creation of free-standing police authorities in 1995/96. In total, local government employment fell during the 1990s by nearly a fifth, though this trend varied significantly from service to service – social services and planning, for example, increasing their numbers. More or less coinciding with the election of the 1997 Labour Government, though, the downward trend reversed. In the public sector as a whole, employment has since risen every year, and in 2005 was 13 per cent higher than in 1998 – more than twice the private sector growth – and in local government 8 per cent higher, though still below the level of the early 1990s (Hicks, 2005).

The gender-based hierarchy – more mirror maze than glass ceiling

At the top of the local authority employment ladder is an echelon of senior managers and salaried professionals. The chief executive, the most senior of all managers, could in 2005 receive a 'pay and benefits package' of up to almost £200,000 depending on, among other things, the size of the authority and its public reputation. For obvious reasons, London boroughs tend to (have to) be the highest payers, and, as shown in Exhibit 13.2, the median salary for a London chief executive was £149,000 – which sounds a lot until you start comparing it with the private sector, where the head of a company with the same turnover and staff would earn more than double this salary. Chief officers, senior managers and senior professionals are also well rewarded for their services. These people have, though, the demanding responsibility of running the local authority or their particular department, advising cabinets and councillors, and managing budgets. With the ever increasing amount of local partnership working, they also liaise closely with a range of other agencies, both private and public.

Senior management in local government is as white male-dominated a world as many other sectors of the UK economy. While women comprise 74 per cent of the total workforce, this numerical dominance is not

---

Exhibit 13.2 Senior management salaries – English authorities, 2005

| CHIEF EXECUTIVES | | CHIEF OFFICERS | |
Median maximum pay	£000s	Average maximum basic salaries	£000s
All authorities	104	Education	93
Shire counties	143	Social services	93
Shire districts	85	Libraries	89
Metropolitan districts	126	Finance	76
London boroughs	149	Housing	76
Unitaries	113	Environmental health	61

Source: Data from EO/IDeA (2005) *Salaries and Numbers Survey of Chief Executives and Chief Officers, 2004/05*

reflected at top management levels. The numbers of women chief executives, chief officers and deputies are slowly increasing – to about 12, 24 and 25 per cent respectively in 2004/05. But while wholly male management teams are commonplace, Shropshire's seven-member team with six women members and a female chief executive was newsworthy enough to warrant a feature article (*Municipal Journal*, 4 March, 2004). And black and minority ethnic (BME) representation at senior management level, lower overall in local government (6.6 per cent) than in the workforce as a whole (8.1 per cent), is minuscule: 1.4 per cent of chief executives and 2.3 per cent of chief officers (*Local Government Employment Digest,* November 2005).

Blatant discrimination may be comparatively rare, but prejudice is widespread and difficult to counter. Carole Hassan, then Watford BC chief executive, argued that local authorities, for all their publicised claims to be equal opportunities employers, are guilty of complacency: 'They think we have got there but we haven't.' She called on organisations like the LGA and the Society of Local Authority Chief Executives (SOLACE) to take action on both race and gender: 'the few senior women in local government are busy mentoring and supporting the others and that puts huge pressure on them. It's less of a glass ceiling than a mirror maze, with new difficulties appearing at every level' (*Local Government Chronicle*, 12 November 1999).

Benefit packages and minimal wages

The work of chief officers is shared with middle-ranking managers and professionals who combine an expert knowledge of a particular service or support function (e.g., finance, law, personnel, IT) with experience and involvement in overseeing the resources and employees of the authority. The number and range of both top and middle management posts are considerable – and their descriptions sometimes beyond parody – as illustrated in the brief selection in Exhibit 13.3. The final element in this group of senior managers and salaried professionals are those with professional training operating at the service frontline, such as teachers, field social workers, environmental health officers and development control planners.

Beneath the top managers and salaried professionals are the 'worker bees': a vast network of employees in a variety of lower-status clerical, manual and non-manual jobs. Local authorities employ some 750,000 administrative, technical and clerical (ATC) 'white-collar' staff – including typists, clerical assistants, clerks in schools, technicians, nursery nurses and welfare assistants. They also employ about a million full-time or part-time manual workers. These are the people who clean streets and schools, are

Exhibit 13.3 Some officer posts and what they pay

	Advertised post (April 2005)	Approx. salary
Warwickshire CC	**Chief Executive** To establish the future governance and leadership role of the authority and strengthen its partnership working with public agencies and the voluntary and private sectors.	£150,000
Rhondda Cynon Taf CBC	**Chief Executive** As 'a true innovator and entrepreneur', you will lead our corporate team, oversee the preparation, implementation and monitoring of our plans, 'keeping the social, economic and democratic needs of our citizens at the centre of our organisation'.	Package up to £120,000
Sunderland City C	**Director of Children's Services** To integrate service delivery across health, education and social services, and 'find new ways of engaging young people, championing consultation exercises that are more than empty gestures'.	£110,000 negotiable
Tower Hamlets LBC	**Service Head – Customer Access** 'A role of this magnitude requires a cross-cutting customer care/services manager to set new standards of customer excellence', including establishing a state of the art customer contact centre.	Package up to £90,000
Stafford BC	**Executive Director, Community Services** 'Outward-facing and usually non-operational', this post's 5 priorities are: our Prosperity Strategy, Waste Management, Public Space Management, Community Safety, and Partnership Working.	c. £80,000
Birmingham City C	**Head of Equality and Diversity** 'To mainstream equality, exploring how we can infuse the Council with a new understanding of what equality and diversity means, and harness them to make this a city of outstanding opportunity'.	Package up to £70,000
Malvern Hills DC	**Head of Business Support and Customer Services** To lead the council – a key member of the Worcestershire Hub – in developing a joined-up approach to customer service and procurement across all the county's councils.	To £54,600
Camden LBC	**Council Tax Manager** To be responsible for the day to day management of council tax arrears from the court stage onwards; also for managing the council tax property team and outside inspectors.	To £39,414
Havering LBC	**Waste Enforcement Manager** With your 'passion for tackling environmental crimes', you will seek a balance between encouragement, persuasion and enforcement to complement other StreetCare and waste management initiatives.	To £28,179

Exhibit 13.4 Some less well paid local government posts

Advertised post (April 2005)	Pay
Cleaning operatives To provide cleaning services in various locations, including libraries, neighbourhood offices, community centres and office accommodation.	£5.65 per hr
Assistant in Charge Supervisory experience required to oversee the service of food to school pupils and be responsible for hygiene and cleanliness of the dining centre. Basic food hygiene certificate required or training provided.	£5.76 per hr
Domestic Assistant, Children and Young People's Division To carry out cleaning duties at an inner-city children's centre to a high standard, ensuring that the centre is kept in a clean and hygienic condition.	£5.78 per hr
Street Cleansing Operative/Driver You must be prepared to walk long distances and work outdoors in all weathers. Full driving licence needed to enable you to cover driving duties when needed.	£940.50 per month
Lifeguards To carry out pool supervision duties in line with established guidelines, ensuring high standards of customer care. A RLSS Pool Lifeguard qualification is desirable but not essential.	£230.08 per week
Library Assistant To work in this busy community library, you will have excellent people skills, an enquiring mind, a genuine enthusiasm for reading plus the confidence to actively promote it.	£10,893– £14,127 p.a.
Learning Disabilities Team Clerk This job involves administrative support, computer inputting and answering telephone calls from the general public. Good organisational skills and excellent communications skills are required.	£11,649– £13,458 p.a.
Teaching Assistant To work in a primary school at Key Stage 1 level in what OFSTED called (in October 2004) 'a good and effective school which gave good value for money'.	£12,018– £14,106 p.a.
Sheltered Housing Warden Experienced Resident/Non-resident warden to provide a quality service to a tenant management co-operative's sheltered housing schemes.	£12,663 p.a.
Playworker: Children and Young Peoples Division You will be expected to work as a member of a team providing a high quality play environment that responds effectively to meet the individual needs of children.	£13,737– £14,664 p.a.

Exhibit 13.5 Some chief executives – four pen portraits

John Best (Milton Keynes) – career-shaping influence of Jellybread
Previous career – 24 years in planning and urban regeneration for three London boroughs – prompted, he claims, by touring when a Sussex University student in the late 1960s with popular blues band, Jellybread (Pete Wingfield as keyboard vocalist). 'I started to notice how communities develop', which sparked lifelong interest in planning and new towns.

Arrived in MK – the UK's fastest growing city – in 1996, becoming CE in 2003. Still a keen jazz musician, playing bass occasionally in a big band, and rationalising its managerial relevance in the 'element of orchestration – getting all players in MK doing something together to look and sound good'.

Susan Law (Managing Director, Doncaster MBC) – experience Down Under
Previous career – Initially in New Zealand, but key experience in Australia, particularly as CEO to Adelaide City Council. Caught in crossfire of that city's troubled politics, resigning mid-contract and going as a World Bank adviser to Cape Town, South Africa. Admits knowing little (then) about UK local government, but was head-hunted when Doncaster's elected mayor, Martin Winter, decided to replace the departing CE with an MD reporting directly to him.

First impressions: the extent of external monitoring. 'I knew central government controls most local government spending, but its impact hadn't dawned on me. I wonder if all this monitoring actually acts as a handbrake on service innovation.'

---

caretakers, council gardeners, home helps and road maintenance operatives. In addition, there is a substantial number of miscellaneous workers whose jobs are neither wholly clerical nor wholly manual: cashiers in canteens, ticket-sellers, pest controllers, and so on. All of these posts, as can be seen in Exhibit 13.4, are remunerated distinctly more modestly – many at rates little above the national minimum wage (£5.05 in 2005), and considerably below even the downwardly revised Council of Europe Decency Threshold of £6.70 per hour, or £255 for a 38-hour week. With many having to rely on state benefits to the low paid in order to survive, the surprise must be not that 2002 saw the first national strike of local government workers for 23 years, but that it has not become an annual event.

To summarise this section, it is clear that councils remain, by any standards, large-scale employers of extremely heterogeneous workforces. They have at the top a range of well-paid senior managers and professionals, and beneath them a vast army of lower-status adminis-

Alistair Neill (Merthyr Tydfil CBC) – 18 months and a pay cut to Chief Exec
Previous career – International private sector, working in Africa, Asia and the USA for Unilever and BP. Speaks German, also French with West African accent. Took a 50 per cent pay cut in 2002 to join Northamptonshire CC as corporate director – 'I wanted a public sector role with an opportunity to connect with government and policy makers and see if I could use my private sector management skills.'

After just 18 months, was appointed CE at Merthyr, smallest and then almost the worst-rated council in Wales. Spearheaded a major turnaround, winning the Leading Wales Award 2005 for outstanding leadership. Vehemently rejects notion of people working in the public sector being born, not made: 'If there's an idea that people should be sacrificing an inordinate amount to work in the public sector, how are you going to get high performers?'

Sheena Ramsey (Knowsley MBC) – from north east to north west
Previous career – Geology degree ('such a man's world') led to Equal Opportunities MA and NE-based local government career. Research officer at Newcastle, equal opps officer at Middlesbrough, then back to Newcastle as, eventually, Assistant CE.

She has a strong personal commitment to equalities and social justice, and, prompted partly by bringing up three young sons, wants to encourage a better work–life balance across the council. 'I see a lot of people working phenomenally hard and very long hours. I want to create a counter-culture to get things done within working hours.'

Sources: Information from *Municipal Journal*, 1 May 2003 (Best); 14 October 2004 (Law); 23 June 2005 (Ramsey); *Local Government Chronicle*, 11 July 2003 (Neill).

trative, clerical, manual and non-manual employees. These people are essential to the process of service provision, yet the financial rewards they obtain are often relatively unattractive. Compare, for example, Exhibits 13.3 and 13.4, and the more than tenfold pay differentials between jobs being advertised at the same time. Employment 'packages' incorporating negotiable benefits such as pension options, private health insurance, and 'company' leased cars are worlds apart from the experience of manual and clerical workers.

The world of senior management

We turn now from those who actually provide the services of a local authority to those whose job is to manage them, and it: the senior officers at the top, rather than the front-line, of the organisation. As departments become ever less tied to single services, chief officers are expected to play a corporate as well as a departmental role, and may well not even come from the department's dominant profession (Stewart, 2000, p. 202). Certainly those at the very top are likely to be appointed at least as much for their managerial skills and experience, including that acquired abroad or in the private sector, as for their professional qualifications and expertise – as is illustrated by Exhibit 13.5's small but colourful selection of chief executives in post in 2005, that at least starts by resembling Manchester United's immortal forward line.

There are at least four distinctive dimensions of the senior management role that bear examination, summarised in Exhibit 13.6.

Exhibit 13.6 The senior management role – four dimensions

- Exercising professional influence
- Supporting, advising and monitoring politicians
- Representing the authority's interests externally
- Managing staff and resources within the authority.

Exercising professional influence

Senior local government officers may now spend most of their time as managers, but still the majority are trained and qualified professionals: solicitors, treasurers, architects, planners, engineers, housing managers, education administrators, social workers and so on. Professionalism in this sense remains a hallmark of British local government, and one of its most powerful forces. We list in Exhibit 13.7 a small sample of the dozens of professional bodies involved in local government – some still very largely, like SOLACE, SOCPO and ACSeS; others, like CIPFA and CIPR, only partly. These bodies are, of course, key members of their respective policy networks and communities (see pp. 187–8), but they have other roles too. They are, as Rhodes noted (1988, pp. 214–15), 'organised as "learned societies", in which capacity they recruit and train personnel, organise conferences and seminars, produce research and publications and, as with any other organised group, proselytise and lobby for their interests'. They are also 'trade unions and ... can use working to rule and strikes as a means of influencing the government. In effect, therefore, the professions can have three bites at the cherry of political influence.'

The influence of senior officers as professionals can thus be considerable, especially within those policy areas where complex technical knowledge is at a premium and of consequential value to central government. As ever, it is important not to generalise: some technical

Exhibit 13.7 Some leading professional bodies – acronym clubs

1. **SOLACE – Society of Local Authority Chief Executives (and Senior Managers)**
   Membership: Acronym is no longer accurate, as any public sector senior managers now allowed in. Has expanded in recent years to become, as well as membership organisation, a flourishing not-for-profit consultancy (SOLACE Enterprises) and a charitable trust (SOLACE Foundation), providing training grants, travel bursaries, etc.
   Provides, for annual sub of £280 +, a newsletter, all kinds of publications and policy papers, a conference, 'networking and influencing opportunities', and a plush and convenient Westminster base – the appositely named Hope House.

2. **SOCPO – Society of Chief Personnel Officers**
   Membership: Again, catchy acronym retained, but in practice now the 'Society of Personnel Officers in [any and all] Government Services'.
   Provides, for the cheapest sub of £90, the usual range of publications, conference, discounts, plus various specialist working groups organised, naturally, on local government lines: task-and-finish groups with a Lead Officer.

3. **CIPFA – Chartered Institute of Public Finance and Accountancy (pron. 'SIPFA')**
   Membership: Has long been split between local government and others. Wanted to extend still further, merging with Institute of Chartered Accountants in England and Wales (ICAEW), but got the cold shoulder. Is more of a training and standards-monitoring body than the others, with own professional qualification, post-grad diploma, etc.
   Provides, for £260 sub, probably the slickest service among local government professional bodies: all the usual perks, plus a good weekly mag, *Public Finance*, and statistical information service.

4. **ACSeS – Association of Council Secretaries and Solicitors**
   Membership: Eligibility criteria almost abandoned in the face of a new army of monitoring, scrutiny, standards officers etc. If you're boss of anything vaguely admin or legallish, they'll take your money. Still largely local government-focused, though, and committed to the democratic provision of local services.
   Provides, for £170 sub, useful 'best practice' notes and guidance, good conference and cute acronym, but not, recently, the higher-profile policy leadership that some members would like. Perhaps the first black woman president, Gifty Edila, will help.

5. **CIPR – Chartered Institute of Public Relations**
   Membership: 8,000 +, but only a small minority of 'communications professionals' from local government – regrettably, considering how much some councils could learn about PR. Still, it has its own sectoral group.
   Provides, for £200 sub, training and development programme as well as usual benefits, and local government group has own quarterly mag, *PR News*, and sponsors Excellence in Communications awards.

professional communities have historically been distinctly more influential than others. Both Dunleavy (1980) and Laffin (1986), for example, contrast the massive influence of local authority highways engineers and surveyors in the development of the motorway programme with the comparatively minor contribution of the housing management professions to the post-war housing boom. The latter was led much more by private sector construction interests and a combination of national politicians and civil servants. Where such professional influence does occur, though, it is more likely to constitute a force for centralisation than for localism, as Rhodes explains (1988, p. 225):

> The consequence of professional influence is the promotion of homogeneous standards, not local diversity. Their locus in policy networks places them *in,* if by origin they were not *of,* the centre. The outcome is centralization by aggregation of interests and nationalization of standards; the source is the professionals employed by sub-central organizations. (emphases ours)

Working with politicians

The relationship between senior officers and councillors is explored in Chapter 15. Senior officers are likely to be involved in the process of developing strategies and policies for the authority. Much of their time is taken up in writing reports for cabinet members, meeting with councillors, and liaising with officer colleagues in other departments to provide policy advice and guidance. They also, necessarily, have extensive *delegated powers* in respect of their particular services – set out nowadays, of course, in the council's constitution. Executive members too have delegated powers now, though, both individually and collectively, and the outcome of the negotiation of particularly the most sensitive of these delegations – planning permissions and certain categories of licence – has provided a new indicator of the officer or member dominance in the running of an authority.

Another recent development has been senior officers' *monitoring role* in relation to the performance of the council and councillors. Part of the Conservative Government's response to the 1986 Widdicombe Committee Report was to require local authorities to appoint a monitoring officer – usually the chief legal officer or council solicitor – responsible for reporting directly to the council on issues of legality, financial probity and alleged maladministration. The Local Government Act 2000 extended these responsibilities, and a monitoring officer is now charged with promoting and maintaining high standards of conduct within the local authority, and with ensuring that executive decisions, together with all relevant background documentation, are made available publicly.

Senior officers stand at the heart of the decision-making processes of local authorities. Their delegated and monitoring responsibilities give them some powers, but above all it is their ability to influence the choices, thinking and approach of leading councillors that gives them real decision-making influence. Their proximity to the formal holders of decision-making authority – executive councillors – gives them an opportunity for influence not afforded to such a degree to employees in the lower ranks of the organisation.

External relations

As indicated even by some of the skeletal job descriptions in Exhibit 13.3, managing relations with the world outside the council has become an increasingly important part of the daily workload of senior officers in an era of growing collaboration, local partnerships and supposedly 'joined-up' government. Links with central government regional offices, local authority colleagues in other areas, conferences and debates within professional associations all contribute to a powerful network of influence for the modern senior officer. They constitute important sources of information and ideas, and provide a national forum in which senior officers can present themselves as policy entrepreneurs and learn from the knowledge and experience of others. More generally, they enable officers to make sense of the local government world and to put the work of their own department, profession and council in a broader context.

As described in Chapter 8, partnerships have become an integral part of the world of local governance. Senior officials in social service departments are thus in regular touch with voluntary groups and agencies. Land-use planners will represent the authority in public meetings and debates. Housing officers will attend numerous meetings with tenants' associations and community organisations. In contrast to the position 30 years ago, these senior officers have come to expect a relatively 'rough ride'. In today's consumer culture, people are less willing to accept professional explanations of what is best, and far more prepared to question the policies and actions of the local authority. The need to consult with the public on a wide range of issues – a key strand of Labour's modernisation agenda – has also meant greater interaction than ever before with the local population.

Internal management

As we have seen, the role of senior staff within local authorities is nowadays a managerial, as well as a professional, one. Effective chief officers and senior managers in local authorities exercise a range of skills – in strategic management, decision-making, political awareness and sensitivity, leadership, business and commercial practice, negotiation – that go far beyond anything required in their professional qualifications.

The new executive structures have, in most authorities, affected the role of senior officers significantly – more so than was sometimes initially understood. Executive members are more involved in day-to-day decision-making and management, and officers correspondingly less so. The tensions inherent in senior officers' responsibilities to serve both the council as a whole and the current political leadership have increased. Inevitably, however, there will continue to be considerable differences in the operational styles and practices of what are, statutorily, identical authorities. It would be both naïve and premature, therefore, to start playing down the influence of senior local government officers in policy-making, whatever the formal position might be. Their knowledge and expertise mean that, along with senior councillors, they remain of central importance.

From model employers to flexible employment structures

For much of the postwar period, local authorities had an image as 'model' or 'good practice' employers, but the period from 1979 ushered in changes. Local government was subjected to commercialism and competition – most notably in the form of compulsory competitive tendering (CCT). With these changes came private sector management ideas and personnel practices such as performance-related pay, staff appraisal procedures, and decentralised negotiating and consultative arrangements. Authorities found it difficult to maintain national pay and conditions in services subject to competitive tender, and there was a movement away from formal systems for the management of industrial relations towards more *ad hoc* approaches reflecting the organisational interests of management (Leach *et al.*, 1994, p. 199).

The realities of CCT meant that it became increasingly difficult for local authorities to maintain the 'model' employer tradition. If the choice were presented as one of aspiring to best employment practice, but at the possible loss of a vital contract and the associated jobs, councillors would understandably fight for the contract. In response to such dilemmas and the changing environment, local authorities developed various ways of introducing greater flexibility into their employment practices.

Chief officers were given greater discretion to employ and deploy staff, with councillors' involvement being confined to the most senior appointments. Contracts and job descriptions became less tightly defined, making it easier for clerical and administrative staff in particular to be transferred between departments, and for new working practices to be introduced. Increasing numbers of chief executives and senior officers were recruited on fixed-term contracts and with company-style benefits packages. In another echoing of the private sector, performance-related pay (PRP) for senior managers was introduced by some authorities – by no means all Conservative – with merit bonuses or awards for exceptional performance. More widespread, and beneficial to both the employees and service users of an authority, were the adoption of more flexible working hours and conditions – flexitime, job-sharing and home-based working all taking off earlier in local government than in the economy as a whole.

Conclusions – how can there be?

This chapter has provided an overview of the local authority workforce: an enormous variety of people involved in delivering services and developing strategic local policies. Many of the human resource and industrial relations issues faced in local government are similar to those found in large-scale private sector organisations. In general, the traditional bureaucratic approaches to personnel management have been replaced by managers with devolved budgets and responsibility for their own staff. The position of local authority managers, however, is complicated by their base within the public sector. Pay settlements can be controlled by national governments, with the effect that overall pay levels fall relative to private industry. Policies of change and 'modernisation' are imposed from above, and issues such as redundancy, competitive tendering, and best value all become the subject of political argument and debate. The management task is further 'complexified' – an ugly, but perhaps less pejorative term than 'complicated' – by the involvement of councillors in the management and oversight of the authority.

It would be miraculous if local government staff were not on occasion to feel dumped upon and demoralised. Yet survey evidence is inevitably ambiguous. Overall job satisfaction levels, perhaps because they are customarily higher among women workers, have long been higher in local government and the public sector generally than in the private sector. Yet the gap effectively has closed in recent years (Gardner and Oswald, 2001), with reported stress levels rising faster in the public sector alongside regular evidence of increasing staff recruitment and retention difficulties (see, e.g., *Local Government Employment Digest*, October 2005). In Exhibit 13.8 we present two examples of almost simultaneous surveys, which, while not utterly irreconcilable, certainly draw very different pictures: in one, relatively high levels of job satisfaction and a positive view of management, particularly in top CPA-ranking authorities; in the other, an undervalued and demotivated workforce, seriously anxious about their personal futures. There are, in short, no neat conclusions, nor could there be. As we warned in the opening paragraph of this chapter, beware of generalisations.

Exhibit 13.8 Job satisfaction – it depends who you ask

With a workforce of over 2.5 million, ranging from highly paid senior managers to at least a quarter of a million women on literally poverty-level wages, it is difficult to draw any general, evidence-based conclusions on topics such as job satisfaction or stress in the workplace. Just *how* difficult can be seen from two 2005 surveys of local government employees, both conducted by MORI, but commissioned by very different organisations with inevitably differing interests: the Improvement and Development Agency (IDeA) and the public service union UNISON, two-thirds of whose 1.3 million members work for local authorities.

IDeA – CPA and Employee Attitudes: This was a systematic telephone survey, using 'snowball'/referral sampling, of 500 local authority employees, 100 each from district councils with CPA rankings of Excellent, Good, Fair, Weak and Poor. The study examined the relationship between councils' CPA scores and their staff's motivation and management, which proved to be a significant one, as can be seen in the lower section of the table.

	Agree (%)	Disagree (%)	Net agree (%)
[X Council] is an above-average/one of the best places to work	53	10	+43
I feel valued for the work that I do	65	20	+45
My pay is fair compared to similar jobs in other organisations	51	33	+18
Senior management have a clear vision of where the organisation is going	64	22	+42

	ALL (%)	'Excellent' (%)	'Poor' (%)
[X Council] is an above-average place to work – agree	53	68	20
I would speak highly of [X Council] to others – strongly agree	33	51	20
I feel valued for the work that I do – strongly agree	18	21	13
I am very satisfied with my present job	30	33	18
[X Council] is focused on the needs of its customers – strongly agree	30	48	13
[X Council] keeps its employees informed – strongly agree	20	31	6

UNISON – Sustaining Communities – Taking the Strain: A survey of 10,000 UNISON members working in local government, which showed, according to the union's Head of Local Government, Heather Wakefield, 'a workforce under pressure, undervalued, understaffed, and under-resourced'. Headline findings given by the union to *Local Government News* (20 September 2005) included:

- 72% of respondents feeling undervalued by their employers;
- 59% having considered leaving their jobs in the previous six months;
- 27% considering themselves fairly paid for the work they do;
- 33% reporting doing unpaid overtime each week – on average 4 to 6 hours, which, the union calculated, amounted to 7 million days of unpaid work;
- 40% having experienced verbal abuse by service users;
- 16% reporting being bullied by their manager;
- 79% worried, and 54 per cent very worried, about the Government's proposed changes to the Local Government Pension Scheme [in particular, removal of the 85-year rule for most members, enabling voluntary retirement on full pension where sum of age + membership equals 85 years].

Chapter 14

Political Parties

Introduction

Like it or not – and we conclude this chapter by examining both sides of the case – political parties and party politics are a central feature of contemporary local government across most of the United Kingdom. Moreover, notwithstanding some important changes and challenges accompanying the arrival of executive-based policy making as well as plenty of sniping criticism of their activities, they will continue to be so for the foreseeable future. In the first part of the chapter, therefore, we look at the current political landscape of local government, and briefly at how that landscape has come to look as it does. We then compare the organisation and impact of the principal political parties, both inside and outside the council. We examine too the role of the national parties and their respective policies in relation to local government.

Party systems and the survival of non-partisanship

It is important to get the balance right when dealing with party politics in local government. Understate its significance, and one risks completely misunderstanding how and where many of the most important council decisions are actually made. Overstate it, and one falls into the trap of assuming that all councils are run on tightly disciplined party lines, and that all decisions are party-based. The truth is that, as with almost everything else to do with local government, the variety of practice is almost infinite. Nothing is universally true of all 440 or so authorities in the country, as can be seen in outline in Exhibit 14.1.

Exhibit 14.1 summarises the range of party, and non-party, systems in Great Britain in 2005/06. In the metropolitan areas of the country, in most English counties and unitaries, and in the larger shire districts, there are *fully developed party systems*. Nowadays five-sixths of all councils come into this category – those in the bottom four main rows of Exhibit 14.1 – and, because they include nearly all county and unitary councils, they touch the lives of almost all British voters. All, or a great majority, of the councillors on these authorities are elected under the labels of national or nationalist political parties and, having been elected, they organise

Exhibit 14.1 Party systems in local government – Great Britain, 2005/06

PARTY SYSTEM AND DEFINITION		ENGLAND					WALES	SCOTLAND	GREAT BRITAIN	
		Unitaries	Counties	Non-Met. Districts	Met. Districts	London Boroughs	Unitaries	Unitaries	Total	%
COMPLETELY/PREDOMINANTLY NON-PARTISAN (60% or more seats held by Independents)		–	–	4	–	1	3	6	14	3
WEAK PARTISAN (20–59% seats held by Independents)		5	–	40	4	1	10	3	63	14
MULTI-PARTY/FRAGMENTED (20% or more seats held by third party/parties)		10	6	38	9	1	3	6	73	17
TWO-PARTY (80% or more seats held by two parties, neither more than 60%)		17	18	66	10	11	2	6	130	29
ONE-PARTY DOMINANT (60–75% of seats held by one party)	Cons	4	8	46	2	4	–	–	64	
	Lab	4	–	9	3	7	2	5	30	117 } 27
	LD	4	1	12	3	1	–	1	22	
	(SNP)	–	–	–	–	–	–	1	1	
ONE-PARTY MONOPOLISTIC (75% or more seats held by one party)	Cons	1	–	15	–	3	–	–	19	
	Lab	1	1	6	5	2	2	4	21	44 } 10
	LD	–	–	2	–	2	–	–	4	
Total		46	34	238	36	33	22	32	441	100

Note: Percentages in these tables may not add up to precisely 100 because of rounding.
Source: Data from Edkins Family Index Page – Local Council Political Compositions (www.gwydir.demon.co.uk/uklocalgov/makeup.htm).

Exhibit 14.2 Party affiliations of councillors, Great Britain, 2005/06

| PARTY AFFILIATION | ENGLAND | | | | | | | | | | WALES | | SCOTLAND | | GREAT BRITAIN | | | |
| | Unitaries | | Counties | | Non-Met. Districts | | Met. Districts | | London Boroughs | | Unitaries | | Unitaries | | 2005/06 | | 1979 | |
	No.	%	No.	%	No.	%	No.	%	No.	%	No.	%	No.	%	No.	%	No.	%
Conservative	778	32	1,147	51	4,833	46	546	22	650	35	109	9	126	10	8,189	37	12,143	53
Labour	808	34	575	25	2,118	20	1,182	48	854	46	479	38	504	41	6,520	30	7,351	32
Liberal Democrat	662	28	470	21	2,391	23	593	24	317	17	149	12	175	14	4,757	22	1,032	4
Nationalist parties	–		–		–		–		–		173	14	184	15	357	2	278	1
Independents and others	159	7	77	3	1,233	12	124	5	40	2	354	28	233	19	2,220	10	2,232	10
Total	2,407		2,269		10,575		2,445		1,861		1,264		1,222		22,043		23,036	

Notes: 'Others' include Liberals, Social Democrats, Greens, Ratepayers' and Residents' Associations, and other small local parties. In Northern Ireland, party affiliations of the 582 district councillors following the 2005 elections were: Democratic Unionist Party 182; Sinn Fein 126; Ulster Unionist Party 115; Social Democratic and Labour Party 101; Alliance 30; Greens 3; Independents and others 25. Figures for the London Boroughs exclude the 157 members of the Common Council of the City Corporation of London, which claims to have no party politics.

Source: Data from Rallings and Thrasher (2005).

themselves into separate party groups. Independents and representatives of local or fringe parties find it hard to get elected to these councils, and in many places are non-existent (see also Exhibit 14.2).

In the more rural areas of England and in Wales and Scotland the picture can be very different. Here, there are many English district and Scottish and Welsh unitary councils with *weak party systems* (14 per cent as defined in Exhibit 14.1) and others that are actually or effectively *non-partisan*, almost all councillors having stood as Independents of some description.

Traditionally, perhaps the best examples of near-complete non-partisanship have been the three Scottish Island authorities: Orkney, Shetland and the Western Isles. But predominantly non-partisan councils are to be found in many parts of the country that are by no means parts of

---

Exhibit 14.3 Four forms of developed party system

1. *Multi-party or fragmented* – relatively few Independents or 'others', but council seats divided among several party groups. Most of these councils will be 'hung' or 'balanced', in the arithmetical sense of there being no one party with an overall majority. Their actual forms of administration can vary greatly – from single-party minority rule, through all possible permutations of 'power-sharing' arrangements. In countries with PR electoral systems multi-party hung councils are the norm, as indicated in the footnote on Northern Ireland in Exhibit 14.4. Our first-past-the-post (FPTP) system reduces their number, but they still make up nearly a third of the total, reflecting the fact that it is far easier for third and minority party candidates to win election in the smaller wards and divisions of local councils than in our much larger parliamentary constituencies. Contrary to what might be thought from their mutual antipathy at national level, in council cabinets and executives in 2005 the parties could be found working together in every imaginable combination: 36 involving Conservatives and Lib Dems, plus possibly other groups; 21 involving Labour and Lib Dems; 11 Labour and Conservatives; and 10 all three.

2. *Two-party* - relatively few third party and Independent members, council seats being split fairly evenly between the two leading parties. Depending on the actual party balance, some of these councils too will be hung. In others control will swing regularly from one party to the other.

3. *One-party dominant* - one party holds a decisive majority of seats, and will expect to run the council most of the time.

4. *One-party monopolistic* - self-explanatory; the extreme product of our electoral system, one party having unbroken, and often effectively unchallenged, control of the council.

any Celtic fringe: Cambridgeshire, Cumbria, Devon, Dorset, Durham, Gloucestershire, Humberside, Lincolnshire, Oxfordshire, Shropshire, Somerset, Staffordshire and Surrey.

This brings us to *developed party systems*, which both arithmetically and organisationally can be divided into at least four types, as in Exhibit 14.3.

Labour's waning local dominance

There are versions of Exhibit 14.1 in this book's previous editions, the most interesting for comparative purposes probably being that for 1996/97, immediately before Labour came to power nationally (Wilson and Game, 1998, p. 260). There were at that time no fewer than 146 'one-party monopolistic' councils, just three of which were controlled by the Conservatives and 126 by Labour, as were 65 of the 97 'one-party dominant' councils. Of the 36 metropolitan districts, two-thirds (24) were one-party monopolies, all Labour; similarly 10 of the 15 in London. There could be scarcely be a more eloquent measure of the transformation of the local political landscape during two terms of national Labour Government. Nearly three-quarters of those one-party fiefdoms have disappeared, and the Conservatives have regained what they would consider their historically rightful position as, numerically, the pre-eminent party of local government – albeit still some way short of what it had been a quarter of a century earlier, as shown in the final columns of Exhibits 14.2 and 14.4.

Parties in power nationally expect to lose a certain number of seats in local elections to protest votes, but the Conservatives by 1996/97 had carried it to an extreme, having lost nearly two-thirds of their councillors and 242 – nearly 95 per cent – of the councils they held when Mrs Thatcher came into office in 1979. By comparison, Labour in its first 8 years of government lost 39 per cent of its councillors and 55 per cent of its councils. The party could, however, fairly point to the country's increasingly pronounced urban/rural and north/south political divisions. The positions that the Conservatives have regained have been predominantly in non-metropolitan England. In London and the metropolitan districts, overwhelmingly in Scotland and Wales, and, just, in the unitaries, Labour was still in 2005 the leading local government party.

There are two other points to note before leaving these three overview Exhibits. The first is that the Conservatives' losses in the 1980s and 1990s were, of course, in many cases not direct to Labour but to the Liberal Democrats or their predecessors. During this period the party moved from the same kind of fringe position locally as it occupied parliamentarily, to centre stage, so that in 2005, apart from the 34 councils it controlled

Exhibit 14.4 Pattern of control of local authorities – Great Britain, 2005/06

PARTY AFFILIATION	ENGLAND														WALES		SCOTLAND		GREAT BRITAIN			
	Unitaries		Counties		Non-Met. Districts		Met. Districts		London Boroughs						Unitaries		Unitaries		2005/06		1979	
	No.	%	No.	%	No.	%	No.	%	No.	%					No.	%	No.	%	No.	%	No.	%
Conservative	11	24	23	68	111	47	4	11	8	24					1	5	–	–	157	36	256	49
Labour	12	26	6	18	22	9	16	44	15	45					8	36	13	41	92	21	113	22
Liberal Democrat	5	11	3	9	19	8	3	8	3	9					–	–	1	3	34	8	2	*
Nationalist parties	–	–	–	–	–	–	–	–	–	–					1	5	1	3	2	*	4	1
Independent	–	–	–	–	7	3	–	–	1	3					3	14	6	19	16	4	68	13
No overall control	18	39	2	6	79	33	13	36	6	18					9	41	11	34	139	32	75	14
Total	46		34		238		36		33						22		32		441		518	

Notes: * less than 1%.

'No overall control' is a purely arithmetical definition of councils on which no single party has more than 50 per cent of all seats. It may therefore include councils on which a single party holds exactly half the seats and, through the casting vote of the mayor or chair of the Council, may be in a position of effective overall control.

Of the 116 non-mayoral English authorities under no overall control, 40 (34 per cent) were governed by minority administrations (18 Conservative, 11 Labour, 10 Lib Dem, 1 Independent), and the remainder by various permutations of power-sharing arrangements: 38 involving 2 parties/groups, 31 involving 3; and 7 involving 4 or more.

In Northern Ireland, where local elections are based on the proportional Single Transferable Vote (STV) system, all 26 councils in 2005 were under no overall control, as defined above, with the exception of Ballymena (DUP).

Sources: Data from Rallings and Thrasher (2005); Edkins Family Index Page – see Exhibit 14.1.

outright, it was additionally involved in the government of about twice that number – the partner of choice, it would seem, of all other parties, whatever they might say about it publicly.

Second, it will be seen that, while the number of Independent-controlled councils has fallen since 1979 by about three-quarters, the number of Independent and minor party *councillors* is almost identical. The decline that we used to record year after year has recently been arrested and reversed – thanks particularly to the emergence of many ultra-local, community and single-issue parties, like some of those in Exhibit 11.9, for example.

The history and spread of local party politics

In fact, the present-day hold of party politics on *so much* of the country's local government is a comparatively modern phenomenon. Party politics *per se* has a history in many towns and cities dating back at least as far as the Municipal Corporations Act 1835 (see Chapter 4), but its spread outside those areas is generally much more recent. We should therefore view the emergence of a more politicised local government as 'a steady long-term trend, beginning in the nineteenth century, spreading in this century first through the major cities and then, if less evenly, to the shires' (Young, 1986a, p. 81). The trend has been well described in recent years, by Young himself and by Gyford (Gyford *et al.*, 1989), who usefully identifies five stages to the story, summarised in Exhibit 14.5.

Our chief concern here is naturally with Gyford's final Reappraisal stage, incorporating as it does both a quantitative extension of the scale of party politics in local government and some fundamental qualitative changes in its character. Much of the quantitative change occurred suddenly and immediately upon reorganisation in the early 1970s. Up to that time about half the councils in England and Wales, and two-thirds of those in Scotland, could be defined as 'non-partisan', in that over half their elected members resisted all conventional party labelling. There was, as ever, an urban–rural divide: between two-thirds and three-quarters of urban councils being run on party lines compared with one-third of county councils and just 10 per cent of rural district councils.

Reorganisation inevitably involved the merging of many previously non-partisan authorities, with others having stronger partisan traditions. The latter almost invariably prevailed, and following the 1973/74 elections the proportions of predominantly partisan authorities rose immediately, to nearly 80 per cent in England and Wales and to over a half in Scotland.

In the succeeding few years this trend continued, the Conservative Party in particular insisting that all party sympathisers stand as official party candidates and not, as often happened previously, as Independents. As

---

Exhibit 14.5 The party politicisation of local government

1. *Diversity* (1835–late 1860s) – many of the new municipal councils dominated and split by party politics, but no uniform national pattern. 'Tories, Whigs, Conservatives, Liberals, Radicals, Chartists, Improvers and Economisers offered varying prescriptions in different towns' (Gyford *et al.* 1989, p. 7). Main divisive issues: role of religion in educational provision; levels of municipal spending; drink/teetotalism.

2. *Crystallisation* (1860s–1900s) – administrative rationalisation of local government accompanied by a channelling of party politics, where it existed, into a predominantly Conservative-Liberal contest. Key catalyst: Joseph Chamberlain's Birmingham Liberal Association (1860s), as both a successful electoral organisation and a radical pioneer of municipal collectivism – local government's proactive involvement in gas and water supply, slum clearance, public health, parks and gardens.

3. *Realignment* (1900s–1940s) – Labour's displacement of the Liberals as the principal radical force in local government, offering 'a distinctive municipal programme calling for better wages and conditions for council workers, the provision of work for the unemployed, public baths and laundries, and adequate housing for working class families' (Gyford *et al.*, 1989, pp. 11–12). Anti-socialist response orchestrated by the Conservative Party through local groups labelled variously Moderates, Progressives, Municipal Alliance and Ratepayers.

4. *Nationalisation* (1940s–1970s) – of local government-run public utilities and hospitals, and of local party politics. Growing involvement of the national party organisations in local government; local elections fought more on national issues and personalities; but most county and rural district councils still organised on non-party lines.

5. *Reappraisal* (1970s onwards) – rapid growth and change in character of local party politics following local government reorganisation. Quantitative change – increasing numbers of party-dominated councils and declining numbers of Independents – accompanied by qualitative change, through the formalisation of local party organisation and the intensification of policy debate.

Source: Information from Gyford *et al.* (1989, ch. 1).

---

already noted, Independent councillors still survive in larger numbers than is often recognised, but Independent councils have been inexorably squeezed, election after election. More recently, they have been squeezed even more in Scotland and Wales by the mid-1990s' reorganisation of local government. In both countries there are now many fewer Independents on the larger unitary authorities than there were previously.

Party politicisation in practice

Counting is easy. But there is a lot more to understanding the party politicisation of local government than simply adding up the numbers of party-dominated councils. If we describe a council as 'party politicised', we should expect to find certain features of organisation and modes of operation. They are not new; they developed gradually, most notably under the direction of Labour's influential London leader, Herbert Morrison, in the 1920s and 1930s. Morrison's model party system, described by one of his biographers, George Jones (1975), comprises at least seven elements, as listed in Exhibit 14.6.

This party political dimension is rarely included in diagrammatic representations of the organisation and working of councils, because, in the past, it would inevitably have complicated an otherwise fairly straightforward, if simplistic, picture of officers and departments servicing

Exhibit 14.6 The Morrisonian model party system

Herbert Morrison, Home Secretary during the Second World War, and deputy prime minister 1945–51, was from 1934–40 Leader of the London County Council, and, before the arrival of David Blunkett, 'the only Labour figure in British politics who reached the top rank of the party through local government' (Donoughue and Jones, 2001, p. 63). It was, though, as the organised and organising Secretary of the London Labour Party during the 1920s that he developed and propounded the following basic precepts of local party organisation:

1. *The selection of candidates* by local committees of party members.
2. *The formulation of a distinctive policy programme* by a local party group, usually comprising a mix of councillors and local party representatives.
3. *The production of a party election manifesto* to which all party candidates are expected to adhere, both during the election campaign and once elected.
4. *The attempted implementation of the manifesto* in the event of the party winning a majority of seats on the council.
5. *The organisation of councillors into party groups* for the purposes of determining cabinet and committee memberships and other positions of leadership and responsibility, developing and co-ordinating party policy, determining strategy and tactics, and ensuring group discipline.
6. *The election of a group leadership,* comprising an individual leader and usually a committee of group executive officers, by members of the party group.
7. *The convening of pre-council and pre-committee party group meetings* to enable party group members to agree on policy and plan their debating and voting tactics.

committees of councillors who made policy decisions that were then publicly approved in full council. We ourselves sought to address this complication and, in the interests of realism, to show not only where party politics fitted into the policy making process, but also how in many councils it in fact drives it (Wilson and Game, 1998, Figure 14.1, p. 268).

The party groups, often omitted altogether, featured almost at the centre of our illustration – as they would also for Copus (2004), a key writer on the topic, who compares the group to a Leviathan, reaching 'into all facets of council politics and into the wider public realm' (p. 93), though whether the analogy is with the biblical sea monster or Thomas Hobbes' all-powerful state is left for the reader to decide.

The party groups and their respective sizes are the direct outcome of the local elections and, unless there is a directly and separately elected mayor, will determine who is to run the council and how. The elected leader of the majority or largest group would generally become Leader of the Council. The majority group's manifesto becomes the council's agenda, to be translated into practical policy proposals by the relevant officers and departments. Councillors of the majority group would generally chair and numerically dominate all committees and sub-committees – as they now take all the seats on the executive or cabinet. Like cabinet members, committee chairs would liaise closely with departmental chief officers in preparing their meeting agendas.

Each public committee meeting – and here we have *the* key difference introduced by executive policy making – would usually be preceded by private pre-committee (caucus) meetings of the different party groups at which they determined their tactics: which issues to focus on, who would speak to them and how they would vote. As yet, we still have no clear overall picture of what has taken the place of such pre-committee meetings: whether, for example, in most councils, party groups still meet to discuss forthcoming executive decisions, and whether group decisions are binding on cabinet members. Until we do, we cannot claim a proper understanding of how councils are *really* working, because, just as with committees, one needs to visualise the 'unofficial' organisation of the political parties superimposed completely on the council's 'official' policy making structure.

A hung council, in which there is no overall majority party, will inevitably operate differently in practice, but not in principle. There may have to be negotiated compromises on manifesto proposals. Executives, as we have noted, comprise members of perhaps three or four parties, and of course no votes in any arena can be won simply by a party exercising tight party discipline over its own members. Officers may find themselves dealing with and briefing spokespersons from two or three different parties. Those parties, though, and councillors' party affiliations, remain at the heart of the policy process.

Organisational and operational differences

Any political party would recognise most of the elements in Morrison's model party system, different though actuality often is from theory. For a start, local parties will inevitably vary in their size, resources and sheer capability – ranging, to use Copus's taxonomy, from the omnipotent, through the 'functioning-mechanistic' and resurgent, to the dormant and downright moribund (2004, pp. 68–70). Thus a dearth of willing and capable volunteers may 'informalise' candidate selection procedures, as we saw in the experience of some of our councillors in Chapter 12 (pp. 250–1). Party manifestos can vary enormously in length and specificity, ranging from almost book-length productions to some that look as if they have been lifted from the proverbial back of an envelope. Party discipline varies too, some groups treating potential or actual voting dissent with considerably greater tolerance than others (Gyford *et al.*, 1989, pp. 172–5; Copus, 2004, pp. 104–11). But there are also some *systematic differences* of formality and emphasis across the political parties.

The fundamental difference between, in particular, the Labour and Conservative Parties derives directly from their contrasting origins and objectives. Labour is a programmatic, constitution-based, ostensibly democratic party whose local operations are governed by a set of *Model Standing Orders for Labour Groups*. Some local parties will adhere more rigidly than others to these Standing Orders, but there is a greater uniformity of practice than among local Conservative parties – more uniformity, for example, in the selection of council candidates, which is by ward parties, but only from a *panel of approved candidates*, drawn up by the local party executive committee from ward party or union branch nominees, the whole process being overseen by the regional party. The Conservative selection process, in comparison, is considerably more relaxed, with ward branches left much more to their own devices and with less emphasis being placed on the prospective candidate's party experience or even membership.

For Labour, as prescribed in the Morrisonian model, policy making, including the drafting of the manifesto, is constitutionally not the exclusive responsibility of the party group on the council, but one shared jointly with the *local party*. Non-councillor representatives therefore have a right of non-voting attendance at group meetings; group nominees are expected to report back to the party, and there are regular joint meetings. For Conservative councillors, policy is determined by the party group, then possibly (or possibly not) discussed with the constituency's Local Government Advisory Committee, if such a body formally exists. Not surprisingly, Labour party groups on councils tend to be run more tightly, with generally more emphasis on internal discipline, than either Conservative or Liberal Democrat groups. Which means, in turn, that there is significantly greater potential for internal party conflict, comparable to that at national level between the Parliamentary Labour Party (PLP) and the Conference-elected National Executive Committee (NEC), with party activists concerned to prevent councillors becoming 'sucked into' the council and being deflected by professional officer advice from manifesto priorities.

The Conservatives, traditionally the party of the status quo, have evolved over a much longer period than Labour and are generally much less rule-bound in both their national and local organisation. There is a model constitution for Conservative groups, produced by Conservative Central Office, but it is not binding and is regarded more as a guide to good practice. Liberal Democrats too tend instinctively to favour structural flexibility and to resist externally imposed discipline, although the influential Association of Liberal Democrat Councillors based in Hebden Bridge (Yorkshire) seeks to foster the virtues of group organisation and coherence.

Leadership differences

A further and obviously related dimension of party difference is that of the parties' attitudes towards leadership. These are as distinctive locally as they are nationally, and, if anything, the differences have grown with the arrival of executive-based policy making, designed as it was to empower local leaders and give them a more visible and accountable public profile. Stoker and his University of Manchester colleagues are the official DCLG-sponsored monitors of the new political management arrangements – Evaluating Local Governance: New Constitutions and Ethics (www.elgnce. org.uk) – and their early findings suggest that, certainly among the great bulk of councils that opted for the leader/cabinet model, party-distinctive styles of leadership have been very much carried forward from the earlier committee era.

Focusing on the three measures of leadership autonomy in the first section of Exhibit 14.7, it was found that in 34 per cent of leader/cabinet authorities the leader was allowed to select cabinet members, in 54 per cent to allocate portfolios, and in 38 per cent to take policy decisions without consultation. Combining these measures into a single continuum, 28 per cent of leaders were found to have no freedom of individual action, while at the other end 16 per cent had, in this defined sense, full autonomy. That 16 per cent, though, was split extremely unevenly, including over a quarter of Conservative councils, one in eight Labour, and no Liberal Democrat councils at all. The comparison between the Conservative and Lib Dem figures is particularly interesting, suggesting that, while Conservative councillors are prepared generally to be deferential towards their leaders,

Exhibit 14.7 Leadership in leader/cabinet councils, by political party

	Cons	Lab	LD
Measures of leader autonomy			
Leader chooses members of the cabinet	55	28	18
Leader allocates cabinet portfolios	67	57	53
Leader takes at least some executive decisions alone	47	31	47
'Concentrated' leadership – leader does all 3 of above	28	12	–
Leadership/scrutiny typology			
Individual leadership + robust scrutiny	25	10	13
Individual leadership + weak scrutiny	(35)	21	27
Group leadership + robust scrutiny	19	(44)	(40)
Group leadership + weak scrutiny	22	26	20

Note: ◯ = modal executive style

Source: Data from Stoker *et al.*, 2003, chs 5 and 9.

Lib Dems will delegate certain executive decision making powers, but not necessarily additional powers of appointment.

Exhibit 14.8 puts a little flesh on the bones of these bare statistics by giving brief characterisations of three of the executive leadership styles identified by Stoker's team. The suggestion, of course, is that leader-dominated executives are likely to be found predominantly in Conservative authorities, and team executives disproportionately in Labour authorities. It may be, though, that the multi-actor executive, which is probably closest to the Westminster cabinet model, will come more into its own as local government becomes increasingly accustomed to its new *modus operandi*.

In the lower section of Exhibit 14.7, Stoker *et al.* incorporate an assessment of overview and scrutiny (O & S) arrangements, in order to provide a somewhat more rounded picture of leadership styles from the viewpoint of the authority. The assessment was based on several factors – the independence of O & S from the executive, its readiness to explore innovative forms of service delivery, and the quality of officer support it received – which could be combined into a crude index of what we have termed 'scrutiny robustness'. Put it together with the 'leader autonomy' index, and you have a 2 × 2 leadership/scrutiny typology, which, as shown by the circled figures in Exhibit 14.7, correlates at least to an extent with these authorities' party control.

If you want to get behind typologies and correlations to real-life leaders, there is something to be said – and not just out of consideration of the libel

Exhibit 14.8 Three executive leadership styles

Leader-dominated executive	Cabinet members work to the leader, who takes responsibility for the overall direction of policy. Role of the cabinet is to advise on policy development and monitor progress of implementation. Can result in fewer full cabinet meetings and more 'bi-laterals' between the leader and individual portfolio holders. Leader will be the key contact for external partners, and may choose to have own independent sources of policy advice.
Multi-actor executive	Cabinet members have extensive delegated powers, operate with considerable autonomy from each other and from the leader, and they themselves are expected to provide leadership in their respective policy areas. They will develop their own networks and meet independently with external partners. Leader's role is to maintain a corporate approach and ensure that cabinet members' efforts join up to form a coherent policy. Individual cabinet members are the 'default clearing point' in decision making.
Team executive	Leader and cabinet work together, with a view to collective decision making. Full cabinet meets regularly and possibly at length, and individual decision making is checked back with the cabinet as a whole. Leader's aim is to ensure and manage consensus, and give a collective drive to council policy.

Source: Information from Stoker *et al.*, 2004, pp. 39ff.

law – for picking on those from the recent past rather than the present day. Which is why, for our illustration of the Conservative Party's receptiveness towards 'leadership from the front', we have chosen Dame Shirley Porter, Conservative Leader of Westminster City Council, 1983–91. She left behind some very prominent and personal legacies of her leadership, including hundreds of business-sponsored white-and-green designer litter bins and modernistic, strategically sited 'Porterloos'. More seriously, she also left some hugely damaging accusations of wilful misconduct for attempting to boost the Conservative vote in marginal wards through the selective sale of council houses – the notorious 'homes for votes' scandal.

It is not the propriety of Dame Shirley's leadership that interests us here, however, so much as its unquestionably individualistic style – visionary or authoritarian, depending on your viewpoint, and your proximity to it:

I am synonymous with Westminster City Council. In my years as Leader I've tried to change the culture at the Council, but ... it's like taking the British Empire and turning it into Great Britain plc. You're changing a cosy establishment of both members and officers. We've had our battles ... I remember asking, 'Why don't we run this Council like a business?' One of my own side, a certain uptight gentleman with a moustache, spluttered, 'This is the Council!' That was the beginning of my wanting to change the way things were run.

Her leadership was summed up by a badge she liked to wear, reading 'YCDBSOYA':

I'll give you the polite version. It means 'You Can't Do Business Sitting On Your Armchair'. My father, Sir Jack Cohen, who built the Tesco supermarket chain, gave one to Callaghan and one to Heath, but I haven't had the temerity to give one to Mrs Thatcher – yet. (Abdela, 1989, pp. 186–93)

The then prime minister used to figure regularly in Shirley Porter's interviews, and there were some striking similarities between the two women's proactive leadership styles: the impatience with the conventions of public administration, the readiness to see their own colleagues as part of the problem as much as part of the solution.

In the other two parties, such highly personalised leadership would be much more risky, as evidenced by their councillors' widespread scepticism towards the whole idea of directly elected mayors. There are plenty of strong and influential Labour leaders around but, out of constitutional necessity and the politician's instinct for personal survival, they will generally take considerable care to carry their party groups with them. They will 'talk the talk' of consensus, teamwork, and even – to use a favourite 'Old Labour' expression – 'comradeship'.

David Bookbinder, Leader of Derbyshire County Council, 1981–92, was a contemporary and in some ways a Labour version of Shirley Porter: an equally high media profile and just as concerned to challenge the 'cosy' culture of local government. But, even in a personal interview, Bookbinder's choice of a first-person pronoun was usually plural:

For years and years it has always been the view that local government is a partnership between the councillors and those professionals employed to deliver services ... Nonsense! The officers have one role and the members have another. The members are elected and the job of any government is to govern ... We have a term – being officered. The officer will get hold of the Chair at a pre-committee meeting, explain to the Chair what they want to do, give them a report, and the Chair will instruct the committee members to deliver what is on the paper. But a member's role is not to say yes or no to the recommendation at the end of the report. We want to say what goes into the sausage machine. We are supposed to be the creators, elected on a political philosophy. We have changed people's quality of life: 80 per cent of children get school meals when it used to be 50 per cent; twice as many old folk are getting home helps; meals on wheels are the same price as when we took control in 1981; we have more nurseries. (Willis, 1990)

Party differences – policies and principles

David Bookbinder's declamation takes us neatly from organisation to policy. Our main political parties do organise themselves and operate differently from each other, but even more obvious are their policy differences.

As we have emphasised throughout this book, local government, its structure, functions and financing, have come in recent years to occupy a prime place on the UK national political agenda. Accordingly, no national party's manifesto is now complete without a selection of pledges concerning the further changes that it will impose on local government, should it be elected to office. The three main party manifestos for the 2005 General Election were fairly typical, albeit without differing from one another quite as markedly as some of their predecessors. As can be seen in Exhibit 14.9, each party had its own proposals for the financing of local government – already under review, of course, by Sir Michael Lyons – for the provision of some of its principal services, and even for the basic structure and organisation of sub-central government as a whole. As a result, the scale, scope and shape of our local government system will all inevitably be rather different at the end of the 2005 Parliament from what they would have been under either a Conservative Government or even some form of joint Labour–Liberal Democrat Administration.

We have argued in previous editions that, unread though they are by the vast majority of electors, these manifestos are important documents – and most certainly the one of the winning party. To demonstrate, we reviewed in 2002 Labour's 1997 manifesto pledges, awarding ticks where they had been implemented and crosses where not. The results were notable in both relevant respects: most of the several strands of what subsequently became known as New Labour's 'modernisation agenda' had in fact been anticipated in its manifesto, and, with very few significant exceptions, the specific commitments in the manifesto had by the end of four years of government been substantially implemented.

Losing manifestos are important too, though obviously in a very different way. They represent publicly defeated – and, by inference, unpopular – programmes, which their authors are generally going to want to change before their next airing. Following the 2005 General Election,

Exhibit 14.9 The national parties' local government manifestos, 5 May, 2005

	Conservatives	Labour	Liberal Democrats
Democracy	Ban Scots MPs from voting on English Bills, including those on local government; elected police commissioners.	Consult over more directly elected mayors; consider 4-yearly, whole-council elections for all; parish councils for London.	Extend STV for Scottish local elections to all GB – and the House of Commons – and the Scottish Parliament and Welsh Assembly.
Regions	Axe unelected assemblies; return regional powers over planning, housing, transport, fire service to local authorities.	Devolve more powers to regional bodies – planning, housing, transport, economic development; review powers of London mayor and GLA.	Give powers of unelected bodies to local authorities; return strategic planning to counties; streamline remaining functions into one agency with executive of elected councillors.
Finance	Retain council tax; offer permanent discount of up to £500 to households where all residents aged 65 +.	Reform council tax after Lyons review; consider £200 refund for every pensioner household paying council tax.	Scrap council tax and replace by Local Income Tax, saving average family £450 overall.
Education	Schools to set own priorities and budgets; funds · allocated by pupil numbers; heads to have full control over admissions and expulsions, and freedom to spend money according to school's needs.	Successful primary schools to become Foundation Schools; all secondary schools to become independent specialist schools; new powers for OFSTED to close failing schools and replace failing managements.	Scrap tuition fees; heads to have LEA support for 'managed transfer' to other schools or specialist units for pupils whose behaviour is unacceptable.
Inspection	Scrap CPA and Best Value; more powers for local communities over planning decisions, with less interference from central government.	Councils to have further freedoms to deliver better services, subject to national minimum standards; reduce bureaucracy by cutting inspectorates and inspection costs.	Free councils from 'stifling controls' of central government; merge 8 inspectorates into one streamlined independent Audit Commission.
Anti-social behaviour	Neighbourhood policing to give local people a say over police priorities; councils to get powers to act against illegal traveller encampments.	Parish council wardens to get the same powers as local authority employees to issue Penalty Disorder notices for noise, graffiti, throwing fireworks.	Big late-night venues to contribute to extra policing costs.

Main source: Information from Rose, 2005.

this jettisoning of defeated policies started almost immediately, with Lib Dem MPs attacking their own party's flagship Local Income Tax pledge, before later in the year new Conservative leader, David Cameron, appeared to be contemplating rewriting not just the policies of his party, but also some of its presumed values.

The contrasts and disputes among the parties can be just as great at local elections. Councils are certainly more restricted and constrained in what they can do than they used to be. They cannot raise taxes as they might wish, and their influence over their major budget expenditures may be limited to the margins, but, as we emphasised in Chapter 10, marginal is not the same as trivial, certainly not to those whose lives are directly affected.

Local elections thus continue to be run by those involved in such a way as to suggest that the outcome makes a difference. Party manifestos and candidates' election addresses are likely to combine some of the national policies headlined in Exhibit 14.9 with references to local issues and circumstances, and the whole atmosphere and conduct of the election will be set by the party defending its record and those that may seriously be challenging it. We have tried to convey something of the flavour of these partisan contests in Exhibit 14.10.

The three elections summarised in Exhibit 14.10 were selected not for their typicality; if anything, quite the reverse. Each contest had its own strong and unique local undercurrents. They were almost entirely party political clashes, but by no means entirely *national* party clashes. In each case what shaped the campaign debate, and probably boosted whatever interest the media and the electorate might have in it, was the record of the *local* parties, the *local* controlling group, the *local* council leadership. As in most elections, most of the votes cast will have been party votes, but, as we saw in Chapter 11, a significant minority of them will have been for different parties than would have been supported in a parliamentary election.

The pros and cons of party politics

It is at election time that we see most clearly both the positive and negative features of the extensive role played by party politics in our modern-day local government. We have already alluded – indirectly in Chapter 3, and directly in Chapter 11 – to some of the claimed positive features, notably the contribution of parties to political education and participation. These, coupled with the other claims set out on the left-hand side of Exhibit 14.11, make an apparently strong case, yet it remains a case that many of us find unpersuasive. When asked their opinions, as in the 1985 Widdicombe Committee survey, the majority of respondents (52 per cent) said they

Exhibit 14.10 Three local elections, 1999

SOUTH STAFFORDSHIRE DC – TAXLESS TORIES' TRIUMPHANT RETURN

Background: A whole-council election in the only West Midlands council to remain Conservative throughout the party's local government meltdown in the mid-1990s. Natural Tory territory – the north-western, owner-occupying, suburban and green belt fringe of the West Midlands. With virtually no black/minority ethnic voters, it seems a world away from nearby Wolverhampton.

Conservative record: Thrift-driven council had contracted out its refuse collection, earned over £50 million from council house sales, and was seeking re-election after 6 years of not charging residents any council tax: the district collected the tax, but it went entirely to the county and parishes. Local issues: whether the no-tax achievement was a result of prudent financial management, as the Conservatives claimed, or service-cutting plus the fact that the district's 27 parishes provide services – village halls, allotments, bus shelters – that elsewhere are district responsibilities. Lib Dems argued, with illustrations, that councillors should live in the wards they represent.

Result: Conservatives re-elected with their previous majority of 6 increased to 20.

UTTLESFORD DC – UNHOLY CON–LAB ALLIANCE SET TO CONTINUE

Background: Where is it? Surrounding Stansted Airport – a rural, historical, predominantly agricultural district in NW Essex. Unquestioningly Conservative until the Lib Dems displaced them as the largest party in previous whole-council elections, in 1995. A brief Lib Dem minority administration was ousted in 1997 by what *they* saw as an 'unprincipled' alliance of Conservatives, Labour and Independents.

Local issues: Usually the airport, any prospective expansion of which will arouse united opposition. But in 2001 the alliance was *the* issue and the debate was heated and personalised. To quote the Lib Dem leader: 'in this council the Labour leader, a funeral director, employs the Tory leader as a pallbearer. If that's not jobs for the boys, I don't know what is!' Nationally targeted council for Lib Dems.

Result: Conservatives and Labour swapped two seats, but no gains for Lib Dems, who did, though, win majority control in 2003.

DONCASTER BC – LABOUR HANG ON IN DONNYGATE

Background: A mining, engineering and horse-racing district in South Yorkshire and traditionally a near-monopolistic Labour stronghold. But acquired a 'Donnygate' reputation as England's sleaziest council following accusations (and convictions) of expenses fraud and planning irregularities by both councillors and officers. Through party suspensions and election defeats, Labour's council majority was reduced to an embarrassing 23.

Local issues: CORRUPTION! – certainly for the still-small Conservative and Lib Dem groups. Labour's third leader in 3 years and several new – and untainted – candidates argued that it was not the only or most important issue, citing the council's good record on service delivery and value for money, as evidenced in the Audit Commission's league tables.

Result: Labour lost a further 6 of the 22 seats contested (one-third of the council only) and had its majority cut to 11 – the lowest since 1976. In 2002, very much as a consequence of these issues, Doncaster became one of the first mayoral authorities (see Exhibit 6.4 above).

Exhibit 14.11 The pros and cons of party politics in local government

The merits and benefits	The counter-claims

The merits and benefits

- *More candidates, fewer uncontested seats* in local elections.
- *More active campaigning*, more information for electors, more debating of the issues.
- *Clarification of the issues*, as the parties are challenged by their opponents to justify their arguments and assertions.
- *More citizen awareness and interest* in local government generally and the local council and its services in particular, resulting probably in a higher electoral turnout.
- *Stimulation of change and initiative* – as parties with their underlying principles and collective resources develop policies to put before the electorate.
- *More opportunities for public involvement in community life.*
- *Enhanced accountability* – as the parties collectively and their candidates individually make public pledges, which, if elected, they must seek to implement, and for which they can subsequently and electorally be called to account.
- *Governmental coherence* – the existence, following a decisive election result, of a single-party administration, clearly identifiable by the electorate and council officers alike, able to carry out the policies on which it was elected.
- *Enhanced local democracy* – the existence of electorally endorsed party policies and programmes, reducing the potential policy influence of unelected and unaccountable officers.

The counter-claims

- *More party candidates, fewer Independents* – the major parties, with their institutional resources, have too much advantage over minority party candidates and Independents.
- *Narrower debating of the issues* – with rounded discussion displaced by the strident adversarial clash of party rhetoric.
- *Less electoral enlightenment* – as uncommitted voters become disenchanted by the polarisation of debate and by politicians' apparent convictions that their party alone possesses all the answers.
- *Electoral boredom* – with electors staying at home, invoking 'a plague on all their houses', or unmotivated by an outcome that seems a foregone conclusion.
- *Less public involvement* – with the many citizens not wishing to join a political party being excluded from areas of local community life.
- *Nationalisation of local elections* – as supposedly local campaigns focus much of their attention on national issues and personalities.
- *Reduced representativeness of councils* – as the winning party takes all positions of responsibility and seeks to implement its policies to the exclusion of all others.
- *Excessive party politicisation of issues* – with the parties feeling obliged to adopt usually adversarial positions on subjects that might more satisfactorily be approached consensually.
- *Reduced local democracy* – as councillors are 'disciplined' into voting with their party, regardless of their personal convictions or judgement.
- *Exclusion of professional advice* - as all effective decisions are made by party groups, usually without the benefit of professionally trained and experienced officers in attendance.

would prefer local councils to be run on non-partisan lines, with only a third (34 per cent) feeling that a party system is better (Widdicombe, 1986d, p. 88). We need to examine, therefore, the other side of the coin, which is why Exhibit 14.11 is deliberately set out as a kind of balance sheet.

Set out in this way, the arguments may indeed seem quite evenly balanced. Certainly, you must form your own conclusions, preferably with reference to your personal experience and impressions. Realists that we are, we would be inclined to point first to the historical trends we identified earlier in the chapter. The comprehensive party politicisation of most of our local government is not only here to stay, but, if the trend towards ever larger and unitary authorities continues, a likely by-product will be a reinforcement of the domination of the national parties of whatever remains of our 'local' democracy.

Finally, enough of academic balance. Like Dire Straits' Mark Knopfler, we are unconvinced of the virtues of fence-sitting: 'a dangerous course; you can even catch a bullet from a peacekeeping force'. We refer, therefore, to the argument we put forward in Chapter 12: that politics, properly understood, is at the very heart of what local government is necessarily about. It is about the management and resolution of the inevitable conflict of local views concerning the provision and distribution of public goods and services. Without necessarily agreeing with the respected colleague of ours who insists that the definition of an Independent is someone who can't be depended upon, we would suggest there is something to be said for these conflicting views being marshalled and articulated openly by consciously accountable party politicians, rather than by self-styled 'non-political representatives', whose motives and policy objectives may be left publicly unspecified.

Chapter 15

Who Makes Policy?

The internal and informal politics of policy making

Chapters 12 to 14 examined three of the key elements in a council's policy making process: elected councillors, the officers who advise them, and the political party groups of which most of them are members. But these were essentially static examinations, or snapshot pictures. In this chapter we bring them together and focus on their collective *raisons d'être*: the actual determination of policy. It is a process that has been transformed structurally by the advent of political executives held to account by an overview and scrutiny regime. Executive members are now personally responsible and accountable for decisions relating to the management and delivery of services in a wholly different way from committee chairs under the previous system.

These changes have not, however, invalidated everything previously written about policy making in British local government: about the centrality and subtleties of the member–officer relationship, the critical importance of a council's 'party arithmetic', and, not least, the attempts by some of our academic colleagues to conceptualise these inter-relationships. The purpose of this chapter, therefore, is to review and, where necessary, refine what we know about the *internal and informal* influences on policy making. We know from several of the chapters in Part 1 that much of the framework of local government policy nowadays is laid down by central government. But we have also seen how local authorities can still pursue policy priorities, respond to specific local circumstances, and launch their own initiatives. This chapter explores the extent to which it may be possible to make some general statements about how, within town halls and county halls across the country, these things are done.

Analytical models

Three main analytical models have been widely used to describe the distribution of power and influence inside local authorities. Each is considered briefly, along with a further model based on insights from central government, before the chapter goes on to emphasise the need to broaden out discussion beyond the limitations of models.

The formal model

This model derives from the 'legal-institutional' approach that once dominated the study of local government. Its proponents saw power relationships in formal terms and focused on the formal structures of decision making – the council, its committees and departments. The model could hardly be simpler: councillors make policy, while officers advise them and carry it out. No overlaps or qualifications are countenanced.

Advocates would argue that, if people understand the formal, legal position, they understand reality. Critics would retort that reality, and certainly political reality, is considerably more complex, as has already been suggested in our discussion of councillor roles in Chapter 12. A model that sees councillors making policy through the council, while officers merely advise and implement, tells us more about what perhaps *should* happen than about what *actually* happens. It simply fails to recognise the complexity within, and the organisational variety among, local authorities.

Yet one must beware of dismissing even an overly simplistic model as worthless. The confrontational Thatcher years saw real assertiveness by councillors of both the New Urban Left and the Radical Right. They set out to run authorities themselves in the way that the formal model delineates. Remember the quote in Chapter 14 from David Bookbinder that could easily have been echoed by Dame Shirley Porter: 'the officers have one role and members have another. The members are elected and the job of any government is to govern'. For a time at least, this model, often dismissed as naive, had its forthright advocates.

The technocratic model

A rival to the formal model has been the technocratic model, which views *officers* as the dominant force in local politics. Their power resides, it is asserted, in their control of specialised technical and professional knowledge, unpossessed by and possibly incomprehensible to part-time, amateur, generalist councillors.

This model too, however, is something of a caricature and should not be accepted uncritically, especially in the age of executive government. Highly paid, professionally trained officers, heading large departments, with all the staff and other resources of these departments at their disposal, can appear formidable to the inexperienced, newly elected councillor entering the council offices for perhaps the first time. But the relationship is not all one-sided.

Plenty of leading and long-serving councillors, particularly those in effectively full-time executive positions, will have the experience, knowledge and political skill to assert themselves effectively in any negotiation with officers. Moreover, even the neophyte councillor comes with that vital source of democratic legitimacy that no officer, however senior, can ever have: the authority of having been *elected*, on what is now an endorsed political platform, to represent all the citizens of their locality.

Exhibit 15.1 is a kind of balance sheet of the respective resources of officers and councillors – a little like that in Exhibit 9.7 in which we compared the resources of central and local government. We argued there that local government has access to more resources than is sometimes suggested, and so it is with councillors in their relations with officers.

It will be apparent from Exhibit 15.1 that it has been the politicisation, and particularly the intensified *party* politicisation of local government since the 1970s or 1980s, that has done more than probably anything else to shift the balance of power between officers and elected councillors. We come back again to the rise during the 1980s of ideologically committed and politically skilful councillors of both the New Left and the New Right, which inevitably served to check any independent policy aspirations of officers. In the 1990s, for example, ruling Conservative Party groups in Westminster LB, Wandsworth LB, Wansdyke DC in Avon and Rochford DC in Essex were notably assertive in the introduction of competitive tendering and the enabling/purchasing philosophy – just as a decade earlier

Exhibit 15.1 The resources of officers and councillors

OFFICERS	COUNCILLORS
• Professional knowledge, training, qualifications	• Political skills, experience; possibly training, expertise, qualifications in own field of work
• Professional networks, journals, conferences	• Party political networks, journals, conferences
• Full-time, well-paid employee of council	• Spends an average of 20 hours per week on council work, far more if on the Executive
• Resources of whole department	• Resources of whole council
• Knowledge and working experience of other councils	• In-depth (possibly lifetime) knowledge of own council, ward, its residents and service users
• Commitment to professional values and standards	• Commitment to personal and political values, to locality and community
• UNELECTED 'servant of the council' – appointed to advise councillors and implement their policy	• ELECTED on political manifesto to make policy and represent hundreds/thousands of residents and service users

the 'municipal left' had introduced public transport and council housing subsidies, and job creation and anti-discrimination policies.

Notwithstanding such examples, the professional and technical knowledge possessed by officers remains a tremendous resource, equipping them to act as powerful policy makers *in the absence* of any positive policy lead from members. Their influence can be especially strong in smaller rural authorities dominated by Independent councillors. As professionals, officers are always there to fill any policy vacuum. It is up to councillors to set their own clear and – recalling Rhodes' observations in Chapter 13 on the centralist inclination of professional influence – localist policy agendas and thus to ensure that there is no vacuum.

The joint élite model

Claiming to be more truly reflective of actual practice than the formal or technocratic models, the joint élite model argued that policy making is dominated by a small group of leading majority party councillors (now invariably located in the cabinet) and senior officers, with minority party and what we now call non-executive members and junior officers at most only marginally involved.

It was an interpretation that found support in several empirical studies. Saunders' research in Croydon (1980, pp. 216–30) revealed a picture of town hall politics where chief officers and political leaders worked as 'close allies' maintaining a powerful control over policy making. Cockburn's study of Lambeth saw the backbencher 'excluded by the high-level partnership between the leadership and senior officers' and consequently taking 'little part in the policy planning process'. Council decision-making was, Cockburn maintained, dominated by 'a tightly-knit hierarchy under the control of a board of directors [the chief officers] in close partnership with a top-level caucus of majority party members' (Cockburn, 1977, p. 169).

But the joint élite model too had its critics, who questioned the virtual monopoly of influence apparently attributed to this élite. Young and Mills (1983) argued, for example, that the very exercise of routinised power by those at the top of a hierarchy makes them less likely *sources of policy change* than those lower down. These 'junior actors' learn from direct operational experience and often have the creative energy necessary for the development of new initiatives. Important though leading councillors and officers in any authority obviously are, a thorough understanding of the policy process requires a recognition that they will rarely constitute a united cohesive group sharing a common agenda. In the real world, relationships are both more complex and frequently characterised by tension and conflict.

A 'dynamic dependency' analysis

Quite apart from their respective limitations, all three of the above models date from the era of the committee system. It is therefore worth noting what might be termed an early 'post-modern' analysis: an attempt to adapt elements of the earlier models, most notably the resource-based technocratic model, to the political management changes introduced by Labour's 'modernisation agenda' – indeed, to local authority differences in the implementation of those changes.

From her perspective as a member of the University of Manchester's Evaluating Local Governance (ELG) project, Gains draws on the literature on central government bureaucratic political relations (e.g., Rhodes and Dunleavy, 1995) that stresses the importance of 'formal and informal institutionalised rules in structuring action and influencing outcomes' (Gains, 2004, p. 94). At the local level, these institutionalised rules would include institutional understandings or 'inheritances' concerning the departmental and hierarchical nature of local government, the under-standing that officers are politically neutral and serve the whole council (Stewart, 2000); also shared 'world views', such as the Thatcher-instilled drive for economy, efficiency and effectiveness, and 'New Labour's 'steering centralism' and its commitment to targets, performance measurement and partnership working.

Gains' 'dynamic dependency' thesis is that all behaviour, including that of councillors and officers, is the outcome of the interplay of these institutional understandings – which in part are institution-specific – and the actors' skill in exercising their respective resources: the political resources of the council leader *vis-à-vis* senior managers, the strength of the party group, and so on (p. 95). Dynamic dependency analysis, Gains suggests, provides a better understanding than more static models of how and why member–officer relations differ both across authorities and over time. More specifically, it can help to explain the 'huge variety of formal institutional arrangements adopted to enact the 2000 Act' that were found by the ELG surveys (p. 98): how, for example, the delegation of decision-making powers to individual portfolio holders is more likely in Conservative and county authorities, why dedicated officer units supporting the scrutiny function are more likely to be established in Labour ones, and that generally officers appeared to have responded initially more quickly and more positively than did councillors to the abolition of the committee system (pp. 98–100).

Like all models, the idea of dynamic dependency has its strengths and its weaknesses. But, unlike the joint élite model, it does not assume shared values or priorities, and it emphasises usefully how local history and political culture will vary along with, for example, the political resources of a council leader, the strength of the party group and the clout of the professional officers. Moreover, it does not see the balance of power between, in our case, officers and members in zero-sum terms, but rather as a dynamic and dependency-based relationship, varying from one institutional setting to another. It thereby adds a helpful nuance to our understanding of local policy making.

Broadening the debate – additional influences on policy making

There is more, though, to an understanding of the distribution of policy influence in a local authority than simply an analysis of the activities of the most senior players. As Stoker and Wilson (1986) show, other factors need to be incorporated if a model is to depict anything like the full complexity of internal power relationships. That is the purpose of the remainder of this chapter: to add to, qualify, and generally complicate the models outlined above, and in doing so to identify some of the additional influences on policy making. Our focus will be on those authorities that now have executive management structures, rather than the 59 smaller English shire districts (populations of less than 85,000) that opted for 'streamlined committee systems', although in practice many of these smaller authorities will face similar influences. Figure 15.1 provides a diagrammatic presentation of the ideas covered, which comprise:

- *Intra-party influences* - relations *within*, especially, ruling party groups, and between groups and the wider party;
- *Non-executive influences* – the evolving roles of 'backbench' or non-executive councillors;
- *Inter-departmental influences* – relations between and across departments and professions;
- *Intra-departmental influences* – relations within departments; and
- *Inter-party influences* – relations *between* party groups, especially in hung authorities, where they have to take account of one another.

The ruling party group and party networks

The ruling party group as a whole, not just its leading and executive councillors, can have a significant influence on policy making. Few party groups are homogeneous. Often there are factions with their own priorities and agendas that make it difficult even in public, let alone in private group meetings, to achieve and maintain unity. The ruling Labour group on Leicester City Council at the end of the 1980s was unusual in the formalisation of its factionalism, and in the fact that the party leader, Peter Soulsby, was one of the few members that belonged to none of them, but it

Figure 15.1   *Power inside local authorities: a diagrammatic representation*

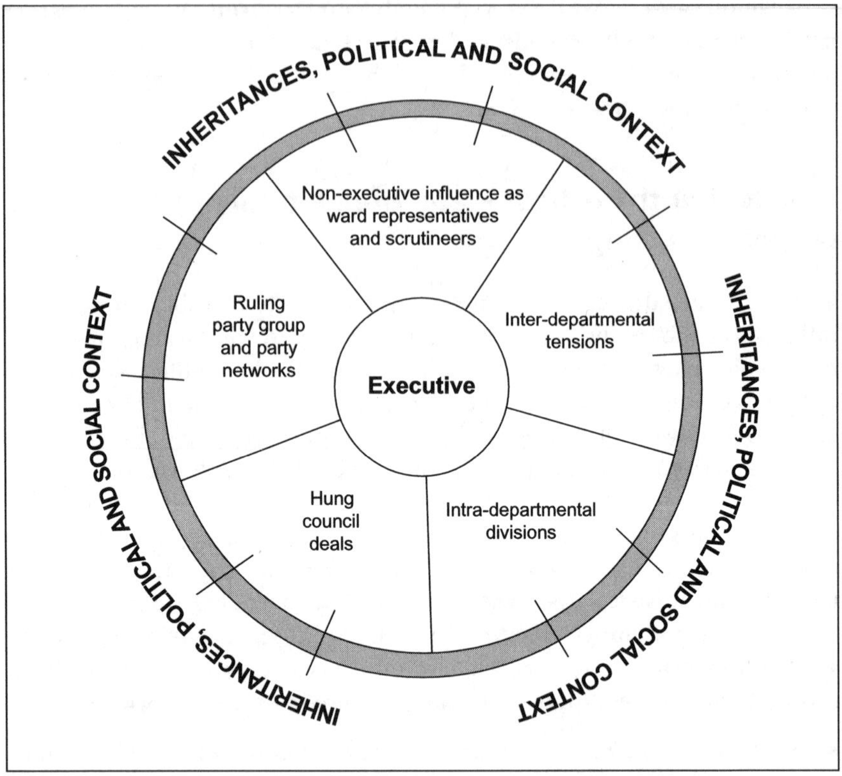

Source: Some of the wording in this figure draws upon Stoker and Wilson (1986).

was by no means unique. There were in effect four caucuses within the group (Leach and Wilson, 2000, pp. 128–9):

- The 'left', about 13 in number, who met in a local pub, with formal agendas, in advance of Labour group meetings;
- The 'black' caucus of about 8 members, including one white Muslim councillor, which also held formal pre-meetings;
- The 'right' – again about 8 members, largely from Leicester West parliamentary constituency, less formally organised than the left and black groups; and
- The 'non-aligned' group, of between 6 and 8 members.

Most party groups operate more informally – even haphazardly – but that does not stop them being a source of policy influence. Policy initiatives can emerge from the backbench/non-executive members of a group, who can also veto or refer back leadership proposals with which they disagree. Stoker (1991, p. 98) notes that, while over many issues and for most of the time, a group may simply endorse decisions taken elsewhere, at the very least senior councillors and officers must be careful not to offend the core political values and commitments of backbenchers. The role of party groups in local policy making is a potentially crucial area for decision-making.

Party groups nowadays expect to be consulted and listened to, and leaders – other than directly elected mayors – have to cultivate their support continuously. Upset just one or two members and they may decide to leave; alienate a majority and *you* may have to. Defections and instances of 'crossing the floor' of the council chamber are numerically far commoner, if less publicised, than in parliamentary politics, as evidenced in almost any local election listings. Even discounting all the plain, unvarnished 'Independents', there will be plenty of candidates describing themselves as 'Independent Conservative', 'Socialist Labour', 'Independent Liberal Democrat', even 'Independent Green', and suggesting that their favoured parties cannot accommodate the ideological purity of their views – or perhaps just them personally.

On occasion, party groups will flex their muscles and remove the group leader. It can be a heartless process, especially when the relevant group meeting comes, as often happens, immediately after an election. The best known, and fascinatingly recounted, case was the then 'Red Ken' Livingstone's displacement of the more right-wing Andrew McIntosh as leader of the Greater London Council in May 1981, within 24 hours of McIntosh having led the Labour Party to electoral victory (Livingstone, 1987, pp. 3–4). A similar fate befell Theresa Stewart, Labour leader of Birmingham City Council for nearly six years, but overthrown by supporters of Albert Bore within days of the May 1999 elections. In 2005, Labour group members on Hull City Council conducted their execution in stages, first removing the power of their leader, Colin Inglis, to appoint his own cabinet, then a fortnight later replacing him altogether with a former leader, Ken Branson. Leaders or executive members who owe their elected positions to their group can expect to be reminded regularly of the fact – which is one powerful reason, of course, why so many councillors oppose the very principle of directly elected mayors, whose first accountability is to the electorate as a whole, rather than to them.

The *local party network* also requires consideration. Links with the wider party organisation can be a valuable resource for individual group members, especially in the Labour Party, where such networks have a greater policy significance, with local election manifestos, for example, being drawn up in consultation with non-councillor party members. It was thus the district parties in Walsall and Rochdale, rather than the party groups on the council, who were the real originators of the decentralisation policies in those boroughs. Local councillors and council leaders must respect the role of the wider movement; disregard can easily lead to conflict.

Non-executive councillors

It might have been better if the essentially parliamentary term 'back-bencher' had never been applied to the very different world of local government, where, in the traditional committee system, no councillor constitutionally had more decision making authority than any other. 'Backbencher' misleadingly and demeaningly suggests a hierarchical role division where none legally existed. On the other hand, 'frontline' councillors, favoured by the IDeA and a few councils (Tameside, Cardiff), seems a bit militaristic for our taste. We shall therefore continue, despite the term's inherent negativity, to talk mainly of 'non-executive' councillors, who now have four distinct roles – as members of the full council, representatives of their wards and constituents, overviewers and scrutineers, and community leaders – through which they can play a part in shaping policy, if not in actually taking policy decisions.

In promoting or defending local ward interests, councillors can sometimes enter the policy arena in a very influential way. In Leicester in 1983, two Asian Labour councillors initiated a campaign that overthrew the majority Labour group's housing policy by blocking a demolition plan in their ward (Stoker and Brindley, 1985). Local ward interests can easily cut across party interests, and in authorities with relatively weak party systems (see Exhibit 14.1) these local interests are likely to be compensatingly stronger. In such circumstances, councillors can, by developing alliances and lobbying, contribute regularly and effectively to the shaping of council policy.

One of the Government's intended by-products of executive local government was the enhancement of councillors' ward and community roles, and of their unique position as conduits of their constituents' views to the council. Freed from at least some of their former committee work, non-executive members are expected to consult with their communities on the development of policy, on the regular reviews of Best Value and the development of the Best Value Performance Plan, and on any other community-relevant initiatives. Councils are charged specifically with ensuring that appropriate procedures are available for members to 'feed-in' the views of their constituents to the policy development process.

These procedures include the council's overview and scrutiny arrangements, which, if properly exercised, are about far more than evaluating existing policy and holding the executive to account *after* the event – knowing whom to blame – important and satisfying though that is. The opportunities are there for the 80 per cent or more non-executive members to contribute *prospectively* to the development of policy *before* it is finalised (see Exhibit 6.6). Overview and scrutiny are rightly presented as an integral part of effective executive government, and their potential impact is almost limitless, because they offer the non-executive members who exclusively run the process the possibility of reviewing, scrutinising, reporting on and making recommendations concerning any past, present or future policy or action of the council, or any matter affecting the council's area or its inhabitants.

For the full potential of scrutiny to be realised in this wide-ranging sense, however, at least three conditions are required. First, councillors themselves must approach the process positively, acknowledging that not being part of the executive can be *empowering* at least as much as disempowering. They must realise too that new skills are likely to be expected of them, which for most will mean serious training. Instead of, as often sufficed in the past, passively processing officer reports, they should now be assessing and probing, working collaboratively to draw out evidence and views from witnesses, and understanding performance indicators, comparative data and financial processes in a way that few will have done previously (Audit Commission, 2001, p. 24).

Second, scrutiny members need to learn not just new skills, but also new ways of working – constructively across the party divide. Their role as scrutineers, even if they happen to be members of the same party as the executive, is not to defend the party line, but to explore, critically if necessary, ways in which the council can better serve its community. It is vital, therefore, that party 'whipping' and tight disciplinary regimes be relaxed – something that does not come easily to members who may have spent their entire adult lives opposing just about everything their political opponents stand for.

Third, effective scrutiny requires, in addition to committed and trained members, *dedicated* officer and resource support – in both senses of the adjective. The executive's demands must not be allowed totally to hold sway. Sufficient and sufficiently senior officers need to be allocated specifically to the scrutiny process, and, like the members, they need to view the assignment positively, and not as some kind of second-class, career-blocking posting, inferior to working for the executive. Adequate financial support is needed too, so that, for example, independent advice can be sought from outside consultants. The appointment of such senior dedicated officers was, initially at least, very much the exception.

None of these conditions is easily met – either by authorities facing additional demands on some of their most valued officers, or by members and officers having to adapt or suppress deep-rooted instincts and work in ways that are bound at first to seem alien. It is small wonder, therefore, that it has been the overview and scrutiny function that almost all authorities, and particularly their non-executive members, have found it hardest to get working effectively (see, e.g., Snape, 2004; Leach and Copus, 2004).

Inter-departmental tensions

Most councils have more than one overview and scrutiny committee or panel, but not one for every major department. In this way, as in several others, local government practice differs from that of the mainly departmentally-linked select committees in the House of Commons. Councils have generally been readier to recognise that many of the most urgent and intractable problems they face – the so-called 'wicked issues' of social exclusion, environmental sustainability, community safety and the like – cannot be pigeonholed neatly into service-specific departments and committees. They have therefore set up more open-ended and flexible scrutiny arrangements, often with some formidably all-embracing titles – such as Bexley's Social Inclusion and Corporate Affairs; Children's, Housing and Social Services; and Environment and Regeneration. Others, like Durham, have linked their O & S committees to their corporate aims: Promoting Strong and Healthy Communities; Looking After the Environment; Building a Strong Economy; Arts, Leisure and the Environment.

Such developments, though, should not be taken to imply that departmental identities and boundaries are no longer of much significance. Departments remain the main units of a council's administrative organisation, and, as ever, they represent different interests and inevitably have different, and potentially conflicting, sets of priorities. Particularly at times of zero growth or service and staffing cutbacks, these differences surface and can lead to arguments across departments in the fight for scarce resources, and conceivably for departmental survival.

There are also instinctive *professional rivalries* – between, for example, the technical departments involved in land development: 'Planners, architects, housing managers, valuation officers and engineers all claim an involvement and there is a long history of rivalry between these professions' (Stoker, 1991, p. 102). Dominance of specific departments and professions will inevitably change over time; unacceptable policies will be delayed and favoured policies will be accelerated. Increased professionalisation within the local government service has meant that inter-departmental tensions are never far from the surface. They will spill over into the policy sphere with some regularity.

According to Pratchett and Wingfield (1996), the dual impact of market competition and the internal reforms associated with the advent of the 'New Public Management' has been some erosion of the public service ethos in local government. The divisions of functions between client and contractor that are engendered by market competition have led to increasingly antagonistic and adversarial relations between different parts of the same organisation, encouraging more reticent and secretive behaviour within local authorities. Employee loyalty is frequently perceived nowadays to be to a specific 'cost centre' rather than to the broader authority.

Intra-departmental divisions

Intra-departmental divisions are a further factor in the policy making equation. Individual departments are frequently no more homogeneous than are party groups. The size and diversity of many departments mean that, in effect, the span of control a chief officer can exercise must be limited, thereby providing junior officers, often with greater technical expertise by virtue of their more recent training, with scope for influence.

Most departments in larger local authorities consist of hundreds, even thousands, of employees in a range of relatively separate hierarchies and organisational divisions. Indeed, given the recent trend of merging departments into a much smaller number of strategic directorates, there is increasing scope for competing priorities and internal friction *within* a single management unit. In 2005, for example, Leicester City Council had a Regeneration and Culture Department, which brought together the former Cultural Services and Neighbourhood Renewal Department and the former Environment Regeneration and Development Department into a unit with more than 3,200 staff and no fewer than six divisions, as follows: community protection and wellbeing; cultural services; environment; highways and transportation; regeneration; resources. As noted in Chapter 6, it is commonplace nowadays to 'streamline' a dozen or more service departments into just four or five multi-functional directorates: Children and Lifelong Learning; Adult Care and Community Services; Leisure, Culture and Property Services, and the like. In such contexts, senior managers play the role of directors of larger groups of more disparate, if related, services than would have been the responsibility of their predecessors.

Divisions within departments can also arise with the spread of decentralised management and service delivery. Area-based housing officers, for example, may develop a dual loyalty: to the local authority but also to their own operational area and its residents. Conflict is by no means uncommon between area offices and central departments, or between a number of decentralised area offices. Nor is it unknown for officers working in decentralised offices to develop close ties with local ward councillors – another source of potential influence for junior officers. Failure to incorporate *junior* officials in any model of decision making inside the town hall is to ignore a group which can, on occasions, be influential.

Hung or balanced councils

The prevalence nowadays of hung or balanced councils – those on which no single party has an overall majority of councillors – raises further questions about the adequacy of the joint élite model, which assumes the existence of a small group of leading majority party councillors. In 1979, 14 per cent of councils were hung; in 2005/06 that figure was more than double – 32 per cent or 139 councils (see Exhibit 14.4). If in future Scotland's introduction of proportional representation for local elections were to spread to the rest of Great Britain, the number of hung councils would be likely to double again, to around two-thirds of the total (Leach and Game, 2000, Ch. 2).

Even in the absence of electoral reform, though, in about a third of councils party groups already *have* to take into account each other's policies and actions; otherwise, any proposal they put forward could in principle be defeated at any time. First, however, they need to determine among themselves how council business is in fact going to be conducted. With a committee system there were several possibilities:

- *Minority administration* – where one party, usually the largest, took all committee chairs and vice-chairs and, in a sense at least, 'governed' as if it had an overall majority;
- *Power-sharing* – where two or more parties agreed to share committee chairs, but without, usually, any more far-reaching agreement on a shared policy programme: a deal or arrangement, therefore, rather than a formal coalition; and
- No *administration/rotating chairs* – where there were no permanently held chairs, the positions being rotated among the parties purely for procedural, rather than policy, purposes.

Executive government changes completely the 'rules of the game', imposing altogether different demands on a hung council and requiring substantially different solutions. Under the committee system there was no easily identifiable 'executive': no functional or constitutional equivalent of a cabinet, with seats and portfolios that could be bargained over in negotiations over the formation of a governmental coalition. With committee chairs having no individual decision making power and relatively little additional remuneration, the arena of coalitional negotiation, in so far as there was one, was the 'legislature' – the council chamber – rather than the executive.

With executive local government – and its generally enhanced remuneration for executive members – the 'no administration' option, for a start, ceases to be either a possibility or, even if it were, an attraction. Councils are required to adopt some form of executive, mayoral or otherwise, and those executive positions offer what coalition theorists would call the twin incentives of *policy influence* and the *benefits of office* (Laver, 1989, p. 19). So, while the negotiations now facing party group leaders on a hung council may appear to resemble those that would have taken place under the committee system, and while even the available options may appear to be similar, what is at stake is very different indeed.

The principal options, as indicated in the notes accompanying Exhibit 14.4, are a one-party cabinet – the equivalent to minority administration – even though that party could be defeated in full council at any time, or some kind of two- or multi-party coalition cabinet. Interestingly, the figures for hung councils in 2005 show a split between these two basic options similar to the one that developed under the committee system as 'power-sharing' became more widespread in the 1990s. In about a third of councils, one party (usually but not invariably the largest) has opted to 'go it alone', and in the other two-thirds some permutation of the parties has negotiated power-sharing arrangements. The second interesting observation, illustrated in Exhibit 15.2, is the apparent disconfirmation of the *a priori* hypothesis that, with the change from committee to executive systems, coalition formation would become more arithmetically rational and therefore predictable.

The UK committee system used to confound any coalition theorists who gave it serious attention. The absence of any executive body or cabinet to act as a significant prize deprived them of their core assumption about politicians being, above all else, office-motivated, and made a nonsense of their typical 'minimal winning coalition' predictions – that parties will form ideologically compact coalitions that win with the fewest members possible. As it was, the forms of administration to emerge on hung councils proved only minimally predictable, and mostly had to be described and explained *post hoc*, usually in terms of local institutional, cultural and, very far from least, personality factors (e.g., Mellors, 1989; Leach and Stewart, 1992). This is not the place for a comprehensive study of coalition formation under executive local government but, to judge from the sample of outcomes in Exhibit 15.2, in this respect not much has changed.

In the case of each major party, it would seem impossible to predict from the arithmetic alone what kind of administration would result from its being the largest single party in a hung authority, or even whether it would itself be part of the administration at all. The notion of the minimal winning coalition would seem, more often than not, to be an irrelevance, and even the idea of maximising the size of the cabinet for party advantage has clearly been resisted regularly.

In Exhibit 15.2, the greatest range of outcomes results from situations in which Labour is the largest party, and there are good cultural and historic reasons for this. Until the early 1980s the Labour Party nationally took an extremely severe view of coalitions and strongly discouraged local party groups from involving themselves in power-sharing arrangements or even

Exhibit 15.2 Hung council administrations, 2005 – how could you guess?

	Cons seats	Lab seats	LD seats	Indep/Other	MWC seats	Actual administration (Cab/Exec. composition)
CONSERVATIVES largest party						
Warwickshire CC	27	23	11	–	32	Cons minority
Bradford MBC	38	29	15	8	46	Cons minority (6-member cabinet)
East Riding of Yorkshire C	29	8	22	8	34	Con/LD/Lab (7/1/1)
Herefordshire (unitary) C	21	4	17	16	30	Con/Ind (5/5)
LABOUR largest party						
Brighton & Hove City C	21	23	3	7	28	Lab minority
Hull City C	2	27	22	8	30	Lab minority
Waltham Forest LBC	18	26	15	1	31	Lab/LD (7/3)
Wirral MBC	21	26	19	–	34	Lab/Con/LD (5/3/2)
Birmingham City C	40	46	30	4	61	Con/LD (6/4)
Leeds City C	24	40	26	9	50	LD/Con/Green/Lab (4/4/1/1)
Lambeth LBC	7	29	27	–	32	LD/Con (6/2)
Redcar & Cleveland BC	13	23	15	8	30	LD/Con/Ind (4/4/2)
Slough BC	8	15	6	12	21	Con/Lib/LD/UKIP/Ind (3/2/1/1/2)
Carlisle City C	20	24	7	1	27	Cons minority
LIB DEMS largest party						
Bristol City C	11	27	32	–	36	LD minority
Bolton MBC	19	20	21	–	31	LD minority
Luton BC	4	21	21	2	25	LD minority
Leicester City C	10	20	24	–	28	LD/Con (6/3)
Bath & NE Somerset C	26	6	29	4	33	LD/Con/Ind (4/4/1)
South Gloucestershire C	21	16	33	–	36	LD/Con/Lab (4/3/2)
Sefton C	19	20	27	–	34	LD/Lab/Con (4/3/3)
Rochdale MBC	9	24	27	–	31	Lab/Con (8/2)

Note: MWC = Minimal winning coalition

Source: Data from Edkins Family Index Page (see Exhibit 14.1 above).

forming minority administrations, and thereby risking dilution of the ideological purity of the party's manifesto. Over the years, that harsh official view has largely disappeared, but the instincts that underpinned it live on, and Labour remains the party most likely to take a stance of: 'If we can't be in control, we'll be in opposition' – which perhaps at least partly explains the several non- or anti-Labour coalitions and the apparently odder position still in Carlisle. To explain, on the other hand, why similar arithmetic in other authorities produces Labour-based coalitions or minority control, one has, as ever, to go back to those 'local factors'.

Any form of hung council administration is likely to involve far more extensive inter-party contact and negotiation than is seen in most majority-controlled councils. Officers too – particularly the chief executive and chief officers – have to assume different roles, working with and briefing spokespersons from possibly several parties rather than from just one. They may, indeed, perform a role of broker, bringing the different parties together in order to negotiate some policy or procedural agreement. And, of course, non-executive members find their position is enhanced, as every council vote becomes precious. Bargaining becomes the order of the day because there is no one-party élite of members who can be sure, unaided, of delivering a policy programme.

Conclusion – constantly shifting alliances

The conceptual models presented in the first part of this chapter – the formal, technocratic, joint élite and dynamic dependence models – provide some useful insights into local policy making, but can appear simplistic. While the arrival of executive government has generally strengthened the positions of leading councillors and senior officers, it is misleading to see the policy process as confined to this élite. While their centrality is not questioned, their exclusive dominance certainly is. Local authorities are political institutions, in both the 'big P' and 'little p' – the partisan and the broader – senses of the word. They incorporate a whole range of additional actors and influences that may impinge on policy making, depending on an authority's traditions, culture, leadership, political balance and so on. The policy process in the real world is a complex and changeable one. It can be regarded as a series of shifting alliances, forming and re-forming over time and from issue to issue. These networks and alliances vary enormously, but they are by no means solely the preserve of the political executive and the officer élite.

Chapter 16

Voluntary and Community Groups – The Exercise of Influence

Bowling in groups

A curiosity of our age of individualised and privatised lifestyles, of PCs, iPods and mobile TV, is not just that organised groups and group activity still exist, but that they have almost certainly increased in recent years. On the face of it, this seems to conflict with the mass of evidence produced by US Professor Robert Putnam in his famous mapping of the alleged breakdown of civic and social community engagement in post-1960s' America, *Bowling Alone* (2000). There is no equivalent body of data for the UK, but what there is would seem to question the direct comparability of the two societies.

The independent Power Inquiry, in common with other recent commentaries, differentiated between *electoral activity* – unambiguously declining – and *pressure activity*, which included a wide array of activities designed to influence decision-making without seeking electoral advantage, and which, if anything, had increased (Power Inquiry, 2004, p. 12). Apparent evidence, directly relevant to our concerns, comes in the form of several detailed studies of group activity in particular regions (e.g., VONNE, 2000; Lewis, 2001; Voice East Midlands, 2003), towns and cities. One such is the Brighton and Hove Community and Voluntary Sector audit (2003), which, for a population of about a quarter of a million, identified 1,524 local organisations. Especially interesting for its comparability across time was the 1998 survey of Birmingham's voluntary sector by Maloney and colleagues. Taking as their baseline Newton's study of Birmingham in the early 1970s, which recorded 4,264 formally organised voluntary associations in the city, Maloney *et al.* (2000) found 5,781 for a population of roughly 1 million, or an increase of more than a third (2000, p. 805). If the largely non-political sports clubs were excluded, the number of groups had more than doubled, from 2,120 to 4,589.

While Putnam might have found such figures surprising, the authors did not, because of the dramatic changes in the local government environment over the intervening thirty years (Maloney *et al.*, 2000, p. 806):

For example, as local government powers and functions have been progressively eroded in traditional service delivery areas such as housing, existing or new voluntary and community organisations have taken over some of these responsibilities and developed new areas of work ... there has been a shift to a more enabling role rather than direct provision of social services. The doubling of the number of groups in the social welfare category [666 to 1,319] reflects the impact of such trends ... Local government has also moved into new policy fields, such as economic development, environmental protection and crime prevention, and has done so in co-operation with a range of 'third force' organisations. (Stoker and Young, 1993)

Here we have, then, our principal interest in this chapter. The actual numbers of what we shall call, following the above authors, Voluntary and Community Groups (VCGs) are secondary, except in so far as they confirm the immense scale of local group activity that is so often overlooked in nationally-focused studies of interest and pressure groups. We shall in fact start with some definitions and categorisations to help make sense of this scale. The greater part of the chapter, though, will be concerned with the differing – and changing – kinds of relationships groups have with their local authorities, and the nature of their influence on policy making and service delivery.

An inclusive definition

For those conducting auditing exercises, and certainly for bodies such as the Charity Commission, precise definitions are obviously important. For us they are less so. As indicated in Exhibit 16.1, we favour the term Voluntary and Community Groups because it is probably the most commonly used nowadays in UK local government, and we define them as *independent, not-for-profit bodies that work in various ways for the benefit of the community*. It is a deliberately simple, inclusive definition, but it serves our purposes, which, we should emphasise, differ somewhat from those of our colleagues who are writing primarily about national government, and who will prefer the terms 'pressure groups' and 'interest groups', and definitions that give greater prominence to political campaigning and policy influence and pay less attention to working *with* government (see, e.g., Coxall *et al.*, 2003, ch. 9; Jones *et al.*, 2004, ch. 11; Budge *et al.*, 2004, ch. 13).

As Exhibit 16.1 makes clear, campaigning counts very definitely as a public-benefiting activity, and the definition thus acknowledges that the many groups who would see themselves as either predominantly service-providing or almost entirely non-political can be drawn into the political process, if only intermittently. Thus a local gardening association resisting

Exhibit 16.1 The Voluntary and Community Sector (VCS) defined

Voluntary and Community Groups – a rough and ready definition:

- not-for-profit organisations,
- independent of government,
- benefiting from some measure of voluntarism,
- adding value to the community through such activities as:
  - providing services,
  - acting as advocates, and
  - campaigning.

Other common labels

- **Voluntary sector** – can seem to emphasise large household-name charities at the expense of the many more small community-based groups.
- **Non-profit sector** – widely used in the USA and internationally; misleading for pedants, suggesting that groups aim only to break even, rather than make a modest surplus: it's the underlying purpose and the non-distribution of profit that are important.
- **Charity sector** – risks getting confused with registration with the Charity Commission. About 170,000 groups are, but more than twice as many are not.
- **Third sector** – sometimes used as catch-all term for everything that isn't done by the market or the state, including the 'informal sector' of personal and family relations. But coming back into favour with the Government (National Audit Office, 2005), so look out for TSOs – not, in this context, trading standards officers, but Third Sector Organisations.
- **Social enterprise sector** – also due to become fashionable, though with different meanings for the different political parties. Suggests a focus more on businesses and income-generation than on service provision.
- **Interest, pressure groups** – little used nowadays in the world of local government itself; much more in political science literature about, predominantly, national and international government. Both terms reflect a concern with groups as policy influencers, rather than potential service providers.

Some figures

- On the narrowest definition – groups registered with the Charity Commission – the VCS contributes around 2.5 per cent of the UK's gross domestic product (GDP); on the broadest definition probably around 9 per cent, making it almost as large as local government.
- Again on the broadest definition, the VCS comprises around 600,000 organisations, employing, on a very rough calculation, around 600,000 paid workers and utilising some 16 million volunteers.
- In recent years the proportion of its income (37 per cent +) that the VCS receives from the Government, in the form of grants and contracts, has overtaken the proportion received from the public in donations and the purchase of goods and services.

a proposal to build a road over its land becomes temporarily a campaigning group. At local level, many groups are precisely such single-purpose groups, which burst into political life only when an issue such as a council planning decision affects them directly.

At the other extreme, our definition can also embrace groups who may become in effect single-issue parties, putting up candidates in local elections against those from larger, nationally-based parties. The argument would be that, while the latter are clearly seeking the responsibility of government, the single-issue groups are using the electoral process primarily as a means of publicising their cause. They may well not field enough candidates to form an administration, even if outstandingly successful, although they can occasionally, like the Independent Kidderminster Hospital (Health Concern) campaigners, find themselves almost inadvertently in government (see Exhibit 11.9).

Insiders and outsiders

There are two main approaches to the categorisation of groups: in terms of who or what they represent, and by the nature of their relationship with government. The first categorisation would differentiate between *sectional/interest* groups, whose principal purpose is to advance the interests of their members – trade unions, business organisations, tenants', residents' and ratepayers' associations, BME (black and minority ethnic) groups, arts and cultural groups, groups for women, gays, lesbians, bisexuals – and *cause/promotional* groups, whose members and supporters are not necessarily the direct beneficiaries of their activities – groups advocating the interests of children, the elderly, the disabled, victims, the homeless and unemployed.

It quickly becomes clear that even this apparently simple distinction is by no means an absolute one, with many groups obviously qualifying for both categories. That, however, goes for almost any attempted categorisation, and certainly, as we shall see, for the one to which we shall give greater attention: the insider/outsider distinction developed and elaborated by Grant (2000). In this case, however, the overlap serves to highlight the very point we are seeking to make.

Insider groups are those with some combination of characteristics that makes them potentially useful to government and therefore worthwhile consulting on a regular basis. *Outsider* groups either do not want to become closely involved with government or do not possess the characteristics to make them useful regular consultees.

There are several characteristics that can make groups attractive to government, or at least make them seem worth cultivating: authority, information, experience, ideological and policy compatibility, and, ultimately, sanctions. The *authority* of a group is its ability to speak on behalf of, and if necessary deliver the support of, a substantial proportion of those it purports to represent. Just how many 'Asian businesses' are members of the Birmingham Asian Business Association, a council's economic development department might reasonably ask, and from which of the city's Asian communities? Is the Midlands Vietnamese Community Association or the Vietnamese Development Centre more representative of both the Buddhist and Catholic sections of that community? Authority is likely to be closely linked with a group's possession of useful *information*, both about its own members and specialist information not necessarily otherwise accessible by policy makers.

Local groups, their managements and leading volunteers can get to know, and be known by, council policy makers far more easily than can their national counterparts operating on the Whitehall and Westminster stage. Reputations – good and bad – can be established and *experience* acquired much more quickly. If council officers are looking for responsive and reliable consultees, or for a group to assist in policy development or service delivery, they are naturally going to turn first to those with whom they have previously worked and who already have, in their eyes, a positive track record.

Being representative, possessing information and having experience are great – for a group that aspires to be an insider. The next test – or perhaps it should really be the first – is whether its ideology, politics and policy interests are at least broadly *compatible* with those of the council, and particularly with the party or parties currently controlling the council. For the political scientists responsible for some of the early group studies in UK local government, this issue of political compatibility tended to be treated as the all-important one.

Newton, in his chapter on 'The Politics of the Four Thousand' groups in Birmingham, described more and less 'respectable' and 'controversial' groups being dealt by the Council in very different ways (p. 67). Those 'so well respected and established within the community that their activity and co-operation with the [Council] is not questioned by any of the party politicians' would have their business handled by officers 'without fear of political repercussions'. By contrast, 'less respectable and more controversial organisations would be handed on to the appropriate council committee', where they would have to take their political chances.

Dearlove (1973), in a contemporaneous study of politics in the London borough of Kensington and Chelsea, found similarly that only a relatively small selection of groups was in fact drawn into the local council's policy deliberations, but used slightly different adjectives to explain their success or otherwise in gaining access. The council's response to groups revolved around councillor assessment of their demands – 'helpful' or 'unhelpful' – and their communication styles – 'acceptable' or 'unacceptable' (ch. 8).

Not surprisingly, groups judged by the ruling Conservative councillors to be the most helpful were those whose demands mirrored most closely the views of the majority group. Thus the Kensington Housing Trust was widely regarded as being 'very helpful', since it contributed towards solving local housing problems, thereby lessening the need for the local authority to build more council houses, and reinforcing the policy priorities and ideological orientations of the ruling group.

By contrast, the 'unhelpful' groups (for example, Kensington and Chelsea Council Tenants' Association, or the Kensington and Chelsea Inter-Racial Council) canvassed demands which only a minority of councillors supported and which ran counter to the policy priorities of the ruling Conservative administration. Such 'unacceptable' demands had necessarily to be channelled through what the ruling group perceived as 'improper' routes – for example, petitions and demonstrations.

There are, of course, plenty of outsider groups today who either choose or are forced to employ 'megaphone methods' to make their voices heard: petitions and placards, letters and lobbies, marches, sit-downs and demonstrations. If you call your group the Animal Rights Militia, Reclaim the Streets, or the Disabled People's Direct Action Network, you will neither expect nor probably want the same reception as, say, the Cats' Protection League, the Bournville Village Trust, or the Birmingham Fellowship of the Handicapped.

Two of the big outsider issues since the 1990s have spawned their own 'umbrella' websites that detail the typical protest methods utilised, with some success, against councils across the country. First, there are the many local anti-incinerator campaigns (www.no-incinerator.org.uk/contacts/html), launched in opposition to councils' plans to reduce their dumping of biodegradable waste by building giant incinerators. The Guildford Anti-Incinerator Network (GAIN) alone logged 84,000 letters of objection, reinforced by a black balloon rally, a community waste workshop, and a parallel campaign in support of increased recycling and composting. Other forms of protest have included demonstrations and marches on Parliament, the dissemination of technical counter-information on the potential danger of incinerator emissions, extensive use of the internet – for both collecting and putting out information, and direct action on construction sites. A second set of campaigns using similar methods have been those to Defend Council Housing (www.defendcouncilhousing.org.uk) against proposals for large-scale stock transfers (see Exhibit 7.8).

Changing relations

It is not, then, that the insider/outsider distinction no longer has any relevance; rather, that, as Stoker (1991, ch. 5) was among the first to note in this context, the world of local government began to change significantly from the 1970s and 1980s onwards and with it the operation of local group politics. The operational relations between groups and their respective councils appear, therefore, very differently to a contemporary observer from how they did to Newton, Dearlove and colleagues. The relatively closed and inward-looking organisations that they encountered have since 'opened out', as Stoker put it, in several distinct ways. There was the growth of a 'community orientation' among both councillors and officers, the greater readiness to look at services from the viewpoint of the users as well as from that of the organisational providers, and the increased commitment to consultation with outside interests (Stoker, 1991, pp. 124–8). Meanwhile, these developments were met by a greater assertiveness and diversity among the local groups themselves, and, in some cases at least, the availability of additional resources. Between them, these trends brought about 'an increased willingness on the part of interest groups and local authorities to share responsibility for the delivery of services' (p. 128).

Interestingly, this greater willingness of the two sectors to operate in concert manifested itself in councils right across the then highly politicised party spectrum, albeit in differing ways. Left-wing Labour authorities, for example, could encourage voluntary sector, cause and community groups that challenged the status quo by providing them with grant funding. Centre-right or Liberal Democrat-influenced authorities were keen to be seen to have good relations with a wide range of groups and to be listening to their concerns. And for Conservatives voluntary groups offered an obvious alternative means of organising the delivery of services and thereby challenging the monopolistic position of the council.

Compacts and contracts

If you wanted a single-item demonstration of the extent to which councils' views of and relations with voluntary and community groups have evolved steadily since the 1970s and rapidly since the mid-1990s, you need look no further than the *Voluntary Sector Compact* that just about every English local authority now has with its own Voluntary and Community Sector. It is easy to be cynical about such documents, especially when they are in the main glossy, saccharinely illustrated, and, initially it seemed, about as toothless as a caterpillar. It is even easier when they derive directly from a New Labour Government initiative aimed unashamedly at persuading the VCS of its role in helping it to deliver the government's own policy agenda. In this instance, though, it is worth also considering the other side of the case.

The 1998 *National Compact on Relations between Government and the Voluntary and Community Sector in England* was produced early in the life of the new Government, and was itself based heavily on the thinking and recommendations of the highly regarded Deakin Commission Report on the Future of the Voluntary Sector (1996). Together with its series of Codes of Good Practice – on BME groups, community groups, consultation, funding and volunteering – the Compact's aim was to change the position of the VCS from one of being variously marginalised and/or patronised by government – not least by local government – to one of working in partnership with it. It thus set down, as have the ensuing local compacts, a list of rights and responsibilities or undertakings to which both sectors should adhere in order to make their relationship constructive and reciprocally beneficial. An inevitably much abbreviated illustration of the nature of those undertakings, and of the overall tone of the compacts is provided in Exhibit 16.2.

As the compacts themselves emphasise, even though any breaches are now referable to the local ombudsman and potentially subject to judicial review, they should not be seen primarily as statutorily binding documents. Rather, they are 'memoranda' or 'frameworks' that represent the product of discussions and negotiations between the respective parties and that are subject to regular review and amendment. Their unenforceability, though, should not detract from the significance of, in particular, some of the governmental undertakings: the explicit acknowledgement, for example, of groups' rights to receive the full cost of their service delivery, relevant information and consultation, and to criticise publicly and campaign against government policy without jeopardising any public funding. As was pointed out, this latter commitment represents a rare example of an invitation to an organisation to bite the hand that feeds it.

The force of such undertakings lies more in the extent to which their breach can cause political embarrassment: to a local authority perhaps a loss of reputation with partner organisations, an adverse impact at a CPA inspection. Certainly, in the early years of the compacts there were relatively few apparently substantiated complaints of groups being threatened or penalised following public criticism of government funders' policies (see Blackmore, 2004, p. 27). It is likely, however, that small local groups will be more nervous of the possible response of their councils than larger groups might be of central government departments, and at both levels it is probable that some funded groups will feel it advisable to operate with a degree of self-restraint. Groups have other reservations too, as we shall see, about both the philosophy and the content of compacts, but Professor Deakin himself, asked to comment particularly on the local impact of one of the principal products of his report, was generally upbeat.

Exhibit 16.2 Outline of a Local VCS Compact

What? Why?

In 1998 the Labour Government formed a *National Compact* with the VCS – to improve their relationship to mutual advantage, and in recognition that voluntary and community groups (VCGs) were increasingly delivering services previously provided by the public sector. All 388 English local authorities agreed to publish *Local Compacts* by 2004/05.

A typical Local Compact between Happitown BC and its VCS

Introduction – emphasising that the Compact is a negotiated, 'living' agreement, setting down shared principles, values and commitments to improve working relations between the Council and VCGs for the overall benefit of Happitowners; *not* anything threatening or legally binding.

Shared principles for joint working – for example:

- An independent, diverse VCS is vital to a democratic and inclusive society.
- In developing public policy and delivering services, the Council and VCGs have distinctive but complementary roles and accountabilities – the Council being driven by statutory duties and government policy; and VCGs by their charitable aims.
- Partnership working between the Council and VCGs will build relationships, improving policy development and service delivery.

Undertakings by Happitown Council – for example:

- To contribute two principal categories of voluntary sector funding:
  o **Voluntary sector grant aid**:
    On a one-off or annual basis, usually less than £10,000; Council to publicise a clear process and framework for awarding grant funding.
  o **Service-level agreements**:
    For the delivery of services by VCGs for and on behalf of the Council; Agreements up to 3 years, subject to annual review of performance, containing clear and agreed specifications of the work involved and of monitoring and evaluation systems.
- To accept the legitimacy of VCGs including the relevant element of overhead costs in their estimates for providing a particular service.
- To recognise and support the rights of VCGs to campaign within the law, and to challenge and criticise central and local government policy, without jeopardising any public funding.
- To consult with the VCS on major issues, wherever possible allowing affected organisations time to consult their members and beneficiaries.

Undertakings by VCGs – for example:

- To have a written constitution, and keep accurate records and financial accounts.
- To demonstrate impacts of funding: clear community benefits in terms of activities undertaken (outputs) and the results of these activities (outcomes).
- To ensure members and supporters are consulted about the group's policy positions, particularly in relation to the Council.

Resolving disagreements – for example:

- Both sides should first seek resolution through informal discussions.
- If necessary, an independent investigator/mediator should be used.
- If the VCS remains dissatisfied, the matter may be taken to the Local Government Ombudsman or the Compact Mediation Scheme run by the Government's Active Communities Unit.

There was today, he felt, a far better two-way relationship between the VCS and councils of all political complexions than had existed at the time of his report, when the Conservative Government saw voluntary groups chiefly as vehicles for delivering policy programmes that Labour councils were attempting to boycott (Brindle, 2004, p. 10):

> Labour councils would have nothing to do with voluntary sector bodies, which they associated with Tory ladies in flowery hats and that sort of stuff. The Tories were almost equally patronising – you know, 'our little helpers'. 'We can entrust you with various things; we'll contract with you to make sure you deliver [public services], but come near us to talk about policy – not a chance'.

Today, with the Government's insistence on councils working in partnership with all other sectors, and VCGs being seen as essential to its mission to improve public service delivery, the *behaviour* of councils towards their VCSs would have been bound to change. But, while as ever with local government there are exceptions, the signs are that underlying *attitudes* have also changed. Groups and their representatives are consulted more regularly and more genuinely on policy issues that have an impact upon them; they are invited to serve on advisory groups and partnership boards; and they generally have a more direct role in helping to develop as well as to deliver local government programmes.

The Leicester-based environmental charity, ENVIRON (see Exhibit 16.3), is one example of the kind of group that could be seen as having a genuinely mutually beneficial relationship with a range of local government agencies. Much of its work is funded by or through local authorities, but many of its projects involve working directly and jointly with council officers. It employs a skilled staff of specialists, part of whose professional function is to provide expert advice, but whose expertise is also contributed through the increasing amount of partnership working in which the group is involved. Environmentally progressive as Leicester City Council is, there must be occasions when ENVIRON finds itself disagreeing over aspects of its chief funder's policy, and certainly over the national Government's lacklustre record on matters of sustainability and climate change, but it would be quite surprising if it felt seriously constrained by the possibility of losing future funding from voicing such criticisms in public.

ENVIRON, however, is these days a large organisation, with an established reputation and a history of successfully managed projects behind it. It is able to seek funding from a wide variety of public, voluntary, private and even overseas sources, and so reduce its dependence

Exhibit 16.3 ENVIRON

What?

An independent charity, founded (from former Leicester Ecology Trust) in 1993, to provide advice on environmental management and sustainability to businesses and local authorities in Leicester, Leicestershire and the East Midlands.

How?

Much of ENVIRON's work is based on partnerships with:

- **Leicester City Council** – involvement from the outset in Leicester becoming, in 1990, Britain's first Environmental City; now a key member of Leicester Environment Partnership, and contributor to the city's Environment and Climate Change Strategies. Many other projects, including Allotments for All, Bikes 4 All, a city-centre bike park, recycling schemes for computers, mobile phones, tyres, etc.
- **Leicestershire County Council** – the Eco-schools Green Flag project – a pupil-led, whole-school environmental management project; provision of environmental education in every school; the Business Resource Efficiency Club; work with the community on numerous nature conservation and recycling projects.
- **East Midlands Development Agency** and **Leicestershire Economic Partnership (LEP)**: ENVIRON drafted the Leicester Environment Strategy on behalf of the LEP and, with the support of the City Council, Leicestershire TEC and Business Link, launched advisory Business Line.

Management

Board of Directors (unpaid) from local government, local businesses, universities.

Staff

40-strong multi-disciplinary team of landscape architects, teachers, ecologists and business managers, supplemented by volunteers, trainees and work placements.

Funding

ENVIRON's 2004 turnover of £1.25 million – 12% up on the previous year – includes an increasing proportion of income deriving from contracts, sales and consultancy. Major funders include: Leicester City Council, Leicestershire County Council, Hinckley & Bosworth and Harborough District Councils; Department of Trade & Industry; Neighbourhood Renewal Fund; New Opportunities Fund; the Big Lottery Fund; SITA Environmental Trust; English Nature.

Other projects

The EcoHouse – an environmental showhome; Braunstone Solar Streets – a project to install photovoltaic panels on houses renovated by Leicester Housing Association; a composting club (The Leicestershire Rotters – naturally) and Rotten Resource Centre; the Green Doctor – providing instant cold cures with practical advice on energy efficiency; and Eco-coffins – use your imagination, or try their website: http://www.environ.org.uk.

on any single source. Smaller and newer groups with neither the established records to impress external funders nor, quite possibly, the administrative skills required to negotiate their bureaucratic systems, are likely to turn initially to their own councils and be proportionately more financially dependent on them.

Our illustrative local compact in Exhibit 16.2 outlines the two principal types of council funding available to VCGs: relatively modest one-off grants to cover operating costs and perhaps some individual projects, and funding through a much more detailed service-level agreement to undertake contractually specified work. Most council websites will give some indication of the approximate numbers of groups that it funds and perhaps its total grant funding in the previous year. Southend-on-Sea BC is one of the commendable few to provide fuller details, and Exhibit 16.4 therefore shows how one body of predominantly Conservative unitary councillors chose in 2005/06 to disburse over £550,000 of what they would call their local taxpayers' money. The list embraces, we venture to suggest, at least some interests that a few decades previously, when one of us happened to be growing up in the borough, would probably not have received such consideration.

VCS dilemmas

When phrases like 'a Compact way of working' start entering the vocabulary of civil servants and local government officers, when there is talk of a strengthened and upgraded 'Compact Plus' and of a Compact Commissioner to oversee relations between public bodies and the VCS, there can be little doubt of the scale of the change that has overtaken the world of local group politics in recent years. Greater recognition, however, has its potential costs for all those involved, and for VCGs it can seem as if they are losing at least as much as they are gaining through closer involvement with their local councils.

There is widespread concern, for example, over the Government's openly *instrumentalist* approach to the VCS: ministers' apparent belief that the sector's prime function is to contribute to the delivery of the Government's agenda and to the meeting of Government targets. In practice, the accusation goes, the Compact rhetoric about valuing a forthright and assertive VCS is just that: rhetoric. Governments – local as well as national – have little genuine interest in the sector's wider contribution to society. Groups that campaign as well as deliver services are still viewed with suspicion, as they were in the past. Government is at best co-opting the sector; at worst, neutering it (Whelan, 1999).

Exhibit 16.4 One council's grant funding of voluntary groups

A selection of the 47 groups, selected from 78 applicants, that received £556,000 in grant funding – usually including a contribution towards operating costs – from Southend-on-Sea (SoS) Borough Council, 2005/06

	£	Purpose of group/grant
SoS Guild of Help/Citizens Advice Bureau	149,000	Free, confidential, independent legal advice
HARP (Homeless Action Resource Project)	112,000	Emergency accommodation etc. for the homeless
Southend Association of Voluntary Services	26,600	Training, support for voluntary/community organisations
Age Concern	25,200	Information, advice to the elderly
Relate South East Essex	22,300	Development of self-help skills within families
Southend Women's Aid	20,600	Victims of domestic violence
DIAL Southend	19,900	Information, advice to people with disabilities
Southend Community Furniture Recycling Project	19,200	Providing affordable furniture
Royal Association for Deaf People	14,700	Counselling sessions, drop-in sessions
South East Advocacy for Older People	12,600	Advocacy service for the elderly
Southend Play Council	11,300	Promoting good quality play provision
St. George's United Reform Church	10,250	Activities for the local community
Southend Vineyard	10,250	Food storehouse for the homeless
Shoebury Information Shop	10,000	Assistance, advice to residents
Parentline plus	9,800	Parenting courses, workshop
Southend Mencap	8,800	Sports club for adults and children with disabilities
Southend Pier Museum Trust Ltd	8,700	Operating costs

Exhibit 16.4 continued

	£	Purpose of group/grant
Business Enterprise Agency of SE Essex	8,200	Business support services
Salvation Army, Leigh-on-Sea Corps	6,500	Meals and activities for the elderly
SoS Sports Council	6,000	Provision of sporting facilities
Southend Carnival Association	5,700	Staging annual carnival
Thursday Club	4,500	Activities for children with learning disabilities
Essex Racial Equality Council	4,100	Promoting good racial and ethnic relations
South Essex Switchboard	3,400	Information, support for lesbians, gay men, bisexuals
Share-IT Community Centre	3,000	Facilities, activities for ethnic minorities
SoS Arts Council	3,000	Developing artistic understanding and appreciation
SoS Disability and Sensory Forum	2,700	Office equipment for groups working with disabled
Volunteer Reading Help	2,700	Volunteers working with disabled, vulnerable children
Hindu Elderly People's Day Centre	2,500	Hall hire charges, administrative support

10 grants of £1,000, including:

	£	Purpose of group/grant
Churches and Refugees Together	1,000	Hall hire, assistance to asylum seekers
National Federation of the Blind of the UK	1,000	Audio description at local theatres

8 grants of £100–£500, including:

	£	Purpose of group/grant
Cruse Bereavement Care	500	Training facilities for volunteer bereavement counsellors
Southend Crime Prevention Panel	500	Neighbourhood Watch Co-ordinators meetings, newsletter

In exchange for this qualification, if not sacrifice, of their independence, VCGs are expected increasingly, by government and consumers alike, to act *as if* they were in fact part of the state sector. Driven by the Labour Government's audit and performance culture, local authorities devise constricting straitjackets of regulation and accountability to safeguard grants and contracts that, groups will allege, often pay less than the full cost of service delivery in the first place. Meanwhile, politicians promise consumers quality public services and a full range of consumer choice – but from VCG staff whom they still expect to be committed volunteers, rather than properly paid professionals.

And when it comes to consultation, the very knowledge and experience that give groups their value as service deliverers may be regarded as a threat by councillors, who, as elected representatives, are inclined to see themselves as the best judges of the needs of 'their' communities. There is in addition the inherent problem for almost any interest group when dealing with governments: that its views can be treated in much the same way as Mandy Rice-Davies, in the 1960s 'Profumo Trial', dismissed the denials of men whom she claimed to have slept with for money: 'Well, they would say that, wouldn't they?' Groups' views are presumed simply from their names.

The Labour Government, in particular, sees its challenge as being in some way to get beyond these groups in order to reach 'ordinary people'. Which creates the paradox that these groups, one of whose key functions is to provide channels of communication between citizens and their governments, are finding themselves circumvented by more innovative and Government-favoured forms of consultation such as focus groups, citizens' juries, citizens' panels, deliberative opinion polls and local referendums (see Lowndes *et al.*, 2001) – devices that prioritise the involvement of individual citizens rather than organised groups (Pratchett, 2004, pp. 227–8).

Conclusion – a more complex world

The pattern of relations between local groups, their councils and other local agencies was probably always more varied and complex than apparently simple classification schemes implied. Certainly, that is the case in today's world of local governance, as voluntary sector groups are funded to deliver services once provided by the council itself, and both sectors find themselves working alongside each other in all-embracing partnerships. These are themes that, prominent though they have already been throughout the book, will be returned to in its final section.

Part 3

From Change to Postmodernisation

Chapter 17

Two Decades of Management Change

Introduction – providing and deciding

We began this book by suggesting that readers' previous experience of local government would probably have been as customers, consumers, clients and citizens. Our ordering of this short, alliterative list was not accidental. The terms cover the two fundamental functions that local government – indeed, any government – performs: the *service* function and the *political* function (Boyle, 1986), or providing and deciding. It *provides* certain goods and services, and it is the setting in which the citizenry collectively debates and *decides* the key issues concerning the public provision of those goods and services – their scale and distribution, their quality, cost and mode of financing. Fundamental as both are, we have already suggested in Chapter 12 that it is the political function that is utterly indispensable. The service function can be – and has been – contracted out, wholly or partly privatised. Remove the political function, though, and what is left is not local government, but, at most, local administration.

Yet the focus of recent national governments, of both major parties, has been disproportionately on the service function – how to provide services more efficiently, more cheaply, more homogeneously, more competitively and more privately. By comparison, the political function – how, collectively, it is decided what services should be provided and how they should be paid for – has been relatively neglected. Put another way, the public, already inclined to think of councils more as service providers than as *their* local government, have been seen first as customers, consumers and clients for those services, and only secondarily as citizens.

The customer/citizen distinction has tended to shape this final part of the book in its previous editions and, indirectly, it will do so again. In the third edition, there were two unevenly balanced chapters: the first on the numerous and radical managerial changes during the Thatcher/Major and early Blair years, and a second, much shorter, chapter about the political changes that comprised New Labour's 'democratic renewal' agenda and that were then just getting under way. In the ensuing four years, two things have happened. Managerial change continued apace, but on the political front, as during the Conservative Governments, not a great deal *new* has occurred. The heralded changes have been implemented, and we have discussed them in the main body of the book: the new council constitutions and hugely important political management reforms – notwithstanding the dearth of elected mayors – in particularly Chapters 5 and 12; the electoral process changes in Chapter 11; and the power of well-being in Chapter 9.

There are likely to be further political changes, or changes with major political implications, in the future – signposted probably in the pronouncements on 'function, form and finance' anticipated variously in a 2006 White Paper and the final report of the Lyons Inquiry. The first Minister of Communities and Local Government, David Miliband, talked, during his brief 2005–06 term of office, of 'the politics of empowerment' and, sounding a bit like a localist Trekkie, a 'double devolution ... to the Town Hall and beyond' (Miliband, 2006) – to which we shall return in Chapter 18. But it seemed unclear – and maybe now, following his removal to another department, we shall never know – precisely what in practice he had in mind. We are left, therefore, with a major chapter – this one – bringing as up-to-date as possible the account of managerial change since the 1980s, followed by an inevitably speculative final chapter about the future of and for our local government – without necessarily taking for granted that it has one.

The Conservatives – CCT and the contract culture

Of the funnel-load of local government changes and reforms introduced by the 1979–97 Conservative Administrations (see Figure 2.1), the most constitutionally significant were arguably those enabling ministers to intervene in the budget-making and tax-setting processes of individual councils. The most far-reaching in practice, however, were probably those associated with Compulsory Competitive Tendering (CCT) – particularly if it is seen, properly, as one strand of the 'New Right' privatisation or contracting-out strategy of those governments. Essentially, the CCT process required a comparison of the costs of continuing in-house provision of specified services with those of any interested private contractors, and the award of the contract to the most competitive bidder. That meant the *lowest* bidder, and councils were prohibited from imposing conditions on such issues as trade union rights, employment protection, sickness benefit, pensions, training and equal opportunities that might have had the effect of restricting or distorting competition. Cost was always the ultimate criterion, rather than quality.

It must be emphasised that it was the *competitive tendering* - the cost comparison – that was made compulsory, *not* the contracting-out of the service, which might or might not eventuate, depending on the competing bids. If, after competition, no alternative bid was received or the in-house bid proved to be the lowest, the local authority continued to provide the service, but in an organisationally different way. The part of the authority carrying out the service became known as a Direct Service Organisation (DSO), and these DSOs were obliged to maintain separate trading accounts, which had to make a specified percentage surplus.

Three Local Government Acts drove the CCT process, steadily extending the services affected from the 'blue-collar' technical to the 'white-collar' managerial: 1980 – the construction and maintenance of housing and highways; 1988 – refuse collection, grounds and vehicle maintenance, building and street cleaning, school meals, sports and leisure management; 1992 – housing management, legal, personnel, financial and IT services. It sounds like an ideological policy and it was, owing much to the New Right 'think tanks' – the Adam Smith Institute, the Institute of Economic Affairs (IEA), and the Centre for Policy Studies (CPS). Their argument, and that of likeminded Conservative politicians, was that the contracting-out of services formerly provided monopolistically by central and local government or by agencies such as the NHS would lead to both improved service quality and reduced costs. It would challenge the 'dependency culture' imbued by the Welfare State and would lead to less, and smaller, government. For local authorities, it would mean their entering a brave new world of *sharing* the provision of services with a range of other bodies – private industrial and commercial concerns, and voluntary organisations. This is how far-reaching it was: the progenitor of local governance and partnership working.

Opponents of CCT, on the other hand, noted its potential to reduce the role not only of elected local authorities but also of trade unions. It was part of the Government's comprehensive attack on trade union power and public sector pay bargaining, and on the strong financial and institutional links between the public sector unions and the Labour Party. More tellingly, it was argued that claimed cost savings from CCT came largely not from increased efficiency, but rather from cuts in employees' pay and conditions, and from safety-challenging changes in working practices.

The impact of CCT – managerial and financial

As with many innovations, the immediate impact of CCT was less dramatic than the more strident claims of either its proponents or opponents had predicted. No near-universal 'takeover' by the private sector materialised, and the overall picture was what you will by now have come to expect – extremely varied from service to service, and from one council to another. Some services were far more amenable to private sector bids than others, but only in building cleaning and construction were more than half of all contracts won by outside bidders. In all services DSOs tended to win a disproportionate share of the larger contracts, so that, while around 40 per cent of the total number went to private bidders, they amounted to only around 25 per cent of the overall contract *value*. In Scotland, both figures were significantly lower, but even in England and Wales more than one in every six authorities had no outside contracts at all. What the Labour Government inherited in 1997, therefore, was, in most authorities, a mixed economy of in-house and external provision.

The financial savings or otherwise achieved by CCT were notoriously difficult to evaluate accurately. Annual cost savings were undoubtedly achieved – perhaps of around 8 per cent overall – but neutral studies suggested that these owed more to the introduction of competition than to the awarding of contracts to private firms. The major savings came from staffing reductions, often by 20–30 per cent, which happened even under DSO contracts; also from the worsened pay and conditions – temporary contracts, cuts in sick pay, holidays and pensions – of those people, disproportionately women, who hung on to their jobs. Then there were cases of service failure – some comic, others tragic (Wilson and Game, 1998, p. 349) – and councils' termination of contracts not being fulfilled satisfactorily.

It might be imagined that, with most larger contracts staying in-house, CCT left much of local government relatively unchanged. By no means. Whether retaining or 'losing' contracts, all authorities had to adapt their patterns of management and organisation in response to CCT quite fundamentally. The major change was the need to separate the roles of client and contractor within the authority. *Clients* are those responsible for the specification and monitoring of services; *contractors* are those responsible for the direct production and delivery of the service. The separation of these roles would be made within a single department or by creating separate contractor departments.

Other managerial trends

The CCT story contains within it a certain irony. It did not spell even the beginning of the end of local authorities as direct providers of services, and in one way it had almost the reverse effect because, in presenting authorities with the challenge of winning contracts in-house, it encouraged them to streamline and strengthen their management systems so that they were better able to do precisely that. The client/contractor split and creation of internal markets were an important part of this managerial reform programme, but there were also several other noteworthy strands.

Customers and charters

Without doubt, one of the most important developments in the public service since the 1980s has been what Skelcher termed 'the service revolution' (1992): the proclaimed commitment to put customers first, or, at least, to label them 'customers' and tell them they are being put first. Traditionally, local authorities have had residents, tenants, clients and claimants *to* whom, rather than *for* whom, they provided services in the way, and to the standards, that they felt most appropriate. Then, prompted to an extent by the private sector, came what was variously labelled the *public service orientation* (PSO) or *customer care*. Councils gradually came to realise that these previously passive recipients of their services should be treated more as customers, with at least a voice, if not totally free choice, and an entitlement to be consulted and even involved actively in decision making.

The practical manifestations of a council's customer focus can be seen today in a host of ways: customer service centres, employing multi-skilled staff; one-stop telephone systems; personal identification of 'front-line' staff; downloadable forms and leaflets; user surveys and residents' questionnaires; advertised complaints procedures; customer care training, neighbourhood forums; public question times at council meetings; even (though this still exceptionally) arrangements for responding to residents' problems outside conventional office hours. And then there are *customer charters* and *service guarantees*.

Charterism has come to be associated with John Major, whose July 1991 White Paper, *The Citizen's Charter*, sought to empower the citizen as an individual service consumer – note the singularising apostrophe – if not more ambitiously as a participant in the collective process of government. In fact, Major's initiative was pre-dated by several mainly Labour councils developing their own charters, customer contracts and redress mechanisms. York City Council's was among the most interesting:

> not merely as an example of local government innovation anticipating a major central government initiative, but because of the way it attempts to weave together the concerns of citizens, customers and community. The commitment to citizenship – to people's *civic rights* as citizens of York – is explicitly stated in terms of rights to know; rights to be heard and to influence; rights to be treated honestly, fairly and courteously; rights to participate and be represented. These general civic rights are subsequently translated into practical entitlements, through, for example, the establishment of:

- area committees where you can have your say about decisions affecting your neighbourhood;
- special arrangements to involve some of the people who are not often listened to: people with disabilities and other special needs.

(Prior, 1995, pp. 91–2, emphasis ours)

The Citizen's Charter movement, with its subsidiary charters for council tenants, parents and other groups, was part of local authorities' recognition that they should try to get 'closer' to those they served. At the very least, local charters clarify the nature of the relationship between an authority and its citizens by using the language of rights, entitlements and responsibilities which can be checked and monitored (Prior, 1995, p. 100). For examples of councils that have remained committed to the idea, search the websites of Broxtowe BC for 'service charters', or Gateshead MBC, and – for just the 240 or so examples – the remarkable Pembrokeshire CC for 'customer charters' (see conference paper by Game and Vuong, 2003, on linked website).

Essentially, though, these documents – like Labour's 1998 *Service First* relaunch of the Citizen's Charter - are about a rather narrow, consumerist concept of citizenship, in which consumerist values are substituted for democratic ones. At their first airing, Miliband's Neighbourhood Charters – setting out 'the responsibilities of service providers and residents for keeping the neighbourhood safe and clean' (Miliband, 2006) – sounded like a recycling of the same formula. Should they materialise, the proof of the pudding, as the original translation of Cervantes' *Don Quixote* supposedly phrased it, will be in the tasting.

Quality systems and quality assurance

If 'customer first' initiatives are to be more than pious rhetoric, there needs to be a genuine institutional commitment and capacity to translate them into service quality. This recognition prompted many authorities to develop quality control (QC), quality assurance (QA), and total quality management (TQM) systems, as means of improving their service quality. The three processes are clearly differentiated and discussed by Skelcher (1992, ch. 8).

Quality control   Is an inspection and checking process which occurs *after* the service has been or is ready to be provided. Its purpose is to measure performance against pre-set standards and thereby identify any failure rate in the service provision. An example would be a post-repair tenant satisfaction survey. Knowledge of tenants' dissatisfaction will, it is hoped, help to improve the service next time.

Quality assurance   Is the attempt to stop sub-standard service being provided in the first place. It involves designing delivery systems and procedures so that a certain standard of service can be guaranteed every time. Originally developed in the manufacturing sector, where product standards can be measured and specified precisely, QA does not translate easily into the local government world of personal service delivery. Nevertheless, the British Standards Institute (BSI) developed a recognised benchmark (BS 5750), against which local and NHS authorities could assess their QA systems, and a number received accreditation. Developing an accreditable QA system can be a protracted and resource-intensive exercise, necessitating as it does the detailed codification of policies, procedures, performance standards and monitoring systems. On the other hand, confronted by, say, a case of alleged child abuse in a council residential home, it is not hard to see it as a worthwhile investment.

Total quality management   Can be seen as making service quality the driving force of the whole organisational culture of the authority – 'a way of involving the whole organisation; every department, every activity, every single person at every level' in the commitment to quality (Oakland, 1989, p. 14). Its demands are obviously immense, which is one reason why Stewart suggests that it 'is often an aspiration imperfectly realised or perhaps understood' (1996, p. 19).

Strategic management

Self-evidently, any authority aspiring to quality management requires a *strategic approach,* ensuring that its multiplicity of activities and policies are consistent, and are all contributing to corporate objectives and values. Nowadays, though, all authorities will seek to take stock of their activities systematically in what is a constantly changing environment, and either set new directions or at least state some vision of where the authority will be in so many years' time, and what it will be doing.

That, in essence, is what strategic management and planning are about: providing information and developing decision making processes that enable elected members and officers alike to set priorities, direct their energies to key issues, and thereby develop a means of coping assertively with change. It can be contrasted with, and is a means of getting away from, the limitations of operational or reactive management (see Wilson and Game, 2002, p. 334). It involves standing back from the everyday pressures of operational management and taking a broader, corporate, longer-term view of the authority and its functions.

As an additional way of fostering strategic thinking and breaking down traditional departmental and professional boundaries, most leading authorities now structure themselves around a small number of *directorates*. These are headed, as noted in Chapter 6, by *Executive/Strategic/Corporate Directors*, who may oversee several combined departments, but are freed from the day-to-day responsibility of departmental management. The intended outcome is a streamlined strategic management team, comprising the chief executive and strategic directors, who are better able to focus on major policy issues and secure co-ordination between services.

Devolved, cost centre management

An almost necessary concomitant of strategic management is a devolution of actual management responsibility. If an authority's overall objectives and policies are to be achieved, they need to be translated into clearly defined targets or key tasks for individual managers. Somebody, in short, has to be accountable. But, to make their accountability meaningful, that person has to have the necessary discretion to deploy financial and other resources in such a way as to attain the specified targets. The principle behind such devolved management is that it releases initiative among middle and junior managers, who would previously have been constrained within a steep management hierarchy, and thereby leads to greater efficiency and, in the case of a local authority, a better quality service to the public.

The managerial logic is the same as that behind the 1980s' Next Steps Initiative within the civil service, which set up separate units or executive agencies to perform the executive functions of government that were previously the responsibility of Whitehall departments. Executive Agencies – ranging from the massive Jobcentre Plus and the Prison Service Agency to the Royal Mint and Public Record Office – remain part of the civil service, but have responsibility for their own financial, pay and personnel decisions. Similarly, cost centre managers, whether within a university or local authority, remain part of the corporate body, but have the authority to use the resources they have been allocated to achieve the key tasks and standards of performance with which they have been entrusted.

Performance management

The establishment of cost centres is likely to lead in turn to performance management (PM): the specification, measurement and evaluation of the performance both of individuals and of organisations. Tasks are devolved to cost centres and expressed in measurable terms, enabling the performance of the cost centre and the cost centre manager to be reviewed regularly, appraised, and then rewarded or penalised accordingly. Generally, when it is the organisation that is being evaluated, the term used is performance review (PR); and when an individual, performance appraisal (PA).

But what, for a service-providing local authority, is 'performance'? For the Audit Commission, the body chiefly responsible for auditing and inspecting, monitoring and measuring the performance of public bodies, it means the '3Es': Economy, Efficiency and Effectiveness, as set out in Exhibit 17.1. Proper measurement of these '3Es', however, is a much more difficult proposition for a political, sometimes monopolistic, multi-service-delivering local authority than for a single-product, profit-maximising manufacturing company. At the very least, the council's political values and objectives have to be taken into account, and these are likely to be considerably more complex than merely the maximisation of profit. There are obvious problems too in even defining, let alone measuring, outcomes of, say, the educational experience, or some of the social services.

Controversial and provocative though they can prove, a wide selection of measures has been used over the years to assess aspects of council performance. As described in Chapter 9, all councils are now required to produce for the Audit Commission and to publish themselves dozens of these mainly Government-defined Performance Indicators (PIs). Initially, in 2000/01, there were for a unitary authority over 200 of these indicators, although gradually and in consultation with local authorities they have been pruned back and focused increasingly on outcomes and effectiveness, rather than on inputs. The lower section of Exhibit 17.1 exemplifies a few of the different *types* of PIs – cost (BVs 33, 86), productivity (76a), time targets (78a), demand for service (170a), quality of service (79a) and policy outcome (38, 197, 82b).

New Labour – Best Value and performance plans

CCT was opposed from the outset by Labour – in Parliament and even more vehemently by the steadily growing numbers of Labour councils. Customer care, quality service, strategic and performance management, however financially and commercially driven they might be considered, are more difficult to argue against, and the New Labour Party being primed for government by Tony Blair had no inclination to try. The Party's 1997 manifesto made clear how, having transferred the first capital 'C' from competitive tendering to something called Best Value service provision, it would work with and build on some of the other parts of the New Public Management edifice (p. 34):

> Councils should not be forced to put their services out to tender, but will be required to obtain best value. We reject the dogmatic view that services must be privatised to be of high quality, but equally we see no reason why a service should be delivered directly if other more efficient means are available. Cost counts but so does quality.

Exhibit 17.1 Performance measurement

Dimensions of performance – the Audit Commission's 3½ Es

- Economy – concerned with *costs* and *inputs*, and with minimising the cost of resources involved in producing any given standard of service.
- Efficiency – *not* about cost *per se*, but the *relationship between inputs and outputs*: producing the maximum output for any given resource input.
- Effectiveness – about the *relationship between intended and actual outputs*, or, put another way, between *outputs and outcomes*.

These are the conventional '3Es' that are at the heart of the Government's whole performance management programme. The sometimes added 4th E is:

- Equity – a measure of how fairly resources are distributed through a population, according to the needs of that population, not of the individual.

Best Value Performance Indicators (BVPIs) and Birmingham City Council's performance, 2003/04

Performance Indicators – examples drawn from the 'suite' of 141 (www.bvpi.gov.uk)	Relevant Es	Birmingham	Average for met. districts
Corporate health (23 PIs)			
BV 9 Percentage of council tax collected in financial year	Effectiveness	94.7%	95.7%
BV 11b Percentage of top-paid 5% of Council staff from black and minority ethnic communities	Equity	13.8%	3.4%
Education (27)			
BV 33 Youth service expenditure per head of population in youth service target age group	Economy	£57	£87
BV 38 Percentage of 15-year-olds in LEA schools achieving 5 or more GCSE grades at A* to C or equivalent	Effectiveness	49.4%	46.2%

Social services (13)				
BV 197	Percentage change from 1998 in pregnancies of 15 to 17 year olds, per 1,000 15 to 17 year old female residents	Effectiveness	−15%	+ 1%
Housing and housing benefit (19)				
BV 76a	Number of effective visits to claimants for fraud detection purposes, per 1,000 caseload	Efficiency	366	210
BV 78a	Average number of days to process new housing benefit claims	Efficiency, Effectiveness	32.0	48.4
BV 79a	Percentage of randomly sampled cases in which calculation of housing benefit is found to be correct	Efficiency, Effectiveness	96.4%	96.1%
Environment (9)				
BV 82b	Percentage of household waste sent by Council for composting or treatment by anaerobic digestion	Effectiveness	2.6%	3.0%
BV 84a	Kilograms of household waste collected per head of population	Effectiveness	453	467
BV 86	Cost of household waste collection per household	Economy, Efficiency	£37.7	£32.5
Transport (22)				
BV 99a	Number of pedestrians seriously injured per 100,000 population	Effectiveness	87.8	64.0
BV 165	Percentage of pedestrian crossings with facilities for disabled persons	Equity	87.6%	76.5%
Cultural and related services (5)				
BV 170a	Number of visits to Council-funded museums per 1,000 population	Effectiveness	944	749

Every council will be required to publish a local performance plan with targets for service improvement, and be expected to achieve them. The Audit Commission will be given additional powers to monitor performance and promote efficiency. On its advice, government will where necessary send in a management team with full powers to remedy failure.

As with most of its manifesto commitments, the Government duly delivered – more completely than many of its supporters might have liked. In early 1998, one of the six 'modernisation' consultation papers outlined what would be a new duty for local authorities – to deliver services to clear nationally and locally set standards by the most economic, efficient and effective means available (DETR, 1998c, para. 7.2). The signal was unmistakable: the Government would rid local authorities of the deeply unpopular and wholly cost-focused CCT regime, but Best Value would prove every bit as centrally prescriptive and potentially even more interventionist. It applied, moreover, to every single service and function.

A lukewarm evaluation

CCT was repealed and Best Value statutorily introduced in the Local Government Act 1999, coming into operation in England and Wales in 2000. Reversing the poll tax story, legislation in Scotland on this occasion came later – in 2003, and with a somewhat less centralist framework. The way in which BV works can be seen in Exhibits 17.2 and 17.3.

As with all the Government's 'modernisation' initiatives, BV has been evaluated, in this case by a team assembled by Cardiff University's Centre for Local and Regional Government Research. Notwithstanding the fact that their subsidiary report of ten case study authorities was affirmatively entitled *Changing to Improve* (Entwistle *et al.*, 2003), their principal conclusions, from a survey of nearly 3,000 officers and members from 314 councils, were distinctly lukewarm. The implementation of Best Value was 'a major challenge for most authorities' (p. 4), particularly for smaller district councils with fewer corporate staff, with cross-cutting reviews proving particularly demanding and taking longer than expected.

On the 4Cs, the evaluation confirmed the by then widely accepted view (see Wilson and Game, 2002, p. 338) that most councils were rather better at consulting and comparing than at challenging and competing. Few were felt to have examined rigorously the underlying need for a service, as opposed to thinking up ways of improving it. Competition too was a tough requirement, particularly for those authorities strongly committed to in-house provision, who had hoped that the disappearance of CCT had seen the end of having to compete constantly with the private sector.

Exhibit 17.2 The Best Value regime

BV's key purpose – to require councils to make arrangements – in the form of an annual BV Performance Plan (BVPP) and regular service-specific and cross-cutting Reviews – to secure *continuous improvement* in the way they undertake *all their service responsibilities,* having regard to their *economy, efficiency and effectiveness.* Councils to review all services regularly to demonstrate to the public and inspectors that they are applying continuous improvement principles.

BV Performance Plans – assess existing performance through national and locally determined BV Performance Indicators (PIs), set future targets, and outline the authority's programme of BV Reviews. Should be the principal means by which an authority is held to account for the efficiency and effectiveness of its services and for its future plans.

BV Reviews – should prompt consideration of radical approaches to service improvement, by asking 'big questions' not normally addressed in day-to-day management. Reviews to follow *the 4Cs*:

- **Challenge** why, how, and by whom a service is being provided and show that alternative approaches to service delivery have been considered;
- **Compare** its performance with that of similar authorities across a range of relevant BVPIs, taking into account the views of both service users and potential suppliers;
- **Consult** local taxpayers, service users, external partners and the wider community in setting new and demanding performance targets and an action plan to deliver continuous improvements;
- **Compete,** wherever practicable, in order to secure efficient and effective services.

Review questions would typically include:

- *What* does the service do now?
- *How well* does it do it, and for what cost?
- *What* do its customers want of it?
- *How well* does it do it in comparison with others?
- *Could* the benefits of the service be obtained in some other way?
- *Could* some other organisation provide it better and/or cheaper?
- *Can* we do the job better (and by how much)?
- *Can* we make customers happier (and by how much)?
- *How* can we get the same benefits to the people while spending less?
- *Should* we be providing the service at all?

Inspection – all council functions are subject to regular inspection by either a special inspectorate or the Audit Commission's Inspectorate. Like CPAs, all inspection reports – over 3,200 by 2005/06 – are published by the Audit Commission, most usefully by the individual authority and 'your local area': www.audit-commission.gov.uk/yourlocalarea/index.asp. For a sense of their flavour, see Exhibit 17.4.

Failing services – the Secretary of State has wide-ranging powers to intervene where an authority is judged by inspectors not to be delivering a BV service, and ultimately to remove responsibility for the 'failing' service from the authority altogether.

Exhibit 17.3 The good, the fair and the ugly

BV Inspections

Score each service/function on two 4-point scales:

- *Quality of the service*: poor = no stars; fair = 1 star; good = 2 stars; excellent = 3 stars;
- *Prospects for improvement*: no; unlikely; probably; yes.

The things they say

The judgements of the inspection teams, composed usually of between 2 and 5 members, are formed during a visit of a few days, on the basis of interviews and perhaps a focus group of staff, visits and 'reality checks', and, of course, much documentation. As even the following ultra-summary extracts show, however, their reports are crammed with quite sweeping observations, impressions and conclusions.

1. *Herefordshire Council – Homelessness and Housing Advice Service*
   Excellent 3-star service that will probably improve

   Good features: accessible service to rural, dispersed community through network of offices and outreach services; maximum use of Council's own well-maintained accommodation, rather than bed and breakfasts; excellent reception facilities, all offices wheelchair-accessible, with toys for children and enthusiastic staff; positive approach to victims of domestic violence; vacant properties let in less than two weeks on average; regular inspection of hostels and other accommodation.

   Likely improvements: more direct support for clients with additional needs in temporary accommodation; collect more monitoring information on issues of disability, race, gender and ethnicity; improved equal opportunities training for staff and elected members.

The case study authorities had never been intended to highlight best, as opposed to possibly typical, practice, but their experience too was double-edged (p. 6):

Examples of challenging practices and 'thinking outside the box' were identified ... [but] evidence from the case studies suggests ... that the kinds of changes were often incremental and rarely involved wholly new approaches to procuring and delivering services.

Many councils reported their elected members as appearing generally to be disengaged from the whole BV exercise, and particularly from the preparation of BV Performance Plans. These were widely seen as documents prepared by officers for the benefit of external auditors, rather than the product of any intense political debate about values, priorities and

2. *Bedfordshire CC – Library Service*
   A good 2-star service that will probably improve

   Good features: responsiveness to public priorities of extended opening hours (incl. Sundays) and IT access; good core book-lending and enquiry service; facilities for children – e.g. homework centres in especially deprived wards, with welcoming, interactive staff; positive work with disabled people through Library Link service; provision of other-language newspapers and free internet access for recent refugees; libraries mostly bright and welcoming (except Bedford Central); good user satisfaction ratings.

   Likely improvements: increase usage and take-up by black and ethnic minority communities, by relevant welcome signs, displays and promotional material; rely less on user surveys and develop more informal user groups.

3. *Castle Morpeth BC – Housing Maintenance and Capital Programme*
   A poor, no-star service, unlikely to improve

   Poor features: no formal maintenance appointments system, too many jobs done on 'urgent' basis; no effective monitoring of contractors' performance; council's 'over-ambitious' modernisation programme will take 100 years to complete, which 'falls a long way short of tenants' aspirations'; uncoordinated maintenance programmes lead to inefficient use of scarce resources; no regular and systematic customer feedback sought; no tenant involvement in development of services or in BV review.

   Improvements unlikely: because no effective system of performance management with tenant involvement yet in place; low staff morale; 'departmentalism' hinders corporate and co-operative working; concerns about capacity of council to drive through the level of change and continuous improvement required by BV.

resource allocation. Councillors and officers alike were critical of the costs and time that the new regime seemed to demand, not least the inspections (p. 7):

Many respondents believed inspection to have been a major driver of improvement in their organisations, but a large proportion felt that the added costs involved had outweighed the benefits.

Beacons of light and LPSAs

Best Value was New Labour's comprehensive assault on local government service provision, applying to all functional responsibilities of all councils. It was backed up, though, by several other more selective initiatives, one of

Exhibit 17.4 Beacon Councils and the IDeA

What are Beacon Councils (BCs)? Councils formally recognised by the Government as 'best performers' or 'leading lights' in a particular service area, who can be used, during the year in which they hold beacon status, to disseminate through various 'learning activities' their experience and best practice to other authorities. The aim of BCs is to raise service quality by enabling all councils to learn from the best.

The Beaconising process
- Each year, Ministers from across government select *themes* in service areas that have a direct impact on the quality of life of local people. Councils apply, singly or jointly, under the themes where they can demonstrate that an excellent service is being provided.

  The 10 themes for the 8th Round of Beacons (2007/08) include electoral services, healthy schools, increasing Voluntary and Community Sector service delivery, the role of elected members as community champions, and preventing and tackling anti-social behaviour.
- Councils are shortlisted by an expert Advisory Panel, supported by the BC team of ODPM civil servants. Shortlisted councils are visited and assessed, and final recommendations for beacon status made to Ministers by the Advisory Panel. There are usually up to 50 BCs per round, selected from, in recent years, more than 200 applicants.
- To be selected, a BC must show:
  - *Excellence* in a beacon theme;
  - *Good* general performance; and
  - *Plans for effective dissemination* – e.g. showcase events, open days, workshops, seminars, mentoring opportunities, etc.

Dissemination and the IDeA – throughout the dissemination process, councils work closely with the *Improvement and Development Agency (IDeA)*. The IDeA was formed in 1999 by the Local Government Association as one of the two successor organisations to the Local Government Management Board (LGMB). The *Employers' Organisation* took over LGMB's pay negotiating role, *IDeA* its management and development role.

IDeA sees itself as a localist counterbalance to the Government's centralised inspection and control regime. In addition to supporting the BC scheme, it runs a voluntary Peer Review Programme for councils, undertaking reviews of councils as a 'critical friend', rather than a regulatory inspector; runs elected member and manager development programmes; and has a useful website to compensate for its computer-unfriendly acronym.

In summary, IDeA is about generating improvement from within local government – to quote the title of a useful article by current Executive Director, Lucy de Groot (2005). Bristol City Council's former Chief Exec, the new executive cabinet decided they didn't (then!) need one of those and removed her – their loss, IDeA's gain.

which, also launched in 1999, was Beacon Councils (Exhibit 17.4) – a scheme for identifying examples of excellent performance in individual local councils and disseminating news of that performance to the rest of local government through open days, publications, conferences and the like.

While beacon schools and NHS beacons were discontinued after a few years, Beacon Councils are seen overall as an ongoing success, particularly by the increasing number of authorities and officers who can speak with first-hand experience. The most recent evaluation survey, by the University of Warwick's Local Government Centre, found far more positive reactions than to Best Value (Rashman and Hartley, 2006, p. 7):

> The vast majority of officers believe it informs best practice (83 per cent), encourages networking with peers (75 per cent), as well as providing models to improve performance (69 per cent) ... Authorities which have been Beacons generally indicate that the costs of their involvement are far outweighed by the benefits of raising the council's profile on the national stage and boosting staff morale.

Beacons, interestingly, received no direct mention in Labour's 2001 manifesto, the generally bland local government section of which suggested that another initiative for rewarding high-performing councils, Local Public Service Agreements (LPSAs), would play a more prominent role in the future, as indeed they have (Labour Party, 2001, p. 34):

> We want to give successful local councils more leeway to meet local needs using a £400 million reward fund. We have piloted local public service agreements to offer new investment and greater financial flexibility in return for higher performance. We will extend this reform to all upper-tier councils. We will offer further flexibility for high-performance authorities, with reformed inspections and more local discretion to encourage civic renewal.

Few in the world of local government, reading that apparently anodyne last sentence, could have imagined that it presaged something that would soon come to dominate many of their professional lives: not beacon status, not even their LPSA – of which more later – but, also otherwise unmentioned in the manifesto, Comprehensive Performance Assessment.

BV Mark II – CPA

The 2001 election was followed by a ministerial reshuffle, Stephen Byers and Nick Raynsford replacing John Prescott and Hilary Armstrong as, respectively, Secretary of State and minister responsible for local government. Both new ministers had served previously as councillors and they at least presented their reform plans in less interventionist language than had their predecessors. The key early policy document was the 2001 White Paper, *Strong Local Leadership – Quality Public Services*, which acknowledged explicitly – almost as if it were news – just how strangulating central government's micro-management of local government had become: over inputs (for example, through controls over council borrowing and ring-fencing of grants), processes (by requiring the production of a myriad of plans or the establishment of partnerships) and decisions (DTLR, 2001a, paras 4.2–4.4):

Over the years, the cumulative effect has become significant:

- the level of ring-fenced grant is in danger of rising to levels that seriously restrict councils' financial room for manoeuvre;
- councils are now required to produce some 66 separate plans and strategies, with top-tier councils alone required to produce more than 40; and
- the Regional Co-ordination Unit has identified some 30 key initiatives targeted at deprived areas and neighbourhoods [Area-based Initiatives – ABIs].

This accumulation of central requirements and initiatives 'can become counter-productive', the White Paper admitted, as could the 'many overlapping performance measurement frameworks ... to monitor local government services' (para. 3.12). In future, therefore, the Government would shift its focus 'away from controls over inputs, processes and local decisions ... to the assured delivery of outcomes through a national framework of standards and accountability (para 1.12). Accordingly, the White Paper set out 'a comprehensive performance framework for improvement, coupled with a substantial package of deregulation'. Not surprisingly, what has become known as Comprehensive Performance Assessment (CPA) has undergone some changes both in substance and in terminology, but, even after the 2005 adjustments necessitated by 'the harder test', the White Paper prototype and the philosophy underpinning it are still clearly recognisable in the regime as outlined in Exhibit 9.3. (For a fuller account of CPA, its methodology and operation, see Game 2006 on linked website.)

We have termed CPA 'Best Value Mark II', which is partly accurate, partly not. CPA did not *replace* BV, but rather *incorporated* it. As described above, BV is a statutory regime, and the basic requirements it makes of BV authorities – the Performance Plan and Performance Indicators, regular service reviews, demonstration of continuous improvement – remain largely unchanged. Most obviously incorporated by CPA was BV's dual scoring system, with 4-point scales for 'quality of the service' and 'prospects for improvement' (see Exhibits 17.2 and 17.3), the huge difference being, of course, that with CPA the final assessment was not of the performance of a single service, but rather of the whole local authority.

In the White Paper, just four of these overall performance ratings were envisaged:

- *High performers*;
- *Strivers* – not top performers, but with proven capacity to improve;
- *Coasters* – not top performers (nor beer mats), and no proven capacity to improve; and
- *Poor performers*.

Unsurprisingly, such a schema proved easy to mock. Within days, the categories had been relabelled – Thrivers, Strivers, Skivers and Divers – which, while frivolous, was arguably less misinterpretable than the original, in which 'coasting' could be taken as complimentary, and 'striving' sounded altogether too stressful. Almost as if prepared for it, ministers changed to the less derisible 5-point scale: Excellent, Good, Fair, Weak and Poor – prompting the cynical suggestion that the whole labelling issue had been a planted concession on the part of a government nervous of its ability to sell a highly controversial policy to sceptical local authorities. The other disarming strategy, of course, was to ensure from the start that there were more apparent winners than losers, for the point of CPA as a driver of continuous improvement was that all assessments would have consequences.

Freedoms, flexibilities and failures

Part of the White Paper's 'substantial package of deregulation' would involve 'freedoms and flexibilities' for all councils: greater freedom to borrow and invest; fewer plans and strategies required by ministers; fewer 'consent regimes', where government agreement is required before action can be taken; and wider powers to provide services for others and to charge for discretionary services. Though such 'freedoms' were possessed already by principal authorities in most purportedly democratic countries, several were for UK councils potentially significant and have been touched on earlier in this book.

CPA, however, was predicated on there being significant *additional* 'rewards' for high-performing councils, and these, the White Paper indicated, would include a freedom from budget- and council tax-capping, less ring-fencing of government grants, further reductions in plan requirements, greater freedom to use income from fines, and a 'much lighter touch' inspection regime.

But if, in this still obviously centrally directed system aimed at improving performance, the 'good children' are rewarded, the poor performers – the 'Poor' or '0-star' councils – must receive, if not punishment, at least a course of corrective therapy. Early indications were that ministers inclined towards a fairly heavy-handed form of *statutory intervention*, externally directed, and leading quite possibly to the 'failing' council being placed in administration or having its functions transferred to other providers. In practice, they opted for a process of *engagement*, tailored to the particular needs of the individual councils – working *with* them to guide, assist and assess their recovery, rather than working them over.

What happens is that the DCLG (previously the ODPM) appoints a *lead official* – usually a former senior local government manager – to assist the council in formulating a recovery plan, identifying external sources of support, and monitoring its implementation. That lead official is supported by an *Audit Commission relationship manager*, who co-ordinates inspection activity for any council (not just those subject to DCLG involvement), and a *Government monitoring board*, comprising the above two officials and other relevant stakeholders, that acts as the formal monitor of the council's performance recovery, and makes recommendations to the minister, other government bodies and inspectorates, and the council itself (Hughes *et al.*, 2004).

There is plenty to admire about CPA and its drive for continuous improvement, at both the high achieving and low achieving ends of the spectrum. Ministers, assisted variously by the Audit Commission, the LGA, the IDeA, and, of course, the generally positive commitment of the local authorities themselves, have created a nationally orchestrated performance management process that is unique and unmatchable in any other large-scale system of local government. If you doubt it, look again at some of the numbers in the third column of Exhibit 12.3 and imagine the governments of those countries trying to run annual CPAs for their thousands of local authorities. They couldn't possibly, but, much more importantly, it wouldn't occur to them to want to. As with the wish to control individual councils' tax and spending levels, it requires both the centralist structure of local government and the centralist cast of mind.

Local Area Agreements – Labour's elephants?

If CPA dominated Labour's second term of government without having had even a mention in the 2001 manifesto, the initiative that ministers apparently saw as the flagship of Labour's third term were Local Area Agreements (LAAs). They come with a respectable pedigree. Local Public Service Agreements (LPSAs), which *were* advertised in the 2001 manifesto,

Exhibit 17.5 Local Public Service Agreements (LPSAs)

What are they? A particular form of central-local partnership between government departments and *individual* local authorities, involving specific agreed local performance goals, government help in achieving them, and cash rewards for success – 'something for something' agreements, to quote the Government.

The 3-part LPSA sets out:

- **The authority's commitment** to deliver, within about three years, a dozen or so *specific and measurable improvements in service performance, over and above* any targets in its BV Performance Plan. The targets, as well as being 'stretching', should be defined precisely and in terms of *outcomes*, not outputs or inputs. They should be council-identified local priorities, discussed with partners, and agreed with the Government.
- **The Government's commitment** to help the authority achieve these agreed improvements, mainly by providing interim *'pump-priming'* grants of £750,000 + £1 per head of population.
- **The Government's commitment** to pay extra *performance reward grants* of up to 2.5% of 2004/05 net revenue expenditure if/when the performance improvements are verifiably attained.

History and significance: 20 authorities concluded pilot LPSAs in 2000/01, later extended to virtually all 150 top-tier authorities. Seen as a key and successful element in the Government's modernisation agenda, a second generation of agreements was negotiated from 2005, with more emphasis on local, rather than national, definition of targets and on partnership working.

An example – Birmingham City Council's LPSA (2005–08)

The Government will pay pump-priming grants of £1.75 mill. in 2005/06 to cover the Council's increased expenditure involved in implementing the LPSA. If all 13 targets are met in full, the Council will receive extra Performance Reward Grants of £34 million.

The Council' performance commitments or 'stretch marks' include:

- To increase the percentage of pupils achieving 5 or more GCSEs at grades A* to C from 51.2% in 2004 to 56% in 2007, instead of 55.5% without the LPSA;
- To reduce the incidence of arson vehicle fires from 2,048 p.a. in 2004 to 1,361 p.a. in 2007, instead of 1,660 without the LPSA;
- To reduce the percentage of young people convicted of an offence who reoffend within 2 years from 46.1% p.a. in 2004 to 39.1% in 2007, instead of 41.1% without the LPSA;
- To increase Council-assisted take-up of new council tax benefit claims by people over 60, from 161 in 2004/05 to 1,751 in 2007/08, instead of 1,147 without the LPSA; and
- To reduce the number of 16 to 18 year olds not in education, employment or training from 13.6% in 2004 to 7.5% in 2007, instead of 9.0% without the LPSA.

Source: Birmingham City Council and Birmingham Strategic Partnership, *Second Generation Local Public Service Agreement, April 2005 – March 2008* (ODPM, 2005).

have proved to be one of the success stories of the modernisation agenda –
see Exhibit 17.5.

The ODPM's evaluation team noted and were impressed by the sheer
scale of the LPSA exercise (ODPM, 2005i, p. 5):

> Negotiating a dozen or so targets covering policies owned by eight
> central government departments with each of 130 local authorities over
> a three-year period was a hugely ambitious undertaking ...

Inevitably, there were difficulties and tensions, unavoidable with a
government that at its heart simply cannot bring itself to trust those it
describes in its rhetoric as its 'local government partners'. Local authorities
thus found themselves on occasion signing up to central government
targets that they considered 'pointless if not unachievable' (p. 5). Such
instances, though, were the exception, and have also been addressed with

---

Exhibit 17.6 Local Area Agreements (LAAs)

What are they? The Government's big 'third-term' idea for improving co-
ordination between local authorities, local agencies of central government –
Primary Care Trusts, Jobcentre Plus, Sure Start, Connexions – and their
partners, to improve the quality and reduce the bureaucracy of local service
delivery. Unlike LPSAs, which are negotiated between individual government
ministers and individual local authorities, LAAs work primarily through
Local Strategic Partnerships (LSPs – see Exhibit 8.5) and Government Offices
for the Regions (see p. 182).

Particular features?

- **Partnership working** – LAA outcomes to be negotiated by all local delivery
  partners, drawing on priorities and evidence from the LSP's Community
  Plan;
- **Simplified government funding** – the Government to 'dramatically simplify'
  the numerous funding streams from Government departments going into
  the same local area, to facilitate 'joined-up' public services;
- **Devolved decision-making** – LAAs 'require central government departments to be more willing to let go of detailed day-to-day control of their
  programmes ... they will need to allow local authorities and their partners
  to decide jointly which priorities best reflect local circumstances'. So said
  the ODPM (2004b, p. 5)!
- **Four national priority functional blocks** – LAAs normally to be structured
  around some combination of four functional blocks:
  (a) Children and young people;
  (b) Safer and stronger communities;
  (c) Healthier communities and older people; and
  (d) Economic development and enterprise.

the shift in emphasis to local priorities in the second generation of Agreements. Generally, LPSAs have been 'welcomed by local authorities which remain largely enthusiastic' (ODPM, 2005i, p. 5):

> The key features of the scheme – the focus on a limited number of negotiated stretch targets, Government support for implementation, and the prospect of a reward – have motivated authorities to participate and strive to succeed.

Presumably feeling itself to be 'on a roll' with LPSAs, the Government decided to combine in 2004/05 its new Agreements toy with its other passion – partnership working – and came up with Local Area Agreements (LAAs), as outlined in Exhibit 17.6. In their rather different way, these are at least as ambitious as LPSAs, but may struggle to receive from local government quite as positive a reception – particularly in two-tier areas

---

History – First 21 pilot LAAs launched in 2004; 87 signed by end of 2005; all remaining LSP areas to be signed up by 2007. Should be increasing alignment of LPSAs and LAAs.

An early example – Coventry Partnership's LAA, 2005–08: *Progress Through Prevention*

- **Overarching theme: Prevention** – Encompasses the aims of preventing decline or waste of potential, and intervening before serious problems arise – whether it be in a neighbourhood, supporting a family, or in the health of young or elderly people.
- **Agreed priority outcomes** – within functional blocks (a), (b) and (c):

  o Getting children and young people to attend school;
  o Enabling children to live in a family situation;
  o Reducing the number of criminal offences;
  o Increasing the number of drug misusing offenders entering treatment;
  o Reducing smoking levels;
  o Keeping older people out of hospital; and
  o Improving people's satisfaction with their neighbourhoods.

- **Examples of key outcomes** – detailed targets to be negotiated –

  o Reduce percentage of half-days missed by school pupils through absence;
  o Reduce percentage of pregnant women smoking in Sure Start Children's Centre areas;
  o Reduce percentage of emergency hospital admissions of over-65s;
  o Increase percentage of disabled children attending mainstream school; and
  o Reduce percentage of 'looked after' children placed more than 20 miles outside the local area.

and those without coherent and effective Local Strategic Partnerships (LSPs).

An early evaluation (ODPM, 2005j) found enthusiasm, even greater than usual variation in the quality of the pilot agreements, and a disconcerting level of perplexity. The enthusiasm verged occasionally on the manic: 'the most exciting government initiative in years' (p. 13) in the eyes of one regional government officer, who should perhaps get out a bit more. The variation is an understandable consequence of the novelty and inherent complexities of the LAA process: the exceptionally wide range of different stakeholders – including Voluntary and Community Groups – the very resource-intensive process of negotiating and agreeing outcomes, the new authority role and additional resourcing required of Government Offices, and the lack of any tangible LPSA-type 'reward'. Being inherent, most of these factors are there to stay, as indeed may be the perplexity encountered by the evaluation team (pp. 5, 20–1):

> Many participants remained confused about the purpose of LAAs throughout the [negotiating] process ... Within particular pilot areas it was not uncommon to find that individual interviewees had quite different views of what an LAA was and how it could benefit their area. One interviewee described it as like 'trying to eat a cloud with a knife and fork'.

Attractive as the metaphor is, the *Local Government Chronicle* cartoonist preferred the old aphorism about the elephant: you cannot define an elephant, but you know one when you see one (see Figure 17.1). The fact is, though, that you *can* define an elephant – mammal with trunk, average adult weight of 3 tonnes, etc. LAAs, by contrast, seem to have the capacity to remain indefinable, even to some of those required to negotiate them.

The collateral costs of service improvement

The second half of this chapter has focused largely on the Labour Government's Modernisation Agenda (LGMA). It is an agenda that has taken at least eight years to evolve, fitfully and often disconnectedly. By the Government's count, however, it now comprises more than 20 separate policies and initiatives, more than half of which are aimed exclusively or primarily at improving services – their quality, cost-effectiveness, responsiveness, inter-connectedness and accessibility. This reflects our assertion at the start of the chapter about the Government's interest in local authorities being much more in their role as providers than as deciders.

Figure 17.1   *Local Area Agreements – you'll know one when you see one*

Source: Local Government Chronicle, 30 June 2005.

Many of these service-directed initiatives have, as we have seen, been evaluated individually, but the Government also commissioned a series of 'meta-evaluations', drawing together the evidence from the relevant individual studies to assess the LGMA's impact on certain 'over-arching areas'. The first of these, unsurprisingly, is service improvement, the others being: accountability, community leadership, stakeholder engagement, and public confidence. It would be worrying indeed, if, after all this attention, there had no discernible improvement in local services, and happily the meta-evaluation was able to find some (Martin and Bovaird, 2005, pp. 12–13):

> The evidence suggests that there have been significant improvements in most services since 2000/2001 ... Like the ODPM's basket of [performance] indicators, CPA scores suggest that overall local government performance has been improving, particularly among the poorest performers. The evidence suggests that ... key elements of the LGMA ... have been important drivers of improvement.

Happily too, the team did not feel that LGMA policies had actually hindered service improvement (p. 15). On the other hand, there had been what militarily might be termed significant collateral damage – or perhaps, to euphemise a euphemism, collateral costs (p. 15):

[T]here is strong evidence of concerns about:

- 'initiative overload' (particularly among smaller authorities);
- what is seen as the increasing level of central control over local councils;
- the ways in which the provision of more joined-up services is made more difficult by what is perceived to be a lack of joined-up working in central government and the inspectorates; and
- the costs of inspection.

Having drawn attention to each of these concerns at different points in the book, we can only conclude that, whatever it may have done for their service delivery, the LGMA can hardly claim to have enhanced local authorities' even more important political function as robust institutions of community self-government.

Chapter 18

The Future or A Future?

We're all New Localists now

Chapter 17 ended by noting some of the conclusions of the meta-evaluation of the Government's modernisation agenda (LGMA). By the Government's own 'official' Best Value and CPA measures, there was confirmation that local authorities had improved and, moreover, had demonstrated the capacity to keep on improving. They had also responded positively to the various other service-related initiatives in the LGMA. At the same time, there was widespread local resentment of ministers' continuing insistence on managing through targetry and inspection, and of their general 'control freakery'.

At some time during its second term of office, even the Government began to acknowledge that its admission in the 2001 White Paper – about the accumulation of central requirements and initiatives becoming counter-productive – had probably been right. At which point, the casual observer could have been forgiven for concluding that unanimity had broken out across the party spectrum and we apparently had a New Localist consensus on our hands. Leading politicians of all stripes seemed to be articulating the same *Weltanschauung*: a similar diagnosis of what was wrong with local government and a similar prescription for rectifying it. By way of illustration, the following speech might almost have been delivered by a frontbencher from any of the three major parties:

> I want to make the case today for what I call 'real localism'.
>
> We must first define one of the real failures of the modern British political system. It is the cycle of centralization. The effect of creeping centralization ... is today suffocating the spirit of local communities, denying local democracy ...
>
> The historic tendency to centralize power, uninhibited by a constitution providing checks and balances, has ... been part of the problem, not the solution. Decisions have been made for understandable, sometimes laudable, reasons. Central government, concerned about issues of equity, of value for money, of citizen empowerment, has seen a fast track to their resolution through central intervention. But the result is not laudable ... when central government is tempted to do too much, in consequence it does not do it well enough.

Our vision is different. It's of diverse, locally provided, locally funded and locally accountable services. It's about devolving both power *and* responsibility. It's about drawing up a new democratic contract with local people, so they can take control of their lives.

We are on the side of the local community and want to give local people more power and control over how their services are run, their neighbourhoods are policed, and their priorities are delivered. Our support for localism, born of experience and strengthened by our values ... is sincere and lasting.

The call for new localism represents a real opportunity for us as a party. This should be natural territory for us. Decentralization ... means resisting the temptation to concentrate power at the centre and trusting the competence of local government.

If our commitment to localism is to be meaningful, local government must be at the heart of it ... We recognize the urgent need to reduce dramatically the burden of central control on local authorities and give them a freedom to innovate and to become effective community leaders.

So our localism is about crafting a new contract between the public and politicians.

That is what I mean by 'real localism'.

Good stuff, isn't it – and, as you may have guessed, delivered in fact by frontbenchers of *all three* parties. Exhibit 18.1 will tell you who said what, although, by the very nature of the exercise, it isn't awfully helpful. As in *Alice in Wonderland*, we have here some classic Humpty Dumpty semantics: when I use a word, it means just what I choose it to mean. Unlike Alice, however, we cannot just look sceptical and move on. We have to try to make some sense of it – starting with a question that, surprisingly often in such discussions, goes almost unaddressed. If all these people see themselves as 'New Localists', who are 'Old Localists'?

Old Localism

Us! If, by chance, you misread those two letters and thought we were referring to the US of A, that would be OK. Any federal system, giving local and state government constitutionally guaranteed powers and status, is in its way Old Localist (OL). But we meant us, ourselves – one albeit slightly more unreconstructedly OL than the other. This book is Old Localist, with its strong emphasis on elected councils and councillors and their democratic accountability, its concern at the imbalance in central–local relations, its critique of central government's financial control and policy direction, its scepticism about the fragmentation of local government services and their costly re-creation through various forms

Exhibit 18.1 Who said what

The nine paragraphs of our composite 'New Localist' speech on pp. 379–80 come from the speeches of seven frontbench politicians in the following order: 1, 2, 3, 4, 5, 6, 7, 4, 1.

1. **Alan Milburn** (then Secretary of State for Health):
   'Localism: from rhetoric to reality' – speech to the New Local Government Network (NLGN), 5 March 2003 (www.nlgn.org.uk – keynote speeches).

2. **Bernard Jenkin** (then Conservative Shadow Secretary of State for the Regions):
   'Radical plans to re-empower local government' – speech to NLGN, 19 April 2004.

3. **David Miliband** (then Minister of Communities and Local Government):
   'Renewing our democracy' – speech to the LGA Annual Conference, 8 July 2005 (www.dclg.gov.uk – search 'Miliband speeches').

4. **Charles Kennedy** (then Leader of the Liberal Democrats):
   'Liberalism and localism' – speech to the Institute for Public Policy Research (IPPR), 8 December 2005 (www.ippr.org.uk – search 'Kennedy speech').

5. **David Cameron** (Leader of the Conservative Party):
   'I say to Liberal Democrats everywhere: join me in my mission' – speech in Hereford, 16 December 2005 (www.conservatives.com – search 'Cameron speeches').

6. **Paul Boateng** (then Chief Secretary, HM Treasury):
   'New Localism' – speech to NLGN, 23 January 2003.

7. **Caroline Spelman** (then Conservative Shadow Secretary of State for the ODPM):
   'We will restore faith in local accountability' – speech to Conservative Party Conference, 5 October 2005 (www.conservatives.com – search 'Caroline Spelman').

of partnership. Old Localists would agree with David Miliband about our system's need of checks and balances, but, apparently unlike him, would like to see some of the principal ones being powerful and therefore politically challenging town, city and county halls.

New Localists see most of this as pointlessly *passé* – more relevant to the discredited aspirations of the municipal left of the 1980s, if not Joseph Chamberlain's municipal socialism of the 1880s, than to the dramatically changed circumstances of the 'noughties'. Though disputing some of the Government's obsession with micro-management and its interventionist excesses, New Localists accept, rather than rail against, its assumed role as principal driver of change at the local level. They emphasise the 'freedoms and flexibilities' acquired by local authorities, rather than the undiluted centralism of the system in which these 'earned autonomy' baubles are awarded only to approved high-performers. They accept that local 'governance' does not necessarily centre on the elected local authority, arguing that the complexity of modern-day problems requires definitions of 'locality' that are broader and more flexible than can be embraced by established democratic institutions. In this book, Chapter 8 in particular is about New Localism, and the latter part of Chapter 17 – especially the final section on LAAs.

Fairly obviously, the tide of contemporary history is a New Localist one. During 2006, several major announcements were due concerning the future structure and operation of local government, and in this chapter we shall speculate about – to pinch the new CPA jargon – the 'direction of travel' that any reform programme may take, and the distance it is likely to reach. Instinct and experience would normally counsel against any mould-shattering expectations, but the then key minister in that important first year of the 2005 Labour Government was David Miliband, whose thoughts and speeches constituted the raw material of what would have been seen very much as 'his' 2006 White Paper – had he not been reshuffled to departmental pastures new, just a few weeks before its scheduled appearance. Known to have an unusually keen interest in institutional reform, Miliband was thought by some to be on the point of producing something, as the Americans say, out of left field.

Localism sings

Though he himself might query the label, Miliband would be taken by most to be a New Localist (NL) – and with justification. In his many deftly balanced statements about the respective positions of central and local government, where inevitably one side of the balance must come first, it was invariably local government's responsibility as an agent to help deliver national priorities that preceded its role as a definer of local needs or a shaper of local priorities. It may be interesting, therefore, to match Miliband's reform ideas – and indeed those in the actual White Paper – against those of Sir Simon Jenkins: author, ex-editor of *The Times*, ex-chair of the Commission for Local Democracy, and about the most radical localist around – mainly OL, though with NL associates.

Jenkins' prospectus – what he calls his attempt 'to make localism sing' (p. 7) – is best set out in the Policy Exchange pamphlet, *Big Bang Localism: A Rescue Plan for British Democracy* (Jenkins, 2004). By pamphlet standards it is lengthy and can only be summarised brutally here, but its thesis is that the deterioration of our local democratic health has become so serious in recent years that it can only be rescued effectively by a transfer of power from the centre to localities that is both comprehensive and spectacular. Hence the requirement of implementation in the form of a Big Bang – rivalling, if not the birth of the universe, then Margaret Thatcher's Big Bang reform of the City of London's financial institutions on 1 October 1986, which transformed irreversibly the restrictive practices of the stock exchange and securities markets.

Compressed down to eight points, Jenkins' post-Big Bang local government would comprise:

1. A structure resembling that existing before the 1974/75 reorganisation (1,857 principal councils in GB in place of the present 442 – see Exhibit 5.2 above). There would still be a mix of unitary and two-tier authorities, following the re-creation of abolished counties and the dismantling of larger rural districts (often with 'artificial' or 'compass point' names – see pp. 38–9 above) into smaller 'real' town or parish councils with which residents can genuinely identify.

2. County and city councils would regain those functions wholly or partly 'lost' to unelected quangos since the 1970s – including planning, roads, the environment, leisure, culture, the police, prison and probation, youth employment and training.

3. A dismantled NHS, with health services to be taken over by counties and upper-tier authorities.

4. Personal social services would become the responsibility of the most local tier of local government – in England, city, town or parish councils.

5. These authorities, however small by current UK standards, would become self-governing entities for services they could reasonably supply on their own – primary schools and elderly people's homes, nurseries and day-care centres, clinics, surgeries. For provision of larger scale services, they would combine with neighbouring authorities as necessary.

6. All these service-providing authorities would be elected, and led by an elected executive – a mayor, elected either directly or (as in France) as the head of a collective cabinet.

7. All authorities to be funded partly by central government through a single general or block grant, but with over half their income (as in the days before the poll tax) coming from a portfolio of local taxes on, for example, property, income, business, hotels, tourism, gambling, vehicle duty, entertainment.

8. A Local Government Commission, independent of central government, would be charged with implementation: negotiating with authorities to determine their internal constitutions and electoral arrangements, and monitoring schemes for local taxes.

Jenkins would argue that, dramatic as the implementation of even half of his programme would be (say, a Big Pop's-worth), it would do no more than bring us a little closer in line with most other West European and Scandinavian systems, and stop us infringing, as we do at present, several of the Articles of the European Charter of Local Self-Government. However, notwithstanding the localist enthusiasms of those Labour ministers quoted in our patchwork speech, it ain't going to happen – at least not in the foreseeable future. So we had better look at what, more realistically, might happen.

Restructuring once again, or is it destruction?

Miliband was, and is, a thoughtful minister. A one-time research fellow at the IPPR, he reads books – academic books – and, even though his speechwriters sometimes seemed unfamiliar with the authors' names, he would refer to them regularly in his speeches: Jane Jacobs' *Death and Life of Great American Cities*, Paul Ginsborg's *The Politics of Everyday Life*; and American social scientists called Robert: Nisbet, Sampson, Putnam. Possibly aided by such reading, he spent his all-too-short time as Minister of Communities and Local Government testing out various reform ideas that appealed to him, to see presumably whether they appealed to anyone else.

He made clear, therefore, on several occasions, his enthusiasm for strong local political leadership in the form of directly elected mayors or even directly elected cabinets – which appealed rather less, it seemed, to his immediate audiences than it did to Conservative leader, David Cameron. He indicated his fascination with French local government, both the 36,000 communes at its heart and its similar number of indirectly elected mayors. And he communicated his interest – either his own or that of his political superiors – in structural reform, which was under 'active consideration', particularly for the 34 two-tier English counties. He used, on more than one occasion, Norfolk as an illustration (Miliband, 2005b):

> Norfolk has 7 district councils and 21 market towns. We need to ask if the best relationship is between the county and the districts or between *one or more unitary authorities and local neighbourhoods*. And, if it is the latter, we need to look at how that relationship works – be it a new role for parish and town councils, a new role for ward councillors, or an innovative new deal for bottom-up accountability. (our emphasis)

There was confirmation, then, of the open secret that further, and perhaps even nationwide, unitaries had not disappeared from the Government's agenda with the defeat of its proposals for elected English regional assemblies. These assemblies, with their accompanying requirement of unitary local government throughout the region, could have spelt the effective end of local government in many parts of the country – as was described emotionally by Lord (Tony) Greaves, also a Liberal Democrat member of Pendle BC, in one of the Lords' debates on the subject:

> I cannot find any polite words to describe the proposals for my part of
> Lancashire. They are ludicrous ... We are being offered ... a unitary
> county council for the whole of Lancashire, from Carnforth and the
> Arnside peninsula in the north to west Lancashire, Ormskirk, Skelmers-
> dale, which is a Liverpool suburb, and up into the hills where I live in
> east Lancashire. We are being offered one local authority for that whole
> area, representing 876,169 electors and a population of about 1.1 million.
> If somebody tells me that is local government, I tell them they do not
> know the meaning of the words in the English language. It is the
> abolition of local government as we know it. (*Lords Hansard*, 16 June
> 2004, Col. 825)

Norfolk's population is a little smaller than Lancashire's – a mere 822,000
– but in area it is almost twice the size, and much of the population live in
its 21 market towns and the small matter of about 540 parishes into which
the county outside the non-parished city of Norwich is divided. It is
difficult to see a single Norwich-based unitary authority, or even two or
three slightly smaller but necessarily entirely artificial unitaries, making
any more democratic sense than Lord Greaves felt a unitary Lancashire
would have done – without some fairly significant change at the genuinely
local level.

For Jenkins, the answer is easy: restructure downwards, not upwards. In
addition to Norwich, Norfolk has two large towns: Great Yarmouth
(49,000 population) and King's Lynn (34,000), and a further twelve of
those 'market towns' – officially defined as between 3,000 and 30,000 –
with populations of over 5,000. Every one of these is a real place, with
which, as Jenkins would put it, its residents identify and the name of which
they would give, if asked on the proverbial Mediterranean beach where in
England they come from: 'Thetford in Norfolk', Dereham, Wymondham,
Cromer, and so on.

In most other European countries, these towns would all be communes
or municipalities with a full range of local government powers and
responsibilities – instead of having to make do with a sub-principal town
or parish council and otherwise suppress their identities within soulless
'compass point' or amalgam districts: North Norfolk, South Norfolk,
King's Lynn and West Norfolk, Breckland. If Miliband, as he looked at
French communes and mused about 'a new role for parish and town
councils', had in mind turning towns like these into serious units of local
government, and not just service outposts of remote unitary councils, that
would indeed have been interesting. There are, however, several reasons
for apprehension – quite apart from Miliband no longer being in a position
personally to implement any such proposal – the first being precisely those
unitary councils.

City regions – a Senior moment?

We indicated above our uncertainty as to whether Miliband's interest in structural reorganisation was his own, or one that he felt bound to advance. Ever since the Redcliffe-Maud Commission in the 1960s, in so far as there has been a collective 'Whitehall' view of these matters, it has favoured an even smaller number of even larger local authorities – if for no other reason than to make life easier for those civil servants whose job it is to deal with them.

Miliband's chief contribution to this debate was to argue that larger authorities are better able to function 'strategically' – thinking first of 'the overall interests of an area, rather than the delivery of particular services, galvanizing all the resources across the public, private and voluntary sector towards a clear vision' (Miliband, 2005a). This focus on strategic capability appeared as if it might lead to two kinds of proposals in the White Paper on structural reform due in Summer 2006: city regions, on a strictly voluntary basis, for some of England's major conurbations, and unitaries, with rather more ministerial force behind them, to replace two-tier counties.

City regions are areas that acknowledge that the economic, cultural and demographic reach of a city can extend well beyond its formal political boundaries. They cover, therefore, a 'core city' plus its 'hinterland' within clearly defined boundaries, based on something like travel-to-work or leisure and shopping patterns. In themselves, city regions are anything but new, but the concept, used in recent years mainly by planners and economists, suddenly acquired a new political fashionability following the defeat of the North East regional assembly referendum in 2004. The modernisation think tank, New Local Government Network, immediately established a City Regions Commission to examine existing models abroad and their possible adaptability to Britain. The Commission reported in December 2005, asserting that:

> City Regions are for many areas the units best equipped to match contemporary travel and lifestyle patterns, and economic development can be aided by allowing cities to work more strategically with areas that fall within their natural orbit.

By this time, Miliband had attended a series of City Summits hosted by each of the eight members of the then ODPM's Core Cities Group – Birmingham, Bristol, Leeds, Liverpool, Manchester, Newcastle, Nottingham and Sheffield – in which he had urged city leaders to come forward with proposals for a new strategic level of governance beyond their cities. The lead they were being encouraged to follow was clearly that of the Greater London Authority, although all involved in this debate were insistent that there is no single model to be followed, that city regions are probably not a feasible proposition even for all core cities, and that, if they are to operate at all effectively, they must be allowed to 'emerge from below', rather than be imposed. Ideally, it is envisaged, they would develop out of councils choosing to co-operate with each other on some major project – such as the Northern Way regeneration initiative already being led by the three northern Regional Development Agencies.

City regions would, in short, work with existing councils, not replace them, and, while ministers might personally wish otherwise, they might well in practice be headed by some form of executive board, rather than a directly elected mayor. The most obvious early candidates were felt to be Greater Manchester, Birmingham and the Black Country, and Liverpool, followed perhaps by Newcastle–Gateshead, Sheffield and Bristol. The resulting asymmetry of arrangements across metropolitan areas is some way from what Derek Senior had in mind when he proposed a tier of city regions in his Memorandum of Dissent to the Redcliffe-Maud Commission back in the 1960s (see p. 56), but he would surely have derived some satisfaction from seeing his concept more prominently on the reform agenda than at any time since then.

Double devolution or increased democratic deficit?

The Redcliffe-Maud Commission's majority solution, it may be recalled, was for an entirely unitary structure of 58 authorities in England, outside the three conurbations of Birmingham, Manchester and Liverpool. It was seen at the time, as one commentator noted, 'to adhere to the unitary principle in spite of, rather than because of, the evidence presented' (Alexander, 1982, p. 32). Yet it is this principle that the Government looks like adhering to in its current reorganisation plans. It is worrying on at least two counts.

The first is the issue of size and scale, to which we have already given plenty of attention. There is little authoritative evidence of any correlation between a local authority's size and its service efficiency and effectiveness. But when you get to the scale even of our existing authorities, let alone the scale, the remoteness, and the reduced councillor representation of a wholly unitary structure, there is inevitably a diminution in *democratic* effectiveness.

The second concern is with what Miliband claimed was the counter-balance to this increase in scale: his intended 'empowerment of neighbourhoods' (2006). It is irresistibly tempting here to remind ourselves that this was the Minister of *Communities* and *Local* Government talking about devolution to *neighbourhoods*, and to query just what it is that distinguishes these three concepts that a visitor from most other polities might imagine to be almost identical. Between communities and neighbourhoods the suspicion must be that, for most current users of the terms, there is indeed very little difference. A test is to take a phrase like 'genuine community-level neighbourhood governance' (Stoker, 2005), and wonder how that would differ from 'genuine neighbourhood-level community governance', or even from sham community-level neighbourhood governance.

More seriously, the difference that *is* clearly discernible, and presumably intended, is between both of these and local *government*. For, by definition, in a unitary system there is only one institution of local government, and, as is clear from his reference to Norfolk, those unitaries that Miliband had in mind were definitely not neighbourhood-sized. Whatever is going to happen at neighbourhood (or community) level, it seems unlikely to take the form of bodies capable of performing what we have termed the political function of local government. As Jones and Stewart put it (2005):

> Neighbourhoods cannot be the basis for local government. They are sub-local entities of towns, cities and counties. They cannot generate a broad local public interest, deciding priorities over a range of concerns, and matching resources to local aspirations ... They can have a useful role in consultation and perform a few useful functions, but not as the main basis for local governing bodies.

Miliband (2006) described his goal as being 'double devolution', by which he meant both central *and* local government devolving powers, 'not just to the Town Hall but beyond, to neighbourhoods and individual citizens ... and communities [or is it neighbourhoods?] having the capacity to take up the opportunities which are offered to them'. He talked of 'empowerment' offering 'people ways of directly influencing the services they receive, through increased voice and choice'. But the choices he then exemplified were mainly choices for *consumers*: direct payments for services; individualised budgets, allowing service users to shape their own service provision; and neighbourhood charters. The enticing new powers for parish councils – the only remaining local government below county-sized unitaries – were consultation rights and the issuing of Fixed Penalty Notices.

It is rash to conclude a book by attempting to interpret speeches anticipating policies yet to acquire even White Paper status, and we would be delighted to have our more downbeat prognostications proved entirely false. But in 2005/06, with a White Paper on structure set to appear several months *before* Sir Michael Lyons' final report on the form, functions and financing of the future local government that that structure was supposed to accommodate, it was easier to see any 'devolution' increasing, rather than reducing, the UK's already gaping local democratic deficit.

Bibliography

Abdela, L. (1989) *Women With X Appeal: Women Politicians in Britain Today* (London: Optima).

Alexander, A. (1982) *The Politics of Local Government in the United Kingdom* (Harlow: Longman).

Allen, H. J. B. (1990) *Cultivating the Grass Roots: Why Local Government Matters* (The Hague: IULA).

Ashdown, P. (2001) *The Ashdown Diaries, Vol. II: 1997–1999* (Harmondsworth: Penguin).

Atkinson, H. and Wilks-Heeg, S. (2000) *Local Government from Thatcher to Blair: The Politics of Creative Autonomy* (Oxford: Blackwell).

Audit Commission (2001) *To Whom Much is Given: New Ways of Working for Councillors Following Political Restructuring* (Abingdon: Audit Commission).

Audit Commission (2005a) *Governing Partnerships: Bridging the Accountability Gap* (London: Audit Commission).

Audit Commission (2005b) *CPA – The Harder Test: Scores and Analysis of Performance in Single Tier and County Councils 2005* (London: Audit Commission).

Ayres, S. and Pearce, G. (2002) *Who Governs the West Midlands? An Audit of Government Institutions and Structures* (Telford: West Midlands Constitutional Convention).

Baggott, R. (1995) *Pressure Groups Today* (Manchester: Manchester University Press).

Bains, M. (Chairman) (1972) *The New Local Authorities: Management and Structure* (London: HMSO).

Barron, J., Crawley, G. and Wood, T. (1987) *Married to the Council? The Private Costs of Public Service* (Bristol: Bristol Polytechnic).

Barron, J., Crawley, G. and Wood, T. (1991) *Councillors in Crisis* (London: Macmillan).

BHHRG (British Helsinki Human Rights Group) (2005) *Articles on UK Postal Ballot Election by Paul Dale and others* – with link to Commissioner Richard Mawrey QC's judgement (www.bhhrg.org/mediaYear/asp).

Blackmore, A. (2004) *Standing Apart, Working Together: A Study of the Myths and Realities of Voluntary and Community Sector Independence* (London: NCVO).

Blair, T. (1998) *Leading the Way: A New Vision for Local Government* (London: IPPR).

Blais, A. and Carty, R. J. (1990) 'Does Proportional Representation Foster Election Turnout?', *European Journal of Political Research*, 18, pp. 167–81.

Blears, H.. (2003) *Communities in Control – Public Services and Local Socialism* (London: Fabian Society).

Bogdanor, V. (2001) 'Constitutional Reform', in A. Seldon (ed.), *The Blair Effect: The Blair Government 1997–2001* (London: Little, Brown), pp. 139–56.

Boyle, Sir L. (1986) 'In Recommendation of Widdicombe', *Local Government Studies*, 12: 6, pp. 33–9.

Brighton and Hove Community and Voluntary Sector Forum (2003) *Economic and Social Audit of the Community and Voluntary Sector in Brighton and Hove* (www.cvsectorforum.org.uk/org/BH_EconAudit_full.pdf).

Brindle, D. (2004) 'Change Agent', *Society Guardian*, 15 September.

Brooke, R. (2005) *The Councillor – Victim or Vulgarian?* (London: LGA).

Budge, I, Brand, J., Margolis, M. and Smith, A. L. M. (1972) *Political Stratification and Democracy* (London: Macmillan).

Budge, I., Crewe, I., McKay, D. and Newton, K. (2004) *The New British Politics*, 3rd edn (London: Pearson Longman).

Burton, M. (2005) 'A Suffolk Swansong?', *Municipal Journal*, 31 March, p. 12.

Butler, D., Adonis, A. and Travers, T. (1994) *Failure in British Government: The Politics of the Poll Tax* (Oxford: Oxford University Press).

Byrne, T. (2000) *Local Government in Britain: Everyone's Guide to How It All Works*, 7th edn (Harmondsworth: Penguin).

Cabinet Office (1998) *Quangos: Opening The Doors* (London: HMSO).

Cabinet Office (1999) *Modernising Government*, Cm 4310 (London: HMSO).

Cabinet Office (2005) *Reform of Public Sector Ombudsmen Services: A Consultation Paper* (London: Cabinet Office).

Campbell, L. (2004) 'The Mother of all Election Campaigns', *Society Guardian*, 14 May.

CEMR (Council of European Municipalities and Regions) (2000) *Women in Local Politics in the European Union* (Brussels: CEMR).

Challis, P. (2000) *Local Government Finance* (London: LGIU).

CIPD (Chartered Institute of Personnel and Development) (2004) *Employee Wellbeing and the Psychological Contract* (London: CIPD).

CIPFA (Chartered Institute of Public Finance and Accountancy) (2004) *Local Government Comparative Statistics, 2003* (London: CIPFA).

CIPFA (Chartered Institute of Public Finance and Accountancy) (2005) *Councillors' Guide to Local Government Finance* (London: CIPFA).

CLA (Commission for Local Administration in England) (2005) *Local Government Ombudsman – Annual Report 2004/05* (London: CLA).

Clarke, K. and Harrison, S. (2004) 'Governing Health and Social Care', in G. Stoker and D Wilson (eds), *British Local Government into the 21st Century* (Basingstoke: Palgrave Macmillan), pp. 120–32.

Clarke, M. and Stewart, J. (1991) *The Choices for Local Government for the 1990s and Beyond* (Harlow: Longman).

CLD (Commission for Local Democracy) (1995) *Taking Charge: The Rebirth of Local Democracy* (London: Municipal Journal Books).

Cochrane, A. (1993) *Whatever Happened to Local Government?* (Buckingham: Open University Press).

Cockburn, C. (1977) *The Local State* (London: Pluto).

Copus, C. (2004) *Party Politics and Local Government* (Manchester: Manchester University Press).

Corina, L. (1974) 'Elected Representatives in a Party System: A Typology', *Policy and Politics*, 3: 1, pp. 69–87.

Corry, D. and Stoker, G. (2002) *New Localism: Refashioning the Centre-Local Relationship* (London: NLGN).

Corry, D., Hatter, W., Parker, I., Randle, A. and Stoker, G. (2004) *Joining Up Local Democracy* (London: NLGN).

Coulson, A. (1998) 'Town, Parish and Community Councils: The Potential for Democracy and Decentralisation', *Local Governance*, 24: 4, pp. 245–8.

Coulson, A. (2005) 'The Death of a Mass Membership Party?', *Renewal – A Journal of Labour Politics*, 13: 2/3, pp. 139–42.

Coventry [Strategic] Partnership (2005) *Progress Through Prevention: A Local Area Agreement for Coventry, 2005–08* (Coventry: Coventry City Council).

Coxall, B, Robins, L. and Leach, R. (2003) *Contemporary British Politics*, 4th edn (Basingstoke: Palgrave Macmillan).

D'Arcy, M. and MacLean, R. (2000) *Nightmare! The Race to Become London's Mayor* (London: Politico's).

Davis, H. (1996) 'Quangos and Local Government: A Changing World', *Local Government Studies*, 22: 2, pp. 1–7.

De Groot, L. (2005) 'Generating Improvement from Within: The Role of the Improvement and Development Agency for Local Government', *Local Government Studies*, 31: 5, pp. 677–82.

Deakin Commission (1996) *Report on the Future of the Voluntary Sector* (London: NCVO).

Dearlove, J. (1973) *The Politics of Policy in Local Government* (Cambridge: Cambridge University Press).

Dearlove, J. (1979) *The Reorganisation of British Local Government* (Cambridge: Cambridge University Press).

DEFRA (Department for Environment, Food and Rural Affairs) (2005) *Defra Classification of Local Authority Districts and Unitary Authorities in England* (London: DEFRA).

Denters, B. and Rose, L. (2005) *Comparing Local Governance: Trends and Developments* (Basingstoke: Palgrave Macmillan).

DETR (Department of the Environment, Transport and the Regions) (1998a) *Modern Local Government: In Touch with the People* (London: DETR).

DETR (Department of the Environment, Transport and the Regions) (1998b) *Modernising Local Government: Local Democracy and Community Leadership* (London: DETR).

DETR (Department of the Environment, Transport and the Regions) (1998c) *Improving Local Services Through Best Value* (London: DETR).

DETR (Department of the Environment, Transport and the Regions) (1998d) *Improving Financial Accountability* (London: DETR).

DETR (Department of the Environment, Transport and the Regions) (1999) *Local Leadership, Local Choice* (London: DETR).

DETR (Department of the Environment, Transport and the Regions) (2000), *Modernising Local Government Finance: A Green Paper* (London: DETR).

DfES (Department for Education and Skills) (2005) *Higher Standards, Better Schools for All* (London: DfES).

DH (Department of Health) (2002) *Social Services Performance Assessment Framework Indicators 2001/02* (London: Department of Health).

DH (Department of Health) (2005a) *Personal Social Services Expenditure and Unit Costs: England: 2003–2004* (London: DH).

DH (Department of Health) (2005b) *Choosing Health: Making Healthy Choices Easier* (London: DH).

DoE (Department of the Environment) (1981) *Alternatives to Domestic Rates*, Cmnd 8449 (London: HMSO).

DoE (Department of the Environment) (1983) *Streamlining the Cities*, Cmnd 9063 (London: HMSO).

DoE (Department of the Environment) (1986) *Paying for Local Government*, Cmnd 9714 (London: HMSO).

Doig, A. (1984) *Corruption and Misconduct in Contemporary British Politics* (Harmondsworth: Penguin).

Donnelly, K. (2004) 'Education: No Longer a Role for Local Government?', in G. Stoker and D. Wilson (eds), *British Local Government into the 21st Century* (Basingstoke: Palgrave Macmillan), pp. 107–19.

Donoghue, B. and Jones, G. (2001) *Herbert Morrison: Portrait of a Politician* (London: Orion Publishing).

Doogan, K. (1999) 'The Contracting-out of Local Government Services: Its Impact on Jobs, Conditions of Service and Labour Markets', in G. Stoker (ed.), *The New Management of British Local Governance* (Basingstoke: Macmillan), pp. 62–78.

DTLR (Department for Transport, Local Government and the Regions) (2001) *Strong Local Leadership – Quality Public Services* (London: DTLR).

DTLR (Department for Transport, Local Government and the Regions) (2002) *Your Region, Your Choice – Revitalising the English Regions* (London: DTLR).

Dunleavy, P. (1980) *Urban Political Analysis* (London: Macmillan).

Elcock, H. (1991) *Local Government* (London: Methuen).

Elcock, H. (1994) *Local Government: Policy and Management in Local Authorities*, 3rd edn (London: Routledge).

Elcock, H., Jordan, C. and Midwinter, A. (1989) *Budgeting in Local Government: Managing the Margins* (Harlow: Longman).

Electoral Commission (2003a) *The Northern Ireland Assembly Elections 2003: The Official Report* (London: The Electoral Commission).

Electoral Commission (2003b) *The Shape of Elections to Come: A Strategic Evaluation of the 2003 Electoral Pilot Schemes* (London: The Electoral Commission).

Electoral Commission (2004) *The Cycle of Local Government Elections in England: Report and Recommendations* (London: The Electoral Commission).

Electoral Commission (2005a) *Understanding Electoral Registration: The Extent and Nature of Non-registration in Britain* (London: The Electoral Commission).

Electoral Commission (2005b) *Election 2005: Turnout* (London: The Electoral Commission).

Ellwood, S., Nutley, S., Tricker, M. and Waterston, P. (1992) *Parish and Town Councils in England: A Survey* (London: HMSO).

Entwistle, T., Dowson, L. and Law, J. (2003) *Changing to Improve: Ten Case Studies from the Evaluation of the Best Value Regime* (London: ODPM).

EO (Employers' Organisation) (2004) *Local Government Employment Survey 2004* (London: EO)

EO/IDeA (Employers' Organisation/Improvement and Development Agency) (2004) *National Census of Local Authority Councillors in England 2004* (London: EO/IDeA).

EO/IDeA (Employers' Organisation/Improvement and Development Agency) (2005) *Salaries and Numbers Survey of Chief Executives and Chief Officers, 2004/05* (London: EO/IDeA).

ERS (Electoral Reform Society) (2005) *The UK General Election of 5 May 2005: Report and Analysis* (London: ERS).

European Union, Committee of the Regions (1999) *Voter Turnout at Regional and Local Elections in the EU, 1990–1999* (Brussels: EU).

Farnham, D. (1999) 'Human Resources Management and Employment Relations', in S. Horton and D. Farnham (eds), *Public Management in Britain* (London: Macmillan), pp. 107–27.

Farnham, D. and Horton, S. (1999) 'Managing Public and Private Organisations', in S. Horton and D. Farnham (eds), *Public Management in Britain* (London: Macmillan), pp. 26–45.

Fenwick, J., Elcock, H. and Lilley, S. (2003) 'Out of the Loop? Councillors and the New Political Management', *Public Policy and Administration*, 18: 1, pp. 29–45.

Filkin, Lord, Stoker, G., Wilkinson, G. and Williams, J. (2000) *Towards a New Localism: A Discussion Paper* (London: NLGN).

Flynn, N., Leach, S. and Vielba, C. (1985) *Abolition or Reform? The GLC and the Metropolitan County Councils* (London: Allen & Unwin).

Fox, P., Lyons, M. and Skelcher, C. (2002) *Continuity or Change? Officers and New Council Constitutions* (London: ODPM).

Gains, F. (2004) 'The Local Bureaucrat: A Block to Reform or a Key to Unlocking Change?', in G. Stoker and D. Wilson (eds), *British Local Government into the 21st Century* (Basingstoke: Palgrave Macmillan), pp. 91–104.

Gains, F., Greasley, S. and Stoker, G. (2004) *A Summary of Research Evidence on New Council Constitutions in Local Government* (London: ODPM).

Gains, F., John, P. and Stoker G. (2005) 'Path Dependency and the Reform of English Local Government', *Public Administration*, 83: 1, pp. 25–46.

Game, C. (1991) 'County Chronicles: A Collective Appreciation', *Local Government Policy Making*, 18: 2, pp. 3–18.

Game, C. (2001) 'Britain's Changing and Unchanging Electoral Systems', in S. Lancaster (ed.), *Developments in Politics: An Annual Review, Vol. 12* (Ormskirk: Causeway Press), pp. 49–75.

Game, C. (2003) 'Elected Mayors: More Distraction Than Attraction', *Public Policy and Administration*, 18: 1, pp. 13–28.

Game, C. (2004) 'Should the Winner Take All, or Even Quite So Much?', in A. Pike (ed.), *The Missing Modernisation: The Case for PR in Local Government Elections* (London: Make Votes Count/Electoral Reform Society), pp. 10–16.

Game, C. (2005) 'The Miscarriage of Elected English Regional Assemblies: The future of democratic decentralization after the North East shouted No!', paper delivered at the IASIA Annual Conference, Como, Italy (unpublished).

Game, C. (2006) 'Comparative Performance Assessment in English Local Government', *International Journal of Productivity and Performance Management (forthcoming)*.

Game, C. and Leach, S. (1995) *The Role of Political Parties in Local Democracy, CLD Report No 11* (London: Commission for Local Democracy/Municipal Journal Books).

Game, C. and Léach, S. (1996) 'Political Parties and Local Democracy', in L. Pratchett and D. Wilson (eds), *Local Democracy and Local Government* (London: Macmillan), pp. 127–49.

Game, C. and Vuong, D. (2003) 'From Citizens' Charters to the People's Panel: 12 years of public service reform in the UK', paper delivered at the International Symposium on Service Charters and Customer Satisfaction in Public Services, City University, Hong Kong.

Gardner, J. and Oswald, A. (2001) 'What Has Been Happening to the Quality of Workers' Lives in Britain?' (working paper) (http://www2.warwick.ac.uk/fac/soc/economics/staff/faculty/oswald/).

Gershon, Sir P. (2004) *Releasing Resources to the Front Line: Independent Review of Public Sector Efficiency* (Norwich: HMSO).

Glaister, S. (2005) 'Transport', in A. Seldon and D. Kavanagh (eds), *The Blair Effect 2001–5* (Cambridge: Cambridge University Press), pp. 207–32 .

Gosling, P. (2004) 'Up, Up and Away', *Public Finance*, 10 December, www.cipfa.org.uk/publicfinance/features_detail.cfm?News_id = 22318.

Goss, S. (1988) *Local Labour and Local Government* (Edinburgh: Edinburgh University Press).

Goss, S. (2001) *Making Local Governance Work* (Basingstoke: Palgrave Macmillan).

Goss, S. and Corrigan, P. (1999) *Starting to Modernise: Developing New Roles for Council Members* (London: NLGN/Joseph Rowntree Foundation).

Grant, C. (2005) 'Who Has Read Lyons' Script?', *Local Government Chronicle*, 8 September, p. 14.

Grant, W. (2000) *Pressure Groups and British Politics* (London: Macmillan).

Gray, A. and Jenkins, W. (1998), 'The Management of Central Government Services', in B. Jones, A. Gray, D. Kavanagh, M. Moran, P. Norton and A. Seldon, *Politics UK*, 3rd edn (London: Prentice Hall), pp. 348–66.

Gray, C. (2002) 'Local Government and the Arts', *Local Government Studies*, 28: 1, pp. 77–90.

Griffith, J. A. C. (1966) *Central Departments and Local Authorities* (London: Allen & Unwin).

Gyford, J. (1984) *Local Politics in Britain*, 2nd edn (London: Croom Helm).

Gyford, J., Leach, S. and Game, C. (1989) *The Changing Politics of Local Government* (London: Unwin Hyman).

Hambleton, R. (2005) 'Biting the Big Apple', *Municipal Journal*, 30 June, p. 23.

Hammond, S. (2005) 'From mill to Mayor', *Asian News*, 29 April, http://www.theasiannews.co.uk/business/s/191/191691_from_mill_to_mayor.html.

Hampton, W. (1970) *Democracy and Community* (London: Oxford University Press).

Heald, D. and Geaughan, N. (1999) 'The Private Financing of Public Infrastructure', in G. Stoker (ed.), *The New Management of British Local Governance* (Basingstoke: Macmillan), pp. 222–36.

Hebbert, M. (1998) *London: More by Fortune than Design* (Chichester: John Wiley).

Heclo, H. (1969) 'The Councillor's Job', *Public Administration*, 47: 2, pp. 185–202.

Hennessy, P. (1990) *Whitehall*, revd. edn (London: Fontana).

Hetherington, P. (2004) 'Inspecting the Inspectors', *Society Guardian*, 15 December, p. 10.

Hicks, S. (2005) 'Trends in Public Sector Employment', *Labour Market Trends*, 113: 12, pp. 477–88.

Hill, D. (1974) *Democratic Theory and Local Government* (London: Allen & Unwin).

HM Treasury (2005) *Public Expenditure Statistical Analyses, 2005* (London: HM Treasury).

Hollis, G., Hale, R., Jackman, R., Travers, T., Foster, G., Thompson, Q., Ambler, M., Gilder, P. and Sussex, P. (1990) *Alternatives to the Community Charge* (York: Joseph Rowntree Trust/Coopers and Lybrand Deloitte).

Hollis, P. (1987) *Ladies Elect: Women in English Local Government, 1865–1914* (Oxford: Oxford University Press).

Home Office (2005a) *Home Office Statistical Bulletin: Police Service Strength, March 2005* (London: Home Office).

Home Office (2005b) *ASBO Statistics, March 2005* (London: Home Office).

Horton, S. and Farnham, D. (eds) (1999) *Public Management in Britain* (London: Macmillan).

Houlihan, B. (1988) *Housing Policy and Central–Local Government Relations* (Aldershot: Avebury).

House of Commons (2001) *Select Committee on Public Administration Fifth Report, 2000/01: Mapping the Quango State* (London: HMSO).

House of Commons (2002) *How the Local Government Act 2000 is Working*, Transport, Local Government and the Regions Committee, Report and Proceedings of the Committee, Vol. 1, HC 602–1, 12 September (London: House of Commons).

Hughes, M., Skelcher, C., Jas, P., Whiteman, P. and Turner, D. (2004) *Learning from the Experience of Recovery – Paths to Recovery: Second Annual Report* (London: ODPM).

IDeA (Improvement and Development Agency) (2005) *Member Allowances Summary (as of 24/2/04)* (www.idea-knowledge.gov.uk/idk/aio/281821).

Jenkins, S. (2004) *Big Bang Localism: A Rescue Plan for British Democracy* (London: Policy Exchange).

Jenkins, S. (2005) 'Respect Starts With You Letting Us Run Our Lives, Godfather Blair', *The Sunday Times*, 15 May, www.timesonline.co.uk/article/0,,2088-1613211,00.html.

Jennings, R. E. (1982) 'The Changing Representational Roles of Local Councillors in England', *Local Government Studies*, 8: 4, pp. 67–86.

John, P. (2001) *Local Governance in Western Europe* (London: Sage).

John, P. (2004) 'Strengthening Political Leadership? More Than Mayors', in G. Stoker and D. Wilson (eds), *British Local Government into the 21st Century* (Basingstoke: Palgrave Macmillan), pp. 43–59.

John, P. and Cole, A. (2000) 'Political Leadership in the New Urban Governance: Britain and France Compared', in L. Pratchett (ed.), *Renewing Local Democracy?* (London: Frank Cass), pp. 98–115.

Jones, B., Kavanagh, D., Moran, M. and Norton, P. (2004) *Politics UK*, 5th edn (London: Pearson Longman).

Jones, G. (1969) *Borough Politics* (London: Macmillan).

Jones, G. (1973) 'The Functions and Organisation of Councillors', *Public Administration*, 51, pp. 135–46.

Jones, G. (1975) 'Varieties of Local Politics', *Local Government Studies*, 1: 2, pp. 17–32.

Jones, G. (1997) *The New Local Government Agenda* (Hemel Hempstead: ICSA Publishing).

Jones, G. and Stewart, J. (1992) 'Selected not Elected', *Local Government Chronicle*, 13 November, p. 15.

Jones, G. and Stewart, J. (2004) 'Power Without Punch', *Local Government Chronicle*, 5 November, p. 24.

Jones, G. and Stewart, J. (2005) 'It's Big, but It's Not Clever', *Public Finance*, 9 December (www.publicfinance.co.uk/features_details.cfm?News_id = 26050).

Keith-Lucas, B. and Richards, P. (1978) *A History of Local Government in the Twentieth Century* (London: Allen & Unwin).

King, D. and Stoker, G. (eds) (1996) *Rethinking Local Democracy* (London: Macmillan).

Labour Party (1997) *New Labour – Because Britain Deserves Better* (London: Labour Party).

Labour Party (2001) *Ambitions for Britain – Labour's Manifesto 2001* (London: Labour Party).

Labour Party (2005) *Britain Forward not Back* (London: Labour Party).

Laffin, M. (1986) *Professionalism and Policy: The Role of the Professions in the Central–Local Relationship* (Aldershot: Gower).

Laming, Lord (2003) *The Victoria Climbié Inquiry: Summary and Recommendations* (Norwich: HMSO).

Lansley, S., Goss, S. and Wolmar, C. (1991) *Councils in Conflict: The Rise and Fall of the Municipal Left* (London: Macmillan).

Laver, M. (1989) 'Theories of Coalition Formation and Local Government Coalitions', in C. Mellors and B. Pijnenburg (eds), *Political Parties and Coalitions in European Local Government* (London: Routledge), pp. 15–33.

Layfield Committee (1976) *Report of the Committee of Enquiry into Local Government Finance*, Cmnd 6543 (London: HMSO).

Leach, R. and Percy-Smith, J. (2001) *Local Governance in Britain* (Basingstoke: Palgrave Macmillan).

Leach, S. (1999) 'Introducing Cabinets into British Local Government', *Parliamentary Affairs*, 52: 1, pp. 77–93.

Leach, S. (2003) 'Executives and Scrutiny in Local Government', *Public Policy and Administration*, 18: 1, pp. 4–12.

Leach, S. (2006) *The Changing Role of Local Politics in Britain* (Bristol: Policy Press).

Leach, S. and Copus, C. (2004) 'Scrutiny and the Political Party Group in UK Local Government: New Models of Behaviour', *Public Administration*, 82: 2, pp. 331–54.

Leach, S. and Game, C. (1992) 'Local Government: The Decline of the One-Party State', in G. Smyth (ed.), *Refreshing the Parts: Electoral Reform and British Politics* (London: Lawrence & Wishart).

Leach, S. and Game, C. (2000) *Hung Authorities, Elected Mayors and Cabinet Government: Political Behaviour Under Proportional Representation* (York: Joseph Rowntree Foundation).

Leach, S. and Pratchett, L. (1996) *The Management of Balanced Authorities* (Luton: LGMB).

Leach, S. and Pratchett, L. (2005) 'Local Government: A New Vision, Rhetoric or Reality', *Parliamentary Affairs*, 58: 2, pp. 318–34.

Leach, S. and Stewart, J. (1992) *The Politics of Hung Authorities* (London: Macmillan).

Leach, S. and Wilson, D. (1998) 'Voluntary Groups and Local Authorities: Rethinking the Relationship', *Local Government Studies*, 24: 1, pp. 1–18.

Leach, S. and Wilson, D. (2000) *Local Political Leadership* (Bristol: Policy Press).

Leach, S., Stewart, J. and Walsh, K. (1994) *The Changing Organisation and Management of Local Government* (London: Macmillan).

Leach, S., Davis. H. and Associates (1996) *Enabling or Disabling Local Government: Choices for the Future* (Buckingham: Open University Press).

Lee, J. (1963) *Social Leaders and Public Persons* (London: Oxford University Press).

Lewis, D. (2005) *The Essential Guide to British Quangos, 2005* (London: Centre for Policy Studies).

Lewis, G. (2001) *Mapping the Contribution of the Voluntary and Community Sector in Yorkshire and the Humber* (Leeds: Yorkshire and the Humber Regional Forum).

LGA (Local Government Association) (2000a) *Real Roles for Members – The Role of Non-executive Members in the New Structures* (London: LGA).

LGA (Local Government Association) (2000b) *A Role for All Members – The Council Meeting* (London: LGA).

LGA (Local Government Association) (2001) *Electoral Reform in Local Government: A Local Government Association Consultation* (London: LGA).

LGA (Local Government Association) (2003) *Powering up: Making the Most of the Power of Well-being* (London: LGA).

LGA (Local Government Association) (2004a) *Proposals for Comprehensive Performance Assessment from 2005* (London: LGA).

LGA (Local Government Association) (2004b) *The Balance of Funding – A Combination Option* (London: LGA).

LGA (Local Government Association) (2005a) *Local Government Matters: Facts and Figures about Local Councils, 2005–2006* (London: LGA).

LGA (Local Government Association) (2005b) *Just Down the Road? The Future of Road Pricing – A Local Government Perspective* (London: LGA).

LGA (Local Government Association) (2005c) *Queen's Speech 2005: LGA Briefing on the Key Bills for Local Government* (London: LGA).

LGA (Local Government Association) (2005d) *Using Prudential Borrowing: One Year On* (London: LGA).

LGIU (Local Government Information Unit) (2003) *The LGIU Guide to Local Government Finance* (London: LGIU).

Livingstone, K. (1987) *If Voting Changed Anything, They'd Abolish It* (London: Collins).

Local Channel, The (2005) *ICT and e-government Development for Small First-tier Councils in the EU 25* (www.thelocalchannel.co.uk/i2010/Docs/IT2010.pdf).

Loughlin, J. (2001) *Subnational Democracy in the European Union: Challenges and Opportunities* (Oxford: Oxford University Press).

Loughlin, M. (1996a) *Legality and Locality: The Role of Law in Central–Local Relations* (Oxford: Clarendon Press).

Loughlin, M. (1996b) 'Understanding Central–Local Government Relations', *Public Policy and Administration*, 11: 2, pp. 48–65.

Loughlin, M., Gelfand, M. and Young, K. (eds) (1985) *Half a Century of Municipal Decline, 1935–1985* (London: Allen & Unwin).

Lowndes, V. (1996) 'Locality and Community: Choices for Local Government', in S. Leach *et al.*, *Enabling or Disabling Local Government* (Buckingham: Open University Press), pp. 71–85.

Lowndes, V. (2002) 'Between Rhetoric and Reality: Does the 2001 White Paper Reverse the Centralising Trend in Britain?', *Local Government Studies*, 28: 3, pp. 135–47.

Lowndes, V. and Sullivan, H. (2004) 'Like a Horse and Carriage or a Fish on a Bicycle: How Well Do Local Partnerships and Public Participation Go Together?', *Local Government Studies*, 30: 1, pp. 52–74.

Lowndes, V., Pratchett, L. and Stoker, G. (2001) 'Trends in Public Participation: Part 1 – Local Government Perspectives', *Public Administration*, 79: 1, pp. 205–22.

Lynn, J. and Jay, A. (1983) *Yes, Minister: The Diaries of a Cabinet Minister, Vol. 3 – The Challenge* (London: BBC).

Lyons, Sir M. (2005) *Lyons Inquiry into Local Government: Consultation Paper and Interim Report* (Norwich: HMSO).

Lyons, M. and Crow, A. (eds) (2004) *Local Government – Past, Present and Future: A Celebration of the 25-Year Writing Partnership of George Jones and John Stewart* (Birmingham: INLOGOV).

McConnell, A. (1999) *The Politics and Policy of Local Taxation in Britain* (Wirral: Tudor).

McConnell, A. (2004) *Scottish Local Government* (Edinburgh: Edinburgh University Press).

MacGregor, J. (2006) 'Local Government Must Now Step into the Breach', *Society Guardian*, 25 January, p. 8.

McIntosh, N. (Chairman) (1999) *Commission on Local Government and the Scottish Parliament*, Report (Edinburgh: Scottish Executive).

Macrory, P. (Chairman) (1970) *Review Body on Local Government in Northern Ireland, Report*, Cmnd 540 (NI) (HMSO: Belfast).

Mahony, C. (2005) 'Culture Vultures', *LGC – Local Government Chronicle 1855–2005*, pp. 49–50.

Maloney, W., Smith, G. and Stoker, G. (2000) 'Social Capital and Urban Governance: Adding a More Contextualised "Top-down" Perspective', *Political Studies*, 48: 4, pp. 802–20.

Marinko, P. (2004) 'High Cost of Inspections', *Municipal Journal*, 14 October, p. 5.

Marsh, D. (ed.) (1998) *Comparing Policy Networks* (Buckingham: Open University Press).

Marsh, D. and Rhodes, R. A. W. (eds) (1992) *Policy Networks in British Government* (Oxford: Oxford University Press).

Marsh, D., Richards, D. and Smith, M. (2001) *Changing Patterns of Governance in the United Kingdom: Reinventing Whitehall* (Basingstoke: Palgrave Macmillan).

Martin, A. (2004) 'The Changing Face of Public Service Inspection', *Public Money and Management*, January, pp. 3–5.

Martin, S. and Bovaird, T. (2005) *Meta-evaluation of the Local Government Modernisation Agenda: Progress Report on Service Improvement in Local Government* (London: ODPM).

Mellors, C. (1989) 'Non-majority British Local Authorities in a Majority Setting', in C. Mellors and B. Pijnenburg (eds), *Political Parties and Coalitions in European Local Government* (London: Routledge), pp. 68–112.

Miliband, D. (2005a) 'Power to Neighbourhoods: The New Challenge for Urban Regeneration' – Speech to the Annual Conference of the British Urban Regeneration Association, 12 October (www.dclg.gov.uk/index.asp?id = 1122747).

Miliband, D. (2005b) 'Local Government Reorganisation', *Local Government Chronicle*, 1 December (www.dclg.gov.uk/index.asp?id = 1161912).

Miliband, D. (2006) 'Empowerment and the Deal for Devolution' – Speech to the Annual Conference of the NLGN, 18 January (London: ODPM – www.dclg.gov.uk/index.asp?id = 1163065).

Miller, W. (1988) *Irrelevant Elections? The Quality of Local Democracy in Britain* (Oxford: Clarendon Press).

MORI (Market and Opinion Research International) (2003) *Ombudsmen Awareness Survey 2003* (London: MORI).

Murie, A. (2004) 'Rethinking Planning and Housing', in G. Stoker and D. Wilson (eds), *British Local Government into the 21st Century* (Basingstoke: Palgrave Macmillan), pp. 133–50.

MLAC (Museums, Libraries and Archives Council) (2004) *A Quiet Revolution* (London: MLAC).

Myerson, J. (2005) 'Lambeth Talk', *Society Guardian*, 23 February, p. 11.

National Audit Office (2005) *Working with the Third Sector* (London: The Stationery Office).

New Local Government Network City Regions Commission (2005) *Seeing the Light? Next Steps for City Regions - Media Release, 13 December* (London: NLGN).

Newton, K. (1976) *Second City Politics: Democratic Processes and Decision-Making in Birmingham* (Oxford: Oxford University Press).

Newton, K. and Karran, T. (1985) *The Politics of Local Expenditure* (London: Macmillan).

Nolan, Lord (Chairman) (1997) *Committee on Standards in Public Life: Report on Local Government* (London: HMSO).

Oakland, J. (1989) *Total Quality Management* (London: Butterworth Heinemann).

ODPM (Office of the Deputy Prime Minister) (2002) *Public Participation in Local Government: A Survey of Local Authorities* (London: ODPM).

ODPM (Office of the Deputy Prime Minister) (2003) *Balance of Funding Review – Minutes of 3rd Meeting, 21 October 2003* (London, ODPM).

ODPM (Office of the Deputy Prime Minister) (2004a) *Memorandum: Poorly Performing Local Authorities – July 2004* (London: ODPM).

ODPM (Office of the Deputy Prime Minister) (2004b) *Local Area Agreements: A Prospectus* (London: ODPM).

ODPM (Office of the Deputy Prime Minister) (2004c) *The Future of Local Government: Developing a 10-year Vision* (London: ODPM).

ODPM (Office of the Deputy Prime Minister) (2004d) *Balance of Funding Review – Report* (London: ODPM).

ODPM (Office of the Deputy Prime Minister) (2005a) *Local Government Finance Key Facts: England: September 2005* (London: ODPM).

ODPM (Office of the Deputy Prime Minister) (2005b) *Report on the 2004 Survey of all English LSPs* (London: ODPM).

ODPM (Office of the Deputy Prime Minister) (2005c) *Private Finance Initiative – What Is Local Government PFI?* (London: ODPM).

ODPM (Office of the Deputy Prime Minister) (2005d) *Housing Statistics 2005* (London: ODPM).

ODPM (Office of the Deputy Prime Minister) (2005e) *Inspection Reform: The Future of Local Services Inspection – Consultation Paper* (London: ODPM).

ODPM (Office of the Deputy Prime Minister) (2005f) *Annual Report 2005* (London: ODPM).

ODPM (Office of the Deputy Prime Minister) (2005g) *Local Government Financial Statistics England No. 16* (London: ODPM).

ODPM (Office of the Deputy Prime Minister) (2005h) *Vibrant Local Leadership* (London: ODPM).

ODPM (Office of the Deputy Prime Minister) (2005i) *National Evaluation of Local Public Service Agreements – First Interim Report* (London: ODPM).

ODPM (Office of the Deputy Prime Minister) (2005j) *A Process Evaluation of the Negotiation of Pilot Local Area Agreements – Final Report* (London: ODPM).

OECD (Organisation for Economic Co-operation and Development) (2005) *Revenue Statistics of OECD Member Countries, 1965–2004* (Paris: OECD).

ONS (Office for National Statistics) (2005) *Labour Force Survey* (London: ONS).

Osborne, D. and Gaebler, T. (1992) *Reinventing Government: How Entrepreneurial Spirit is Transforming the Public Sector* (Reading, Mass.: Addison-Wesley).

Parris, M. (2005) 'The Birmingham Case Is Simply Vote Rigging, and at the Highest Level', *The Times*, 26 March, p. 21.

Paterson, I. V. (Chairman) (1973) *The New Scottish Local Authorities: Organisation and Management Structures* (Edinburgh: Scottish Development Department).

Perri 6, Leat, D., Seltzer, K. and Stoker, G. (2002) *Towards Holistic Governance: The New Reform Agenda* (Basingstoke: Palgrave Macmillan).

Phillips, C. (2000) *Birmingham Votes, 1911–2000* (Plymouth: LGC Elections Centre).

Pollock, A. and Price, D. (2004) *Public Risk for Private Gain?* (London: UNISON).

Power Inquiry (2004) *The Decline of Political Participation in Britain: An Introduction* (www.powerinquiry.org).

Pratchett, L. (2000) 'The Inherently Unethical Nature of Public Service Ethics', in R. A. Chapman (ed.), *Ethics in Public Service for the New Millennium* (Aldershot: Ashgate).

Pratchett, L. (ed.) (2000) *Renewing Local Democracy? The Modernisation Agenda in British Local Government* (London: Frank Cass).

Pratchett, L. (2004) 'Institutions, Politics and People: Making Local Politics Work', in G. Stoker and D. Wilson (eds), *British Local Government into the 21st Century* (Basingstoke: Palgrave Macmillan), pp. 213–29.

Pratchett, L. and Leach, S. (2004) 'Local Government: Choice Within Constraint', *Parliamentary Affairs*, 57: 2, pp. 366–79.

Pratchett, L. and Wilson, D. (eds) (1996) *Local Democracy and Local Government* (London: Macmillan).

Pratchett, L. and Wingfield, M. (1996) 'The Demise of the Public Sector Ethos', in L. Pratchett and D. Wilson (eds), *Local Democracy and Local Government* (London: Macmillan), pp. 106–26.

Prior, D. (1995) 'Citizens' Charters', in J. Stewart and G. Stoker (eds), *Local Government in the 1990s* (London: Macmillan), pp. 86–103.

Putnam, R. (2000) *Bowling Alone: The Collapse and Revival of American Community* (New York: Simon & Schuster).

Rallings, C. and Thrasher, M. (1997) *Local Elections in Britain* (London: Routledge).

Rallings, C. and Thrasher, M. (2001) 'Aspects of Voting at the Local and General Elections, 2001', Paper presented at the *Elections, Parties and Polls Conference*, University of Sussex, 2–4 September.

Rallings, C. and Thrasher, M. (2003) *Electoral Cycles in English Local Government* (Plymouth: LGC Elections Centre).

Rallings, C. and Thrasher, M. (2004) *Local Elections Handbook 2004: The 2004 Local Election Results* (Plymouth: LGC Elections Centre).

Rallings, C and Thrasher, M. (2005) 'Strength in Numbers', *Local Government Chronicle*, 12 May, pp. 26–7.

Rallings, C. and Thrasher, M. (Annual) *Local Elections Handbook* (Plymouth: LGC Elections Centre).

Rallings, C., Thrasher, M. and Downe, J. (2000) *Turnout at Local Elections: Influences on Levels of Local Registration and Electoral Participation* (London: DETR).

Rallings, C., Thrasher, M., Cheal, B. and Borisyuk, G. (2004) 'The New Deal for Communities: Assessing Procedures and Voter Turnout at Partnership Board Elections', *Environment and Planning C: Government and Policy*, 22, pp. 569–82.

Rao, N. (1994) *The Making and Unmaking of Local Self-government* (Aldershot: Dartmouth).

Rao, N. (2005) *Councillors and the New Council Constitutions* (London: ODPM).

Rashman, L. and Hartley, J. (2006) *Long-term Evaluation of the Beacon Scheme: Survey of Local Authorities – Final Report* (London: ODPM).

Raynsford, N. (2004) 'The future of local government', Speech to *Local Government Chronicle Policy Forum*, 15 March.

Raynsford, N. (2005) 'The New Wave of Local Partnerships' – Speech to NLGN Conference, 23 March (www.dclg.gov.uk/index.asp?id = 1122790).

Redcliffe-Maud, Lord (Chairman) (1969) *Royal Commission on Local Government in England 1966–1969, Vol. I Report*, Cmnd 4040 (London: HMSO).

Rhodes, R. A. W. (1986a) *The National World of Local Government* (London: Allen & Unwin).

Rhodes, R. A. W. (1986b) *Power Dependence, Policy Communities and Intergovernmental Networks*, Essex Papers in Politics and Government, No. 30 (University of Essex).

Rhodes, R. A. W. (1988) *Beyond Westminster and Whitehall* (London: Allen & Unwin).

Rhodes, R. A. W. (1997) *Understanding Governance: Policy Networks, Governance, Reflexivity and Accountability* (Buckingham: Open University Press).

Rhodes, R. A. W. (1999a) 'Foreword: Governance and Networks', in G. Stoker (ed.), *The New Management of British Local Governance* (London: Macmillian), pp. xii-xxvi.

Rhodes, R. A. W. (1999b) *Control and Power in Central–Local Government Relations*, 2nd edn (Aldershot: Ashgate).

Rhodes, R.A.W. and Dunleavy, P. (1995) *Prime Minister, Cabinet and Core Executive* (London: Macmillan).

Robinson, D. (Chairman) (1977) *Remuneration of Councillors: Vol I: Report; Vol II: The Surveys of Councillors and Local Authorities*, Cmnd 7010 (London: HMSO).

Rose, D. (2005) 'Same Goal, Different Approach', *Municipal Journal*, 21 April, p. 10.

RPA (Review of Public Administration) (2005) *The Review of Public Administration in Northern Ireland: Further Consultation* (Belfast: RPA).

Saunders, P. (1980) *Urban Politics: A Sociological Interpretation* (Harmondsworth: Penguin).

Scottish Executive (2004) *Joint Staffing Watch, Survey, December 2004* (Edinburgh: SE).

Seitz, R. (1998) *Over Here* (London: Phoenix).

Sharpe, L. J. (1970) 'Theories and Values of Local Government', *Political Studies*, 18: 2, pp. 153–74.

Shaw, K. and Davidson, G. (2002) 'Community Elections for Regeneration Partnerships: A New Deal for Local Democracy?', *Local Government Studies*, 28: 2, pp. 1–15.

Skelcher, C. (1992) *Managing for Service Quality* (Harlow: Longman).

Skelcher, C. (1998) *The Appointed State* (Buckingham: Open University Press).

Skelcher, C. (2004a) 'The New Governance of Communities', in G. Stoker and D. Wilson (eds), *British Local Government into the 21st Century* (Basingstoke: Palgrave Macmillan).

Skelcher, C. (2004b) 'A Commentary on "Partnership Problems"', in M. Lyons and A. Crow (eds), *Local Government – Past, Present and Future: A Celebration of the 25-Year Writing Partnership of George Jones and John Stewart* (Birmingham: INLOGOV), p. 58.

Skelcher, C. and Davis, H. (1995) *Opening the Boardroom Door: The Membership of Local Appointed Bodies* (London: LGC Communications/Joseph Rowntree Foundation).

Skelcher, C. and Davis, H. (1996) 'Understanding the New Magistracy: A Study of Characteristics and Attitudes', *Local Government Studies*, 22: 2, pp. 8–21.

Skelcher, C., Weir, S. and Wilson, L. (2000) *Advance of the Quango State* (London: LGIU).

Smith, B. C. (1985) *Decentralization: The Territorial Dimension of the State* (London: Allen & Unwin).

Smith, G., Stoker, G. and Maloney, W. (2004) 'Building Social Capital in City Politics: Scope and Limitations at the Inter-organisational Level', *Political Studies*, 52: 3, pp. 509–30.

Smith, P. (1999) 'Countdown to the Relaunch of Clause Zero', *Local Government Chronicle*, 8 January, p. 8.

Snape, S. (2004) 'Liberated or Lost Souls: Is There a Role for Non-executive Councillors?', in G. Stoker and D. Wilson (eds), *British Local Government into the 21st Century* (Basingstoke: Palgrave Macmillan), pp. 60–75.

Snape, S. and Dobbs, L. (2003) 'The Scrutineer: The Impact of Overview and Scrutiny on Councillor Roles', *Public Policy and Administration*, 18: 1, pp. 46–62.

Snape, S. and Taylor, P. (2003) 'Partnerships Between Health and Local Government: An Introduction', *Local Government Studies*, 29: 3, pp 1–16.

Snape, S., Leach, S. and Copus, C. (2002) *The Development of Overview and Scrutiny in Local Government* (London: ODPM).

Social Exclusion Unit (2001) *A New Commitment to Neighbourhood Renewal: National Strategy Action Plan* (London: Cabinet Office).

Stanyer, J. (1999) 'Something Old, Something New', in G. Stoker (ed.), *The New Management of British Local Governance* (Basingstoke: Macmillan), pp. 237–48.

Stewart, J. (1990) 'The Role of Councillors in the Management of the Authority', *Local Government Studies*, 16: 4, pp. 25–36.

Stewart, J. (1996) *Local Government Today: An Observer's View* (Luton: LGMB).

Stewart, J. (2000) *The Nature of British Local Government* (London: Macmillan).

Stewart, J. (2003) *Modernising British Local Government* (Basingstoke, Palgrave Macmillan).

Stewart, J. and Stoker, G. (eds) (1995) *Local Government in the 1990s* (London: Macmillan).

Stoker, G. (1990) 'Government Beyond Whitehall', in P. Dunleavy, A. Gamble and G. Peele (eds), *Developments in British Politics 3* (London: Macmillan).

Stoker, G. (1991) *The Politics of Local Government*, 2nd edn (London: Macmillan).

Stoker, G. (ed.) (1999) *The New Management of British Local Governance* (London: Macmillan).

Stoker, G. (ed.) (2000) *The New Politics of British Local Governance* (London: Macmillan).

Stoker, G. (2002) 'Life Is a Lottery: New Labour's Strategy for the Reform of Devolved Governance', *Public Administration*, 80: 3, pp. 417–34.

Stoker, G. (2004a) *Transforming Local Governance: From Thatcherism to New Labour* (Basingstoke: Palgrave Macmillan).

Stoker, G. (2004b) *How Are Mayors Measuring Up?* (London: ODPM).

Stoker, G. (2005) 'Super-sizing the Cities', *Public Finance*, 4 March (www.nlgn.org.uk/nlgn.php).

Stoker, G. and Brindley, T. (1985) 'Asian Politics and Housing Renewal', *Policy and Politics*, 13: 3, pp. 281–303.

Stoker, G. and Wilson, D. (1986) 'Intra-Organizational Politics in Local Authorities', *Public Administration*, 64: 3, pp. 285–302.

Stoker, G. and Wilson, D. (1991) 'The Lost World of British Local Pressure Groups', *Public Policy and Administration*, 6: 2, pp. 20–34.

Stoker, G. and Wilson, D. (eds) (2004) *British Local Government into the 21st Century* (Basingstoke: Palgrave Macmillan).

Stoker, G. and Young, S. (1993) *Cities in the 1990s* (Harlow: Longman).

Stoker, G., John, P., Gains, F., Rao, N. and Harding, A. (2002) *Report of the ELG Survey Findings for ODPM Advisory Group* (Manchester: Evaluating Local Governance, New Constitutions and Ethics, Department of Government, University of Manchester).

Stoker, G., Gains, F., John, P., Rao, N. and Harding, A. (2003) *Implementing the 2000 Act with Respect to New Council Constitutions and the Ethical Framework: First Report* (London: ODPM).

Stoker, G., Gains, F., Greasley, S., John, P. and Rao, N. (2004) *Operating the New Council Constitutions: A Process Evaluation* (London: ODPM).

Sullivan, H. and Skelcher, C. (2002) *Working Across Boundaries: Collaboration in Public Services* (Basingstoke: Palgrave Macmillan).

Taafe, P. and Mulhearn, T. (1988) *Liverpool – A City that Dared to Fight* (London: Fortress Books).

Taylor, B. and Thomson, K. (1999) *Scotland and Wales: Nations Again?* (Cardiff: University of Wales Press).

Temple, M. (1996) *Coalitions and Co-operation in Local Government* (London: Electoral Reform Society).

Tomaney, J. (2004) 'Regionalism and the Challenge of Local Authorities', in G. Stoker and D. Wilson (eds), *British Local Government into the 21st Century* (Basingstoke: Palgrave Macmillan), pp. 167–81.

Travers, T. (2004) *The Politics of London: Governing an Ungovernable City* (Basingstoke: Palgrave Macmillan).

Travers, T. (2005a) 'It's Now or Never', *Public Finance*, 7–13 October, pp. 26–8.

Travers, T. (2005b) 'Local and Central Government', in A. Seldon and D. Kavanagh (eds), *The Blair Effect 2001–5* (Cambridge: Cambridge University Press), pp. 68–93.

Travers, T. and Esposito, L. (2003) *The Decline and Fall of Local Democracy: A History of Local Government Finance* (London: Policy Exchange).

Travers, T. and Esposito, L. (2004a) *I'm a Councillor, Get Me Out of Here! England's System of Local Government Finance* (London: Policy Exchange).

Travers, T. and Esposito, L. (2004b) *Nothing to Lose but Your Chains: Reforming the English Local Government Finance System* (London: Policy Exchange).

UNISON (2002) *Privatising Halls of Residence* (London: UNISON).

UNPAN (UN Online Network in Public Administration and Finance) (2005) *International Public Sector Indicators – Basic Data on Government Expenditure and Taxation, 1990–2002* (www.unpan.org/statistical_database-publicsector.asp).

Vize, R. (1994) 'Northern Ireland: The Acceptable Face of Quangos', *Local Government Chronicle*, 25 November, pp. 16–17.

Voice East Midlands (2003) *Mapping the Black and Minority Voluntary and Community Sector in the East Midlands* (Nottingham: Nottingham Research Observatory).

VONNE (Voluntary Organisations' Network North East) (2000) *The Contribution of the Voluntary and Community Sector to the Economic Life of the North East Region* (Newcastle Upon Tyne: VONNE).

Walker, D. (2002) *A Critique of New Localism* (London: Catalyst).

Walsh, K. (1995) 'Competition and Public Service Delivery', in J. Stewart and G. Stoker (eds), *Local Government in the 1990s*, pp. 28–48.

Walsh, K. (1996) 'The Role of the Market and the Growth of Competition', in S. Leach, H. Davis and Associates (eds), *Enabling or Disabling Local Government* (Buckingham: Open University Press), pp. 59–70.

Wanless, D. (2002) *Securing Our Future Health: Taking a Long-term View* (London: HM Treasury).

Watt, P. (2004) 'Financing Local Government', *Local Government Studies*, 30: 4, pp. 609–23.

Weir, S. and Beetham, D. (1999) *Political Power and Democratic Control in Britain: The Democratic Audit of Great Britain* (London: Routledge).

Weir, S. and Hall, W. (eds) (1994) *EGO TRIP: Extra-governmental Organisations in the UK and their Accountability - Democratic Audit Paper, No. 2* (Colchester: University of Essex Human Rights Centre)'.

Wheatley, Lord (Chairman) (1969) *Royal Commission on Local Government in Scotland, Report*, Cmnd 4150 (Edinburgh: HMSO).

Whelan, R. (1999) *Involuntary Action: How Voluntary Is the Voluntary Sector?* (London: IEA Health and Welfare Unit).

Widdicombe, D. (Chairman) (1986a) *The Conduct of Local Authority Business: Report of the Committee of Inquiry into the Conduct of Local Authority Business*, Cmnd 9797 (London: HMSO).

Widdicombe, D. (Chairman) (1986b) *Research Volume I – The Political Organisation of Local Authorities* (by S. Leach, C. Game, J. Gyford and A. Midwinter), Cmnd 9798 (London: HMSO).

Widdicombe, D. (Chairman) (1986c) *Research Volume II – The Local Government Councillor*, Cmnd 9799 (London: HMSO).

Widdicombe, D. (Chairman) (1986d) *Research Volume III – The Local Government Elector*, Cmnd 9800 (London: HMSO).

Widdicombe, D. (Chairman) (1986e) *Research Volume IV – Aspects of Local Democracy*, Cmnd 9801 (London: HMSO).

Willis, J. (1990) 'David Bookbinder: Behind the Mythology', *Local Government Chronicle*, 12 January, pp. 24–5.

Wilson, D. (2004) 'New Patterns of Central–Local Government Relations', in G. Stoker and D. Wilson (eds), *British Local Government into the 21st Century* (Basingstoke: Palgrave Macmillan), pp. 9–24.

Wilson, D. and Game, C. (1994) *Local Government in the United Kingdom*, 1st edn (London: Macmillan).

Wilson, D. and Game, C. (1998) *Local Government in the United Kingdom*, 2nd edn (London: Macmillan).

Wilson, D. and Game, C. (2002) *Local Government in the United Kingdom*, 3rd edn (Basingstoke: Palgrave Macmillan).

Wood, B. (1976) *The Process of Local Government Reform, 1966–74* (London: Allen & Unwin).

Young, K. (1986a) 'Party Politics in Local Government: An Historical Perspective', in Widdicombe (1986e) (London: HMSO).

Young, K. (1986b) 'The Justification for Local Government', in M. Goldsmith (ed.), *Essays on the Future of Local Government* (Wakefield: West Yorkshire Metropolitan County Council), pp. 8–20.

Young, K. (ed.) (1989) *New Directions for County Government* (London: ACC).

Young, K. (2005) 'Local Public Service Agreements and Performance Incentives for Local Government', *Local Government Studies*, 31: 1, pp. 3–20.

Young, K. and Mills, L. (1983) *Managing the Post-Industrial City* (London: Heinemann).

Young, K. and Rao, N. (1997) *Local Government Since 1945* (Oxford: Blackwell).

Index